DATE DUE

POLICE
IN AMERICA

THE POLICE
AND THE CRIME PROBLEM

Thorsten Sellin, Editor

ARNO PRESS & THE NEW YORK TIMES
NEW YORK, 1971

Reprint Edition 1971 by Arno Press Inc.

Reprinted from a copy in
The University of Illinois Library

LC# 78-154589
ISBN 0-405-03385-0

Police In America
ISBN for complete set: 0-405-03360-5
See last pages of this volume for titles.

Manufactured in the United States of America

The Police and The Crime Problem

The Annals

VOLUME CXLVI NOVEMBER, 1929

EDITOR: THORSTEN SELLIN
ASSOCIATE EDITOR: JOSEPH H. WILLITS
EDITORIAL COUNCIL: C. H. CRENNAN, DAVID FRIDAY, A. A. GIESECKE, CHARLES G. HAINES,
A. R. HATTON, AMOS S. HERSHEY, E. M. HOPKINS, S. S. HUEBNER, CARL KELSEY,
J. P. LICHTENBERGER, ROSWELL C. McCREA, ERNEST MINOR PATTERSON,
L. S. ROWE, HENRY SUZZALLO, T. W. VAN METRE, F. D. WATSON

THE AMERICAN ACADEMY OF POLITICAL AND SOCIAL SCIENCE
3622–24 LOCUST STREET
PHILADELPHIA
1929

EUROPEAN AGENTS

ENGLAND: P. S. King & Son, Ltd., 2 Great Smith Street, Westminster, London, S. W.
FRANCE: L. Larose, rue Soufflot, 22, Paris.
GERMANY: Mayer & Müller, 2 Prinz Louis Ferdinandstrasse, Berlin, N. W.
ITALY: Giornale degli Economisti, Milano, Via Canova, 27.
SPAIN: E. Dossat, 9 Plaza de Santa Ana, Madrid.

CONTENTS

PAGE

FOREWORD... v

PART I. THE ORGANIZATION AND THE FUNCTIONS OF THE POLICE

MUNICIPAL POLICE ADMINISTRATION.. 1
    Bruce Smith, National Institute of Public Administration, New York City

THE SHERIFF AND THE CONSTABLE.. 28
    Raymond Moley, Professor of Public Law, Columbia University, New York City

THE STATE POLICE... 34
    Major Lynn G. Adams, Superintendent, Pennsylvania State Police, Harrisburg, Pennsyl-
    vania

FEDERAL POLICE... 41
    Albert Langeluttig, Member of the Chicago Bar; Associated with Moses, Kennedy, Stein
    and Bachrach, Chicago, Illinois

THE PRIVATE POLICE OF PENNSYLVANIA..................................... 55
    Jeremiah P. Shalloo, Instructor of Sociology, University of Pennsylvania, Philadelphia,
    Pennsylvania

THE CONTROL AND THE DISCIPLINE OF POLICE FORCES........................ 63
    Donald Stone, National Institute of Public Administration, New York City

POLICE STATISTICS.. 74
    Bennet Mead, United States Bureau of the Census, Washington, District of Columbia

THE ANNUAL POLICE REPORT... 90
    L. S. Timmerman, National Institute of Public Administration, New York City

THE POLICEWOMAN.. 104
    Eleonore L. Hutzel, Deputy Commissioner of Police, Detroit, Michigan

THE POLICE, CRIME AND POLITICS... 115
    Charles E. Merriam, Professor of Political Science, University of Chicago, Chicago, Illinois

THE INTERNATIONAL ASSOCIATION OF CHIEFS OF POLICE AND OTHER
    AMERICAN POLICE ORGANIZATIONS...................................... 121
    Lent D. Upson, Director, Detroit Bureau of Governmental Research; Chairman, Ad-
    visory Committee, Committee on Uniform Crime Records, International Association
    of Chiefs of Police

POLICE JOURNALISM IN THE UNITED STATES................................. 128
    Donald Young, Assistant Professor of Sociology, University of Pennsylvania, Philadelphia,
    Pennsylvania

PART II. PROBLEMS OF POLICE PERSONNEL

THE POLICEMAN'S HIRE... 135
    William C. Beyer, Director, and Helen C. Toerring, Staff Member, Bureau of Municipal
    Research, Philadelphia, Pennsylvania

THE USE OF SCIENTIFIC TESTS IN THE SELECTION AND PROMOTION OF
    POLICE... 147
    L. J. O'Rourke, Director of Personnel Research, United States Civil Service Commission,
    Washington, District of Columbia

PSYCHOLOGICAL METHODS IN THE SELECTION OF POLICEMEN IN EUROPE 160
    Morris S. Viteles, Ph.D., Assistant Professor of Psychology, University of Pennsylvania,
    Philadelphia, Pennsylvania

POLICE TRAINING... 166
    Cornelius F. Cahalane, Police Consultant, New York City

THE POLICE TRAINING SCHOOL.. 170
    George T. Ragsdale, Director, Police School, Louisville, Kentucky

THE ENGLISH POLICE SYSTEM... 177
   A. L. Dixon, C.B., C.B.E., Assistant Secretary at the Home Office, London, England

THE SCHOOL OF CRIMINOLOGY AND OF SCIENTIFIC POLICE OF BELGIUM 193
   Dr. Gustave De Rechter, Director, School of Criminology and of Scientific Police of Belgium, Brussels, Belgium

CRIMINALISTIC INSTITUTES AND LABORATORIES............................ 199
   Dr. Siegfried Türkel, Vice-President, *Académie Internationale de Criminalistique;* Scientific Director, Criminalistic Institute, Police Department, Vienna, Austria

PART III. THE TOOLS AND THE TECHNIQUE OF CRIMINAL INVESTIGATION

CRIMINAL IDENTIFICATION... 205
   J. Edgar Hoover, Director, Bureau of Investigation, Department of Justice, Washington, District of Columbia

THE TECHNIQUE OF THE AMERICAN DETECTIVE........................... 214
   Duncan Matheson, Captain of Detectives, San Francisco, California

THE TECHNIQUE OF INVESTIGATION OF THE ENGLISH DETECTIVE........ 219
   F. J. Crawley, Chief Constable of the City and County of Newcastle, England

THE TECHNIQUE OF CRIMINAL INVESTIGATION IN GERMANY............. 223
   Dr. Robert Heindl, Legation Councillor, German Foreign Office; formerly Commissioner of Police, Berlin, Germany

SCIENCE AND CRIMINAL INVESTIGATION................................. 237
   Harry Söderman, D.Sc., Lecturer on Police Technique, Law School, University of Stockholm, Stockholm, Sweden

MEDICAL SCIENCE IN THE SERVICE OF THE STATE: WITH ESPECIAL REFERENCE TO THE INVESTIGATION OF DEATHS......................... 249
   George Burgess Magrath, A.M., M.D., Instructor in Legal Medicine, Harvard University; Medical Examiner for Suffolk County, Boston, Massachusetts

PSYCHOLOGY IN CRIMINAL INVESTIGATION.............................. 258
   John A. Larson, Ph.D., M.D., Henry Phipps Psychiatric Clinic, Johns Hopkins Hospital, Baltimore, Maryland

BOOK DEPARTMENT.. 269

INDEX TO SUBJECTS.. 283

INDEX TO NAMES... 288

FOREWORD

IT has become almost fashionable to call the police to task for the existence of crime in our country. That this responsibility is in part properly placed there can be no question, for inefficient police service, whether it is in the form of inadequate patrol or the absence of good detective work, necessarily weakens the barrier raised by society against crime, professional crime in particular. Yet, the criticism must not be overstated. The police, after all, is an agency of public service which, like other such agencies, mirrors the opinion and the attitudes of the group which instituted and maintains it. In the last analysis, an inefficient police force is symptomatic of public apathy, which we can hardly expect the police to remedy.

This volume is offered as a contribution to public education. It is hoped, of course, that the police may find in it some helpful ideas, but its primary purpose is to give a wide circle of intelligent readers a conception of the problems which face the police and of the handicaps which the latter must overcome in solving them. An attempt has been made to cover all important phases of police work as it relates to the repression and the prevention of crime. The latter, and extremely important phase of police activity, has unfortunately received too little attention in this volume. This is due, in part at least, to the fact that an article on "Social Work by the Police" has failed to arrive in time for inclusion.

I wish to express my gratitude to all who have freely given of their time and their knowledge in the preparation of these articles, and particularly to the many foreign contributors who, although less directly interested in the project, have generously given us the benefit of their experience. To Mr. Bruce Smith, of the National Institute of Public Administration, New York City, I owe a special debt for expert advice which has greatly aided me in planning the volume.

THORSTEN SELLIN.

Municipal Police Administration

By BRUCE SMITH

National Institute of Public Administration, New York City

THE rôle of police in modern society steadily tends to become more difficult. Viewing the rudimentary police organizations of a little more than a century ago, one is filled with wonder that their work was not more defective than it actually proved to be. There seems to be only one satisfactory explanation. The police of that day were almost exclusively "thief-takers." In other words they were ranged against a fairly definite group of offenders who plied their criminal trades entirely outside of the law. The urgent need for protection made the ordinary citizen a natural ally of the police even when the latter did not enjoy any large degree of public confidence.

GENERAL CONSIDERATIONS

It is not so today. The police no longer confine their attention to groups and individuals who are essentially outlaws. The police function has come to involve intimate regulation of the day-to-day life of nearly every person with whom the police officer comes into contact. Inevitably there has followed an ill-defined yet none the less positive reaction against police restrictions. In the last analysis, this unfavorable result has been due more to the increasing complexities of daily life than to any failure of the police to adjust themselves to the new conditions.

There have, of course, been such failures of adjustment, although they would appear to have been a result rather than a cause. For it must be remembered that police are creatures of legislative enactments, and that their control has sometimes been dictated by some of the wildest vagaries of the legislative imagination. This definition and restriction of powers has at times been carried so far, and the police have found themselves confined within such narrow limits in both administration and criminal investigation, that they have made furtive, and occasionally open efforts to circumvent the laws under which they operate. Laws and ordinances which were unpopular have been ignored, and others which were persistently violated have only occasionally been enforced. For the most part, such departures from the legislative intent have been dictated by practical, rather than corrupt, considerations. In either case, however, they have had a most unfortunate effect upon both police and public. The standard of performance which the penal law should provide has been taken away, the police have drifted with the tides of expediency, and the public, viewing all this, has drawn its own conclusions.

The press, as the mouthpiece of the public, through which the latter hopes and expects to find its views coherently expressed, has scarcely done its part. The most enlightened editorial policies, through which might be secured able discussion of police problems, have often been offset by a news policy designed to appeal to the unschooled and the ignorant. But even editorial policies have frequently been at fault in condemning the police when they were right, and praising them when they were wrong. So there have been few influences at work for the instruction of the public in the realities

1

and the objective standards of police duty.

Nor have we been able to profit greatly from foreign experience, because of the greater simplicity of the police problem there. We can turn with a considerable degree of confidence to European practices concerning police organization and technique, but we can discover little there which has a direct bearing upon our problems of "law enforcement" and the relations of police, press and public. Legislative self-restraint across the seas has succeeded in avoiding most of the pitfalls into which we have blindly stumbled.

The plight in which American police forces recurrently find themselves has a serious effect upon police administration. Being denounced both when they act vigorously and when they adopt a more complaisant attitude, consistent performance is thrown to the winds, each day's work is done without relation to any larger program, and the police force, from top to bottom, becomes chiefly engaged in propitiating those who possess the greatest power to do them injury.

The achievements of American police forces under these adverse circumstances are truly amazing. Foreign observers who perceive the essential unsoundness of much of our legislative provision and police organization are impressed with the quality of work performed by individual police officers. These last represent both the strength and the weakness of our system of crime repression, because while they are responsible for occasional brilliant results, their numbers are relatively so few and their influence upon the entire police organism so slight that they can never be counted as important factors in the effort to improve police service.

Such improvement is now, as in the past, largely dependent upon influences which lie outside the rank and file. Until the statutory basis of police forces is radically revised, the police administrator and the policeman alike will be hedged about and confined in their efforts. Until that revision is accomplished, the work of improving the details of police administration and police duty will necessarily rest upon insecure foundations.

SCOPE AND CHARACTER OF POLICE DUTIES

An outstanding feature of police administration in the United States is its local character. Although the Federal government maintains a number of specialized agencies for the enforcement of particular statutes or groups of statutes, and a few states have placed relatively small but well-organized state police forces in the field, the largest part of the burden of protecting life and property rests squarely upon the municipalities.

The complexities of our Federal union have been reflected in the number and variety of police forces which have sprung up to meet real or imagined emergencies, and have continued to exist almost as a matter of course. This result has come about more by chance than by design. At no time in our history has there been any official effort to define the scope of police activity and to work out a coherent plan for its functioning.

The earliest public police agencies to appear on this continent are still represented by the sheriff, the town constable and the village marshal. Our conception of the police function has been moulded by them, and it is only within recent years that there has been any marked departure from these primitive forms.

Accepted ideas concerning the scope of police duty have followed an even less clearly defined course. As an abstract proposition, the field of the police may be viewed as embracing all, or nearly all, of the administrative powers of government. It has therefore been easy, and has doubtless appeared quite natural, to charge the police with the performance of a wide variety of functions, some of them quite beyond police capacity, and many of so burdensome a nature as to divert the attention both of police administrators and of the rank and file away from the fundamental business of protecting life and property. The following list includes some of the more common of such special activities:

1. Licensing: public hacks and drivers; pawnbrokers, secondhand shops, and junk dealers; pool rooms, dance halls and public exhibitions (including moving picture and stage censorship); Sabbath entertainments; parades; private watchmen, private detectives; railroad police; street vendors.

2. Traffic regulation: immediate control over use of highways both by vehicles and by pedestrians; sometimes extended to include power to designate parking areas, one way streets, and other matters which are legislative in their nature.

3. Public ambulance service.

4. Supervision of paroled convicts.

5. Inspection: exhibition and meeting halls; elevators; storage of liquids and inflammables; oil pollution.

6. Registration of voters and verification of poll lists.

7. Enumeration of inhabitants (police census).

8. Ice breaking in navigable waterways.

9. Examination of prostitutes for venereal diseases.

10. Temporary lodging for the homeless.

11. Emergency relief for the destitute.

12. Free employment agencies.

13. Neighborhood entertainments.

14. Dog pounds.

Not all police departments, of course, exercise each and every one of the foregoing functions. Nevertheless, the list shows the wide range of police duties which are seldom considered when the task of the police is in process of appraisal. These varying responsibilities, some having an intimate relation to the police field and others quite remote from it, raise one of the major problems of police administration. At a time when police and crime problems are of a most pressing nature, it may prove desirable to review the basic ideas upon which our police forces rest, and perhaps to redistribute some of these duties among those governmental agencies best fitted to administer them. In view of the defined limits of this number of the ANNALS, the present discussion will be confined to those features of police organization having the most intimate bearing upon crime control. It will be well to remember, however, that back of them lie these other questions, the solution of which is matter of the greatest moment in some police jurisdictions.

GENERAL ASPECTS OF POLICE ORGANIZATION

The considerable degree of freedom which municipalities enjoy in managing their police forces naturally results in many varieties of police organization. Even where the city charter or other state enactments prescribe the general form of arrangement, there is no recognized system of universal application throughout a given state. It follows that systems of organization are almost as numerous as the municipalities themselves. Few of these variations are of any major import, however, and it is quite possible to name and briefly describe those general forms of organization upon which nearly all of our municipal police forces are constructed. It will be observed that each of these types or systems is chiefly concerned with *control* of police and, hence, with responsibility for its administration.

This matter of police control has always bulked large in the public consciousness. Whatever the original thought may have been, it is clear that we now think of police control as involving a large degree of popular or democratic control; that is to say, there is a conscious effort towards insuring that the police force shall in all respects and in all events be subject to civil power. This profound distrust of an armed, uniformed and disciplined body has been reflected in the steps which have been taken to guard against oppressive police action. In the early days of American police forces, it was not uncommon for the rank and file to be popularly elected, just as many of our rural constables are elected. This was popular control with a vengeance. When that method eventually destroyed itself or became impracticable in the larger cities, recourse was had to devices which would render the administrative head responsive to popular sentiment. The efforts directed to this end are still apparent and they have had a far-reaching effect upon police administration.

THE MUNICIPAL COUNCIL AND POLICE CONTROL

The most common type of police control is now largely confined to the smaller cities, towns and villages. It places the supervision and management of the police force in the hands of a committee of the municipal council, which in turn issues its decrees to a functionary who is generally known as the chief of police. A somewhat similar scheme is followed in many English police jurisdictions with satisfactory results. The political traditions of the United States have, however, prevented a corresponding success in this country. The restricted field in which the English watch committee voluntarily operates finds no counterpart here. Our police committees are not content to confine themselves to broad

questions of public administration affecting the police. They are prone to use their powers in such a way as to regulate the functioning of the police department in the greatest detail. Appointments, promotions, assignments and transfers, disciplinary action and the disposition of individual cases are handled by it as a matter of course. In some instances the police committee has been employed by the council as a convenient instrumentality for the geographic distribution of patronage. In Camden, New Jersey it was common practice for each member of the municipal council to control all police personnel matters affecting his own ward. Thus, if a police vacancy occurred in a given ward, the councilman representing it enjoyed the privilege of designating the recruit to fill it. An identical policy was followed with respect to promotions, assignments and indeed all of the details and ramifications of police management. The police department was thereby placed under the control of a considerable number of masters and ceased to be a coherent public agency.[1]

THE POLICE BOARD

A second form of control is intimately related to the one just described. It substitutes for the councilmanic committee a separate and special police board, made up of individuals who are not members of the local legislative body. This scheme has enjoyed a wide prevalence in the past and despite a pronounced tendency toward other forms it is still fairly common. Its use seems to have arisen from a commendable desire to "take the police out of politics." The most ludicrous efforts were made to this end, all of them being aimed at mechanical devices for removing police administration from

[1] When Camden adopted a commission charter in 1923, these practices disappeared.

political control. Experiments were conducted in organizing the boards on both a bi-partisan and a unipartisan basis. Sometimes there were boards which one was asked to believe were truly non-partisan both in character and operation.

Nearly all such efforts have met with dismal failure. Where bi-partisan boards were set up, the hope was encouraged that the partisan groups represented on it would offset each other. A number of differing results followed, depending upon local conditions or the precise constitution of the board. In some cases the political party enjoying majority representation quickly took command of affairs and relegated the minority party to the background. Sometimes there was a more equal division of control, in which event the management and spoils of the police department were parcelled out among the adverse groups represented. One effect of this was to create a system of political quotas which were carefully observed in making appointments. While the results were what might have been expected, they occasionally had unexpected features. Thus, when Cincinnati employed the quota system, the number of republican aspirants for appointment was always more numerous than the number of democratic aspirants, owing to the overwhelming numerical superiority of the republican party in that city. It was not long before young aspirants, of republican persuasion, were enrolling with the democratic party in order that they might qualify for the much shorter democratic "eligible list," and hence more quickly and easily secure appointment to the police force.

Still a third result followed bi-partisan control. It has happened, though rarely, that the two opposed groups have deadlocked a police board.

Then there was chaos, with conflicting orders issued to the chief, appointments, promotions and pay-rolls held up, and the entire scheme reduced to manifest absurdity.

The Commissioner of Public Safety

The advent of commission government has introduced an entirely different plan of police control. The popularly elected commissioner of public safety exercises not only legislative power as a member of the city commission, but also plenary control over a number of city departments, usually including police, fire, health, welfare and building inspection. This loose collection of agencies is supposed to be related in some occult way, because each one performs a part of the public safety function. In practice, their administration is only remotely related. The effort to bring them together under unified administrative supervision springs largely from the fact that the limited number of commissioners under commission charters makes some kind of grouping absolutely necessary.

Commission government has achieved few successes in the police field. The chief, as the experienced head of the force, is usually displaced from all but the most routine duties of administration, by the inexperienced and nontechnical commissioner of public safety. The chief may acquiesce, and usually does. His eyes are fixed upon the date when he can retire upon pension, and it would be foolhardy for him to risk everything in a test of strength with his superior. If he resists at all, it is furtively. He knows the game better than the safety commissioner and can partially offset the latter's policies by indirect methods of his own. Sometimes, however, the chief is made of sterner stuff, and a head-on collision with the commissioner takes place.

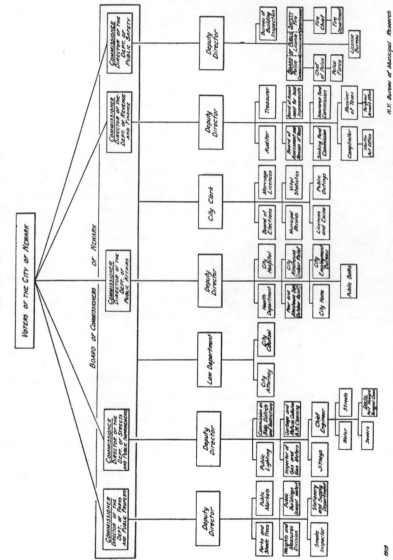

Chart Showing Typical Organization for Police Control Under Commission Government Charters

Then the police department finds itself in its familiar position as the outstanding local political issue. We quote from a report of the Schenectady County (New York) Grand Jury, dated October 20, 1926:

We find the personnel of the [Schenectady] Police Department thoroughly demoralized. There is an utter lack of discipline, of respect for superiors, and little spirit of coöperation. Having had these facts clearly demonstrated to our body, we set about to discover the cause in the hope of finding a remedy.

The cause is without question a spirit of friction and discord between the Commissioner of Public Safety and the Chief of Police. This has spread throughout the rank and file of the department, breeding disrespect in the ranks for the Chief of Police, and holding generally this office in contempt. We find that the Chief of Police has been shorn of most of the authority and powers incident to his office by the Commissioner of Public Safety, with the result that the City of Schenectady benefits but slightly from the ability and experience of the Police Chief.

We find that authority in a uniformed force, over the personnel of that force, should rest somewhere. In deciding the question as to whether it should rest with an experienced, trained police official, or an untrained, inexperienced layman, of short term of office, we are inclined to the former. Under our police rules and regulations in the present instance, the department is run otherwise, and to the detriment of the department.

We find that transfers, details and assignments have been made by the Commissioner, over the head and against the advice and consent of the Chief, which fact has been quickly learned by the persons affected. We find that charges preferred by the Chief and filed with the Commissioner have been disregarded or disapproved of without hearing in the regular way and without calling the Chief in support of these charges. We find particularly that the men chosen by the Chief to work under his direct supervision have been transferred without cause or reason, and others placed there against the consent of the Chief. We find that the unfavorable opinion of the Chief of Police has been courted and encouraged by the Commissioner among the rank and file of the department. We find that permissive orders have been signed by the Commissioner contrary to good police practice against advice of the Chief. We find that private detectives have been working in that city under the direction of the Commissioner unknown to the Chief of Police, at a great cost to the taxpayers, the amount of which is as yet unascertained, and the result of whose work is entirely negligible. We find that the Commissioner assisted Diamente Ragucci in obtaining an interview with William Ross, alias Willie the Wop, a notorious criminal, now confined at Clinton Prison, Dannemora, by communicating with prison authorities, although the Commissioner knew in advance that Ragucci intended publishing any statements he might obtain from Ross reflecting on the Chief of Police. An affidavit reflecting on the character and fitness of the Chief was published by Ragucci in the *Schenectady Gazette* further breathing disrespect and unrest. We find generally arbitrary and officious interference in the business of the Police Department by a Commissioner, however honest and well intentioned, resulting in great harm generally. Without further recital of our findings in this matter, we are of the opinion that the morale of the men of the Department has been undermined; that lack of discipline has been encouraged; that the proper functions and duties of the Chief of Police have been taken away without adequate reason; that disrespect for the office of the Chief has been fostered. We find that the Police Department is in about the state it found itself at the time reorganization was made necessary following the murder of Captain Youmans, and unless this condition is heeded and immediate steps taken to remedy the situation, the citizens of the City generally may have great cause for regret.

This investigation is unique in the fact that none of the officials involved or mentioned are accused or suspected in any way reflecting on their character, honesty, or integrity. This has been freely admitted by all witnesses. It is also freely admitted that the Chief of Police is a man of great experience and training, and competent for the position he holds. We are then met with the question, why has all this discord arisen, and in what manner has the Chief inspired it. The only explanation that has been given after days of cross-examination is that he is a strict disciplinarian and requires obedience of subordinates and compliance with rules. After carefully examining the testimony, we are inclined to the opinion that these are qualifications for the position rather than faults and in any event scarcely any adequate reason or excuse for the actions of his superior.

The foregoing excerpt is remarkable not only for its frankness in dealing with the facts developed by the inquiry, but also for its grasp of the real meaning of the issues involved.

American experience makes it abundantly clear that control by commissioners of public safety offers no solution of our problems of police organization. Unlike the other systems here under analysis, the persistence of this type of control is largely dependent upon the form of local government under which it operates. Earnest efforts have been made to define the respective spheres of the commissioner of public safety and the chief of police. That the distinctions thus drawn have not greatly influenced practical administration is no reflection upon the abstract validity of the conclusions which have been reached. Our local politics being what they are, when we place power and opportunity in the hands of an official, we must expect him to exercise it without much regard for such philosophical limitations as we may place upon him as an afterthought. It would therefore seem as though these conflicts between commissioner and chief are destined to continue so long as commission government endures. Happily for the future of police administration, there are abundant indications that the commission plan is rapidly declining in public favor.

CONTROL BY THE EXECUTIVE

The several forms of organization which recognize police as an executive arm remain to be considered. In all of these the mayor or city manager is the superior police authority, with the chief or commissioner in immediate command. Of this method it may at least be said that it recognizes in some degree the principle of executive responsibility. Sometimes, however, the application of that principle is more apparent than real. Where the chief of police is in immediate and full command, the civil service law not frequently accords him a tenure so carefully protected that the mayor cannot, as a practical matter, remove him for any but the most serious personal or official faults. General incompetence, as evidenced by a whole series of official lapses, is rarely held to be sufficient ground for removal.

On the other hand, if the scheme contemplates partisan management by a non-technical commissioner, the administrative evils described above are quite likely to characterize the police department. In some cities (for example, New York, Chicago, Detroit, Buffalo), the commissioner has been drawn on occasion directly from the professional police force and the advantages of technical qualified supervision thereby secured. While this method obviously has much to commend it and in a few cases has given satisfactory results, the fact should be stressed that there is seldom very much continuity of administrative policy under this method. The chief or commissioner holds office entirely at the pleasure of the city's chief executive, and experience has shown that he is quite likely to be displaced with each

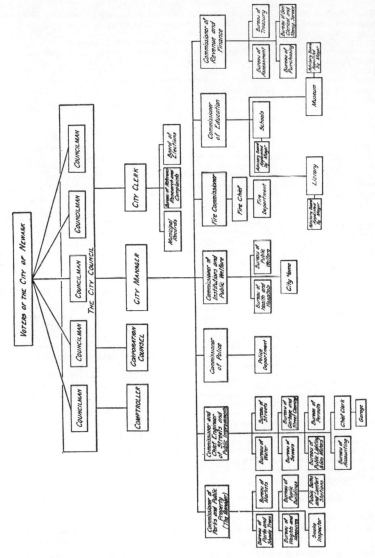

Proposed Commission-Manager Plan
Newark N.J.

Chart Showing Typical Organization for Police Control Under City Manager Charters

N Y Bureau of Municipal Research

1919.

change of administration at the city hall.

We are thereby faced with an apparent conflict between executive responsibility, on the one hand, and experienced administration, on the other. The task of reconciling these two principles in their practical application represents one of the major problems of American police administration.

At this point the question might fairly be raised why this should be a distinctly American problem. The British and the continental police forces—some of them operating under régimes which are quite as democratic as ours—do not seem to be confronted with the same difficulty. The foreign police administrator, whether recruited from civil life or from the rank and file, enjoys a large degree of political independence and security of tenure, and at the same time recognizes his responsibility to the executive. There may be, and there probably are, a considerable number of reasons for this difference, but they all serve to emphasize the usual influence which local partisan politics exercises upon municipal administration in the United States. While the ways and means for correcting this condition quite clearly lie outside the scope of police administration, there is nothing to prevent the invention or the adaptation of methods which will tend to make police management more frequently successful.

MODIFYING THE TENURE OF THE POLICE ADMINISTRATOR

For example, an approach to the reconciliation of executive responsibility and experienced administration might be made by effecting certain changes in the tenure of the police administrator. At the present time, the latter is either a political "bird of passage" with an average tenure, judged by available data, of less than two years, or he is selected by cut-and-dried methods from among the higher officers of the force and accorded a tenure so secure that it is almost impossible to dislodge him. In other words, the alternatives lie between a non-professional, inexperienced and temporary police commissioner, and a permanent professional head who only in rare instances rises above the general level of the force from which he is drawn.

These two alternatives, however, do not exhaust all of the possibilities. In view of the fact that no satisfactory tests for the selection of police administrators have ever been devised, some striking departure from present methods clearly will be desirable. It will not be necessary to provide a kind of civil police dictator who is beyond the reach of popular control. That way lies disaster. Security of tenure might conceivably be purchased at too great a price, and official incompetence be too well protected against vigorous and responsible executive intervention. But if the administrative head is selected without regard to previous residence or official incumbency, is appointed without fixed term, and provision made for his removal only after due notice of the charge and a public hearing, then adequate safeguards both for the public and for the administrator will have been provided. The grounds for removal need not be restricted. It will be enough if the charge and the specification are clearly stated. Whatever the reasons for removal, whether they relate to official acts or to those committed in a private capacity, it is important that the removal shall be effected only after the entire matter has been sufficiently dramatized to capture and hold public attention. Complex devices only serve to confuse popular understanding, but a simple drama, consisting of complaint, answer and final judgment, will meet with no difficulty in holding public attention for the brief period required to accomplish an orderly removal.

The effects of such a scheme must be fairly obvious. In the first place, it would throw open the doors of police administration to a somewhat larger group than are now available in many cities. The outstanding police administrators of the present day have been drawn both from the police force and from civil life. The qualifications involved embrace general personal capacity and intelligence, ability to handle men, and a general knowledge of police practice and procedure. The last named, of course, can only be acquired through actual experience, but it can be learned. There is no mystery about it. If an occasional able civilian is placed in charge of the police force and left there long enough to acquire a knowledge of its technical phases, there is no reason why he should not prove as satisfactory as a professional policeman in the same post.

In the second place, the plan briefly outlined here will place the head of the police force at least on a parity with the rank and file in the matter of tenure. "Orders will be orders" when the administrator is not viewed by the rank and file as a merely temporary figure. Progress will thereby be made towards establishing a consistent and effective discipline.

Finally, the way will be opened towards the development of something like a science of police administration. In the United States there has been a fair degree of continuity in the service of the rank and file, even though many police administrators arrive and depart from public office with a rapidity which is kaleidoscopic. The development of police administration has thereby been greatly retarded. But,

in the matter of police practice and procedure, in which the professional policeman has had an opportunity to apply the results of years of practical experience, there has been developed a body of knowledge concerning ways and means of repressing crime which is quite equal to that produced under foreign systems. The present state of the "science of police administration" on the one hand, and of "the policeman's art" on the other, are in such striking contrast as to carry their own lesson. There is no substitute for informed and intelligent leadership.

Although other papers in this number of the ANNALS deal extensively with questions of personnel management, it is necessary to give them at least passing notice here, for if we are to develop professional police administrators, they must, in the nature of things, be given the ways and means by which their policies may be carried into effect by the rank and file. No exaggeration is involved in the statement that the direction and the control of personnel constitutes one of the most important and also one of the most difficult problems with which the police administrator is confronted. But we have inverted our merit system and have given to the rank and file a certain measure of freedom from political influence which ordinarily is not shared by their chief. To expect superior results from such a scheme is to demand too much from human nature. The *leader* must also *command,* and his commands must be supported by something more substantial than a mere confident reliance upon the good intentions of all mankind. Whatever may be the future development of our civil service systems, whatever steps may be taken for a more scientific method of selection and promotion, it seems clear that the police administrator must be given a more decisive rôle in the selection, promotion and discipline of the rank and file.

DEPARTMENTAL ORGANIZATION

The internal organization of police departments is conditioned in each particular case by the scope of its responsibilities. If it is burdened with a wide range of inspectional duties of such technical nature that they must be performed by specialized personnel, the problem of organization becomes greatly complicated and may prove well-nigh impossible of solution. But, even when the force is confined to the most rudimentary of police services, grave problems arise in distributing responsibility for immediate supervision. The organization charts appearing herewith depict the situation in a number of American cities. Although local conditions sometimes have a far-reaching effect, these examples all depict the underlying problem. In every city of considerable size, it becomes necessary to consider how many divisions and bureaus may be placed under the *immediate* supervision of any one superior. In some cases the police administrator has such immediate supervision over as many as twenty distinct units, whereas his aides and bureau chiefs will ordinarily be responsible for not more than four or five. Right here may be found one of the serious weaknesses of police administration, since the very form of organization imposes an impossible task upon the head of the force. It can only be corrected by a careful grouping of related activities, and the allocation of each group to a deputy or other subordinate of the chief. By such means, instead of fifteen or twenty distinct units, the divisions directly responsible to the chief may be reduced to five or six in number: the patrol force; the detective division; the division of records; the services of transportation, com-

munication and supply; inspection and training; and police surgeons.

The results secured from such a redistribution prove large when compared with the ease with which the change may be made. For the administrative head cannot become involved in adjusting all of the complex inter-relations of daily activities without surrendering to routine in the end. When that surrender takes place the administrative head ceases to be a leader and becomes merely a cog in the machine. Farther down in the official hierarchy, the number of subordinate units may be increased, until, at the very bottom, where the units to be supervised are not bureaus but individuals, they may reach a considerable number. But at the top, the lines of authority should converge upon a mere half dozen men, who alone report directly to the administrative head. The latter is then left free to experiment and test, to adapt and apply various means to a given end. Intelligent leadership may thereby be made effective.

RELATIONS WITH SHERIFFS AND STATE POLICE

The relations between municipal police forces and certain county officials may conceivably have a bearing upon police organizations of the future. In some of the larger cities, such as New York and St. Louis, which include one or more counties within their boundaries, the sheriff has been relieved of his police function either by law or practice. In most instances, however, the sheriff exists side by side with the urban police force, and may, if he chooses, act independently of the latter. Since the sheriff's office is ill-designed for systematic policing, there is little actual conflict between the two agencies in routine police work. But when an outstanding crime cap-

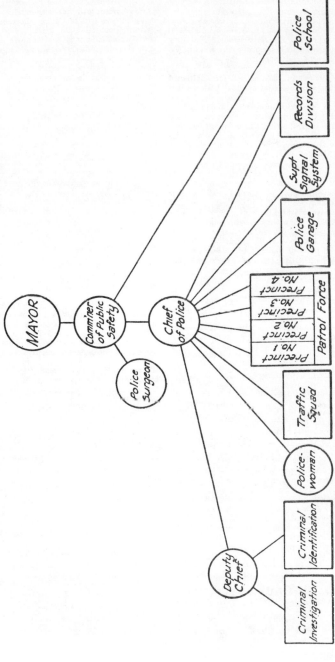

CHART SHOWING THE HIGHLY CENTRALIZED ORGANIZATION OF THE SYRACUSE POLICE BUREAU
Larger cities commonly have a similar organization in exaggerated form

tures popular attention, the sheriff will occasionally grasp the opportunity to take an active and dramatic part in the investigation which follows. While it must be conceded that this practice is largely confined to the smaller municipalities, the latter are far more numerous than the larger cities and their need for effective police action no less important.

A somewhat similar type of intrusion appears in connection with industrial disturbances. In such cases, if the local police force is unable, through lack of man-power, adequately to guard industrial property, recourse may be had to the sheriff. Although the latter is even less prepared to detach regular officers than is the municipal police, he can always fall back upon the time-honored practice of designating special deputies. The latter, who become police officers by the most simple of processes, are entirely untrained in the restrained use of the large powers conferred upon them and easily fall under suspicion of being strike-breakers. In unusual cases, the sheriff may even contract with the plant-owners to provide a given number of special deputies at a per diem rate in excess of that for which they may be readily secured. Any surplus constitutes his own compensation. Special deputies recruited in this fashion are quite likely themselves to become a serious threat to law and order. The task of the municipal police in holding the scales of justice in balance as between employer and striker, is then most difficult to perform.

Until the time arrives for consolidation of police forces by counties or even larger areas, there would seem to be only one means for meeting this problem. Its solution will involve statutory restriction upon the use of special deputies within corporate limits, and an interchange of municipal police in times of great stress. The latter is authorized by the laws of Illinois, and if systematically developed would doubtless prove to be a distinct advance over the roustabouts and gunmen who are now occasionally vested with temporary police authority.

Where state police forces are in operation, a new set of difficulties arise in connection with industrial disturbances. The local police naturally resent what they consider the intrusion of the state police, as a reflection upon their own ability to handle the situation, and the popular mind accepts the appearance of the state police as a deliberate attack upon what is vaguely known as "home rule." Even though we view this sentiment of local independence as mistaken in its application, it is so deep-rooted that it cannot readily be changed and will continue to exercise an extensive influence upon state police administration. So long, however, as the state governments are ultimately responsible for the maintenance of law and order within their borders, they will and must continue to apply repressive measures when local police are inactive or overwhelmed, either through the state police or the militia. Under these circumstances, it would appear that the solution of the matter will ultimately depend upon the measures taken to strengthen municipal police forces, by a formal or informal consolidation of their effective strength over a considerable area.

RELATIONS WITH CORONER

Although the office of coroner is destined eventually to disappear, its roots lie deep in the past, and it may be expected to exercise a steady, though perhaps diminishing influence upon homicide investigations for many years to come. The coroner system takes a number of differing forms, not all of which have an undesirable effect upon police work.[2] But as originally introduced into our county governments, and as a matter of prevailing practice today, the coroner is an elected functionary who combines in himself the techniques and some of the functions of the police, the prosecutor, the court and the pathologist. He is usually accorded by law an exclusive right to the official custody of the bodies of persons who have met with violent or suspicious deaths. But, the local police and the prosecutor also have a function to perform and a responsibility to discharge. As a matter of common practice, all three conduct active and independent investigations. If the homicide has been committed in a village or other small community. there may on unusual occasions be added the sheriff and the state police, each pursuing his own line of investigation but all subject to such restrictions as the coroner may see fit to impose upon them. It seems clear that a more orderly and systematic procedure can only be introduced at the expense of the ancient perogatives of the coroner. The changes which have been proposed include means for assuring a higher degree of technical qualification for the coroner, or as an alternative, the abolition of the office and the transfer of its functions to the prosecutor.

POLICE AND PROSECUTOR

Relations of police and prosecutor have an even more extensive influence, because they are not confined to any particular variety of criminal case. The theoretical plan upon which these two public agencies act is somewhat as follows: To the police is delegated the duty of conducting the investigation,

[2] State of New York; *Report of the Special Joint Committee on Taxation and Retrenchment, 1923*, p. 51.

locating witnesses, accumulating evidence, and apprehending the accused. With these things accomplished, the case is turned over to the prosecutor for further action, and the police step into a passive rôle. What actually happens, however, is that the prosecutor exercises a preponderant influence upon the conduct of the police investigation, sometimes from the very outset. The stages by which this result is brought about vary somewhat in order and importance, but may, nevertheless, be generally described.

In the first place, the prosecutor, in nearly all American jurisdictions, is an elected officer. He conducts a vigorous and popular campaign for election and makes certain vague or definite pledges with reference to the kind of law enforcement which will characterize his administration. Something of this sort seems to be expected of him by the electorate. The mass of voters are quickly and easily stirred by appeals to their reason or their prejudice. The issue of an election of a prosecutor is therefore quite likely to turn upon questions of "wet," "moist," "dry," or "bone-dry" enforcement of the prohibition law; suppression of commercialized vice or "outward order and decency"; a policy of "no quarter" for gunmen, or a Christian application of the "Golden Rule," and similar alternatives.

Now it is quite true that the laws of state or nation have already declared the public policy with respect to such questions, but to the local communities are given such wide powers of administration that it is almost inevitable that the manner and the extent of their exercise should be made a political issue by candidates for prosecutor. The popular choice is thereby made to turn upon questions of statecraft, rather than upon technical qualifications or disinterested administration.

The prosecutor takes office with a more or less clear-cut mandate from the people of the county. Under these circumstances, his influence over the police department is likely to be very great. If the latter proves reluctant to follow the new leadership, there are a number of ways in which it can be forced into line, as through the influence of party organization and the partisan press. Furthermore, the prosecutor himself holds the key to the courts, and can in a measure determine the what, when and how of their functioning. Police administrators who have been tossed about in a few such conflicts, and who have not either lost their jobs or resigned in disgust, arrive at last at the complacent philosophy that they will give the public what it appears to want *at the moment*. They will tolerate or suppress according to the apparent drift of the latest election returns, and will forget, if they ever understood, the social advantages of a vigorous and consistent administration of the penal law. The control of police and law enforcement becomes definitely removed from police headquarters. It is quite likely to be found in the office of the prosecutor, who, as likely as not, is thinking rather of his chances of election to the governorship, than the day-to-day problems of criminal prosecution.

It must not be concluded that this is the only way in which prosecutors usurp the police function, or that the police are not sometimes themselves at fault. Even usurpation by the prosecutor may be tinctured by a commendable vigor in performing a public service. Thus, it is not uncommon to find the prosecutor actively participating in the investigation of criminal cases and even formally taking charge of them as a matter of lawful right. To one familiar with the laborious technique of such inquiries, the spectacle has its humorous features. After all, the prosecutor is merely an attorney-at-law who has been raised to his present station by a popular plurality. As a criminal investigator, he is the merest amateur,[3] but as a lawyer he is presumed to know the value of evidence, a field of knowledge of which the police are occasionally quite ignorant. Under such circumstances, the prosecutor has an answer ready: the police only deal with the superficial aspects of the case; they are content if they can lay their hands on a suspect and care little for the niceties of procedure which may mark the difference between a successful and an unsuccessful prosecution; or the statements of witnesses are so carelessly prepared that they are valueless in a court of law. Where such complaints are well-founded, as they sometimes are, the burden of correcting the fault clearly lies on the police.

But, the prosecutor may go even further. He may have detectives detailed from the police force to his own office, where they work to all intents and purposes as a separate agency, or he may even recruit an entirely independent body of criminal investigators. Where prosecutors have been notably strong, and the police notably weak and politics-ridden, as in Kansas City, Missouri, the public learns in time to turn to the former in reporting offenses, with the result that the police are left entirely without official knowledge of the commission of certain crimes, on the solution of which they might, conceivably, shed some light.

[3] Even an amateur, of course, may be capable of positive brilliancy. See, for example, *The State* vs. *Harold Israel, Journal of Criminal Law and Criminology*, Vol. XV, No. 3, p. 406; in which Mr. Homer S. Cummings, State's Attorney of Fairfield County, Connecticut, succeeded, after a long and patient inquiry, in clearing a youth of murder, for which the latter had already been arrested and formally charged by the coroner.

This duality of police leadership is an especially serious matter because the present drift and tendency is directly towards the further aggrandizement of the prosecutor at the expense of the police. Unless this is checked, the prosecutor will eventually become the virtual head of the police department, and an elected and transitory head at that. In view of the difficulties which have surrounded police administration in the past such a contingency would without any doubt be fraught with the most undesirable consequences. Police would be linked up more closely than ever with local partisan politics, and the present slow drift towards professional administration definitely reversed.

CHECKING INTERFERENCE BY PROSECUTOR

There are several ways in which this tendency may be checked. One method, of course, would consist in developing a professional leadership of the police department which would be sufficiently secure in its tenure actively to combat intrusion by the prosecutor. The feeble efforts towards that end and the meagre results secured have already been described.

Another means, which is rather more promising of early effect because it is not dependent upon legislative approval, would consist in enlarging the scope and enriching the technique of criminal investigation. This course will involve considerable improvements upon prevailing detective practice. At the present time, criminal investigation in the United States is largely dependent upon two old and familiar devices; the professional or non-professional "stool-pigeon," and the liberal use of the "third degree." It so happens that both of these are of such nature that they can rarely be employed effectively by the prosecutor. If the informer is produced in open court as a witness, it may be with danger to his personal safety, and his future usefulness to the police is in any case certain to be impaired. Detectives are, therefore, reluctant to disclose such sources of criminal information. Likewise, confessions under suspicion of having been extorted by fear or force have little value in the eyes of trial juries and are likely to recoil upon the prosecution. It is, therefore, only by enlarging the scope and increasing the certitude of criminal investigations that police departments can hope to deprive the prosecutor of his one legitimate excuse for intruding upon them.

To the established methods of criminal identification, now rapidly becoming universal, must be added the newer *modus operandi* systems, forensic ballistics, and the painstaking study and analysis of all the many physical traces which may be left at the scene of a crime. A settled policy of systematic search for latent fingerprints will in itself go far towards strengthening the case for submission to courts and juries, because the latter are now quite ready to accept them at face value, and their admissibility in evidence is firmly established as a matter of law. Police training schools may also contribute their share by placing emphasis upon the law of evidence, and the purely practical considerations with which it is surrounded.

Along with these refinements of technique, must go a larger degree of supervision over individual investigations. Too often the chief of detectives confines his attention to those cases which receive the greatest publicity from the press, and exhausts his energies in the first hand investigation of such cases. If the investigating personnel of a police force actually receives day-to-day supervision from the chief of detectives and his immediate aides, the latter will enjoy few opportunities to pursue their own favored inquiries. Even the simplest kind of assignment records and progress reports, if closely and intelligently controlled, would yield impressive results in the vast majority of American police departments.

POLICE AS PROSECUTORS

The foregoing proposals are directed at the means which may be employed by the police in resisting, or making unnecessary, frequent interference by the prosecutor in the conduct of police work. There remain to be considered, what steps should be taken to remove the possibility of conflict. In this connection, the fact should be emphasized that so long as police and prosecutors are separately constituted, there is bound to be an overlapping of interest and of activity by the two agencies. It follows that conflict in criminal investigations is a natural and inevitable part of our prosecutor-police system. To draw a sharp and arbitrary line of demarcation between the fields of the two agencies has already proved ineffective. It would therefore appear that if conflict is to be prevented—and it should be prevented in the interests of successful crime control—one of these two agencies must be definitely subordinated to the other, since both cannot be master in the same field. To place the police under the administrative control of the prosecutor would tend to perpetuate existing evils and would almost certainly bar the way to technical and professional leadership of the force. The only alternative will be to recognize that prosecution is an inseparable part of the police function and to organize the police department accordingly. Although this proposal will appear to be somewhat radical on its face, it must be conceded that the chief objection to it will arise from the reluctance of the American people to surrender the power they now enjoy to dictate at the polls when law enforcement is to be lax, and when it is to be vigorous. That attitude, however, represents one of the underlying faults in our criminal justice system, because it renders an abstract and disinterested administration of the law either supremely difficult or altogether impossible.

It may be objected, also, that American police departments are not yet prepared to wield any such extensive power with restraint and a sense of civic responsibility. As to the great mass of police forces this position is well taken, although restraint and a responsible attitude cannot well be developed so long as the police play a minor and passive rôle in the prosecution. And there are even now a few police forces which have developed a sufficiently professional approach to the problems of administration to make this departure well worth attempting.

There will be no dearth of foreign models, of which one will warrant special attention. Under the English system, the police regularly engage a firm of barristers to prosecute the general run of criminal cases. When unusually difficult cases arise, special counsel may be employed for the purpose, and it is only in the gravest offenses that the director of public prosecutions, a Crown officer, may intervene and exercise the privilege of designating counsel. The fact that English police administration is largely decentralized, as here, would render this plan of prosecution easily adaptable to our own governmental structure. In view of the continuing difficulties arising from prosecution by an elective officer, who owes no administrative responsibility to any executive authority, some effort to develop a closely articulated instrumentality and a consistent procedure is of prime importance to the future of criminal justice in this country.

THE POLICE AND THE PUBLIC

Up to this point, we have been chiefly concerned with questions of police organization and function and their general bearing upon actual police work. With few exceptions, these matters, which intimately affect the performance of police duty, nevertheless lie quite without the scope of police responsibility. Where defects have been indicated, they may be corrected, for the most part, only by some authority which is superior to the police department; by the city or state governments, or by the electorate. From the very fact that they are not a primary responsibility of the police, the latter have been prone to ignore them; to accept the means and methods provided by law on the casual assumption that they are the surest and best; or when recognized as faulty, to withhold criticisms in the belief that any opinions which might be volunteered would be either misinterpreted or thoughtlessly rejected. It is easy to see the benefits which might follow from a more general confidence in the police, and equally easy to understand the reasons why popular confidence has been withheld in some instances. Enough has already been said to show the handicaps under which the police labor, owing to faulty organization and allied matters. Some have been thoughtlessly imposed, while others have been deliberately invented as means whereby the police might be prevented from committing abuses of power and authority. The conclusion is inescapable that the police must take the initiative in regaining public confidence as a step preliminary to the removal of some of these burdens.

In what ways can this be accomplished? What, in the last analysis, are the reasons for public dissatisfaction? It is probable that there are many, some of them vague, some fairly distinct in their outlines. First and foremost should be placed the popular suspicion, only occasionally well founded, that the police force is a hierarchy of corruption, which is cunningly employed for the collection of graft. This opinion has a considerable historical basis and became crystallized in a time when it had more foundation than is now the case. But, it may justly be objected that this suspicion is not by any means confined to police activity; that other municipal departments have been proved to be subject to the same charge; and that it therefore does not constitute a sufficient ground for singling out the police for special lack of confidence. Next may be mentioned the almost necessary unpopularity of police work, involving as it does restriction upon the complete freedom of action of the individual. The universal employment of traffic control has tended to make this problem even more acute, since all citizens, without distinction, now feel the weight and pressure of police restrictions, and even a hint of overbearing demeanor by traffic officers is quickly resented and long remembered. Police departments have not been slow to sense the danger, however, and have quite generally impressed the rank and file with the importance of a civil and even courteous attitude towards the general public. In some police departments it is literally true that a charge of incivility against a policeman is viewed as being a matter of grave import, which if established may involve a more severe administrative penalty than would unauthorized absence from post, or slight intoxication. This change in the official attitude is too recent to have influenced all members of a given police force, but because its effect is cumulative the next decade should see a marked improvement in.this phase of the relations with the public.

The solution of such difficulties is fairly obvious. It will involve a steadily improving attitude of the police towards the public from which restoration of public confidence may be expected to follow almost as a matter of course. But, this is more easily said than done. The old and unfavorable police tradition retards many administrators in their efforts towards placing police service on a new basis. Moreover, they are faced at every turn with conditions which are not even remotely within their control; with the uncertainties which surround their official tenure; with unsuitable or unsound methods of recruiting and promotion, which are frequently turned over to a civil service commission; with systems of police discipline which are nothing short of absurd; and with a scheme of administrative checks and balances which renders vigorous and informed leadership a manifest impossibility.

POLICE TRAINING

Despite these influences, the situation is not altogether desperate, for it must be remembered that police are only just emerging from a time when they were viewed as being little removed from the unskilled worker. We have recruited the rank and file in a manner which has suggested that physical fitness was not only the prime, but the sole desideratum. Then, having placed the new patrolman in a uniform and equipped him with a night stick and a service revolver, we have been accustomed to send him out into the night, with little or no supervision, in the belief that the uniform, the badge and the gun have endowed

him with a technical expertness which would be equal to the almost unregulated discretion which accompanies them. Sometimes a superior takes him in hand, imparts to him the sage advice of an elder and regales him with the distilled wisdom derived from many years of police work. This ceremony may last anywhere from ten minutes to an hour, rarely longer. At its conclusion, the recruit is to all intents and purposes a policeman. At all events, he is assigned to police duty.

Sometimes the ceremony—it is little else—is even more brief. In a certain city located in New York State, the commissioner of public safety has boiled down the whole matter of preliminary instruction to a few sentences. His methods are so striking and novel that they may best be described in his own words:

I say to him (the recruit) that now he is a policeman, and I hope that he will be a credit to the force. I tell him that he doesn't need anybody to tell him how to enforce the law; that all he needs to do is to go out on the street and keep his eyes open. I say: "You know the Ten Commandments, don't you? Well, if you know the Ten Commandments and you go out on your beat and you see somebody violating one of those Commandments, you can be sure that he is also violating some law."[4]

The time is not far distant when this would have represented a fair example of the official attitude towards police training. That it is no longer a fair example is due not to the fact that it has virtually disappeared, because it has not. But, within recent years there has been a pronounced swing towards formal police training, a development so definite and positive that it has set many old-time police officers thinking in new terms. Formal instruction in the policeman's art has

[4] New York State Crime Commission, 1927; *Report of the Subcommission on Police*, p. 27.

been an outstanding police achievement of our time—perhaps *the* achievement. It has arrived none too soon. The rank and file, being provided with no standards, have naturally provided standards of their own. Being unschooled in discipline, they have proved incapable of administering discipline to the public with satisfaction.

The police schools are changing all that. The best of them succeed in inculcating a sense of responsibility which can go hand in hand with self-confidence in the exercise of newly acquired power.

Such schools, however, are still relatively few. There are still a number of the larger cities which do not maintain satisfactory training courses for police. Pedagogical method is lacking, as well as a sufficient number of texts having local application. Time and continuing effort will cure such defects, but when one turns to small municipalities and to those of even moderate size, one finds a condition which is not so easily met. In the municipal police force, less than two hundred strong, it is next to impossible to maintain an effective training unit. Clearly some means must be found either for grouping such communities in a coöperative effort, or the state government must step in and supervise the instruction of the rank and file. The first alternative has already been accepted in the state of New York, with results that are thoroughly impressive. If this experiment works as well in other jurisdictions—it is impending in Michigan—there will be no need for turning to the second alternative, which will almost certainly be resisted by some cities. Experience has shown, however, that the possibility of state interference often stimulates local initiative, and it may well prove to be the case in the matter of police training. Certain it is that the

systematic instruction not only of recruits but of veteran policemen and precinct officers offers one of the most promising means towards restoring public confidence upon a foundation which cannot be easily shaken.

THE TECHNIQUE OF CRIMINAL INVESTIGATION

There are, nevertheless, other causes for public dissatisfaction and lack of confidence. Thus, the public mind and conscience is distressed by occasional evidence of prisoners being wantonly manhandled, the application of the third degree in extorting confessions, and similar practices. It is quite useless if one argues—as one can argue—that laxity of prosecution and the indifference of magistrates sometimes drive the police to extreme and extralegal methods, or to point to the fact that the police rarely extort "confessions" from wholly innocent persons. Such arguments are unavailing. Public sentiment has crystallized on these matters—here, as in England—and the only question which is left for the police to decide is the ways and means by which effective police work may be done without recourse to such measures.

It is, unfortunately, true that many police departments would be left without familiar weapons if they were deprived of "stool-pigeons" and forced confessions, and these will, therefore, not be lightly discarded. But the day of their disappearance may be hastened if the police will accord more respectful regard to the inherent possibilities of latent fingerprints, firearms and bullet identification, the *modus operandi* system, and the painstaking search for other traces which are now largely ignored or too hastily cast aside.

When the time comes that criminal investigation operates upon a more scientific basis, when the rubber hose and even more severe devices may at last be relegated to police museums, it seems reasonable to suppose that public antipathy to police investigations will be replaced by individual assistance to the agents of law and order. The police now complain, and rightly, that their work is done against an undercurrent of popular displeasure, and that they do not now receive the aid which could and should be volunteered by persons having knowledge of value to those conducting investigations. The wise police administrator will withhold his recriminations, however, and will strive to place the technique of detective inquiry upon a new and higher plane. With that accomplished, a larger degree of coöperation from individuals may well be secured without further effort.

THE PUBLIC AND POLICE PROTECTION

The third major reason for lack of confidence in the police arises from a feeling of personal insecurity; from a belief that one is insecure in his life and his goods, and a conviction that the police are responsible. This conclusion may or may not be just. That some of our cities have witnessed an extraordinary increase in crimes of violence, particularly those in which firearms are used or displayed, may not be doubted, even in the absence of reliable and comparable crime statistics. But it is equally true that the so-called current disrespect for law does not always result in an abnormally high crime rate. It may also be argued that to hold the police department responsible for the crime rate is like holding the health department responsible for the death rate, since both of these public agencies deal with natural and inevitable human phenomena. Moreover, the police, as we have seen, are not solely and exclusively responsible for the administra-

tion of the criminal law. They share it with many other justice agencies, and their field is in some respects so restricted and circumscribed by law and practice that the full power of police authority is seldom applied.

Over against this view stands the fact that the police constitute the first line of defense against crime and occupy a much larger part of the public consciousness than any other instrumentality of justice. Relatively few citizens can recall ever having seen a judge; fewer still, a prosecutor, coroner, sheriff, probation officer or prison warden. The patrolman is thoroughly familiar to all. His uniform picks him out from the crowd so distinctly that he becomes the living symbol of the law—not always of its majesty, but certainly of its power. Whether the police like it or not, they are forever marked men.

THE VANISHING PATROLMAN

How have police forces met this situation? What have they done to give the citizen a sense of security and a reliance upon the one visible instrument of justice? The householder's common complaint to the patrolman that "You're never here when I want you" brings the retort that "You never want me when I'm here." Both statements have a certain accuracy, and while seemingly opposed, may be readily reconciled. Upon them hangs the explanation of what has been happening to police patrol and the effect of this development upon public understanding and support.

Uniformed patrol is a vanishing institution. The repressive influence of the uniformed police officer is gradually, but none the less surely, being withdrawn. Robberies, burglaries and felonious assaults are almost never knowingly committed in the full view and presence of a policeman, nor even in the immediate neighborhood of the spot where he happens for the moment to be. When "on view" arrests are made for these crimes, it is usually because the police have appeared on the scene unexpectedly and without warning.

No one can measure the repressive effect of uniformed patrol, but that its influence in discouraging criminal acts is very great does not admit of the slightest doubt. Professional police officers are in entire agreement on this point. When they speak of "crime prevention" they often refer to this *repressive influence* rather than to efforts directed at the removal of the underlying causes of criminal conduct. Uniformed patrol is in fact fundamental to successful police work. Not only does it serve to discourage the commission of criminal acts and thereby serve the primary end of police protection, but it also provides the means for securing a highly miscellaneous kind of information which, nevertheless, contributes to successful criminal inquiry. The patrolman is the eyes and the ears of the police department.

Yet, in the face of these facts and of this unanimity of judgment among police officers, there is an almost universal tendency towards the dispersion of the patrol force. In city after city we find the same general condition, and it is rare indeed that more than one fourth of the uniformed force is actually available for patrol duty. This means that under the prevailing three-platoon laws, only about one twelfth of the total force is actually on patrol at any given time. The thin blue line has been stretched to the breaking point. Why this condition, which on the face of it, and by general agreement, is unsound and positively dangerous?

In the last analysis, it all goes back to the fact that about ninety per cent of the police budget is expended for personal service—for the salaries of the rank and file, precinct officers, and their superiors. The rising scale of police salaries has therefore heavily influenced the police budget and has made mayors and municipal councils reluctant to authorize increases in numerical strength. While this influence towards retrenchment has been making itself felt, other influences have been at work, which have enormously increased the demand for police service. The largest and most universal of these new demands has been created by the traffic problem. But there are others which also are highly important. Patrolmen are detailed to the offices and the homes of city officials, to dance halls, ball parks, amusement centers, industrial plants, and many other public and private places. Sometimes it seems as though everybody "with influence" were striving to secure the gratuitous services of one or more policemen. Provision for full compensation to police on sick leave or the disability roll has not been balanced by a corresponding care in the protection of the force against malingering, and police surgeons tend more and more to render free medical service instead of exercising medical supervision and discipline. The organization of the police department, already loose, becomes overburdened with a variety of new offices and bureaus, which fit into no general scheme and plan, which duplicate in part the work of existing agencies, and which divert and absorb their share of the patrol strength. Temporarily disabled men are sometimes brought into headquarters and clerical work discovered for them. Before the disability has terminated, a clever fellow thus specially detailed can invent a perfectly amazing variety of paper work which may serve as a reason for not returning him to the arduous duties of patrol. He secures a typewriter, then an assistant, then an office, and in time he has a "bureau," and he is its chief!

EFFECTIVE PATROL IMPERATIVE

Meanwhile, and in the face of this kind of patrol dilution, the decimated ranks are supposed to carry on. The burden of patrol supervision by lieutenants and sergeants is shifted to the police telegraph boxes, which record at one or more central points the duty calls made by patrols. In many instances, this central record showing the places and times of routine duty calls, is never examined and checked in order to determine whether the patrolman was actually on duty, or was in his "coop," or off post altogether. Thus, with both men and machines available to assure the physical presence of the patrolman at a given time and place, in actual practice patrol supervision has largely failed because chief reliance was placed upon neither by the administrative head.

Other kinds of plant and equipment also have their influence. Thus, the number of district stations may have an important bearing upon patrol quotas, because every such structure requires from twelve to fifteen to operate it throughout the twenty-four hours of the day. Thier chief value lies in their use as convenient means for the distribution of patrols to assigned posts, and as centers from which response can be made to emergency calls. Thirty years ago, the size of police districts was necessarily small, and the number of district stations correspondingly large, because of lack of rapid transit. In these days of traction companies and motorbus lines, motorized police equipment, police telegraph boxes, recall signals, and direct radio communication with patrol cars in case of emergency, the whole basis for a large number of police districts is destroyed.

The time has definitely arrived when we must cease to view the patrol force as a mere reservoir of inert man-power, to be drawn off and diverted for the purpose of staffing every new activity with which the police may be entrusted. The integral strength of that force should be protected at all costs, because when it is weakened, police headquarters is deprived of its senses of sight and hearing, and the community loses the only considerable repressive influence upon crime which the police can provide.

It is doubtful whether a single experienced police officer can be found who will differ with this general conclusion. Why then, it may be asked, has protective patrol sunk to such a low state? The most obvious rejoinder to this query is that, as already shown, many municipal police departments are placed under the administrative control of amateurs rather than professional policemen. But even where the latter find themselves in the saddle, one can but sympathize with their strenuous efforts to avoid being unhorsed. The hand of the politician has always been prominent in police management, and the publicity value of police novelties is well understood in many city halls. So it happens that the prospect for patrol rehabilitation is not especially encouraging under existing forms of police control. The immediate outlook would be better, however, if professional police administrators accorded to this matter the attention which it deserves and lost no opportunity to raise their voices, however feeble for the moment, in defense of an institution of which they well know the value. The needs of protective patrol are so urgent as to warrant all the police and private influence which can be brought to bear in its behalf.

PATROL SYSTEMS

Assuming the existence of an adequate patrol force, in what manner is it to be employed? In the United States we have been prone to adopt only the more obvious methods. Our patrol posts have been confined to three general types, the "circular," the "straight-away," and the "fixed" post. Although the extent and shape of the territory to be covered varies under each of these, they are alike in that they all assume that only one man shall be made responsible for a given area. No fault can be found with this principle of single responsibility; when supported by rigid patrol supervision, it has yielded generally satisfactory results. Its weakness lies in the fact that it presupposes that the individual patrolman will be assigned to an area for which he can actually be held responsible; that the extent of the patrol post will be no greater than he can control at all times. But when the patrolman is given an area containing ten or even twenty linear miles of streets, the whole theory of responsibility breaks down because it is recognized as unfair and impractical to attempt to apply it. The patrolman cannot cover more than a small part of the post in an hour on foot, and even if mounted on horse, motorcycle, or bicycle, or patrolling in a motor car, the effect of routine will inevitably lead him to confine his attentions to some streets and thus to neglect others. Thus it comes about that while the entire area is protected in theory, certain large parts of it may never witness the passing of a uniformed patrolman. The latter are unquestionably left without protection, except in name.

A system which has been carefully worked out and applied in England seeks to meet this condition.[5] This

"sector plan," as it may be called, consolidates several patrol posts into a single unit and assigns a number of patrolmen to cover it by *prearranged routes* and *simultaneously*. Each patrolman is provided with a route card which shows the course to be followed and a time schedule for arriving at certain control points. In this way does headquarters assure itself that the entire area is in fact being covered.

The system has other features which are no less important. In recognition of the fact that uncertainty and the element of surprise are essential characteristics of successful patrol, the routes and schedules are changed daily, four or five sets of the latter being available for each sector. Another interesting feature of this plan is its flexibility. Since prearranged routes are followed there is no necessity that all should be started at one time. So the three distinct "shifts" or "platoons" into which the twenty-four hours are usually divided are discarded altogether. Patrolmen report for duty at many designated hours throughout the day and night, thereby avoiding dispersion and concentration of the patrol force thrice daily which is a characteristic of all American systems and which leaves large portions of the city entirely unprotected at the hours when reliefs are being effected.

An entirely different English method, known as the decentralized box system, is also aimed at the same mark.[6] Under this scheme a booth (of the kind familiar to many American police forces) is placed on each patrol post, which serves as the local office of the constable on duty. From it he communicates with his district station, and at it all orders are left by couriers from headquarters. The distinctive feature

[5] Colonel Alfred Law, *Police Systems in Urban Districts.*

[6] Frederick J. Crawley, "Decentralization and the Police Box System," *The Police Journal* (London), Vol. I, p. 118, 1928.

of the system is the fact that sergeants and constables report for duty, not at the district station, but on post. The points where the constables are to report "on" and "off" duty are determined by schedule, and change daily. The sergeant meets and inspects only one constable of his platoon at these times, although he visits all several times during his tour of duty. Since the constable cannot know whether the sergeant will be waiting for him at the relieving point, it is contended that all constables will appear on post and leave the relieving points strictly according to the time schedule.

It will be noted that both of these patrol systems represent an effort to avoid the clockwork precision of routine patrol and relief which is characteristic of the beat-and-relief plan so widely employed. Since under them the professional criminal cannot forecast when the constable on duty will be at any given point, they undoubtedly mark great advances over the older forms. That they operate without confusion is beyond question although to put either into effect requires both study and application. The "decentralized box system," however, is so readily adapted to American conditions, and might be so quickly and easily installed in most police departments, that it should commend itself to the early attention of our police administrators.

RECENT POLICE PROGRESS

A close scrutiny of police progress since the turn of the century discloses a rather brief list of changes which may confidently be appraised as advances. It is actually confined to three items—criminal identification, police training, and the use of modern means of transport and communication.

The future of criminal identification seems assured. The simplicity of the fingerprint system and its ready acceptance by courts and juries have greatly stimulated its use, and the provision of a central clearing house in the United States Department of Justice for these and other records promises a rapid growth and extension, until its use becomes at last universal. Police training has also made great strides, the chief problem now consisting in the discovery of the best means for the technical preparation of recruits in small police departments. Likewise, motor patrol, telephone, telegraph-typewriter, light and sound signals and the radio are now more or less generally accepted, even though not universally employed.

The list of constructive changes really ends there. But with these problems approaching the point where they may be accepted as solved, other and more difficult questions press forward for attention.

Despite the many studies which have been made of police organization and control, little progress has been made towards a more reasonable and workable system. The reason for this is not difficult to find. Without exception, all proposals for improvement in organization and control have necessarily been aimed at the weakening or the elimination of political influences. But, the police force is too important an adjunct to the political machine to be lightly surrendered by it. Perhaps no such surrender will take place without a last struggle for mastery; and that may be delayed until the crime problem becomes so acute that the popular will makes peremptory demand for these fundamental changes. If such a time ever arrives, it may even prove feasible to revise the whole scheme and plan of municipal police service, to enlarge the areas of local police jurisdiction, and to make the whole responsible in some degree to a central coördinating authority.

Meanwhile, the tasks of the police administrator and of the police critic are much alike; to enlarge the powers and the responsibilities of police leadership; to introduce scientific methods into criminal investigation as rapidly as they can be absorbed; to improve steadily the quality and the extent of police training; and, in all things, to lose no opportunity to advance a little here, a little there, and always in the right direction.

The Sheriff and the Constable[1]

By RAYMOND MOLEY

Professor of Public Law, Columbia University, New York City

IF, by some magic, the enormously energetic and forthright Henry II could visit an American court house, his interest would probably be challenged immediately by the presence of the sheriff in the most commodious and comfortable quarters of the building. His thoughts might find expression in some such manner as this:

Seven and a half centuries ago I returned to England from the continent. Numerous complaints were immediately made that my sheriffs had fallen into bad ways. They were charged with oppression and extortion. I made inquiry and found the charges true. Many of the miscreants I dismissed, and the remainder I reduced in power and importance by my Assize of Northampton. Before the end of my reign it was clear to the wisest of my advisors, that the office was on its way to decline and death. Now I find it not only in existence but marked with the greatest prosperity. Its functions in a new world are not unlike its duties in my own time. Its power is less, but it seems to have survived the vicissitudes of the centuries better than even the Kingship, which I held myself. This is the most amazing of all the wonders of the modern world. It is an office truly touched, it seems, with the magic of immortality.

An answer to this perplexed statement might be made in these terms. After the end of Henry's reign the decline of the sheriff continued. Judicial powers, and later, financial powers were taken away. The name lived but the substance passed. The decline, while very pronounced, extended over such a long span of years that the greatest of English legal scholars has said that "the whole history of English justice and police might be brought under the rubric, The Decline and Fall of the Sheriff."[2] Today in England the sheriff is a dignified and gentlemanly nonentity who guarantees for one year the proper performance of work in which he plays no part. An under-sheriff performs legal routine chiefly in relation to civil proceedings such as the summoning of jurors, the execution of civil judgments, and the returns of the results of parliamentary elections. In America, the office in the early days found some rehabilitation in Virginia, for a few generations approximating the greatness of the medieval office itself. When the tide of civilization drifted westward and a frontier society found itself far removed from central authority, the county sheriff actually became a peace officer. He protected rough extemporary communities from lawlessness, and caught the imagination of the chroniclers and litterateurs of the Wild West. But this flare of the old glory was soon extinguished. Wherever civilization has come to be highly developed in America, the office of the sheriff has slowly approximated a profitable but worthless sinecure.

It has lived only because it is a rich prize for a powerful party system. Its simple and perfunctory duties require no knowledge or skill, but its emoluments are princely. In many of the great counties with a population of

---

[1] In part a reprint of Chapter Five of the author's *Politics and Criminal Prosecution*. Pp. xiv, 221. New York City: Minton, Balch & Co., 1929.

[2] Maitland, *Justice and Police* (London, 1885), p. 69.

from five hundred thousand to three millions, a term as sheriff yields a considerable fortune. Ample political figures have found the office to their liking. President Cleveland held the office of sheriff of Erie County (Buffalo), and Alfred E. Smith, after many years of loyal service in the New York legislature, was sheriff of New York County for a term. But its incumbents are usually party hacks who pay for the nomination by contributing to the party treasury liberal portions of the rich and really unearned fees of the office. No one doubts that the routine duties of the office could be performed at less cost; no one defends the retention of the office as one of the outstanding elective positions of the county; and few remain to claim that as a police officer the sheriff is either adequate or passable. Prohibition has intensified the nuisances of the office. In many counties hordes of deputy sheriffs "search and seize" for the fees that the law permits. Tourists are annoyed by unskilled traffic deputies who make unnecessary arrests for the fees that come to themselves and to grasping justices of the peace. In many instances of industrial warfare temporary deputies, hired because they were imported professional plug-uglies or resident yokels eager for casual employment, have wrought havoc with the possibility of adjusting peaceably the economic questions at issue.

Lord Coke defined the three important functions of the sheriff as, the serving of the processes and writs of the court, the execution of the decrees of the court, and the conservation of peace within the county.[3] These are about what the law requires the sheriffs of the United States to do today.[4]

In pursuance of the first and second of these duties he carries into execution all orders of the court, both prior to and following the decree or judgment. He serves summonses to defendants, warrants of arrest, subpoenas to witnesses, writs of attachment, and other orders. He summons jurors and during the trial has a limited custodial power over the jury. After the judgment he collects the amount due under the judgment, if necessary by the seizure and the sale of property. In some states he attends court and serves as a bailiff. In criminal cases, he has the custody of the accused and temporarily of the convicted. Sometimes he hangs criminals sentenced to death. As custodian of the accused he is the keeper of the jail and is liable for the reasonable care and preservation of the life and health of the prisoners. Largely because of the profits inherent in the fee system of compensating county officers, the function of process server and jail keeper have largely supplanted that of peace officer. The sheriff is not likely to direct his energies with interest and vigor to the least profitable of his duties, and as a result his value as a peace officer has become negligible. A few states and a small number of large counties in other states have freed themselves from the fee system of compensating the sheriff. In these instances, however, the salary fixed is usually larger than that of other county officers, and in many cases the attempt to abolish the fee system has not disturbed some of the sheriff's more profitable perquisites. A large majority of American sheriffs are still under the fee system. This means that in general the elected[5] sheriff runs the office much like a private business or government monopoly. He serves

[3] Coke Litt., 168.
[4] They occasionally have duties in connection with the elections, and in a very few states assist in the administration of tax laws.

[5] The sheriff is elected in every state except Rhode Island. His term in many states is two years, and in almost an equal number, four years.

processes of the court in both civil and criminal cases, attends court, and executes its decrees, and the law provides quite liberal fees, which he collects from the county treasury, from the individual concerned or from some other source. In some states these services extend even to the hanging of condemned prisoners in the county jail.[6] He keeps the county jail and derives a profit therefrom, as we shall explain presently. Under the fee system he usually hires and pays his own deputies and other assistants out of his profits. In like manner he pays for the automobiles used and the gasoline consumed. In many states he must make an accounting, in whole or in part, but in others these financial transactions are entirely his own concern and when he leaves the office he takes his books with him.[7] The profits from this office range from two or three thousand dollars a year in the small counties to sums in the large counties that have been reliably estimated as approximating one hundred thousand dollars a year. The sheriff of New York County until recently received an income reliably estimated at seventy thousand dollars a year. Such a county as Shelby (Memphis) or Davidson (Nashville) was said by those in good position to know to have yielded more than twenty-five thousand. It is not strange that such a colossal plum has been so valiantly and successfully protected by the political parties. The office of sheriff of New York County, for example, has always been regarded by Tammany as one of its choicest possessions. After Alfred E. Smith's long service in the New York Assembly, the party, full of

a sort of astonished gratitude because of the fact that so much service had been given without a suspicion of improper reward, gave him the nomination for sheriff of New York. As a wise member of the Tammany Society explained,

Al had been an assemblyman, and when others had capitalized their opportunities, he had worked hard and taken nothing. Meanwhile his family grew beyond his modest means. So we gave him the nomination for the office of sheriff to reward his honesty, help him raise his family, keep him in public life and help the looks of the ticket.

The office in those days was said to be "worth" more than fifty thousand dollars a year.

The service of writs by the sheriff is not only expensive, but often very inefficiently done. Gilbertson writes that in studying the office in Kentucky he found a thrifty sheriff permitting court writs to accumulate until he had a considerable number to serve in certain distant parts of the county. He also reports that in another county writs of the court were frequently permitted to pass into the hands of people who happened to be going in the direction of the residence of the person to be served.[8] Almost everywhere the law deems court writs of such importance that they must be carried in the personal custody of a sheriff or his deputy. It is ironical that the sheriff and his deputies, chosen haphazardly and not infrequently from the most unreliable elements in the community, are thus legally declared more trustworthy than the carefully chosen civil servants of the United States Post Office Department.

The most indefensible aspect of the

---

[6] In one instance the fee for this is ten dollars.

[7] In Missouri where I conducted the study of the office for the Missouri Crime Survey, this was true in all but five counties. Such information as it was possible to collect concerning the profits of the office was volunteered. There was practically no public record.

[8] *The Government of Kentucky*, by the Efficiency Commission of Kentucky, Vol. 1, p. 575. See also *The County*, by H. S. Gilbertson (New York, 1917).

sheriff's office is the manner in which he is usually permitted to reap profits from his custody of the county jail. A fixed amount, usually from forty to seventy-five cents "per day per prisoner," is appropriated from the county treasury and given to the sheriff for feeding the prisoners in the jail. Whatever profit he can make under this arrangement is his own. A powerful economic motive is thus provided to starve the prison population, and in many counties prisoners have given remarkable evidence of ability to sustain life on a minimum of food. In one county a reliable investigation indicated that the cost of feeding a prisoner was eight cents a day while the sheriff received forty-five. In many counties the sheriff is permitted, either directly or through concessionaires, to sell special articles of food, tobacco or other "luxuries" to the prisoners. He is thus permitted to starve them to the point where they or their friends purchase food to supplement the daily ration. He thus enjoys the extraordinary privilege of reaping a profit not only from starvation but from the relief of starvation. A judge who was a member of a committee of judges investigating the feeding of jail prisoners in one of the largest cities of the United States said that in his opinion the sheriff of that county was profiting at the rate of ninety thousand dollars a year. Prohibition has accentuated this problem still more because of the fact that Federal courts find it necessary to "farm out" short term prisoners to county jails. The Federal government attempts to inspect and regulate the conditions under which these prisoners are kept, but with indifferent success.

A serious question bearing upon the enforcement of criminal law is how the sheriff performs the third of Coke's subdivisions of his office, that of conservator of the peace. This function is thus described by the United States Supreme Court:

As conservator of the peace in his county or bailiwick, he is the representative of the King, or the sovereign of the state for that purpose. He has the care of the county, and though forbidden by the Magna Carta to act as a justice of the peace in the trial of criminal cases, he exercises all the authority of that office where the public peace is concerned. He may *upon view*, without writ or process, commit to prison all persons who break the peace or attempt to break it, he may award process of the peace, and bind any one in recognizance to keep it, he is bound, ex officio, to pursue and take all traitors, murderers, felons, and other misdoers, and commit them to jail for safe custody. For these purposes he may command the "posse comitatus" or power of the county; and this summons every one over the age of fifteen years is bound to obey, under pain of fine and imprisonment.[9]

There has been a great deal of controversy, particularly since the advent of national prohibition, as to just how much initiative the sheriff must exercise in matters affecting the violation of criminal law. A Tennessee case reviewed much of the law on this question and decided that while the sheriff is not bound to do detective work or to employ deputies to do it, he must, "when he has notice that an offense is being committed . . . act in prevention and suppression."[10] It is, however, unnecessary to pursue the legal point as to whether he has or should have the power to act as a police official. The fee system, which we have described, effectually diverts his interests from the active duties of preventing crime and detecting and arresting criminals. As one sheriff puts it:

[9] *South* v. *Maryland*, 18 How. 396 (1856).
[10] *State* v. *Reichman*, 135 Tenn. 685 (1923). See also *Scougale* v. *Sweet*, 124 Mich. 311 (1900).

If I pursue a robber and after much effort capture him, I receive only seventy-five cents from the county as an arrest fee. I get that much from every subpoena, from every jury summons and every warrant. The amount which I receive from police work does not pay for the gasoline which I use in the pursuit, to say nothing of the time my deputies use and which I must pay them for.

Another difficulty which a sheriff meets in some jurisdictions is the danger that he may be removed from all participation in a case in which he has actively assisted in detecting the defendant and making his arrest. The laws frequently provide that he shall be disqualified from acting in a case in which he is prejudiced. Prejudice has been interpreted to mean unusual activity in making an arrest. Such removal from a case means the loss of all the fees involved in it, including that which is paid for attendance upon court. This substantial danger of loss deters sheriffs from any undue activity and usually limits them to the actual serving of a warrant of arrest.

The enforcement of criminal law suffers not only in the legal limitations imposed by the law upon the sheriff but in the incapacity of most of those selected for police work.

King John was forced in the Magna Carta to promise not to make men "justiciaries, constables, sheriffs, or bailiffs, unless they understand the law of the land, and are well disposed to observe it." The sovereign American democracy imposes no such restriction upon itself, and unfortunately in many cases observes no such admonition. Men become sheriffs and constables if they can get enough votes, with the simple restriction that they be citizens, and, in some instances, voters. The former occupations of the sheriffs of Missouri in 1925 were as follows:

Farmer	24	Penitentiary	
Policeman	6	guard	2
Merchant	4	Tinner	1
Contractor	3	Barber	1
Salesman	3	Butcher	1
Miner	3	Lumberman	1
Drayman	2	Mechanic	1
Stockman	2	Storage	
Carpenter	2	business	1
Liveryman	1		
Blacksmith	1		

The public offices which they held were:

Constable	9	Circuit Clerk	1
Deputy sheriff	8	County Deputy	1
Chief of police	6	Post Master	1
Sheriff	3	United States	
Assessor	1	Marshal	1
Mayor	1	None	28
Collector	1		

Their tenure limited by the state constitution to one consecutive term, effectively prevented ninety per cent from serving over one term of four years. Their ability to protect the public from criminals was described by a very able and courageous governor as "abject failure."[11]

The inadequacy of the sheriff, moreover, would become apparent even in the absence of these legal and political limitations. It would probably result from the fact that the county has ceased to be a practical unit for police purposes. Automobiles and good roads have completely revolutionized values of distance. The argument for a larger policing unit for rural areas is well nigh conclusive. The Missouri survey established through a questionnaire that even the sheriffs hold to this view. But the objections of organized labor and the penury of rural legislators stand in the way of the logical next step, the establishment of state police. In states which find it impossible to adopt state police there should be some effort to rehabilitate the

[11] Message of Governor A. M. Hyde, 1923.

sheriff as a peace officer. This could perhaps be done most effectively by sweeping legislation taking from the office all of its functions except that of conservator of the peace. His duties as a process server should be vested in a court officer, a bailiff, and the custody of the jail and the execution of court orders in some other court agency, appointed by the trial court of the county. The sheriff thus shorn of duties which have little to do with police could find time and inclination to protect lives and property from crime. He should, of course, be appointed, perhaps by the county judge and be paid an adequate salary. While such a compromise would yield rather indifferent results, it is about the only type of rural police protection that can reasonably be hoped for in certain states.

The American constable is completely hopeless as a peace officer. His duties and powers bear the same relation to the township or town as the sheriff's have to the county. He serves the justice of the peace as process server and as high executioner. The office is as deserving as in the days when Dull and Dogberry were created to provide mirth for the Elizabethans. With the establishment of a county court of inferior criminal jurisdiction the constable should disappear.

The State Police

By Major Lynn G. Adams

Superintendent, Pennsylvania State Police, Harrisburg, Pennsylvania

THE writer has been informed by the editor that there is to be an article in this number of the ANNALS which will cover the subject of the sheriffs and the constables as peace officers. He can not, however, start the subject properly without briefly referring to both of these peace officers.

The offices of both the constable and the sheriff are ancient, dating back at least to the reign of Alfred, the Saxon King, in England in the ninth century. In the United States, these offices are filled by election for a term comparatively short, rarely over four years. In some states, the sheriff may not hold office more than four years and may not succeed himself in office in successive elections. The constable may succeed himself in office but he must appeal to the voters of his township periodically for reëlection. Special qualifications for the work to be performed are not necessary and these considerations enter little into their selection. In most states, the sheriff depends upon the fee system for his compensation; in a few, he receives a fixed salary. The constable depends entirely upon the fee system and both officers have civil duties to perform in addition to their police duties. Their spheres of jurisdiction are limited and their activities are individual with but faint traces of coördination and coöperation.

In the period of history before the era of railroads with its closely scheduled trains, interurban trolley cars, automobiles and good highways, the criminal's activities were confined, by a lack of mobility, to small areas. Because of this condition, it was relatively easy for the individual police officer to keep his eye on those of criminal propensities and observe each stranger that chanced to appear in the community. For the same reason, it was not difficult to trace the movement of individuals suspected of crime. Thus, the officer chosen by election and without special qualifications was able to give fairly satisfactory service. I say "fairly" advisedly, naturally having in mind the feuds and the disorders that developed in states like Kentucky and West Virginia, and in Pennsylvania where industrial disputes brought disturbances that amounted almost to civil war.

NEED FOR GOOD RURAL POLICE

Increased transportation facilities created a condition where, by his mobility, the criminal could live quietly in one community and commit his depredations in another. His ability to strike and get away with small chance of being recognized or having his movements traced by individual police officers or by a small group of officers whose jurisdiction was limited to a town or county, has driven home to the people the necessity of coördinated police organization; and the writer believes that the term "State Police" in the near future will bear an entirely different significance from what it does today. At present, these conditions have made it so very apparent that the rural districts can no longer depend upon an untrained individual to attend to their protection that many states have organized state police forces with

34

the primary purpose of giving police protection to areas lying outside municipal jurisdiction, and with the secondary function of coöperating with the various police authorities of the state, giving aid where more than normal police power is required, as frequently occurs during disasters by flood, fire, or explosion, during threatened lynchings, or where the local authority is not sufficiently strong to maintain peace and enforce the law.

European countries have not been as slow as the United States in recognizing the necessity for having police systems made up of specially trained men, coördinated by centralized control. In nearly every country in Europe there is some form of state police. European countries with colonies and dominions in other parts of the world have transplanted the state police system in some form in these colonies and dominions. We find such organizations in the various subdivisions of the Commonwealth of Australia as early as 1821; in Canada, in 1873, when the famous Royal Northwest Mounted was organized by Sir John McDowell; in South Africa; in fact, everywhere the British Empire extends, the necessity of a well-organized police system made up of disciplined and specially trained individuals has been recognized. The new Free State of Ireland has recognized and acknowledged the soundness of the organization of the old Royal Irish Constabulary by adopting the system in its newly organized government.

STATE POLICE IN THE UNITED STATES

The United States adopted this system in the Philippine Islands when it organized the Philippine Constabulary in 1901, during the administration of Governor-General William Howard Taft, present Chief Justice of the United States Supreme Court.

The recognition of the necessity of such police organization has been slower in the various states of the United States. Texas was first with its loosely organized "Rangers," made up of men best qualified for their work by their physical stamina, courage, and ability to meet the gunman and the desperado at their own game, with the chances of success in the ranger's favor. Massachusetts later created a state detective force, which was a partial acknowledgment of the necessity for the state to

TABLE I—COMPARISON OF PERSONNEL OF SOME STATE POLICE FORCES

	Pennsylvania	New York	Massachusetts	Connecticut	New Jersey
Commissioners or Superintendents.........	1	1	1	1	1
Deputy Superintendents..................	1	1	...	1	1
Troops, Companies or other sub-divisions....	6	6	9	9	4
Inspectors.............................	...	...	27	1	...
Captains..............................	6	6	1	1	4
Lieutenants...........................	7	18	12	9	8
Detectives............................	...	...	16	...	...
Sergeants-major.......................	...	...	...	...	1
First Sergeants.......................	5	6	...	...	4
Sergeants.............................	26	60	..	9	34
Corporals.............................	52	72	...	...	35
Troopers, Patrolmen, Privates.............	325	394	208	105	192
Total.............................	421	556	264	125	278

supply a specially trained force for the purpose of detecting crime and apprehending criminals. In 1905, the legislature of the Commonwealth of Pennsylvania created the state police force, upon the recommendation of Governor Samuel W. Pennypacker.[1] Since that time, Massachusetts has added a uniformed patrol force to its detective organization, and Connecticut, Maine, Michigan, Maryland, New Jersey, New York, Rhode Island, and West Virginia have created state police forces. With slight variations, the state police of Pennsylvania is typical of forces of similar character in states where the idea has been adopted.

TRAINING STATE POLICE IN PENNSYLVANIA

In the Pennsylvania organization, the personnel is carefully selected from male citizens, over twenty-one and under forty years of age, who have had education equivalent to two years in high school. They are tested for intelligence and resourcefulness. Political affiliations are not considered. The applicant for appointment must be five feet eight inches or over in height, weigh at least one hundred and forty-five pounds and be physically sound in every respect. He must give the names of three representative citizens as references as to his character and worthiness. His history is carefully investigated by an officer of the force. After his selection, he is appointed probationally and sent to a training school that has two purposes: first, to discover any weakness in character that might make him undesirable as a policeman; second, to teach him the fundamental subjects necessary and to develop him physically and increase his skill in all manner of physical combat and self-defense. His course of mental instruction includes courtesy;

[1] See Act 227, P. L., approved May 2, 1905.

the criminal, fish, game, forestry and traffic laws of the state; criminal procedure; rules of evidence; methods of criminal investigation; recording and reporting investigations; identification of criminals; general police methods, including the handling of crowds, mobs and patrols; geography, particularly that of the state; first-aid to the injured; personal hygiene; and use and care of equipment. The physical course includes cavalry drill and horsemanship; drill dismounted; acrobatics, mounted and dismounted; boxing, wrestling and jiu-jitsu; swimming; rifle and pistol shooting; and the use of other weapons such as machine guns and tear gas. Each student must qualify with seventy per cent or better in each subject at an examination held each month, or be dropped as undesirable.

This course of instruction is intensive and carried out under strict military discipline, on a schedule that begins at six A.M., and ends at ten P.M., daily, throughout the course. It covers a period of four months. It is the aim of the instructors to cause each student to do some stunt in horsemanship or acrobatics each day that tests the courage and determination of the student, with the idea of driving those lacking these necessary virtues out of the service—the theory being that a man who is dealing with criminals must be equipped to demonstrate successfully his superiority and that this demonstration inspires confidence and respect in the minds of the public and the criminal; that self-confidence developed in the policeman prevents him from committing impulsive acts and at the same time causes him to act with decision and confidence in an emergency.

After the probationer has been graduated from the training school he is sent to a troop where he remains on probation for an additional month during which he performs police duty in company with experienced policemen. His superiors carefully observe his conduct with a view to further instruction and to discover undesirable traits of character. The elimination effected by this course has amounted to more than fifty per cent of the candidates in a single class of recruits and for this reason the personnel of the organization has developed an *esprit de corps* born of the knowledge that only those worthy may wear the uniform.

PROMOTION AND DISCIPLINE

After one year's service, the state policeman is qualified to take examinations for promotion to the next higher grade. Each year competitive examinations are held and the four highest men in each troop are sent to a school of instruction of prospective non-commissioned officers; from these, all promotions are made to fill the vacancies that occur in the grade of corporal. Vacancies in the grade of sergeant are filled by competitive examination from the grade of corporal; and, in like manner, the lieutenants are selected from the grade of sergeant. All promotions are strictly on a merit basis.

While full authority to hire and discharge, promote and demote, lies with the superintendent, he rarely exercises summary authority. A system of court-martial is set up within the organization in which the court hears and records evidence and passes sentence subject to review and approval by the superintendent.

ORGANIZATION AND EQUIPMENT

The organization of the force is military in character, consisting of headquarters, one school troop and five police service troops. The school troop consists of one captain, two

lieutenants, one sergeant and two corporals. These officers and non-commissioned officers constitute the instruction force of the training school. Each police service troop consists of a captain, a lieutenant, a first sergeant, five sergeants, ten corporals and sixty-five privates. Headquarters consists of the superintendent and the deputy superintendent, with an accounting and recording organization and a bureau for criminal identification and information with identification experts and clerks.

The state is divided into five districts with a troop assigned to each district and a troop headquarters and barracks are maintained in each district. Each troop or district establishes and maintains substations of from three to five men each, located at strategic points. Each station and substation conducts patrols and investigations in the surrounding area. The activity of the substation is directed by a sergeant or a corporal, the activities of stations are supervised and coördinated by the captain of the troop; the activities of all are supervised and coördinated by headquarters.

The personal equipment of a state policeman consists of uniform blouse and breeches; shirt; campaign hat, helmet or cap; buckskin gloves or gauntlets; puttees; shoes; overcoat; rubber coat; Sam Browne belt and revolver holster; service revolver; carbine; handcuffs; billy; badge; whistle and chain; state police notebook and receipt book—all furnished by the state. In addition to this personal equipment, there is furnished special equipment including a certain number of sub-machine guns, tear gas projectors and tear gas hand grenades, first-aid material, and so forth, located at each station and substation in readiness for emergencies requiring their use.

Transportation equipment consists

of horses, automobiles and motor-cycles. In the earlier days of the Pennsylvania state police, horses alone were used, but good roads made the use of motors imperative and the horse has been superseded except for observation patrols, crowd control, and in make subsistence allowances, while in another the men pay a mess assessment out of their salary and the state pays living expenses when the officer is on duty apart from his regular mess. The following table gives an approximate comparison:

TABLE II—APPROXIMATE COMPARISON OF SALARIES PAID BY SOME STATE POLICE FORCES

	Pennsylvania	New York	Massachusetts	Connecticut	New Jersey	West Virginia
Base pay of:						
Trooper	$1,400	$ 900	$1200–1500	$1,200	$1,600*	$1,200
Corporal	1,500	950	1320–1620	1,800	1,800*	1,320
Sergeant	1,700	1,100	1440–1860	2,300	1,900*	1,380
First Sergeant	2,000	1,200	1800–2340	2,600	2,000	1,440
Lieutenant	2,200	1,800	2040–2400	2,900	2,400	2,100
Captain	3,000	3,400	3180–3720	3,600	3,000	2,400
Maximum to be added for continuing service	600	600	600	600	600	......
Free provision of:						
Uniform and personal accessories	Yes	Yes	Yes	Yes	Yes	Yes
Subsistence	No**	Yes	Yes	Yes	Yes	Yes
Quarters	Yes	Yes	Yes	Yes	Yes	Yes
Annual salary of commissioner or superintendent	7,500	10,000	5,500	4,000	5,000	......
Deputy or assistant	5,500	4,500	....	......	3,500	......

* When on detective work, receive increase of $60 annually.
** Men at substations are reimbursed for subsistence, but must pay pro rata share of troop mess, approximately $200 yearly.

country not feasible for motors due to roughness of terrain.

Communication is by telephone between stations and substations. There is intercommunication by radio between district stations and headquarters. Headquarters maintains a radio broadcasting station for the use of the department and the rest of the state government.

COMPENSATION

It is difficult to compare the rates of compensation of the various state police forces, for several different reasons. Among them is the fact that some states pay for subsistence, others

PENSIONS

In the matter of pensions, no two state police organizations are comparable. In Pennsylvania, the workmen's compensation provisions of the state government apply to state policemen when they are injured or killed in line of duty. This is a fairly satisfactory arrangement. Retirement is provided for in like manner, namely, through the "State Employees' Retirement Fund," but, inasmuch as the employee must serve thirty years and be at least sixty years of age to be eligible, this retirement fund is of little use to the Pennsylvania State Police where the duties are too arduous to be performed by a man much past the age of fifty years.

In New York, Massachusetts and Connecticut, much the same situation exists as is found in Pennsylvania.

New Jersey has provided pensions for the immediate families of men disabled in line of duty and has also provided for their retirement—at three quarters of the amount of their salary at the time of retirement—after a period of twenty years' service, provided that the person desiring to retire is over fifty years of age.

ENLARGING THE SCOPE OF STATE POLICE FUNCTIONS

The principal reasons for inefficient police work throughout the entire United States are to be found in the following conditions: (1) unsatisfactory personnel; (2) inefficient administration and leadership; and, (3) lack of coördination.

Let us begin by examining the reason for the first condition. We find that the compensation of a policeman is small; that the field of advancement is extremely limited; that in a large number of instances there is little certainty of steady employment due to political displacement; and that there is little or no assurance of comfortable and honorable retirement after the age of effective service. The young man who is honest, intelligent, ambitious and industrious can not be expected to look upon the police calling, as it is now constituted, with any degree of favor.

Now let us examine the cause of the second condition. We first find that there are but few places where administrators and leaders can be trained for the service. Most executives come from other walks of life, and probably would not have accepted appointment as police administrators had they been successful in their former callings. Successful men can not afford to subject themselves to political whim and even though a successful business man undertakes this task he soon finds that police administration and direction is a task worthy of special preparation backed by broad experience. It frequently happens that about the time the successful business man has learned "what it's all about," he finds himself cleaning out his desk to make room for his successor—who may be a former army officer of excellent reputation, but who is liable to repeat the experience of the more or less successful business man. The point is, police administration is not something that anyone can do successfully, without special preparation or experience.

Let us now turn our attention to the third condition, namely, lack of coördination. At the present time, we have in one state nine hundred and thirty-six cities and boroughs, with an equal number of police forces numbering from one man to four thousand. Each is strictly concerned in the police activities of its own locality and but little concerned about what is happening in neighboring towns and rural districts. In addition to the police of the towns, we have the township constable, the sheriff and his deputies and the county detective each working independently with very little coöperation. The writer knows of a case where a criminal committed crimes in several towns during the same day. The police chiefs of these towns only learned about the crimes through the newspapers the following day. Unless there is centralized authority, there can be little coördination.

The state is the only subdivision of government that can remedy all of the evil conditions found in our present police system. A state-wide police organization would provide a field of advancement that would appeal to the honest, ambitious and energetic young man as a field of service. It could hold out to him the assurance of a pension in the event of his becoming disabled, and an honorable retirement in his old age. It could provide for proper training by establishing special schools for recruits and executives. It could coördinate the efforts of the whole organization by centralized control to the extent that crimes committed in rural districts would be given as much consideration as those committed in the largest cities. It would be able to maintain a corps of expert specialists, ready for service in any part of the state where their services might be required. Such an organization seems to the writer to be the only logical solution to the modern police problem.

BIBLIOGRAPHY ON THE SUBJECT OF STATE POLICE

The State Police, by Bruce Smith. Published by Macmillan & Co., New York, 1925.

Justice to All, by Katherine Mayo. Published by Houghton Mifflin Co., Boston, 1920.

The Trooper Police of Australia, by Arthur L. Haydon. Published by A. C. McClurg & Co., Chicago, 1912.

The Riders of the Plains, by Arthur L. Haydon. Published by The Copp-Clark Co., Toronto, 1910.

Policing the Plains, by Roderick G. McBeth. Published by Hodder and Stoughton, New York, 1921.

Laws of New York—Chapters 315, 481, 676.

Laws of Massachusetts—Chapter 343 (1929).

Laws of New Jersey—Chapters 102 (1921); 271 (1922); 310 (1926); 228 (1928); 219 (1928); 61 (1929).

Federal Police

By Albert Langeluttig

Member of the Chicago Bar; Associated with Moses, Kennedy, Stein & Bachrach, Chicago, Illinois

FOR want of a better designation, "Federal Police" is here used to describe collectively a number of organizations of the National Government whose duties comprehend, in whole or in part, the suppression of crimes defined by Federal statute. As here used, "police" describes activities which are performed by persons of average intelligence without special professional or technical training and which result, as a rule, in prosecutions for crimes in the Federal courts. This excludes regulation, administrative supervision, and the work of such organizations as the special agents of the Bureau of Internal Revenue, who must be expert accountants.

There are four organizations which perform exclusively police duties. These are: (1) the Bureau of Investigation of the Department of Justice; (2) the Secret Service of the Treasury Department; (3) the Customs Border Patrol; and, (4) the Immigration Border Patrol. Four organizations perform, in varying proportions, police duties and regulatory duties. These are: (1) the Prohibition Unit; (2) the Narcotic Unit; (3) the Customs Service; and, (4) the Bureau of Immigration. The Coast Guard combines with the humanitarian service of saving lives and property at sea, the police duty of preventing smuggling, principally of alcoholic beverages. One organization, the Division of Inspectors of the Post Office Department, performs principally the duty of administrative supervision, but a substantial amount of its work comprises the detection and the suppression of various crimes connected with the mails.

Department of Justice—Bureau of Investigation

The Bureau of Investigation of the Department of Justice is the only general police force employed by the Federal government. It performs exclusively police duties and its jurisdiction is the entire field of crime defined by Federal law. It, of course, pays less attention to those crimes which have special organizations for their detection but it does not entirely exclude such crimes from its field of interest.

The headquarters of the bureau is divided into seven divisions, three administrative and four technical. These divisions are designated officially by numbers, but they also have descriptive names. They are:

1. Office of Director (Division 1)
2. Administrative Division (Division 5)
3. Division of Mails and Files (Division 7)
4. General Intelligence Division (Division 2)
5. Theft and Frauds Division (Division 3)
6. Anti-Trust Division (Division 4)
7. Criminal Identification Division (Division 6)

The director of the bureau receives nine thousand dollars a year, the same as an assistant attorney general. He supervises the general operation of the bureau and its field force. He attends personally to all matters of personnel. The Administrative Division attends to the clerical matters relating to personnel and generally supervises the routine administration of the bureau. The Division of Mails and Files receives all the mail that is directed to the bureau. It is there opened, recorded, and filed after reference to the proper technical division of the bureau for attention.

The three technical divisions are divisions 2, 3 and 4. Their descriptive names give some idea of the work which they perform. To each is assigned a more or less associated group of Federal crimes. As the reports of cases being investigated come in, they are referred to the division having that particular sort of case in charge. By this means ramified criminal conspiracies are disclosed and the activities of agents in various parts of the country working on the same conspiracy are correlated.

The Criminal Identification Division is the great central depository and clearing house for criminal records. Although the exchange of records is purely a matter of comity, the Bureau of Investigation enjoys complete coöperation with the police chiefs throughout the country.

The Bureau of Investigation employs one hundred and thirty-six persons in its headquarters. It divides the United States and Alaska into thirty districts. In each of these districts, at some convenient point, is a field office. At the present time the field force includes four hundred and sixty persons, consisting of two hundred and eighty-five investigating agents, seventy-three accountants, and one hundred and two stenographers, translators, telephone operators and clerks. Preference in the appointment of agents is given to men with some legal training; more than one third of the agents are so qualified.

An agent is permanently assigned to each district and put in charge. The other agents circulate throughout the United States from district to district as investigations require. When an agent goes into a district, he must report immediately to the agent-in-charge and keep the latter informed of his movements. The agent-in-charge is responsible for the conduct of each case that is being investigated in his district. He makes to the bureau a semimonthly report of each case. When these reports reach Washington, they are referred to the division of the bureau charged with the general supervision of that particular subject. Here the information throughout the country is compared and the various threads of the criminal plot are disclosed as described above.

The average annual salary of the special agent of the Bureau of Investigation is thirty-one hundred dollars.

TREASURY DEPARTMENT—SECRET SERVICE

The Secret Service Division of the Treasury Department grew out of the necessity for suppressing counterfeiting. The first appropriation of ten thousand dollars for this purpose was made in 1860 and was used to pay rewards and services rendered by individuals, without organization. When the greenbacks and the war bonds were issued during the Civil War, counterfeiting increased and Congress in 1864 appropriated one hundred thousand dollars for the suppression of counterfeiting. Under this appropriation the Secret Service was organized. The headquarters of the Secret Service Division includes a chief, an assistant chief and nine other employees. The United States is divided into thirty-five secret service districts, each with an agent in charge. Each district has a number of subdivisions with one or more agents in each. While territorial jurisdiction is not enjoined by law, the agents are, as a rule, confined to their respective districts. By this means, traveling and subsistence expenses while attending court are held to a minimum, the agent working on a case usually residing where it is tried. The field force includes about one hundred and thirty-seven agents and five undercover men or informants.

The activities of the Secret Service Division are well outlined in the appropriation act for 1929, as follows:

Suppressing Counterfeiting and other crimes: For expenses incurred under the authority or with the approval of the Secretary of the Treasury in detecting, arresting, and delivering into the custody of the United States marshal having jurisdiction dealers and pretended dealers in counterfeit money and persons engaged in counterfeiting, forging, and altering United States notes, bonds, national bank notes, Federal reserve notes, Federal reserve bank notes, and other obligations and securities of the United States and of foreign Governments, as well as the coins of the United States and of foreign Governments, and other crimes against the laws of the United States relating to the Treasury Department and the several branches of the public service under its control . . . and for no other purpose whatever except in the protection of the person of the President and the members of his immediate family and of the person chosen to be President of the United States.

The limitation on this appropriation, confining the fund so strictly to counterfeiting matters, results in some very weird occurrences and prevents coöperation with services outside the Treasury. Ever mindful of an overtechnical and often whimsical Comptroller General, a secret service agent's first inquiry must always be, "Does the appropriation act cover this?" With a criminal almost in his hands, an agent discovers that a forgery is not involved; there is only a robbery of a government office involving hundreds of thousands of dollars. He must cease his work and communicate with his superiors. By the time the interdepartmental communication finds its destination in Washington and the local agent of the proper department is on the job, the criminal has disappeared. It seems that this is a frequent occurrence.

The annual salary of the director of the Secret Service is seventy-five hundred dollars; the average salary of the agents is three thousand dollars.

TREASURY DEPARTMENT—BUREAU OF PROHIBITION

The Bureau of Prohibition comprises two distinct organizations. The enforcement of both the liquor prohibition acts and the anti-narcotic acts are within its jurisdiction.

Anti-narcotic legislation began in 1909 with the prohibition of the importation and the use of opium for other than medicinal purposes. This was followed by an act regulating the use of smoking opium and the Harrison Anti-Narcotic Act, which provided for the registration and the taxation of the users and the dispensers of narcotics, authorized the employment of chemists and agents by the Commissioner of Internal Revenue, and appropriated one hundred and fifty thousand dollars for enforcement.

The administration of the wartime prohibition act devolved upon the Bureau of Internal Revenue. In 1919, the prohibition amendment was adopted and the Volstead Act, carrying an appropriation for its enforcement, went into effect on January 16, 1920. In the appropriation act for 1921, the enforcement of the prohibition act was joined with that of the anti-narcotic acts. Both organizations were, at first, assigned to the Bureau of Internal Revenue. Later, a separate bureau was created.

The Prohibition Unit

The Prohibition Unit performs two functions. It supervises and regulates the legal use of alcohol and attempts to suppress the use of that liquid for beverage purposes. The keys to the entire prohibition organization are the administrators in the twenty-five districts into which the United States and its possessions are divided. Under their supervision both the permitted use of alcohol is regulated and the enforcement of the prohibitive laws carried on. The Washington organization serves the purpose of a clearing house and a general supervisory force, but the real work is done by and under the administrators.

The Bureau of Prohibition is presided over by a commissioner. All persons connected with the bureau, excepting the commissioner, are appointed under the civil service laws. Under the immediate control of the commissioner, an assistant commissioner heads the Administrative Division of the bureau. The commissioner directs the carrying out of the policies prescribed, renders decisions in complicated cases, and supervises the organization and administration of the offices of the prohibition administrators throughout the United States. The Administrative Division has charge of matters pertaining to estimates of appropriations, allotments of funds to the several districts, personnel, space, equipment and general administrative work. The total force of the prohibition organization numbers forty-one hundred and thirteen persons, of whom three hundred and eleven are stationed in Washington.

The Law Division is presided over by a chief counsel and includes seventeen attorneys. The Law Division prepares opinions and holdings on prohibition law and regulations. It conducts correspondence involving questions of law with other departments, prohibition administrators and other prohibition officers, and makes recommendations for compromises in prohibition cases and on applications for pardons and paroles.

The Technical Division of the bureau conducts laboratories at Washington and various other cities. The Washington laboratory analyzes and passes upon the fitness of preparations to be manufactured with distilled spirits, including specially denatured alcohol. Samples taken as evidence in enforcement work under the national prohibition act are submitted to the various laboratories either in Washington or in the field. This division has supervision of work growing out of the provisions of the prohibition act relating to the production and the use of industrial alcohol and those relating to the permissive use of intoxicating liquors. It also administers certain features of the general internal revenue laws relating to bonded warehouses and to those distilleries still operating under the law.

The Audit Division assesses taxes and penalties in all cases involving liquors and narcotics. It acts on claims for the abatement, the refund or the remission of taxes or penalties levied on distilled spirits and wines and makes recommendations on offers in compromise of liabilities incurred under bonds of hospitals or scientific institutions for the use of tax-free alcohol. It examines and audits returns and accounts of intoxicating liquors rendered by persons required to keep accounts by law.

Continental United States is divided into twenty-three prohibition districts and, in addition, Hawaii and Porto Rico each constitutes a district. At the head of each district is a prohibition administrator. In most of the districts there are two assistant administrators. One of them has charge of the "permissive" work. He and his subordinates regulate the legal use of alcohol. The other assistant has charge of enforcement and is chief of Federal prohibition police in his district. A number of deputy administrators are assigned to each prohibition district. They are assigned to seats of judicial districts other than the ones at which the prohibition administrators have their headquarters. They represent the prohibition administrators and are charged principally with the expedition of prohibition cases in the courts of the districts to which they are assigned. The prohibition administrators have also the assistance of a group of attorneys in each district to advise them and prepare prohibition cases for the courts. The chief attorney in each district has charge of the revocation of permits and supervises the work of the agents with a view to the presentation of cases to the courts.

Besides the enforcement group in the various prohibition districts, there is a Special Agents' Force operating under a chief of special agents directly from Washington. For purposes of administration, the United States is divided into ten special agency districts with a special agent in charge of each district. To this force is assigned the investigation of complicated cases running through several prohibition districts and even foreign countries. The special agents circulate throughout the country where their investigation leads them. They report to the special agent in charge of the district in which they happen to be operating. He supervises their work while they are in his district and reports the progress of the case to the chief in Washington. This force has a personnel of one hundred and eighty-four persons.

It would be a work of supererogation to describe the activities and the methods of the prohibition police. The reader is referred for this information to the current issue of any newspaper.

One comment should be made on the organization of the prohibition force.

This organization performs two functions and it is to be noted that the two activities are kept distinct. The distinction between the quasi-judicial activities involved in the permissive work and the executive activities in the enforcement work cannot but be apparent. The complete divorce of this ill-mated couple is highly desirable. It is impossible for one person properly to perform or supervise the performance of both judicial and executive duties at the same time. It would be as wise to combine the judiciary and the police in a large city as it is to allot both the permissive and the enforcement duties to the prohibition administrators.

The Narcotic Unit

The Narcotic Unit is a part of the Bureau of Prohibition. The granting of permits to prescribe and deal in opiates is in charge of the collector of internal revenue. The investigational work in connection with the issuing of permits is performed by the Narcotic Unit; but its chief work is the suppression of the illegal use of narcotics, so that the work of this organization is almost entirely police.

The Narcotic Unit is presided over by a deputy commissioner of prohibition. His headquarters includes forty-seven persons besides himself.

All work incident to the administration of the Harrison Narcotic Act and the permissive features of the narcotic drugs import and export act, including the supervision of the work of the narcotic field force, is performed by the Narcotic Division. The headquarters of this division has two sections: (1) Returns and Auditing; and, (2) Administrative. The Administrative Section supervises the activities of the narcotic field force, the enforcement of the regulations for the use of narcotics, and personnel matters. The Returns and Auditing Section supervises and checks the returns, made by the collectors of internal revenue, of permits to use opium, and audits the vouchers of dispensers of narcotics and the returns of importers, manufacturers and wholesale dealers.

The legal work of the Narcotic Unit is performed in the Law Division of the Bureau of Prohibition.

The field force of the Narcotic Division includes fifteen agents in charge, two hundred and forty-nine agents, and forty-four clerks. The United States and its territories are divided into fifteen narcotic districts, in each of which is located a field office under an agent-in-charge with a small force of agents and clerks. Each field office supervises the legal use of opium in its district and seeks to prevent its illegal use. The same criticism cannot be leveled at the Narcotic Unit as at the Prohibition Unit. It confines its activities to investigational work, leaving judicial functions to others.

The Commissioner of Prohibition receives an annual salary of nine thousand dollars, the deputy commissioner in charge of the narcotic unit sixty-two hundred dollars. The average salary of both the prohibition agent and the narcotic agent is twenty-five hundred dollars. The salaries of the prohibition administrators range from five thousand to sixty-five hundred dollars; of the assistant administrators, from thirty-two hundred to fifty-six hundred dollars; and of the deputy prohibition administrators, from twenty-seven hundred to forty-seven hundred and fifty dollars.

TREASURY DEPARTMENT— COAST GUARD

The Coast Guard is included in a discussion of Federal police because it complements on the sea the work of all the police organizations on land. Un-til the advent of prohibition the principal work of the Coast Guard was humanitarian. This work included assisting ships in distress, the conduct of an international ice patrol and a derelict patrol.

In addition to this humanitarian work the Coast Guard was, before the War, called upon to do certain patrol work of a police character. Attached to the Treasury Department, they were convenient assistants in the prevention of smuggling—before prohibition and immigration restriction, a minor matter so far as sea patrolling was concerned. The Coast Guard also is charged with the enforcement of treaties and laws relative to pelagic sealing and halibut fishing. This is work of a police character, as is also the patrolling of regattas and marine parades.

This police work, while important, did not besmirch the good character of the Coast Guard, nor take much of its energy. With the advent of prohibition and alien exclusion laws and the employment of the Coast Guard in their enforcement came a tremendous enlargement of its police duties, so that now more than half of the money spent on this organization and more than half of its personnel and equipment is employed in the prevention of smuggling of liquor and, in a much less degree, of aliens.

The commandant of the Coast Guard bears the rank of Admiral. He is assisted by a large force of officers and civil employees in maintaining and directing this other navy of the United States. Besides the Washington headquarters, the operative units of the Coast Guard are twenty-two cruising cutters, first class; fifteen cutters, second class; twenty-four destroyers, thirty-eight harbor cutters and launches, two hundred and fifty-five patrol boats, one hundred and twenty-one picket boats and skiffs, two hundred and fifty-one active and twenty-six inactive Coast Guard Stations, sixteen section bases, a Coast Guard academy and a depot. The personnel consists of four hundred and three commissioned officers, one hundred and five cadets, nine hundred and twenty-six warrant officers and ten thousand eight hundred and forty-five enlisted men.

It is unfortunate that the recent and sudden enlargement of the police work of the Coast Guard has resulted in forcing into its ranks untempered human material so fast that the good name of the organization has been too often blackened by hasty and fanatical action. The question arises whether or not the humanitarian and the enforcement work should be assigned to different organizations. It is fortunate that each of the land police forces has not its own navy; but it may be suggested that if the land forces be combined into one Federal police force, there should be a close connection with a similar force on the sea and that both forces be under the direction of one head and charged with the single duty of detecting crime.

TREASURY DEPARTMENT—BUREAU OF CUSTOMS

The Bureau of Customs with a commissioner at its head, is charged with the collections of customs duties imposed by the tariff acts on imports of merchandise into the country. Its primary duty is, therefore, regulative. To perform this duty the nation is divided into forty-seven customs districts, with a collector and a force of subordinates assigned to each. This organization handles the regulative work of the bureau. The staff in each district includes an officer, whose title, or one of whose titles, is that of surveyor. This officer has charge of a force of guards, inspectors and examiners of passengers' baggage. The work of these employees may be classified as police, for it results in the discovery of many infractions of law that lead to penalties and forfeitures. At New York alone, there is a force of one hundred and forty guards who are assigned particularly to the duty of detecting diamond smuggling. Through this port comes the greater part of the smuggled diamonds that go to make up the tax exempt fifty per cent of the diamonds that enter the United States.

Besides the guards and the inspectors at the various ports of entry, there are two organizations in the customs service whose duty it is to combat the ancient crime of smuggling. These are the special agency service and the customs border patrol.

The customs border patrol is a fairly recent addition to the service. It is one of the results of prohibition. At its beginning it was paid from prohibition appropriations although it has always been a part of the customs service. Its main duty still is the detection of liquor smuggling but its list of duties includes the detection of smuggling of all kinds at the land borders.

To each collection district which includes part of the land border of the nation, seventeen in all, a group of border patrolmen is assigned. They work under the supervision of the collector. Border patrolmen are assigned to meet all persons as they cross the border, whether on foot, in automobile, by train or by other conveyance, and ascertain if such persons are attempting to bring in intoxicants or merchandise upon which duty has not been paid. The customs and the immigration border patrolmen work in close coöperation. An automobile entering the country, for instance, along one of the numerous highways or across one of the bridges is met by an immigration patrolman and a customs patrolman; quite often, a prohibition officer makes up a trio. Or, along the less frequented parts of the border such a group may be seen tracking down one of the more desperate bands of smugglers of human beings, intoxicants, narcotics or other merchandise. At the end of 1928, there were three hundred and sixty border patrolmen on the Canadian border, one hundred and thirty-four on the Mexican border, ten in Massachusetts, and ten in Florida.

The special agency service is a hybrid organization. It supervises and corrects the organization of the collectors' offices, audits their books and accounts, and otherwise requires efficient organization of collectors' offices and work. This is, of course, made necessary by the fact that collectors of customs are political appointees. This supervisory work results in the detection of some crime within the service, such as embezzlement, conspiracies to defraud the government by undervaluation, and similar frauds which might arise in a large organization so far-flung and with so much power. In addition to this supervisory work, the special agency service is charged with the detection within the country of all crimes defined by the customs laws. These include smuggling, undervaluation and "dumping."

The special agency service divides the United States into nine districts and, in addition, Canada forms a district with headquarters at Montreal. The force is made up of seventeen special agents and one hundred and thirteen customs agents. Thirty special agents of the customs are specifically authorized by statute. Customs agents are provided for by the annual appropriation acts. These are distributed as the amount of business requires. Each

district has a supervisor who reports directly to a deputy commissioner of customs.

The special agency service presents a problem of organization that bears study. Like the post office inspection force it combines administrative supervision with police work. The post office force realizes the undesirability of this combination. It is doubtful if it is any more desirable in the customs service.

The average annual salary of customs agents and special agents is forty-eight hundred dollars and of the customs border patrol agent twenty-four hundred dollars.

Department of Labor—Bureau of Immigration

To the Bureau of Immigration of the Department of Labor is allocated the duty of enforcing the immigration laws. Its work includes: (1) the regulation of immigration into the country; (2) the expulsion from the country of those who enter unlawfully or whose sojourn here, although they entered lawfully, has become unlawful because of the commission of crime or for some other reason; and, (3) the exclusion of those who seek to enter the country surreptitiously.

The activities of the Bureau of Immigration performed in connection with the regulation of legitimate immigration into the country are not such as may be called police activities. The unlawful sojourn in, or unlawful entry into the country, however, are criminal acts and the discovery of such acts requires police and detective activities of the highest sort.

The field establishment of the Bureau of Immigration has two parts, the Immigration Service and the Border Patrol. The immigration service is charged with the regulation of immigration and the expulsion of aliens who have already entered. Only one-half of the activities of the immigration service, therefore, may be classed as police. The border patrol has the single function of protecting our borders from the invasion of those to whom our ports have been closed, either because they come from unassimilable nations or because the quota of immigrants from their country has already been filled. The activities of the Border Patrol are, therefore, entirely police.

The immigration service divides the entire territory of the United States, including Alaska, Porto Rico and Hawaii but excluding the Philippine Islands, into thirty-five immigration districts. There is also a Chinese office in New York which is organized like a district but concerns itself only with Chinese immigrants. Each district is in charge of a commissioner, a director, or an inspector-in-charge. To each district is assigned an appropriate number of immigration inspectors. Most of these are proficient in the general duties of the service but in the places where they are needed there are inspectors specially trained in Chinese and Oriental matters and in contract labor matters.

To each immigration district which includes a part of the land or the water border of the United States, eleven in number, is assigned a section of the border patrol. This section operates under the general charge of the immigration officer in charge of the district.

The Commissioner General of Immigration is appointed by the President, by and with the advice and consent of the Senate. The remainder of the Washington headquarters and the entire field organization are under the civil service. The entire field service is distinctively uniformed.

At the head of the bureau in Washington is the Commissioner General of Immigration. Under him work an assistant commissioner general and a chief supervisor. The chief supervisor circulates throughout the country and checks up on the organization and the offices in the various immigration districts. The assistant commissioner general is the chief administrator. Under his direction work the division chiefs of the following divisions: (1) Accounts and Personnel; (2) Correspondence; (3) Mails and Files; (4) Statistical; (5) Law; (6) Chinese Exclusion; (7) Transportation and Deportation; (8) Contract Labor; and, (9) Office of Special Representative of Seamen's Work.

The Law Division is headed by a lawyer receiving an annual salary of three thousand dollars. This three-thousand-dollar-a-year lawyer provides the legal advice for the immigration service, legal advice which affects the happiness of so many human beings. The Transportation and Deportation Division conducts the concentration of deportees and their movement in groups to ports of departure.

The immigration service consisted on June 30, 1928, of nineteen hundred and forty-nine persons. Of these, eight hundred were immigrant inspectors. The balance was made up of clerks, guards, matrons, laborers and other servants and supervising personnel. The last consisted of nine commissioners, nine assistant commissioners, two supervisors, twenty-five district and thirteen assistant district directors.

The border patrol consisted on June 30, 1928, of one supervisor, six assistant superintendents, twenty-eight chief patrol inspectors, one hundred and sixty-six senior patrol inspectors, five hundred and four patrol inspectors and forty-two clerks, laborers, etc.

The police work of the immigration service is, of course, not fully able to expel all aliens, unlawfully in the country. No police force, however efficient, has yet succeeded in suppressing crime completely. Indeed, no attempt is made by the immigration service to comb the country and ferret out each alien who is here unlawfully in a technical sense. As long as an alien who is in the country unlawfully conducts himself otherwise in a peaceful manner and does not become so prominent as to be brought to the attention of an immigration inspector, the likelihood of his being deported is not very great. It is only when the unlawful resident commits a crime, or becomes important enough to have enemies who know his past, or takes too prominent a part in labor organization matters that he is likely to find himself haled before a board of inquiry and on his way back to his homeland.

The work of the border patrol is more like that of the policeman who familiarly walks the beat. At each international bridge or highway, the entrant into the United States is met by an inspector. Each train that crosses the border is visited by an inspector. Of course, the mountain pass and the desert is not neglected, nor is the secluded bay or harbor. The smuggler of human cargo is just as skillful as the smuggler of the old sort and he is met by just as skillful opposition as the smuggler of gems. The smuggler of human contraband is likewise just as desperate as the smuggler of old, and although the border patrol is still quite young, its list of casualties is already large.

The work of the Bureau of Immigration is very vital. Its control over the lives and happiness of a large number of human beings must be very wisely exercised. The force accorded the findings of the various immigration authorities by the Supreme Court of the United States puts into the hands of the immigration service great power

for evil. There are those, whose opinions are worthy of respect, who question the validity of the findings of the immigration service in many cases. When one realizes the power of the immigration inspector and then looks at the salary schedule, one shudders. The commissioner general receives eight thousand dollars, the chief of the service at New York receives sixty-five hundred dollars and the chiefs of the other districts receive forty-six hundred dollars or less. The average pay of the immigration inspector is twenty-three hundred and fifty dollars and of the border patrol inspector, two thousand dollars. The personnel of the service fully realize their power, and the men such salaries attract do not fail to make their importance felt. When one approaches an inspector, one gets the impression that, whether one is a native-born citizen or not, one's sojourn in the United States is a matter of grace—sometimes, the grace of the immigrant inspector.

THE POST OFFICE DEPARTMENT— DIVISION OF INSPECTORS

The Post Office Department is the one that comes most continually into contact with the average citizen. Its offices are found in every village and hamlet in the United States. The Postmaster General, upon whom falls the care and supervision of this great system, is kept by the rural congressman continually aware of his responsibility.

The inspection service originated as a means of supervising the internal administration of the postal system. The office of chief inspector first received congressional recognition in the appropriation act of 1886. It had existed, in fact, for a number of years before, at least as early as 1878.

The duties of the Postmaster General are no longer confined to seeing that mail is collected and delivered. They now include the administration of many criminal laws connected with the mails, such as transmission of obscene literature and fraudulent schemes, mail rifling and post office robberies. Along with the enlargement of the duties of the Postmaster General went the enlargement of the functions of his inspection force.

The chief inspector is in immediate charge of the Division of Post Office Inspectors. His headquarters numbers eighty-nine persons and his field force, fifteen inspectors-in-charge and five hundred and twenty-five inspectors. The Washington headquarters has the following sections:

1. Administrative Section
2. Accounting Section
3. Review Section
4. Miscellaneous Section
5. Depredation Section
6. Fraud Section
7. Foreign Section
8. Supply Section

The Administrative Section supervises the activities of the inspectors and the Washington headquarters, and controls the personnel of the organization.

The Accounting Section has charge of all accounting matters of the division and supervises the investigations of claims for reward made by individuals who have assisted in the apprehension of persons charged with postal crimes.

With the exception of the Supply Section, the other headquarters sections are employed in supervising the cases which the inspectors investigate and report on. The Review Section reviews and checks all classes of cases in which collections have been made or valuable articles recovered. The technical sections perform functions similar to the technical divisions of the Bureau of Investigation of the Department of Justice.

The United States is divided into fifteen postal inspection districts, each with an inspector-in-charge and a force of postal inspectors. Postal inspectors are appointed from the civil service lists. Before being eligible, they must have served four years in the regular postal service. The Postmaster General nominates a group to take the examination, and from the successful candidates, inspectors are appointed according to the grades obtained. The force includes a mechanic, a draftsman and an architect. Otherwise there is no specialization among the inspectors, each being called upon to make investigations of any class of case that might arise. Except in cases of crimes, the inspectors can take no definite action as the result of their inspection. Their duty is to inform the departmental officers of the operations in the field, so that the latter may take definite action. The inspectors do not consider themselves as detectives in any sense. They maintain that this designation should be reserved for the plain clothes policemen. They forewarn a post office of their visit and seek to maintain cordial and confidential relations with the postal force.

The activities of the inspectors fall into three categories, as follows: (1) administrative inspection of post office and postal accounts; (2) installation and instruction in the use of machinery and technical systems; and, (3) detection of crime.

Criminal investigation carried on by the post office inspectors includes larceny of mail, burglary of post offices, robbery of postmen, trains, and other conveyances, and wilful transmission of forbidden matter in the mails. Although the inspectors express a strong opposition to being classed as detectives, more than one-third of their activity is pure criminal investigation.

In his annual report for 1921 the

Postmaster General included the recommendations for the reallocation of the work of the inspectors made by a commission consisting of the chief inspector, the solicitor for the Post Office Department, and a group of experts outside the service. The commission recommended, in substance, the transfer of criminal investigation work to the Bureau of Investigation of the Department of Justice. This very intelligent recommendation has not yet been heeded. The post office inspectors still spend much of their time doing detective work for which they are not best fitted and which they can do less efficiently because their principal work requires activities and methods of approach wholly different from the work of a police or detective force.

The chief inspector receives an annual salary of seven thousand dollars and the inspectors in charge forty-five hundred dollars. The average salary of the inspectors is thirty-eight hundred dollars.

THE SOLUTION—CONSOLIDATION

This study of the police organizations of the National Government suggests the establishment of a single Federal police force for the detection of all Federal crimes. Although one should hesitate to recommend very emphatically so radical a change, this is the only conclusion that can be reached after a careful study of the problem. A unified Federal police force is the only sound solution viewed from the point of view either of governmental efficiency or of social expediency.

There are two powerful forces and one reason for the present situation. The reason is an historical one. The government has grown up as it is; why rip up the roots of the ages—even if they are poison ivy? The two forces opposing the change are powerful enough to delay for many years, if not defeat entirely, the proper correction of a bad situation. The first of these forces is bureaucracy. The placeman will fight hard for his job and give a thousand reasons, or alleged reasons, why his job is important. The appended table tells the story in figures. In that table an attempt has been made to number the force engaged entirely in police duties. Where an organization has several functions a conservative estimate has been made of those that may be allotted entirely to police duties. In the case of the Bureau of Investigation, the figure for the Washington headquarters does not include the force allotted to the Bureau of Identification. This is, or was until recently, a unified service. The Prohibition Bureau has recently started its own bureau of identification with the only purpose, apparently, of spending its lavish appropriations. The table presents a convincing picture of the wastefulness of the overhead of the Federal police force. With a headquarters force of one hundred and fifty persons; with a field supervisor in each judicial district, of which there are about ninety, with at most twenty-five others filling supervisory positions; with a force of not more than three hundred clerks, laborers, etc., in the field offices; and with a slight increase in the number of assistant district attorneys, the entire Federal police force would be properly commanded and adequate salaries could be paid to attract good men for the supervisory positions.

The second force opposing a consolidation is the group interested in the fanatical enforcement of a particular law. It may be stated as a reason for each department's having a detective force to suppress crimes defined by the laws which that department administers, that a close association between the administrator and the detective is desirable. As a matter of fact, there is now no more efficient suppression of crime by those departments which have their own police force than by those which rely entirely on the Bureau of Investigation. The real purpose in the mind of those who avow this reason is the fear that their pet statute will get a balanced consideration by a general force, supervised by one who views the entire situation and allots to each duty its proper weight, instead of a fanatical and unbalanced consideration by a force to which one crime, and one crime alone, is antisocial. It is hard to conceive of a more improper influence on the citizen than being stopped by a Federal officer and find him to be an immigration officer who boldly announces, "I am not looking for liquor, I'm looking only for aliens." A Federal police should be interested in the equal enforcement of all Federal laws.

Another alleged reason for the present division is the need for specialization. In a unified force, any necessary specialization could be adequately provided for. Indeed, with the larger numbers in the training school and under unified supervision, those with special aptitudes would be more quickly recognized and placed.

CONCLUSION

Besides the saving in overhead expense, the provision of adequate salaries for supervising personnel and the even-handed enforcement of all laws instead of the fanatical enforcement of some, there are other reasons in favor of a unified force. First, entirely incompatible duties will not be delegated to the same men. The problem of the proper organization of the quasi-judicial administrative duties performed by many organizations in the Federal government is intriguing; but surely there should be no close associa-tion of the quasi-judicial administrator and the policeman or his superior. It is scarcely less undesirable to mix the duties of administrative supervision with those of police. The approach of the administrative supervisor, such as the post office inspector, is entirely different from that of the detective. One comes announced and with an attitude of helpfulness; the other acts efficiently only with surprise and suspicion.

Second, a unified force will justify an adequate training school. The Bureau of Investigation has an excellent training school now but the small number of entrants into the service does not justify a really adequate institution. Of course, the institution could be used by all the forces without consolidation but such a use would support the idea of consolidation too much for the present bureaucrats; and, besides, the entrance requirements into the various services are now so different as to make the use of a single school difficult.

Third, a unified Federal police force is the only organization that can properly coöperate with state police. At the present time there is no organized coöperation between Federal and state police. Whatever coöperation exists is a matter of agreement between the local supervisor of one of the Federal organizations and the local police authorities or state's attorney. It is little wonder that the local authorities make little progress with coöperation. The number of local chiefs representing the Federal strong arm is bewildering, if not exasperating. Besides, it is asking a good deal for state authorities to master the intricacies of the Federal appropriation acts and the jurisdiction of the various forces. If there were one person to whom a local officer could go, when a case arose where Federal and state law should coöperate, there would be coöperation, but as things now are such an officer must be an expert in Federal criminal laws as well as in Federal appropriation statutes to know where to seek Federal aid. On the other hand, even if they would, most of the Federal organizations are prevented from properly coöperating with state authorities. Their funds are appropriated for the enforcement of certain laws and any cost of coöperation must be borne by the agent who coöperates. Then again, with so many responsible for coöperation, responsibility is assumed by none. The Bureau of Investigation coöperates as far as it can. Its Division of Identification enjoys complete coöperation with local police; but except for this, its force is so small and its organization so incomplete that any real coöperation with state authorities is impossible.

The logic of a unified police force, however, cannot be pushed too far. The subordinates of the surveyors of customs should not be included in a consolidation. Their activities are too intimately bound up with the necessary routine of customs administration to permit their police function to predominate over their customs function. While their duties are police in the sense that a traffic officer is a policeman, they are not really detectives or police in the sense in which that term is used herein. Of course, the discovery of contraband as goods pass through the customs may be called detective work but it is really discovery as the result of inspection, not of investigation.

The present organization of the Coast Guard should probably not be disturbed. Humanitarian and police duties are not incompatible and the present organization is large enough, if adequately supplied with funds, to justify a proper training school and gradations that make a career in the service attractive. While police duties, finally, must be performed on both land and sea, the similarity of the descriptive name of the duties does not take account of the many essential differences in training and organization required on land and sea.

PERSONNEL—FEDERAL POLICE

Organization	Head-quarters Force	Field Super-vision	Attorneys, Clerks, etc., in Field	Police
Bureau of Investigation......................	97	30	102	285
Secret Service..............................	11	35	13	137
Prohibition Unit............................	119	187	759	1,684
Special Agency Service of the Bureau of Prohibition	1	9	52	124
Narcotic Unit..............................	40	15	44	249
Customs Agents	1	10	....	130
Customs Border Patrol.......................	...	...	....	504
Immigration Service.........................	30	20	100	300
Immigration Border Patrol...................	...	35	42	670
Post Office Inspectors.......................	49	7		310
Totals.................................	348	348	1,112	4,393
Coast Guard...............................	67	209	....	6,093

The Private Police of Pennsylvania

By Jeremiah P. Shalloo

Instructor of Sociology, University of Pennsylvania, Philadelphia, Pennsylvania

TO discuss a subject such as that of private police without limiting the area surveyed would be difficult without very extensive and time-consuming research. For this reason, it has seemed wise to limit this article to one state. It is hoped that the problems found in Pennsylvania may throw some light upon conditions elsewhere.

It would be well at the outset to point out that the term private police is somewhat misleading if not wholly contradictory. If police power can issue only from the governing authority or a representative of that authority, in this instance the State, it follows that all those upon whom the State confers police power become a part of the executive power of the State and should be subject to the State. In other words, they become an integral part of the police power of the State and can in no way be divorced from that power save by relinquishing such delegated power or by revocation by the State. Despite the fact that the State delegates full police power to private individuals in the employ of bodies other than those under the control and direction of the State, the State exercises no control over these individuals in Pennsylvania and such as are commissioned are responsible only to their private employers who compensate them for their services.

Much criticism has been leveled at the private police of this Commonwealth and most of it has been justified, particularly that aimed at the Coal and Iron police. Millions of dollars worth of property are in need of some sort of protection and the system of practically selling police power at five dollars a head has become established in this state to provide such protection. Pennsylvania is unique in this respect as no other state has any organization comparable to the Coal and Iron police. In fact, many of the Secretaries of State in this Union apparently never heard of private police if one may judge from the replies sent the writer to inquires made. Most of them declared there was no private police or confused the term with state police.

The private police are in reality public officers in the employ of private corporations or public authorities acting in private capacities. Their function is simply the protection of property. Yet they are empowered to maintain peace and order. They are empowered to arrest on view anyone trespassing on company property. In short, their police power is identical with that of a uniformed policeman on the streets of Philadelphia and they may arrest not only upon company property but anywhere in the county where their commissions are recorded.

The only basis upon which a distinction may be made between public and private police is upon the basis of purpose. Private police are hired by private concerns for the sole purpose of guarding and protecting the employer's property, are compensated by the company employing them and are responsible only to the employer. The above argument holds true for railroad police and other private police as well.

THE PRIVATE PATROLMAN

There is another type of police—the private patrolman. These are simply individuals who decide to set themselves up in the business of watchmen by securing a number of residents in a block or square in the city to subscribe for their services. Having assembled the necessary number of signatures they petition the Mayor or the Department of Public Safety for a licence to patrol the section. The detective bureau of the police department investigates the individual applying and if he is found satisfactory a license is granted him for one year. Department stores are permitted to employ a number of store police on practically the same basis. There are some three thousand private patrolmen in the city of Philadelphia and their compensation is based purely on a business arrangement depending upon the service rendered. These men have no power outside the section for which they are licensed and usually turn over the arrested offender to the city authorities. They are responsible only to their employers and their license may be revoked by the city for cause shown.

THE PRIVATE DETECTIVE

Private detectives, although usually catalogued as private police, are in reality not police at all and have no power of arrest other than that which inheres in the individual by virtue of his citizenship in the Commonwealth. They may, however, serve warrants in criminal cases upon order from the court. These fall into two classes: those who hold licenses and conduct agencies and those who are operatives.

A person applying for a detective's license must post a bond of two thousand dollars and pay a fee of twenty-five dollars. The license extends for three years. These licenses are issued by the Court of Quarter Sessions and may be revoked by the court for cause shown. The application must be filed in the office of the Clerk of Quarter Sessions two weeks before the granting of the license and advertisement must be made once a week for two weeks in a newspaper of general circulation in the county.

The operatives are not required to pay any fee or to post any bond. They are exactly the same as employees in any industrial concern. Most of them are used for shadow work, theatres, attendance at ball games, social gatherings, and industrial under-cover work. The matter of records is a sensitive subject with detective agencies. The record usually consists of the original report in long hand by the operative who has been assigned a number, such as "B-3." The subject is also numbered and the client likewise. When the report is turned in at the end of the day the original is drawn up in duplicate. One copy is sent to the client and the other is placed in the agency's files. These are not accessible to anyone but the state authorities or to an accredited investigator upon order from the court. Compensation of operatives ranges between five dollars and ten dollars per day. The amount to be charged depends upon the nature of the case. The State has nothing whatever to do with fixing the charges to be made by a detective agency for its services. In New York State if the license is issued to a corporation the bond is three thousand dollars and the fee three hundred dollars; if issued to an individual, the bond is two thousand dollars and the fee two hundred dollars. These are granted by the State.

Regarding the kind of work done by detective agencies, it is difficult to get any reliable facts. Most of them claim they do not handle "domestic cases." In New York any agency not handling such cases is likely to pass out of existence in a short time. It is safe to say that they all handle some of this kind of work. The charge that many of the smaller agencies are simply blackmailing organizations is probably true, but how this may be proved is not easy to see since no records are available and all the information which one may obtain must come from ex-employees with a grievance. A person defrauded prefers no publicity.

The William J. Burns International Detective Agency took over the work of the American Bankers Association in 1909 when the Pinkertons were replaced. There are some twenty-seven thousand banks in the United States, of which number twenty-three thousand are members of the Association. The Burns agency furnishes protection to these banks for a contracted amount. The signs which appear on bank doors, grocery shops, and so on, that this place is protected by such and such an agency may mean nothing. It may mean that a patrolman visits such places at definite times or it may be simply a "psychological service." Some companies keep a regular force of patrolmen for their subscribers and when extra protection is desired they send men to the bank or the building for a stated period. The Holmes Electric Protective Service maintains a small force for such purposes although most of the work is purely mechanical. By means of an elaborate and delicate set of electrical devices it is possible for the central office to know immediately if anything takes place within a building where their instruments are installed, regardless of the distance. These watchmen have permits to carry guns and have police power upon the property where they are stationed. They rarely bring an offender to the police station but turn them over to the city authorities and appear in court against them. These men are paid usually at the rate of one dollar per hour.

RAILROAD POLICE

In the case of railroad police, the Pennsylvania Railroad issues to each patrolman a book of instructions covering every phase of his job. His duties, powers and prerogatives are carefully set forth. When to arrest and when to refrain from arresting are explained in clear-cut language. According to the Heagie report, which will be mentioned later, there were three hundred and sixty-nine policemen on the Pennsylvania system in Pennsylvania on March 1, 1928. These men are organized on a military basis with captains, lieutenants and privates, even as the Coal and Iron police and the state police. Their functions are described as purely protective. According to Superintendent Buzby, prevention rather than apprehension is the policy of the Pennsylvania Railroad police. There are also a number of plainclothes men travelling on the trains to prevent gambling and disorderly conduct. The age requirements are twenty-one to forty-five, although there is a gradual scaling down of the upper limit at the present time. Patrolmen are paid a monthly salary of one hundred and forty-five dollars to start and may advance to one hundred and sixty-five dollars per month. Further advancement either in rank or salary is purely a matter of ability. Other private police are those employed by charitable organizations, for prevention of cruelty to children and by water companies for protection of fish. These totalled only ninety-one on March 1, 1928.

INDUSTRIAL POLICE

The real interest, however, in the private police of this state lies in the so-called industrial police or Coal and

Iron police. Liberal journals and intelligent editors and clergymen have denounced the Coal and Iron police and have repeatedly pointed out the necessity for curbing them. To them have been charged some of the grossest and most flagrant violations of human rights since Torquemada, and their methods have been likened, with a great deal of truth, to those used by the Spanish Inquisition. There can be no question but that the Coal and Iron police do constitute a very serious menace to the welfare of families, especially in the soft coal region. Usually possessing no knowledge of the common decencies and totally unaware of the fundamental liberties, these creatures, it is charged, have ridden with shoes of iron over the rights of citizens unfortunate enough to reside within their jurisdiction. Inasmuch as every citizen agrees that the tactics of these police are an indictment of the State of Pennsylvania, the question inevitably arises "Why not abolish them"? As an academic problem this might easily be solved, but as an actual, practical problem it is not quite so easy. It might not be unwise at this time to know a little more about their origin.

Private police made their appearance officially in this State in 1865 when railroads were granted the right to hire guards, to be known as railroad police and possessed of all the powers of a policeman of the city of Philadelphia. The following year, on April 11th, the Coal and Iron police were created by an Act, supplementing the Act of 1865. By this latter Act the Governor was authorized to appoint police upon request from any person in possession of collieries, furnaces or rolling mills, stating that more protection was needed or desirable. The only criterion, even as today, was necessity. There was no fee and no bond required.

A list of names was sent to the Governor, who turned them over to the Commission Bureau with an order that so many commissions be sent to such and such a company. Nothing was known of the history of the men being commissioned. It was simply a case of filling an order sent to the State by a private corporation or employer. These men were permitted to carry guns and all the rest of the paraphernalia of a first class policeman, and their authority was absolute throughout the county in which they were employed. They were theoretically, even as at the present time, employed for "the protection of the property" of the employing company, but under the statute their police power was just as great off the property as on it. This is still true despite recent legislation, which will be discussed a little later.

In 1871, in the general fee bill, commissions were listed at one dollar. The commission extended until annulled. During the Pennypacker administration it was decided to fix the term of the commission at one year. The employers fought strenuously against any change and finally settled upon five years. Governor Pennypacker compromised and the term was fixed at three years, which duration continues to this day.

No change occurred until June 8, 1923, when the fee was raised to five dollars per commission. The form of the application was also changed and the applicant was required to be a citizen of the United States, a citizen of the State of Pennsylvania, and a resident of the Commonwealth for at least one year immediately preceding his application for a commission. He must also furnish two reputable references. He must give, in addition, an account of his employment for three years prior to his application for a commission.

These police were commissioned only for the counties in which the employer's property was located and subscribed to the constitutional oath which accompanied the commission. The recorder of the county sent the oath to the office of the Secretary of the Commonwealth where it was placed on file. A certified copy of the oath made by the recorder of the proper county was filed with the commission in every county in which the property of the employer was located or for which the policeman was appointed and in which it was intended he should act. The present application does not differ materially except in the matter of the bond.

According to the report drawn up by Mr. Heagie, of the Governor's office, for the information of the Governor when the Mansfield bill and the Musmanno bill were under discussion in the legislature last March, there were in this State on March 1, 1928, 2,474 Coal and Iron policemen in the bituminous fields and 812 railroad police. It is a practical impossibility to give the exact number of police commissioned with any degree of recency because the nature of the public record prevents it. The persons whose names appear upon the public record may, or may not be, still in the employ of the company. Many commissions have been returned and have not yet been cancelled on the record, or it may be that a number have not yet been returned. It is possible to know how many were issued, but that gives little information as to how many are at present employed. In his report Mr. Heagie listed the fifteen companies employing the greatest number of private police. For our purposes only the five largest need be mentioned. The Carnegie Steel Company headed the list with four hundred and seventy-five private police; the Pennsylvania

Railroad, three hundred and sixty-nine; the Hudson Coal Company, two hundred and fifteen; Bethlehem Steel, one hundred and seventy-two; and the H. C. Frick Coke Company, one hundred and thirty-two.

During the Pinchot administration, under the leadership of Dr. Clyde L. King, then Secretary of the Commonwealth, an attempt was made to eliminate the undesirables in the private police and to clean up what was admittedly a rather dirty condition. To this end Sergeant George W. Freeman of the state police was appointed a special investigator for the Secretary's office and given a free rein to investigate every individual applying for a commission. Sergeant Freeman personally knew many of the Coal and Iron police and was in a position to cancel or recommend granting or renewal. Many commissions were cancelled and many more refused. In the reports turned in to the Secretary there are glaring instances of abuse of power and actual crime committed by these alleged guardians of the law. The companies employing Coal and Iron police were ordered to clean up the situation or the State would step in and clean it up. Some improvement was noted. But it was impossible to make any permanent improvement. The difficulty lay deeper. The system and not the men employed were responsible. The State and not the employers were responsible. If the State was willing to sell its sovereign power for five dollars it could be expected that nothing but violence and corruption must follow. Magistrates and squires divided fines with arresting officers, it was claimed. In one instance, three or four hundred Russians attending a picnic aroused the ire of a Coal and Iron policeman and were all arrested, charged with disorderly conduct. When brought before the squire they were each fined ten dollars and costs. There was nothing to do but pay or go to jail, and these illiterate foreigners, with no knowledge of their rights and still living under the czarist psychology, obeyed. Many such stories are told. Company towns entirely enclosed by high wooden fences reminded one of feudal days. There was no law there except company law. In some cases one was not permitted to enter these towns. The lord of the domain was the Coal and Iron policeman with his badge, club and gun.

LEGISLATIVE REFORM MEASURES

On the night of February 9, and the early morning of February 10, 1929, John Barcoski,[1] a miner-farmer of Santiago, Pennsylvania, was so brutally beaten by a lieutenant and two patrolmen of the Coal and Iron police, in the employ of the Pittsburgh Coal Company, that he died. This murder outraged every law-abiding citizen in Pennsylvania and demands were made that the private police be abolished at once. Representative M. A. Musmanno, in whose legislative district the murder took place, introduced a bill into the House of Representatives on March 13, designed to curb the power of the Coal and Iron police and to restrict their authority to the property of the employing company. In Section Ten of the bill he defined their powers and added:

. . . but such powers and prerogatives except in the case of express companies shall be exercised only upon the property of the corporation, association, individual or company for which or for whom he was appointed and upon any public highway upon which such property may abut within one thousand (1000) feet from any building, structure, works, plant or equipment

[1] The three policemen accused of killing Barcoski have since been acquitted of murder but are now held by the State for involuntary manslaughter.

that may be located on said property except that such policeman may guard payrolls in transit at any place or the transmission lines of any electric power company.

This excerpt does not appear in the Mansfield bill, which was approved. Section Eleven of the Musmanno bill stated:

All persons arrested by policemen appointed under this Act shall be taken before committing magistrates or to jails, lockups or station houses and the keepers thereof shall receive all persons arrested by such policemen for the commission of any offense against the laws of this Commonwealth.

Section Eleven of the Mansfield bill, which is the law governing private police in Pennsylvania at the present time, reads:

The keepers of jails, lock-ups or station houses shall receive all persons arrested by such policemen for the commission of any offense against the laws of this Commonwealth.

The impossibility of restricting Coal and Iron police to a piece of real estate, while still possessed of full police power throughout the county in which the property is located, was recognized by Representative Musmanno and he yielded to the arguments of his colleagues when the bill was being debated before the Committee of the Judiciary General on March 27, 1929. He proposed at that time to strip the private police of all police power and designate them simply as watchmen. This was voted down.

With respect to Section Eleven, he declared it was a very serious mistake to omit the first part which, had it been in force, would have prevented the Barcoski murder which took place in private barracks. Except for these two omissions, the Musmanno bill and the Mansfield bill, which Governor Fisher approved on April 18, 1929, are identical.

The chief difficulty which will arise relative to the enforcement of the Mansfield bill will hinge upon the interpretation of Section Ten, which confers upon police appointed under this Act "the powers and prerogatives conferred by law upon the members of the police force of cities of the first class and upon constables of this Commonwealth." A first class city is defined as one with more than one million population.

Since railroad police and Coal and Iron police derive their powers from the same Act, authorities as to one are applicable to the other.

In *Bunting* v. *Pa. R.R. Co.*, 284 Pa. 117, 120, the Supreme Court ruled:

The authority of officers appointed under this Act [1865, P. L. 225] is not limited to offenses committed against the railroad. Their powers are general, as the Act expressly confers the right to arrest all persons engaged in the commission of any offense against the laws of the Commonwealth which may be committed on railroad property. In making arrests for violation of law not immediately concerning property of the railroad company, these officers act not as agents of the company, but as policemen.

The courts have apparently been unwilling to define the powers of these policemen,—in the comparatively few instances that question has been raised before them. . . . In an opinion rendered February 24, 1926 (7 Pa. D & C 596), Deputy Attorney General Campbell concluded, "the only limitation upon the exercise of [their powers as Philadelphia policemen] is that they shall not extend beyond the county or counties within which the individual policeman has been qualified to act by the filing of his commission and a copy of his oath of office with the recorder of the county." . . . He concluded that they may exercise their powers whether on or off the property of the company for which they were appointed as state officers, but were not subject to call or control by local police authorities. This would seem to be a proper construction of the law in view of the repeated statements of the courts that they are public officers,—although the wording of the act might be construed to permit arrests committed on or near company property only. The point does not seem to have been passed upon by our courts.[2]

Both bills contain a bond requirement. For every private policeman commissioned the employing company must furnish a corporate bond of two thousand dollars. This bond requirement, while outwardly an advance over the former methods, is actually no improvement. This bond is for the assurance of faithful performance of duty, but if the commission is revoked for cause the company merely calls upon the bonding company. The same is true with the blanket bonds issued to banks. There is nothing in the bond requirement which in any way improves the situation except that a little more care may be taken in the selection of policemen. The Mansfield bill was approved April 18, 1929.

A new bureau has been created, known as Industrial Police, and Captain Lumb, a former state trooper and Commandant during former Superintendent Groome's absence, has been appointed secretary. All applications are now investigated through this new office. The state police are the investigating agents and monthly reports must be sent from the various private police forces to the Governor. To put teeth in the new law, Governor Fisher has issued a set of regulations. Among them one finds the injunction to submit monthly reports. The color of the uniform is designated as forest green with dull bronze buttons. The shield must be worn in full view and must have "Industrial Police," written on it together with the company's name and number. A military cap is

[2] From a statement drawn up by Representative M. A. Musmanno.

prescribed. Regulations issued to the private police of every company must be submitted to the Governor. The first regulation is far from clear:

Industrial Police must confine their activities as such strictly to the protection of the property and facilities of the concerns for which they are respectively appointed, and to the preservation of order upon or in connection with such property or facilities.

What is meant by "protection" is not clear. Regulation Nine also presents difficulties from the legal point of view. "Industrial Police shall not use undue violence in making arrests, unnecessarily display or use weapons, or use profanity." What is the meaning of "undue violence"?

Such is the situation from the legislative angle at the present time.

Is the Problem Solved?

Major Lynn G. Adams, Superintendent of the state police and probably more familiar with the problem than anyone in the state, has expressed the opinion that the new legislation will have very little effect upon the system. As long as private interests can secure police authority for their own purposes; as long as these men are dependent upon private interests for their living; as long as police, commissioned by the state, remain responsible to private corporations, just so long will there be abuses and evils to correct. He suggests that the state enlarge its state police force so that the entire state will be policed. Pay the men more than a starvation wage. Put police work on a par with the professions, and have young men of ability upon the force. Eliminate the problem of a dependent old age and offer some incentive for competent young men to apply for admission. He frankly admits that some of his own men have been guilty of abuse of power, but wherever found they have been dis-

charged. His suggestion, then, is to put the responsibility for law and order upon the state police by developing a larger constabulary and having barracks at danger points.

The head of a large coal company's private police told the writer, in June, that the coal operators would gladly discard the Coal and Iron police if the State would offer some real protection. He even went so far as to say that the operators would pay a special tax for state protection. He said: "These men cost a fortune. We pay sergeants one hundred and ninety dollars a month; corporals, one hundred and seventy-five dollars a month, and privates, one hundred and sixty-five dollars a month, and maintenance. And some of the men we get are worth nothing." When asked why deputy sheriffs were not hired, he replied: "Those fellows are simply bums, wardheelers, grafters. They know nothing of police work and are only looking for a little easy money. We pay plenty for them. What the sheriff pays them we do not know."

The net result of all the State's efforts to curb the power of the private police is nothing. The problem of the private police in the mining regions will never be solved, according to competent critics, until the Coal and Iron police are stripped of their police power and become simply industrial guards or watchmen. To this proposal the operators reply that with the type of person employed today in the mines it is impossible to handle the situation and be assured that valuable property will not be destroyed in times of emergency unless there is a police force for the specific purpose of protecting the property. The tendency to identify every foreigner with anarchism or Bolshevism is undoubtedly the main reason for the fear that resides in the mind of every operator.

The Control and the Discipline of Police Forces

By Donald C. Stone

National Institute of Public Administration, New York City

IN a dozen obvious ways the discipline of a police force is indicated by the mere appearance of the policeman on duty. It is reflected in his general bearing, in his relation towards superiors, and in the attitude with which he performs his duties. To know why a police force is well disciplined is, however, quite a different matter. A practical police officer has said, "A disciplined patrolman possesses that indefinable something which makes him responsive to orders and authority." [1] To determine what this "indefinable something" might be, takes us to the root of police organization and into the various angles of police control. Disciplinary action or the use of punishment for breach of rules, neglect of duty, or general incompetence is but one phase of the problem.

In the past, police administrators have treated the subject of police organization largely as a theoretical question or have ignored it altogether. They have failed to see the vital effect it may have upon the control of the force. Factors, such as the division of authority between the chief and a civilian police board or public safety commissioner; the vesting of disciplinary powers in a civil service commission, committee of council, or court; the failure to consider police service as a professional undertaking; and, the lack of adequate means for controlling the rank and file in the performance of duty may prove a permanent stumbling block to a well-disciplined force. It is the practical phases of such

[1] Cornelius F. Cahalane, *The Policeman*, p. 12.

questions and their effect upon police discipline which concern us here.

COMMISSIONS AND BOARDS OF POLICE

One common method of dividing police authority is to place the force under the general supervision of an administrative board or a committee of council. The powers of such a board vary widely. They may confer extensive authority not only over policies but over the day by day management of the force. Generally, the board is given authority over the appointment, promotion, punishment and removal of personnel.

The extent to which the board exercises these administrative powers must necessarily weaken the respect borne to the police chief and his deputies. The rank and file are in fact serving two masters—the chief and the members of the board. In so far as they serve the board, the chief will find it proportionately more difficult to maintain an effective discipline. Without authority there can be no control.

Moreover, the board as an administrative agency has never proved a success. It is too unwieldy. Unless one member is able to dominate it, which would defeat the purpose of board control, it is likely to be deadlocked or unable to agree on any progressive action. This impotency and the frequent inability to perform even routine matters can hardly command the respect vital to good discipline.

In an attempt to remove the police from politics, some cities provide that the members of the board shall represent existing political parties as equally as possible. This practice either tends towards stagnation of police action or serves as a clever means for distributing patronage equitably.

CONFLICT BETWEEN CHIEF AND COMMISSIONER OF PUBLIC SAFETY

Another means of dividing executive control is to place a commissioner of public safety in charge of what are called the safety functions; namely, police, fire, health, building regulation and public welfare. Under this arrangement the chief of police is made a subordinate of the commissioner.

Although there may be some theoretical similarity between these so-called *safety functions*, it does not extend into the practical phases of routine administration. The methods and the technique for managing a health or building department differ entirely from police requirements. The fact that both firemen and policemen wear uniforms can in no wise be interpreted to mean that their administrative problems are similar. Yet many cities continue to treat these activities as identical and place upon some layman's shoulders the impossible task of becoming proficient in them all overnight, and—for fear that he might learn something about them—the most effective means are provided for supplanting him every year or two.

Almost invariably the commissioner will concentrate his attention upon the police, as this is the most interesting function and also the most useful for personal and political reasons. He more readily accepts the technical nature of the health, the building regulation, and the fire departments, leaving them pretty much in the hands of their trained directors. As a result public safety commissioners have injected themselves more and more into the routine management of the police

force and have wrested from the chief that control which he must have inviolate if he is to maintain a well-disciplined force. The commissioner may make assignments or promotions over the head of the chief. He may dismiss charges against the men. Perhaps he will develop an interest in the detective bureau and supersede the chief in formulating its policies and selecting its men.

Under such conditions a personal conflict between the chief and the commissioner is ever in the offing. If each enjoyed unlimited tenure of office, satisfactory adjustments might occur more often. But, with new commissioners and chiefs arriving with great frequency, the maintenance of a harmonious *modus vivendi* becomes impossible. Friction and discord may result not only between the chief and the commissioner but throughout the rank and file, as they strive to serve two masters.

There is but one remedy for this condition. The position of public safety commissioner should be abolished and the entire control of the force placed in the hands of a single administrative head. It is submitted that a trained and experienced chief of police, either uniformed or civilian, is the logical person for this authority. If the so-called safety activities need any coördination the mayor or the city manager is the proper official to supply it.

THE CIVILIAN COMMISSIONER OF POLICE

A somewhat similar division of authority may arise in those cities which place a civilian commissioner of police over the chief. In contrast to the public safety commissioner, the police commissioner is expected to give his full attention to police matters and therefore can much more readily become a professional police administrator. Perhaps the greatest gains in American police administration have been due to two or three of New York City's civilian commissioners. Fortunately, the police commissioner there is given such extensive powers that he is virtually the chief of police as well as the commissioner. Though their achievements may have been greatly due to their personal qualifications, the success of these commissioners would have been less likely, if not impossible, had they not been vested with complete authority over the force.

In contrast to New York the majority of cities with civilian commissioners have so divided the authority between the commissioner and the chief that neither is really responsible. For example, the city of Rochester carries this division of authority to an absurd extreme. Under the city manager, the chief administrative officer of the city, is a commissioner of public safety. Subordinate to the commissioner is a director of police. Finally, under the director's supervision is the chief of police. With each officer superior to the chief taking a share of authority, the chief is shorn of all but a semblance of control over his subordinates. Truly it is a question whose subordinates they are. With an unfortunate selection of a commissioner, a director, or a chief the friction between them could quickly throw the entire force into a state of discord.

Not only by police boards and commissioners does the chief of police find himself deprived of authority. Anomalous as it may seem, it is from civil service commissions that chiefs may have most to fear. With the well-intentioned purpose of keeping politics out of the police and making merit count, major powers over the selection, the promotion, and the removal of the force are conferred upon the commissions. As a result, policemen in cities having commissioners of public safety are not asked to serve two masters but three—the commissioner, the chief and the civil service commission.

EVILS OF DIVIDING AUTHORITY OVER DISCIPLINARY ACTION

The power to put punishment into effect, swiftly and certainly, as well as to instill the fear of it, must always be the most potent force in promoting good discipline. In private undertakings punishment for breach of duty is considered such a matter of course and so inevitable that the necessity of its use is consequently minimized. In police service where rewards for good service are less certain, and where strict adherence to duty is of paramount importance, the disciplinary use of punishment is even more vital. In spite of this, its effectiveness is vitiated by delay and division of authority. Disciplinary powers which should remain inviolate within the police department are transferred to civil service commissions, committees of council, or to courts. These agencies seldom have the viewpoint of the police. In practice they have been extremely sentimental over the thought of a man's losing his position and not at all sentimental concerning the deteriorating effect of continuing him in the service. This has gone on to such an extent that the law in some places practically considers the policeman's right to his job as inalienable, not to be separated from him except under the most solemn rites of judicial process.

Methods of removal or other drastic disciplinary actions vary from department to department. Police officials are seldom restricted in the use of reprimands and light penalties. More often, though, the final authority for suspensions and removals has been transferred totally or in part to the bodies mentioned above. Frequently the police cannot remove a man from the force, no matter how serious the offense, but must refer the matter to the civil service commission or some other specified agency. In place of his rôle as police executive the chief must assume somewhat the position of a plaintiff at a trial, sometimes begging, even imploring, the trial board to impose a penalty.

In other departments discipline has not been so far removed from police authorities. Very often, however, the accused is given the right of appeal to either the civil service commission, the council committee, or a court of law. Review by a court is even more to be condemned than civil service review, for the court is farther removed from administration and less apt to appreciate the practical aspects of police work. It is particularly a menace when it decides on the weight of evidence, in addition to reviewing the procedure by which the punishment or the removal was imposed. By so doing it strives to substitute its judgment for the police official's in regard to a man's usefulness on the force.

The protection from politics, possibly gained by giving these corollary agencies the power of review, is far outweighed by the police administrator's loss in control of discipline. Bruce Smith succinctly describes the evils of such checks upon police authority.

The administrative head often withholds his hand through fear of reversal in the courts. He knows, either by report or from actual experience, that it takes but a single striking reversal of his judgment to impair not only his prestige and official control but also the whole day-to-day discipline of the police force. The essence of a sound discipline inheres in its constant application.[1]

[2] *Report to the Commission of the Subcommission*

The continuing of unsuitable men on the force because of barriers and hazards in removal cannot but foster an undisciplined rank and file. The chief is denied a powerful means of obtaining attention to duty, corruption is more likely, and the very fibre of the department is weakened with a resulting loss of public confidence.

The personnel files of many departments reveal men who not only have been suspended but also discharged and reinstated from six to a dozen times. Frequently the number of men reinstated in a single year equals or even exceeds the number removed. In Buffalo, to take a random example, there were eight separations from the force and eleven reinstatements during the year 1922. From 1922 to 1926 the total number resigned, dropped, and dismissed was seventy-three, whereas there were thirty-eight reinstatements.

In Kansas City and St. Joseph, Missouri, the partisan police boards dismiss and later reinstate large portions of the forces. Although the members of the force are protected after the probation period by the necessity of formal charges and a hearing, the requirement means nothing because the police boards are permitted to reduce forces for economy. Bruce Smith found long lists of discharged policemen upon this pretext, to be later reinstated when the political wind blew more favorably.[3]

On the other hand, police chiefs have been entirely too passive to these reinstatements, many failing to make any vigorous opposition. Others have reinstated men when the decision lay entirely in their own hands. Police boards, civil service commissions, council committees and courts cannot be held entirely responsible for a practice

on Police, The Crime Commission of New York State, p. 24.
[3] *Missouri Crime Survey,* Chapter 1.

which police chiefs, through their own incapacity or lack of foresight, may have brought on themselves.

POLICE EXECUTIVE MUST BE SOLE AUTHORITY

The conferring of disciplinary powers upon civil service commissions has been tried and found wanting. Raymond Fosdick says:

Too often, civil service is a bulwark for neglect and incompetence, and one of the prime causes for departmental disorganization. Too often does the attempt to protect the force against the capricious play of politics compromise the principle of responsible leadership, so that in trying to nullify the effects of incompetence and favoritism, we nullify capacity and intelligence too.[4]

The conclusion that police discipline must be removed from civil service commissions might not be so well defined if these commissions had protected the force "against the capricious play of politics." Commissions, however, are about as apt to be governed by political factors as are police departments. Their record certainly shows this to be the case. The same political authority usually appoints both. How, therefore, can one assume that it will not use the one for political purposes if it would so use the other? Assuredly not on the grounds that the civil service system is inherently free from politics, for too often the name *civil service* or *merit system* really serves as a cloak to cover up its real nature. The mere passing of a law will not in itself prevent the commission from being as partisan in exercising its selective and disciplinary powers as the police. Being entirely free from responsibility for police service and largely ignorant of its needs, the chances are that it will be more partisan. At any rate, commissions have devised most novel methods by means

[4] *American Police System*, p. 284.

of which the intent of the civil service law has been completely evaded.

It is not proposed here to eliminate technically qualified civil service commissions entirely from police matters. Such commissions should supplement rather than supplant police authorities in the administration of personnel. Final authority must always rest in the police, particularly in disciplinary matters. The commission should be obligated to consult the police on every measure proposed, otherwise the practical aspects of policing will be pushed into the background. Police management cannot yet be reduced to terms of examinations, efficiency ratings and other mechanical devices. How the man stands up in the line of action is the real question. Only the police can answer that.

Conferring complete authority over discipline upon the police administrator does not mean that this power is to be used in secrecy. The accused should have an opportunity to state his side of the case, but to police authorities only. His claims may be made a matter of written record. There is no harm in requiring the police to file papers with the civil service commission. There the interest of the civil service commission must end except as the commission may benefit therefrom in improving selective methods so as to prevent undesirables from getting into the service.

If a dismissed policeman wishes a public hearing, it should be granted. However, this hearing should be before police executives who have the final and the sole authority. This is the only guarantee necessary and it will be much less political or biased than when the matter is referred to a foreign agency.

An interesting method of disciplining is practiced by the state police of Massachusetts. A trial board of officers of almost equal rank to the defendant is selected. When the regulations were formulated, the commissioner of the force reserved to himself the right to rehear cases and change penalties, fearing that the trial board might be too lenient. In actual practice he found it necessary to review the penalties, but not in the way he anticipated. In almost every case the board tended to be too severe. This placing of disciplinary action in the hands of the troopers themselves has gone a long way to build up their *esprit de corps*.

Great discretion is needed by the police executive in selecting the form of punishment to be imposed, or it may defeat its own end. Oral and written reprimands or warnings are the most common, and perhaps the most abused. Putting a man on the carpet offers the official a splendid opportunity to obtain the offender's viewpoint. Misunderstandings of long duration may be cleared up if the official will trouble himself sufficiently to discuss the matter frankly and with consideration.

The practice of inflicting fines is to be severely condemned. The burden of the punishment usually falls on the policeman's family rather than on him. Suspension without pay is not in the same category, for it is the suspension part which is the real punishment.

Reduction in rank for the purpose of punishment is particularly apt to break the offender's spirit and cause him to lose interest in the service. In the future his relationship with his official associates will constantly be a source of great embarrassment.

The system of giving demerits for cases of improper conduct has proved unsuccessful. It attempts to supplant judgment by a purely mechanistic device. Of course this does not mean that these cases should be omitted from the personnel records. In an improved form the demerit system allows merits for unusual performances. Service or efficiency rating plans are an outgrowth of the demerit system and likewise have met with very little success. This is partly due to the adoption of impractical plans. The army ranking scale based upon a man-to-man comparison and a graphic system as used in Cincinnati have shown the best results.

In any of these disciplinary measures it is of utmost importance for the police authorities to convince the offender that he is receiving a square deal. If the latter feels that his side of the matter is brushed away without due consideration or that he is treated in a high-handed manner, only continued resentment and future difficulties can ensue.

The problem of reinstatement should also be grasped firmly. No member of the force who is dismissed or who resigns while charges are pending should be eligible for reappointment or reinstatement. The rigid adherence to such a rule will repay a department many times. It is seldom likely that those whom it has been necessary to dismiss will ever make good policemen. More serious than this is its demoralizing effect upon the other members of the force.

Disbarring persons who resign while charges are pending is exceedingly important. Many of these resignations are accepted by the police administrator to avoid the danger of having his decision reversed by a court or a civil service commission. The accused knows that a new chief or commissioner will soon be in office. Never having been tried, his chances of reappointment are not beclouded by his record.

IMPORTANCE OF THE RECRUITING PROCESS

Civil service advocates seem a bit illogical in their emphasis upon the removal phase of personnel administration. If the commission adopts methods which will select good men, why need it have fear of dismissals? Besides, if party preferences of candidates have nothing to do with their selection, how can it have much bearing upon removals? It is like locking the door after the horse is stolen.

Adequate measures to prevent the unfit from getting on the force should form the first line of defense in reducing the need for disciplinary action. To delay until men have been recruited, trained and placed in active service before removing incompetents is inefficient and expensive. Bruce Smith is very definite on this matter:

Even a stern discipline and a most vigorous weeding out of ineffective or undesirable members cannot offset the palpable weaknesses in the system of selection now employed. The elimination of an undesirable applicant before appointment, or shortly thereafter, probably has more value in maintaining the morals of such a body than the most unrelenting system of disciplinary penalties.[5]

The first step is the application of vigorous examinations (intelligence, aptitude, and medical) upon a large number of high grade candidates. By no means should the examinations require a knowledge of police affairs; their period of training will give them that. The possibility of measuring a man's prospective worth as a policeman by means of written examinations is still largely undeveloped. However, the absurdity of selecting policemen on the basis of arithmetic, spelling and geography tests is evident. Yet this is done by the majority of civil service commissions.

Character investigations are even more important. Dismissals are largely necessitated by problems of character. Obviously such dismissal

[5] *Illinois Crime Survey*, p. 344.

would be unnecessary if the men requiring them were disqualified at the start. Police administrations and civil service commissions alike have brushed the matter of character investigations aside as though it were of no importance. For example, the rules for recruiting policemen in one of the largest cities in the country provide that the candidate must furnish two character references and if these prove unsatisfactory, he must give two more. This appears to be a pretty good guarantee that no candidate will be disqualified from the character standpoint.

Police departments should not accept a man until they feel reasonably certain that he has integrity, moral courage, resourcefulness and other necessary characteristics which cannot be measured by written examination. Personal interviews must be made with those who are most likely to have an unbiased judgment of the man. Character investigation of references themselves may be necessary. No matter what methods are adopted, the police authorities should have the final decision on the qualifications of a man.

In those departments which subject their men to a period in the police training school, a second opportunity is provided for eliminating the unfit. Examinations and critical observation by the instructors should be applied with the definite purpose of selecting the most fit.

The probationary period is the last possible place to eliminate the unqualified without the involved process of hearings, trials and reviews. Not until the recruit is sent into the firing line of actual police duty comes the real test of his aptitude for police work. His proficiency in written examinations may there prove of little practical value.

The probationary period varies from city to city; in some two months, in others three, four, or six, and upwards to a year. In state police forces it ranges from four to six months. In almost all cases it is sufficiently long to give a thorough trial. With the exception of two or three state police forces, few departments have critically reviewed the recruits while on probation. When asked why he fails to take advantage of this period, the chief is likely to shrug his shoulders or say, "My deputies do not recommend them for removal." The civil service commissions or the courts cannot be blamed for this.

THE PROFESSIONALIZATION OF THE POLICE

Policing our great cities is no longer a "watch and ward" affair. A policeman today must be armed with science as well as with a gun. Not only must he be versed in criminal investigation and identification, traffic control, patrol methods, criminal procedure and prosecution, and first aid, but he should have a rudimentary knowledge of criminology and of sociology as well. At the same time he must be a two-fisted guardian of the peace and a practical social worker. The demands upon the police administrator are even more exacting, calling for greatest managerial ability.

In European cities, police administration is recognized as a profession, calling for extensive training and experience. Administrators take up police work as a life career. Not being subject to the vagaries of politics and vested with ample authority over their men, their forces have far surpassed those in America in quality of service and discipline.

In America, the splendid discipline of the state police agencies of Pennsylvania, New York and Massachusetts may well serve as a model. The commissioner or superintendent has been vested with all necessary powers. Forthwith he has undertaken to professionalize the service much as in European cities. Politics have not urged him to concentrate on meeting popular demands. Being free to give his entire energy to constructive police duty, the rank and file know that he is working in their interest. As a result he can demand discipline and obtain it. Fortunately, he need not often *demand* it; it is created by the professionalized character of the service.

Administrators who take up police work as their life profession are likewise needed at the head of our municipal police forces. Undoubtedly a higher grade of ability can be obtained from civilians trained in police administration. His present short tenure of office and the injection of politics will always block professional ends. Those recognized by the current administrative head for good service may be plowed under by his successors. The patrolman knows not whether his enforcement of a law will bring commendation or condemnation. He sees blanket orders and clean-up campaigns which are not meant by those dictating them. In some departments, it is even expected that certain orders be disobeyed. If they are obeyed and the patrolman interferes with protected gambling and liquor interests, dives and speakeasies, he may be sent to "patrol the bushes" or given other handicaps. A well-disciplined man cannot survive in such an atmosphere. It is such obstacles as these which now block the professionalization of American police forces.

Health departments furnish a splendid example of a professionalized public service. The health officer is recognized as a technician. Only men trained in public health are eligible for the position. His subordinates likewise must be trained and competent.

The politicians have learned that the public will not tolerate any tinkering. As a result, the ethics and the discipline of the service are of the highest. Police service also deals with a social ill whose solution is just as difficult and even more complex. The sooner this is recognized, the sooner will effective police forces be placed in the field to combat the ever increasing crime problem.

CHIEF AS A LEADER OF HIS SUBORDINATES

The rules and regulations of police departments set forth in unquestionable terms that it is the first duty of the patrolman to give unqualified obedience in the performance of duty; to carry out orders promptly, even blindly; and, humbly to subordinate his ideas and opinions to those of his superiors. How much more is it the duty of superiors to be tolerant, coöperative, and reasonable! Almost any group of men will respond when their superior takes them into his confidence, is sympathetic, and leaves the way open for them to come to him when they are in difficulty. Evidently, police officials do not appreciate this, for they frequently deal with their men harshly and with aloofness, employing what might be called the blood-and-thunder method. The attempt to enforce discipline entirely with fear is doomed to failure since the rank and file are necessarily beyond official surveillance during much of their duty.

Moreover, the chief in large departments is seldom available to the rank and file for matters of advice. The rules require patrolmen to take up grievances or other matters with sergeants or with their captain. If the latter considers it important enough he may confer with his official superior, and so on, till it may reach the attention of the chief. The grievance or problem may be such that the patrolman cannot approach his immediate superior, or experience may have taught him that he will get little satisfaction in that way.

The chief or his deputy, in all but the metropolitan departments, should hold himself open to consultation by any of his subordinates on questions of professional or personal importance, which cannot be handled by the man's immediate superior. The chief need have no fear of being overwhelmed by visits from his men. He can control that. The important thing is that they should feel free to go to him. The same necessity for accessibility applies even more strongly to district captains and the detective chief. Although some of their problems may not seem important to police officials, they are to the patrolmen, and it is of patrolmen that the force is largely composed.

R. A. Reiss, the eminent Swiss authority, makes the following statement concerning the chief of police.

He should be on good terms with his personnel, at the same time enforcing a vigorous discipline. For the good of the service, he ought not to consider his personnel as mere subordinates, but as his collaborators on whom depends the success of his mission.[1]

The failure of chiefs to supply their men with up-to-date copies of the department's rules and regulations often leads to friction in the relationship between patrolmen and their superiors. As the chief executive of the force, it is for him to provide a manual of regulations to which all ranks can refer for a definition of their duties, rules of procedure, and the authority of each in the giving of orders. This manual should be so devised that new regulations can be currently added to it. With such a manual the official relationship between patrolman and superior will not

[1] *Contribution à la Réorganisation de la Police.*

be so accidental, with each attempting to show as much authority and lack of obligation as possible. In addition to requiring his force to be instructed in these rules, the chief should teach all officers the art of giving orders and how to obtain both the obedience and the good favor of their men.

CONTROL OVER MEN ON DUTY

The isolated manner in which a patrolman patrols his beat calls for extraordinary means of supervision. No matter how competent the patrolmen may be, they cannot be left hour after hour to their own devices. Alertness and aggressiveness in the performance of duty calls for a continuous accounting of the men by means of inspections, call boxes, recall signals and written reports.

The most effective system of controlling men on the beat is to place six or eight beats in charge of a sergeant. The sergeant, or roundsman as he is sometimes called, is then held responsible for the patrolling of these beats. It is his job continually to inspect the patrolmen, encourage and advise them in their work, and to take charge of any emergency which may arise. The more the patrolman is kept on his toes by such means the better work will he perform.

The success of patrol supervision depends in large measure upon the attitude and the ability of the sergeants. They must have such a high sense of duty that they will report or discipline patrolmen when they violate rules or neglect duty. The sergeant should guard against undue familiarity with them. This does not mean that he should hold himself aloof or adopt high-handed methods. These never gain the respect necessary for any permanent form of discipline.

In the majority of European cities, the roundsman is the crux of the whole patrol problem. In contrast, American cities either do not recognize his importance or have so detailed their sergeants to other matters that they play a negligible part in the supervision of patrol. The sergeants must be inspected as well as the patrolmen. This is the duty of the lieutenants or captains. Again, in turn, the captains need supervision by inspectors or the chief, the latter being the pivot upon which the whole force rotates. Discipline in the line of duty will, therefore, depend largely upon the definiteness with which he assigns responsibility to his subordinates and establishes means of controlling their performances.

Mechanical means of communication are being increasingly employed to control the patrolman on the beat. By requiring him to report to headquarters every hour or half hour by means of patrol or call boxes, there is greater assurance that he is physically present on his beat. Recall or flash systems by means of which the patrolman is reached from headquarters are an added guarantee. Communicating with patrol cars by radio is no longer just an experiment but is proving of very practical success in Detroit and other cities.

The decentralized police box system devised by Chief Constable Crawley of Newcastle-upon-Tyne is finding great favor in English cities. Under this plan, the constables go directly to their boxes (small booths) and from there report by telephone to headquarters. It is no longer necessary to retain numerous district stations, thereby releasing many men for more hours of actual police duty. By means of periodic calls to headquarters, recall signals and inspections, the constables are thoroughly controlled.

The filing of the patrolman's and the detective's daily reports makes these men more accountable for their activities. A further example is the use of detective assignment records to inform the chief of detectives what results each man is obtaining in the investigation of cases.

The foregoing are but a few suggestions of the many devices a police executive may adopt to control his men. Important though these devices may be, they cannot offset the necessity of placing the force completely in the hands of a single and trained administrative head and clothing him with such authority over his subordinates that he can be held accountable for their official acts.

Police Statistics

By BENNET MEAD

United States Bureau of the Census, Washington, District of Columbia

POLICE statistics, which form one of the principal classes of criminal statistics,[1] include all quantitative information concerning police organizations and their activities. As thus defined, police statistics include both the data compiled by all classes of police agencies and the information compiled by other agencies concerning police work. This article is, however, limited to the consideration of data officially compiled and no attempt will be made to cover the statistics compiled by crime commissions and similar bodies. The chief emphasis will be placed on statistics of city police departments rather than on state and national organizations engaged in police work. State police agencies are concerned chiefly with special types of work, such as traffic control and prohibition enforcement. The various Federal police agencies are also highly specialized. The city police departments, however, deal with every variety of crime and delinquency, and are the outstanding public agencies in the United States which deal with crime.

This article is also limited to a survey of those police statistics which relate to crime and delinquency and does not attempt to cover such activities as traffic control. During recent years, the regulation of traffic has steadily increased in importance in many localities and tends to overshadow the older functions of the police in preventing crime and apprehending criminals. Our concern is mainly with the basic

[1] The other two classes are judicial statistics and penal statistics.

function of the police in protecting the community against crime.

CLASSES AND FUNCTIONS OF POLICE STATISTICS

The existing statistical data compiled by the police include the following principal classes:

(1) Number and types of offenses known to the police; (2) offenses cleared, by arrest of the offender or otherwise; (3) persons arrested or charged, and their disposition; (4) property stolen and recovered; (5) personnel: size, character, and distribution; (6) type and extent of equipment; and, (7) cost of conducting work.

The principal purposes served by police statistics are, as follows:

(1) To show the prevalence of crime during a given period, such as a month, a quarter, or a year, in each city and state, and in the country as a whole; (2) to show the trend of crime in each geographic area during successive periods, that is, to measure the increases or decreases which occur monthly, quarterly, or yearly; (3) to measure the results accomplished by the police in dealing with crime; (4) to furnish data concerning the characteristics of offenders and their social and economic condition; (5) to show, in part, the economic loss resulting from crime, and the cost of conducting police work.

The measurement and the comparison of different police agencies as to their efficiency would be perhaps the most important function of police statistics, if satisfactory indices of police efficiency could be developed. At present, however, there are such marked variations in the crime conditions of different cities and in police organization, policies, and methods, that no satisfactory conclusions can be reached as to the relative efficiency of police departments. It may be possible in the future to develop accurate measures of police efficiency; such measures must be regarded as future objectives rather than present possibilities. In view of the importance of the matter, examples will be given in this article to illustrate the difficulties and the obstacles which prevent us from measuring police efficiency. For the present, it is sufficient to mention a few of the more important factors entering into the problem, which would need to be definitely measured on a uniform basis before police departments could be rated as to efficiency.

(1) The character of the population of each community as to sex, race and age composition; (2) the industrial character of each locality; (3) the situation of each city or state with reference to other cities and states; (4) the physical character of each locality, whether hilly or level, and so on; (5) prevailing climatic and weather conditions; (6) prevailing types of housing, whether mostly detached dwellings, rows of dwellings, or apartments; (7) the available resources and mechanical equipment of each police department; and, (8) the size and the character of the police personnel.

It is evident that only a few of these factors can be measured exactly or expressed in such terms that they could be used in computing an index of police efficiency.

In this article, the principal types or classes of police statistics will be considered with reference to their value for the purposes mentioned above, especially for measuring the prevalence of crime, the trend of crime, and the cost and the results of police activity. The

bearing of the statistics on police efficiency will be indicated, so far as feasible. The principal statistics on the cost of police work will be summarized and examples of other important types of statistics will be presented.

EFFORTS TO STANDARDIZE POLICE STATISTICS

At the convention of the National Police Association held in St. Louis in 1871, a resolution was adopted declaring it to be one of the purposes of the association "to procure and digest statistics for the use of police departments." Since the organization of the International Association of Chiefs of Police in 1894, criminal records and statistics have been frequently discussed at the conventions of the association. In 1922, the association endorsed a system of crime records which has since been widely adopted by police departments. In 1926, a booklet was published by the United States Bureau of the Census, entitled "Instructions for Compiling Criminal Statistics." [2]

At the 1927 convention of the International Association of Chiefs of Police, a committee was appointed to formulate a complete standard system of police statistics. This Committee on Uniform Crime Records has recently completed its report which outlines an excellent system of record forms, and forms on which local police departments could furnish data for state-wide and nation-wide compilation. The Committee has also recommended a standard annual police report.[3]

[2] This booklet was largely prepared by Professor Sam B. Warner (now of the Harvard University Institute of Criminal Law) as Director of the Committee on Records and Statistics of the American Institute of Criminal Law and Criminology. It suggested a few of the more essential statistical tables which it would be desirable for each police department to publish annually.

[3] See article on The Annual Police Report, by Mr. L. S. Timmerman.

In preparing this article, many valuable suggestions have been received from the publications of the Committee on Uniform Crime Records. The work of this committee stands as the culmination of the movement started fifty-eight years ago to develop an adequate system of police statistics in the United States.[4]

PREVALENCE AND TREND OF CRIME— METHOD OF MEASUREMENT

Statistics of the number of offenses known to the police form the best available means of measuring the extent of crime at a given time, and the changes from time to time in the prevalence of the more serious offenses against persons and against property. It is, of course, impossible to obtain complete statistics of crimes committed, since many crimes remain undiscovered, and many more crimes are known only to private individuals and are not reported to official agencies.

[4] The Committee on Uniform Crime Records was made up of Commissioner Wm. P. Rutledge of Detroit, Chairman; Chief Jacob Graul, Cleveland; Commissioner James Higgins, Buffalo; Deputy Superintendent John H. Alcock, Chicago; Commissioner Alfred F. Foote, Boston; and Chiefs Thomas Healy, New Orleans; George G. Henry, Baltimore; L. V. Jenkins, Portland, Oregon; and August Vollmer, Berkeley, California.

Among the members of this committee, Chief Jenkins had been chairman of the section of the Association which prepared the standard record system in 1922, and Chief Vollmer was an active member of the Committee on Records and Statistics of the American Institute of Criminal Law and Criminology which outlined the plan for police statistics in the Census Bureau manual. Thus the Committee on Uniform Crime Records was linked, through two of its members, with the two leading committees responsible for previous efforts to improve police statistics.

The research work of the Committee on Uniform Crime Records was directed by Mr. Bruce Smith, police expert of the National Institute of Public Administration. A committee of Federal officials and of specialists in various phases of criminology acted as technical advisors to the committee.

There are wide variations in the completeness with which different classes of offenses are reported to the police. It is probable, for example, that in most localities the great majority of homicides are officially recorded. On the other hand, many cases of embezzlement and of petty theft are not reported. The Committee on Uniform Crime Records has recommended that statistics of offenses known to the police be compiled for only eight classes of "major offenses," which are as follows: (1) murder; (2) manslaughter; (3) aggravated assault; (4) rape; (5) robbery; (6) burglary; (7) larceny (except automobile theft); and, (8) automobile theft. The committee, as a result of its investigations, believes that reasonably complete information can be obtained for these groups of offenses but that satisfactory data cannot now be secured for other offenses under the conditions existing in the United States. While this conclusion is, no doubt, well founded, it is interesting to note that in other countries the official statistics of offenses known to the police may cover a wide range of offenses. In England, for example, all "indictable offenses" are covered. Comprehensive crime statistics have been compiled for many years on a nation-wide basis in Canada, England, and the principal countries of Europe.

The Committee on Uniform Crime Records has worked out a standard procedure for the centralized recording of offenses by police departments, and for uniform reporting, monthly and annual, to a national bureau which is charged with the task of compiling criminal statistics for the country as a whole. At the present time, only a few police departments in the United States publish satisfactory data concerning offenses known to the police.

A beginning has been made toward

the development of state-wide police statistics in New York and Massachusetts, but the development of nation-wide statistics of offenses known to the police remains a task for the future.

In order that statistics of offenses known to the police may be as accurate as possible, it is desirable to compile data concerning offense reports which are found upon investigation to be unfounded or erroneous. The total number of such unfounded reports should preferably be deducted from the total of each class of offenses before computing ratios of offenses to the population. At present, however, several of the cities for which statistics are available do not publish comparable data on unfounded cases. It has therefore seemed advisable in this article to use figures representing the full number of reported offenses.

In the case of many minor or petty offenses, the only available means of measuring their prevalence is through statistics of arrests, or of persons charged with the offenses. Leading examples of such offenses are: drunkenness; disorderly conduct; vagrancy; and, violations of traffic laws. Obviously, statistics of the number of persons charged with these offenses do not represent the full number of cases in which these offenses are committed. But they do represent, for all practical

TABLE 1—COMPARATIVE CRIME RATES IN SELECTED CITIES: 1928

Population, and Number of Major Offenses Known to the Police per 100,000 Inhabitants (a)

City	Estimated Population (b)	Total (c)	Homicide	Robbery	Burglary	Larceny (c)	Automobile Theft
United States:							
Detroit, Michigan.........	1,378,900	1,189.1	12.8	56.4	39.7	1,014.7	816.5
Cleveland, Ohio (d).......	1,010,300	560.6	13.1	117.3	208.4	51.2	558.3
Baltimore, Maryland......	830,400	1,170.5	26.9	40.6	270.5	658.2	314.3
Buffalo, New York.........	555,800	536.3	24.7	43.5	154.0	244.7	413.1
Rochester, New York......	328,200	943.0	8.2	13.1	208.4	515.8	264.5
Canada: (e)							
Montreal, Quebec.........	618,506	(f)	(f)	16.2	241.1	899.3	(f)
Toronto, Ontario..........	521,893	(f)	(f)	13.8	140.1	893.9	(f)
Winnipeg, Manitoba.......	191,998	(f)	(f)	26.7	371.4	2,096.9	(f)
Vancouver, British Columbia	117,217	(f)	(f)	50.3	422.3	1,866.6	(f)
Hamilton, Ontario.........	114,151	(f)	(f)	26.3	82.4	340.8	(f)
Ottawa, Ontario...........	107,843	(f)	(f)	6.5	165.1	1,157.2	(f)
Quebec, Quebec...........	95,193	(f)	(f)	....	26.3	98.8	(f)
England:							
London..................	7,783,062	204.1	0.6	0.4	44.0	108.6	23.7

(a) Based on data in tables 9 and 10 taken from 1928 annual reports of police departments; and for Canada, from annual report, "Criminal Statistics," issued by Dominion Bureau of Statistics.

(b) Estimates for United States by Bureau of the Census, as of July 1, 1928. Estimates for Canada as given in annual report, "Criminal Statistics."

(c) Exclusive of automobile theft in the United States, but includes automobile theft in Canada. Total also includes offenses not separately shown in this table.

(d) Data cover felonies only.

(e) Data cover the calendar year 1927.

(f) Figures not available.

purposes, the number of cases coming to the official notice of the police. The use of arrest statistics for measuring the prevalence of minor offenses, as well as for other purposes, will be discussed in a later section.

CRIME RATES IN DIFFERENT CITIES

It is feasible to present in this article statistics of offenses known to the police, in proportion to population, for only five cities in the United States, and for only a few of the principal offense groups. These figures are presented in Table One, which is based on the data published in the 1928 reports of the police departments in the cities represented. Corresponding official data are also given for the seven leading cities in Canada, and for London.

In addition to the cities covered in Table One, corresponding statistics of the number of offenses known to the police are presented elsewhere in this report for Los Angeles, California (See Table Nine). It is, however, not feasible to compile crime rates for Los Angeles, since no official census estimate of the city's population is available.

Owing to differences in the scope of the statistics for the various cities it is doubtful how far the figures in the "total" column in Table One are really comparable. It would be very hazardous to proclaim, on the basis of these figures, that Detroit had a higher total crime rate than any other city for which statistics are shown in the table. Nor can we safely conclude that Buffalo had the lowest recorded crime rate. The contrast between the rates for these two cities is especially striking since their reports are among the first which have been published in substantial accordance with the standards for annual police reports, as recommended by the Committee on Uniform Crime Records. Detroit has been

compiling statistics of offenses known to the police for a number of years, but the Buffalo police department has only recently begun such compilation. Accordingly, the marked difference between the rates for the two cities may be due, at least in part, to the more complete recording of offenses in Detroit.

In Cleveland and Baltimore, data concerning offenses known to the police have been compiled for about the same length of time as in Detroit, and they should be about equally complete for all three cities. The Cleveland statistics are restricted to felonies. This limitation, however, affects only larceny, of the offense groups shown in Table One.

More satisfactory comparisons can be made for specific offense groups than for the total of all offenses. Baltimore has the highest rate for homicide, closely followed by Buffalo. The rates for Detroit and Cleveland are about one half as great and the rate for Rochester about one fifth as great as the rates for Baltimore and Buffalo.

The robbery rate is largest for Cleveland, while Detroit has a rate less than half as large. Baltimore and Buffalo have rates about one third of the Cleveland rate. Rochester has by far the smallest rate, only one ninth of the Cleveland rate.

For burglary, Baltimore has decidedly the largest rate, and Cleveland and Rochester have rates about three fourths as large as the Baltimore rate. The rate for Buffalo is about one half of the Baltimore rate. Detroit has the lowest burglary rate, about one seventh of the rate for Baltimore.

The larceny or theft rate is by far the largest for Detroit, while the rate for Baltimore is about two thirds as large, and the rate for Rochester about one half as large. The Buffalo rate is less than one fourth of the rate for Detroit.

The Cleveland larceny rate is not comparable with the rates for other cities, since it represents only grand larceny, while the other rates cover petty larceny as well. The great majority of thefts are petty. In Detroit, for example, "simple" or petty larcenies formed six out of seven of the larcenies represented in Table One.

Automobile thefts are here shown separately from other thefts, in accordance with the offense classification recommended by the Committee on Uniform Crime Records. This separation is made because police experience demonstrates that many reported automobile thefts are not actual thefts, but represent cases of temporary unauthorized use of property.

Frequently, even when theft is the actual object of the offender, it is difficult to secure a conviction for larceny, and the court charge is likely to be reduced to the lesser offense of using property without permission.

Of the cities represented in Table One, Detroit has much the largest rate for automobile thefts. The Cleveland rate is less than three fourths and the Buffalo rate one half of the Detroit rate. The rate for Baltimore is about two fifths as large and the Rochester rate is less than one third as large as the rate for Detroit.

The principal figures in Table One for cities in the United States may be summarized as follows: Detroit had the largest rates for larceny and automobile theft; Cleveland had the highest robbery rate; Baltimore had the largest homicide rates and burglary rates. Thus, for each offense group, the highest rate is found for one of the three cities which lead in population.

Rochester, which is the smallest of the cities covered in Table One, had the smallest offense rates for homicide, robbery, and automobile theft. These comparisons are by no means conclusive, but they appear to indicate a positive correlation between the crime rate and the size of the city considered —that is, the larger the city, the higher the crime rate.

These statistics for a few cities are illustrative of the type of comparisons which can be made between the larger cities, and between states, whenever similar data are available for a number of states. It should be emphasized that to be exactly comparable such data must be recorded and classified on a uniform basis. It is essential that all offenses made known in any way to the police—or to other law enforcement officials—be not only recorded, but also reported to a central record office in each city. It is essential that each type of illegal act be included under the same heading, regardless of the terminology which may be customary in each state and city.

With reference to the interpretation of crime rates, they should clearly be regarded as morbidity and mortality rates are regarded in the public health field. A high crime rate should be considered as the product of many conditions in the life of the community, among which police efficiency is very important but not necessarily the principal factor. As an illustration of the need for careful analysis of the influence of social conditions in producing criminality, census statistics show that, in the country as a whole, the homicide death rate is about eight times as large for negroes as for the white population. Obviously, a relatively high homicide rate is to be expected in a city with a large negro population.

TREND OF CRIME IN DETROIT

By way of illustrating the use of statistics of offenses known to the police for measuring the changes from year to year in the prevalence of crime, Table

Two is presented. This table shows the ratio to population of offenses known to the police in Detroit, for each year from 1924 to 1928. Rates are here given for all of the major offense groups recommended by the Committee on Uniform Crime Records, except that the rates for murder and manslaughter are combined under the head of "homicide." Table Two is a condensed version of Table IV–C of the 1928 report of the Detroit Police Department.

and rape, the rates showed an upward trend from 1924 to 1928. For both robbery and burglary, the trend was steadily downward. The rate for robbery was only two thirds as large in 1928 as in 1924; and for burglary the rate was only two fifths as great in 1928 as in 1924. For larceny, the rate increased until 1926, then decreased rapidly. In 1928, the rate was about four fifths as large as in 1924.

As indicated above, comparison of the crime rates in different cities throws

TABLE 2—CRIME RATES IN DETROIT, MICHIGAN: 1924 TO 1928

Number of Each Class of Major Offenses Known to the Police per 100,000 Inhabitants (a)

Offense	1924	1925	1926	1927	1928
Grand Total...............	2,110.6	2,401.4	2,175.4	1,904.3	1,747.5
Automobile Theft............	620.1	872.8	501.7	499.5	593.2
Other Offenses.............	1,490.5	1,528.6	1,673.7	1,404.8	1,154.3
Homicide (b)................	12.8	12.6	17.0	10.0	8.5
Aggravated Assault...........	42.3	38.0	44.1	44.5	47.2
Rape........................	10.7	12.6	11.5	12.8	16.9
Robbery.....................	74.2	61.7	63.6	56.6	53.8
Burglary....................	89.5	43.5	39.0	35.3	38.4
Larceny.....................	1,261.1	1,360.2	1,498.4	1,245.5	989.5

(a) Rates taken from Annual Report of Detroit Police Department, 1928, p. 13. These rates differ from those given for Detroit in Table 1, due to the use of differently estimated population figures.

(b) Exclusive of negligent homicide, for which figures are not available except for 1928.

The combined rate for all of the major offenses was decidedly higher in 1925 than in 1924, but it has declined steadily since then and was about one sixth less in 1928 than in 1924. The rate for automobile theft also reached its highest mark in 1925, and was only slightly lower in 1928 than in 1924. The total for all offenses (except automobile theft) reached its peak in 1926, but declined sharply in 1927 and in 1928. For homicide, the peak rate was also reached in 1926, and the 1928 rate was one third less than the 1924 rate. For both aggravated assault

little light on the relative efficiency of police departments. The statistics for Detroit serve to illustrate the fact that a marked downward trend of specific crime rates in a given city may indicate increased efficiency of the city's police department. At the same time, the fact that the trends vary so widely for different offense groups shows the influence of many other factors in addition to police efficiency. For this reason, crime rates are less useful for measuring the effectiveness of police work than other data to be discussed later.

RESULTS OF POLICE WORK

The best available means of measuring the effectiveness of the police in dealing with crime is to compare the number of offenses cleared by arrest (or its equivalent) with the total number of offenses known to the police. It is important that the unit of measurement be the *offense*, rather than the offender. In many cases, two or more arrests are made in connection with one offense. In other cases, two or more crimes may be the work of a single offender. In general it is probable that the number of arrests for major offenses is greater than the number of crimes cleared by arrest. For example, in Detroit, in 1928, there were 8,654 persons apprehended for major offenses, as against 5,541 offenses cleared. As an indication of the large number of cases in which persons are arrested but not prosecuted, it may be noted that 3,815 of these 8,654 apprehensions were dismissed by the police.

Statistics of crime clearances must be compiled on a uniform basis to be of value for comparative purposes. The Committee on Uniform Crime Records lays particular stress on this point in its report and emphasizes that no offense should be classified as cleared, unless it has been officially declared cleared by an authorized high police official, over his signature.

In order to secure the highest possible degree of accuracy, it would be desirable to compare the number of offenses cleared by arrest with the number of actual offenses, first deducting the number of reported offenses which police investigation has shown to be unfounded.

The unfounded cases form a strikingly large proportion of the total reported automobile thefts. For example, the Detroit statistics for 1928 show 2,895 unfounded cases, out of 11,259 automobile thefts. For other offenses, however, the percentages of unfounded cases are small. Out of 16,397 offenses known to the Detroit police in 1928, exclusive of automobile thefts, only sixty-four were unfounded.

TABLE 3—CRIME CLEARANCES IN SELECTED CITIES: 1928

Percentage Which Number of Offenses Cleared by Arrest Formed of each Class of Major Offenses Known to the Police (a)

City	Total (b)	Homicide	Robbery	Burglary	Larceny (b)	Automobile Theft
United States:	%	%	%	%	%	%
Detroit, Michigan........	29.7	76.8	49.8	54.9	23.9	5.9
Cleveland, Ohio..........	45.3	91.7	29.5	23.7	33.5	11.3
Los Angeles, California....	11.1	(c)	19.4	10.9	6.0	(c)
Baltimore, Maryland.....	39.6	94.2	56.4	31.6	33.6	(d)
Buffalo, New York.......	64.1	23.3	45.0	56.0	67.6	16.5
Rochester, New York.....	(e) 12.8	(f)	(f)	15.5	4.8	10.8

(a) Based on data in Table 9, taken from annual report of police department of each city.

(b) Exclusive of automobile theft.

(c) No data available.

(d) Data as to clearances by arrests not available. Recoveries made by police in 97 per cent of cases.

(e) Based on total of those classes of offenses for which clearances were reported.

(f) Percentage not shown, as base is less than one hundred.

CRIME CLEARANCES IN DIFFERENT CITIES

In order to present comparable data for all of the six cities, it has been necessary in this article to compare the number of offenses cleared with the total number known to the police. The percentage of offenses cleared by arrest, in 1928, is presented on this basis in Table Three.

There is a strikingly wide variation in the percentage of crime clearances, whether we compare one city with another or one offense group with another. For the total of all offenses, except automobile theft, the percentage of clearances ranges from a maximum of 64.1 per cent in Buffalo to a minimum of 11.1 per cent in Los Angeles. For homicide, the percentage is highest for Baltimore, and lowest for Buffalo. For robbery, the highest percentage is found in Baltimore and the lowest in Los Angeles. For burglary, the percentage of clearances is highest in Buffalo and lowest in Los Angeles. For larceny, the largest percentage is in Buffalo and the smallest in Rochester. For automobile theft, the percentage of clearances is strikingly low in every city covered. Buffalo has the largest percentage, 16.5; while Detroit has the minimum of only 5.9 per cent.

TREND OF CRIME CLEARANCES IN BALTIMORE

The progress made from year to year in accomplishing better results through police activity is effectively shown by comparative statistics of crime clearances. Such a comparison is shown in Table Four for Baltimore, covering the years 1924 to 1928. The offense groups in this table do not fully correspond with the list of major offenses recommended for statistical purposes by the Committee on Uniform Crime Records.

TABLE 4—CRIME CLEARANCES IN BALTIMORE, MARYLAND: 1924 TO 1928

Percentage which Number of Offenses Cleared, Formed of Each Class of Major Offenses known to the Police (a)

Class of Offense	1924	1925	1926	1927	1928
Total (b)................	% 32.9	% 34.6	% 39.5	% 38.3	% 39.6
Homicide................	94.3	94.7	97.2	95.0	94.2
Robbery.................	54.6	59.9	56.4	49.7	56.4
Burglary................	25.5	28.1	30.6	33.7	31.6
Larceny (b).............	29.0	30.3	34.8	33.4	33.6
Fraud...................	55.7	47.1	60.4	56.6	66.2
Embezzlement...........	(c)	(c)	90.3	87.4	90.1
Automobile Theft (d)..........	96.7	97.1	96.3	97.8	97.0

(a) Computed from data in Table 11, from annual reports of the police commissioner for the city of Baltimore. Percentages derived from "total complaints," and complaints for which arrests were made, for all offense groups except automobile theft. See note (c).

(b) Exclusive of automobile theft. See note (d).

(c) Percentage not shown, as number of offenses was less than one hundred.

(d) Figures represent percentage which automobiles recovered during the year formed of the number reported as stolen. Figures are *not comparable* with figures given for other offenses.

For the total of all offenses except automobile theft, the percentage of clearances increased steadily from 32.9 in 1924 to 39.6 in 1928. There are, however, decided differences between the specific offense groups in respect to the percentage of crimes cleared. For homicide, there was a slight increase from 1924 to 1926 in the percentage of clearances, then a decrease to 1928. But it is obvious that when more than ninety per cent of crimes are cleared, as in the case of homicide, it is difficult to secure appreciably better results or even to maintain from year to year such a strikingly high percentage of clearances as in 1926.

For robbery, the percentage of clearances was slightly higher in 1928 than in 1924, but it shows no definite upward trend since it reached a maximum in 1925; it dropped to the lowest point in 1927. For both burglary and larceny, the percentage of clearances increased decidedly between 1924 and 1928. For fraud, the percentage of clearances was lower in 1925 than in 1924, but rose to its highest point in 1928. Significant figures for embezzlement can be presented only for three years, and these figures fail to show any definite trend.

No figures concerning clearances by arrest are available for automobile theft in Baltimore. Only slight fluctuations are apparent in the percentage of stolen automobiles which are recovered. This percentage was over ninety-six during the entire period from 1924 to 1928.

These statistics show definite gains in the results accomplished by the Baltimore police in the detection and apprehension of criminals. If compiled on a uniform basis from year to year, such statistics for a given city afford a valuable index of police effectiveness,—an index which is obviously more significant than can be obtained merely through crime rates, such as were presented above (Table Two) for Detroit.

RECOVERY OF STOLEN PROPERTY

Comparative statistics relative to the recovery of stolen property provide a useful index of the results of police activity in dealing with robbery, burglary, larceny, and other offenses against property. The recovery of stolen property is a police function fully as important as the apprehension of the criminal. The success of the police in recovering stolen property should therefore be measured in order to cover adequately the results of police work.

Statistics of this character must be compiled on a uniform basis to be of value. Stolen and lost property should so far as possible be separately tabulated. It is essential that the same value be assigned to each article or piece of property both in the tabulation of stolen property and in the tabulation of recovered property. If, for example, it is learned that the actual value of a piece of recovered property differs from the value as previously reported by the owner, a correction should be made in the stolen property record. Furthermore, all stolen property which is recovered should be included in the tabulation of stolen property even when not previously reported as stolen. It is important, also, to tabulate separately any recovered property which has not been stolen in the particular city. On account of the special problems involved, the value of stolen and of recovered automobiles should be tabulated separately from other classes of property. It is also very desirable that property values be correlated with the type of offense and with offense clearances.

At the present time there is little uniformity in the methods of recording and classifying data concerning stolen property. It may be noted, for example, that in many police reports the stated value of recovered property exceeds, by a wide margin, the value of the property reported as stolen. Where this condition exists, it is obvious that the "stolen" and "recovered" values are not properly comparable.

There are a number of city police departments which now compile accurate and useful statistics of stolen property. For example, Los Angeles shows, for each of the principal classes of offenses against property, the total value of property stolen and of that recovered, the number of cases cleared by arrest in which property is recovered, and the number of cases with recovery of property but no arrest. Partial and total recoveries are separately tabulated. Rochester publishes data showing the average amount stolen and the number of cases in which property is recovered, and also classifies burglaries according to the amount stolen. Cleveland classifies robberies and burglaries according to value stolen in correlation with the location and the time of day when the offense was committed.

In view of the wide differences in the methods of compiling and presenting data on stolen property, it would be hazardous at the present time to compare the figures for different cities. Furthermore, statistics of property values must be used with particular caution for measuring police effectiveness. This is especially true where the statistics show merely the total values of property stolen and recovered. For example, such figures for a given city and a particular year might show that a much smaller percentage of property was recovered than in the previous year. But this apparently poor showing might be due to the failure of the police to recover property stolen in a few crimes involving large amounts, while the police may have recovered property in a larger percentage of cases than in earlier years. It is evident that, in appraising the success of police activities, the percentage of cases in which recoveries are made should be given at least as much weight as the percentage of value recovered.

The Committee on Uniform Crime Records has suggested the inclusion of statistics of property stolen and recovered in the annual reports of police departments. But influenced, no doubt, by the difficulty of developing uniform statistics on this subject, the Committee has not recommended that such statistics be compiled at present on a state-wide or nation-wide basis.

From the standpoint of the victim of crime, recovery of his property is of greater importance than punishment of the offender. Therefore, in spite of the obstacles to be overcome, it seems highly desirable to promote the standardization of this class of police statistics with the hope that adequate data for wider areas can be developed later.

PERSONNEL AND EQUIPMENT

In order to judge the effectiveness of police activity, it is necessary to consider not only the quantity of work performed, but the size of the force engaged, its distribution, and the kind and amount of equipment available. With respect to personnel, the Committee on Uniform Crime Records has recommended that police departments in their annual reports show the members of the force, classified by grade; the distribution of each grade among districts or precincts, special bureaus or other administrative units; and, the salary range of each grade. The committee also recommended that changes during the year in the authorized and actual strength of each grade of the police force be shown. These proposed statistics are highly desirable, but for appraising the work accomplished, in relation to the work to be done and the force used, it is desirable to know the average number of police officers actually available at a given time for patrol duty and for each principal type of special duty.

Suppose, for example, two cities, A and B, have police forces of equal size; and that city A uses the "three platoon" system, that is, divides its force into three parts, each of which is on duty eight hours; while city B uses the "two platoon" system, with two twelve-hour shifts. The number of men on duty at a given time will evidently be fifty per cent larger in city B than in city A.

In the Detroit police report for 1928, it is stated that out of a total of 2,675 patrolmen on the force, an average of only 1,188 were available for patrol duty, after deducting those on special duties and those absent on leave, sick or injured. But only between three hundred and five hundred men are on duty at any given time, the number being greater at night than by day.

In the 1928 report of the superintendent of police of Washington, District of Columbia, he points out (Page 2) that only about one eighth of the patrol force is actually on patrol duty at one time and comments, as follows:

It is submitted that the only equitable method for computing the number of police officers per square mile, or per unit of population, is the method herein adopted, namely, that of taking only the actual number of men on duty.

Information concerning type of equipment is also essential for measuring the working capacity of a police department. The actual effectiveness of the police patrol work cannot be judged merely from the number of men available without considering the extent to which automobile and motorcycle patrol has superseded foot patrol.

In a section to which motorcycle patrol is adapted, one motorcycle patrolman can cover the same area as several foot patrolmen. Recently Chief August Vollmer, of Berkeley, after a survey of police work in a middle western city, was reported in the newspapers to have stated that the police problem of the city could be efficiently handled by a much smaller force, at less expense, if up-to-date methods and equipment were introduced.

In view of the numerous complications indicated by such examples as have been cited, it will evidently be difficult to develop statistics of police force and equipment from which exact comparisons can be made between different cities. For the present, it may be necessary to recognize that only approximate comparisons are feasible. All of the members of a police force are engaged, indirectly if not directly, in the task of law enforcement. This is true of the members of a city detective bureau, and other specialized units, quite as much as of the patrol force. It seems legitimate, therefore, to compare the total force of a city with the volume of work performed, as measured by such facts as the number of crime clearances, the number of pieces of stolen property and their value, and the number of persons apprehended and charged. In accordance with this view, the Committee on Uniform Crime Records has recommended, for nation-wide collection, information as to the total size of each police force. This information is to be appended to the monthly report to the national bureau concerning offenses known to the police. The collection of more detailed data as to personnel, and of any data as to equipment, has been wisely postponed for future study and development.

Before leaving the subject of police personnel, it should be mentioned that nation-wide statistics of city police personnel, classified by grade, were formerly included in the annual reports on statistics of city governments, published by the Federal Bureau of the Census. These statistics were published for each year from 1903 to 1907, but were eliminated, together with other non-financial data, when the scope of the report was narrowed to cover only financial statistics.

PERSONS CHARGED WITH CRIME

Nature and functions of data.—Statistics of persons charged with crime form one of the chief classes of police statistics, and cover both those persons who are arrested or taken into custody, and also those notif ed, cited or summoned to appear for trial. A common example of the police notice or citation is the "tag" or ticket used to order traffic violators to appear for trial. The summons is a court order, which may be used instead of a warrant for arrest in cases where the offense is not grave, and the person charged may be expected to comply with the summons.

It is to be noted that the unit of measurement, in statistics of persons charged, is the *person* and not the offense—which is the unit in statistics of offenses known to the police, and of offenses cleared. Thus if two or more persons are implicated in a single offense, each of them will be counted separately; and if one person is charged at one time with two or more offenses, he will be counted only once.

Statistics of persons charged, in order to be of value for comparative purposes, must include *all* persons charged, and not merely those taken into custody. Many police departments publish statistics of arrests, but do not compile any data concerning persons notified, cited or summoned. Where the latter groups are included in the statistics, they are frequently not separated from the persons arrested. Hence, the scope of the statistics often may not be clear.

Distinction should also be made between persons arrested and formally charged with offenses, and those arrested "on suspicion" or "for investigation" but released without being formally charged. In some cities such arrests are quite numerous; while in other places they are infrequent. In order to insure a fair comparison between cities, the detailed statistics (as to sex, race, age, and so forth) of persons charged should not include those arrested and released without formal charge or prosecution.

The Committee on Uniform Crime Records has recommended that annual statistics be compiled concerning:

(1) Persons released without formal charge or prosecution;

(2) Persons charged:

    (a) Arrested;

    (b) Notified, cited, or summoned.

(3) Persons found guilty:

    (a) Of the offense charged;

    (b) Of a lesser charge.

It is recommended by the Committee that these statistics be compiled for persons charged with each important class of offenses, including the major offenses listed previously (see page 76) and also the following minor of enses: assault (not aggravated); forgery and counterfeiting; embezzlement and fraud; carrying weapons; sex offenses, other than rape; offenses against the family and children; violations of drug laws and liquor laws; driving while intoxicated; drunkenness; disorderly conduct and vagrancy; gambling; violations of traffic and motor vehicle laws; other offenses; "suspicion."

Data concerning persons charged are of value for the following purposes:

(1) To measure the prevalence and

the trend of minor offenses; (2) to measure the volume of work done and the results accomplished by the police, especially in reference to minor offenses; (3) to show the characteristics of offenders and the factors responsible for criminality.

In discussing the use of statistics of persons charged for the purposes indicated under headings (1) and (2), it is necessary to deal further with certain functions of police statistics, which have already been considered with special reference to the more serious offenses. In the present section the chief attention will be given to the minor offenses.

Use for measuring incidence of minor offenses.—Statistics of persons charged are of little use for measuring the prevalence and the trend of the major offenses, such as homicide, robbery, burglary and larceny. As a rule, the number of arrests is far smaller than the number of major offenses committed. In addition, experience demonstrates that the ratio of arrests to offenses may fluctuate considerably from year to year. In any case, as indicated in a previous section, the number of offenses known to the police if correctly compiled, forms an accurate index of the occurrence of the principal major offenses.

The situation is different, however, with certain minor or petty offenses, of which cases coming to the notice of the police are most likely to result in the arrest or the notification of the offender. Thus the number of persons charged not only constitutes the only available means of measuring the prevalence, and the trend of these offenses, but may form a fairly accurate index. For example, the number of arrests for drunkenness may, where police policy tends to be drastic, represent practically all cases of intoxication in public places. In any case, the figures

represent the cases in which official notice is taken of public drunkenness.

It is apparent, however, that under other conditions, the number of persons charged may be much smaller than the number of times a given kind of offense has come to official notice.

In order that statistics of persons charged may form even an approximate index of the prevalence of offenses, it is essential that uniform policies and practices in making arrests or bringing charges be followed in various localities, and in a given locality for various years. For example, if it is the practice in city A to bring charges against all intoxicated persons found on the streets, while in city B, charges are made in only fifty per cent of the cases and the rest are released when sober, it is evident that comparison of the numbers of persons charged would lead to quite erroneous conclusions as to the prevalence of drunkenness in the two cities.

Great care is necessary, therefore, in the interpretation of all existing statistics of persons charged, and especially of "arrest" statistics. There is little uniformity in the practice of different police departments in making arrests and in bringing charges. Furthermore, there are frequently drastic changes in the policy of a given police department which may cause spectacular increases or decreases in the number of arrests for a given offense, with no equivalent change in the prevalence of the offense.

A striking case in point is the current bitter controversy between the advocates and the opponents of prohibition concerning the significance of the marked increases in arrests for drunkenness which have occurred in many localities during recent years. Members of the "dry" faction insist that this increase does not represent a corresponding increase in the amount of drunkenness but reflects the adoption of more drastic policies in dealing with offenders, with the result that many of them are now arrested who formerly would have been handled without arrest. The "wets," on the contrary, declare that there has been little change in police policies and that the arrest statistics reflect an actual increase in the occurrence of drunkenness.

The great influence of police policy in such matters may be indicated by citing certain statistics from the 1928 report of the Detroit police department. From 1914 to 1918, this department usually held drunken persons until sober, then released them without trial. In 1918, 11,518 persons were thus released, as against 1,933 who were held for trial. In 1919, this practice was abandoned and the number of drunken persons held for trial increased to 6,249, more than three times the number held for trial in 1918 but only about one half of the total number arrested for drunkenness in 1918. Late in 1926, the former policy of release without trial was resumed, with the result that the number of drunken persons held for trial dropped from 14,624 in 1926 to 4,313 in 1927, while the number arrested, but released without trial, was 710 in 1926 (between December 14 and 31), and rose to 17,721 in 1927.

In this instance, the changes in police policy are clearly stated in the report. Hence the effects of such changes on the statistics can be estimated. But, in the reports of many other police departments, inspection of the figures may point to probable changes in arrest policy, though no definite conclusions can be reached as to just what these changes have been or how great have been their effects. Consequently many, perhaps most, of the statistics of persons charged, or of arrests, which are now available in police reports, cannot be safely used to measure the prevalence or the trend even of minor offenses.

Use for measuring results of police work.—Statistics of persons charged are of decided value, when properly compiled and applied, for showing the volume of work performed by the police and the effectiveness of police activity.

In the first place, for each class of major offenses, the number of arrests may be compared with the number of offenses known to the police. This comparison is, however, much less significant than the comparison of crime clearances with the total offenses known to the police. (See page 81.)

Secondly, for all offense groups, the number of persons charged may be compared with the size of the police force in a given city. This comparison may be made most effectively by calculating the ratio of the number of persons charged to the total number of members of the police force. Such a comparison is at best approximate. In general, the ratios for different cities cannot safely be compared, owing to differences in policies and conditions. Such differences might, for example, account for the fact that a given city had a ratio twice as large as another city. For a given city, however, so long as no appreciable changes are made in arrest policy, the effectiveness of the police may be judged by the trend from year to year in the ratio of the number of persons charged to the total police force.

Third, comparison may be made between the number of persons *found guilty* of various offenses and the *total number charged*. This comparison is best expressed in terms of the *percentage* which those found guilty form of the total number charged. The work of the courts and the prosecuting officials, as well as the police, is reflected in this comparison, which should there-

fore be regarded as an index of the
entire work of law enforcement, rather
than a mere measure of police work.

*Use for showing characteristics of
offenders.*—Statistics of persons charged
can be used for showing the distribution of the criminal and delinquent
classes as to sex, color, age, country of
birth, and other facts. For this purpose, such statistics would be far more
valuable than statistics of prisoners,
which cover only a part of the offenders.[5] Many police departments now
compile social statistics of persons
charged. The Committee on Uniform
Crime Records advocates the development of such statistics on a uniform
basis, by police departments having the
necessary statistical organization. But
the collection of nation-wide statistics
of the characteristics of persons charged
is set forth as a future objective. This
seems the only feasible course, in view
of the difficulties of compiling satisfactory data of this sort.

There is some prospect that during
the next few decades, at least a few
progressive police departments may
undertake the intensive scientific study
of the individual offender, with a view
to learning the personal causes of
delinquency and thus lay a basis for
more effective treatment. Such a
development, even if confined to a few
large cities, would throw much valuable
light on the individual and social causes
of criminality. The case histories of
offenders built up by such studies may
in time become the source of statistics
concerning such facts as the mental and
emotional characteristics of offenders,
and their habits of behavior. The
time seems ripe for such a development.
But no one can forecast how rapidly it
will come nor to what extent it will be
under police auspices.

[5] At the present time, the census statistics of
prisoners are the only criminal statistics compiled
on a nation-wide basis in the United States.

COST OF CITY POLICE WORK

The annual census reports on financial statistics of states and of cities
having a population of thirty thousand
or over, present nation-wide data concerning the cost of police activities by
public agencies.

The cost of conducting police departments during 1927, in cities of
various sizes, is shown in Table Five,
which also gives the estimated general
population of the cities represented.

The figures in Table Five show that
the per capita cost of police work increases, in general, as the size of cities
increases. The cities having from
thirty thousand to fifty thousand inhabitants have decidedly the smallest
per capita costs of operating and maintaining police departments, of providing pensions to retired and disabled
members of the police force, and of improving the plant and equipment used
for police purposes. For each successive class of cities of larger size, the
per capita rates for all three classes of
expenditure become heavier.

If the costs for cities having five
hundred thousand or more inhabitants
be compared with the costs for cities of
thirty thousand to fifty thousand it is
apparent that the per capita cost of
operation and maintenance is nearly
twice as large, the cost for police pensions is over three times as large, and
the cost of improvements is nearly
three times as large. These comparisons suggest that as the individual city
grows larger, the need for public protection of life and property, and for
regulation of individual conduct in the
public interest, tends to increase faster
than the population.

TREND IN COST OF CITY POLICE WORK

Financial statistics of cities are available for most of the years since 1903.
The statistics of the annual cost of po-

TABLE 5—COST OF POLICE WORK: 1927 FOR CITIES OF 30,000 AND OVER,
CLASSIFIED BY POPULATION (a)

Group (by Population)	Estimated Population (b)	Payments for operation and Maintenance of Police Departments		Payments for pensions and Gratuities for Policemen		Outlays for Land and Improvements	
		Amount	Per Capita	Amount	Per Capita	Amount	Per Capita
Total...............	42,716,411	$184,501,599	$4.32	$12,702,560	$0.30	$5,874,280	$0.14
I. 500,000 and over....	19,484,900	113,272,622	5.81	9,083,689	0.47	3,566,502	0.18
II. 300,000–500,000.....	4,146,700	17,153,715	4.14	1,276,572	0.31	803,293	0.19
III. 100,000–300,000.....	9,990,835	30,631,153	3.07	1,448,941	0.15	919,929	0.09
IV. 50,000–100,000.....	5,954,691	16,041,511	2.69	610,135	0.10	421,222	0.07
V. 30,000– 50,000.....	3,139,285	7,402,598	2.36	283,223	0.09	163,334	0.05

(a) Data from 1927 annual census report on financial statistics of cities, and relate to the fiscal year of each city.
(b) Figures represent estimated population at middle of each city's fiscal year.

lice work from 1903 to 1927 are summarized in Table Six. No figures are given for the years 1914, 1920, 1921, and 1922, either because no census was taken for these years, because the census was seriously incomplete, or because the cost of police work was not separately tabulated. It is to be noted also that the reported cost of operation and maintenance in 1909 and 1910 is not exactly comparable with the figures for other years, since the cost of pensions cannot be separated from the reported cost of operation and maintenance for these years. Separate figures concerning the cost of pensions are not available from 1909 to 1915, and outlays for improvements to police establishments were not separately tabulated for the years prior to 1907, nor for 1913.

The annual cost of operating and maintaining police departments, in cities of thirty thousand and over, was nearly five times as large in 1927 as in 1903. This tremendous increase was due, in part, to the fact that the number of cities which are included in the

statistics increased from one hundred and fifty in 1903 to two hundred and fifty in 1927. Another factor was the large growth in population of the cities which were covered both in 1903 and in 1927. But even on a per capita basis, the cost was nearly two and one half times as large in 1927 as in 1903.

The cost of police pensions increased even more rapidly than the cost of operation and maintenance, and was nearly seven times as large in 1927 as in 1903; while the outlays for improvements to police establishments show nearly a four-fold increase during the twenty years from 1907 to 1927.

As shown in the third column of Table Six, from 1903 to 1906 the cost of police work formed an increasing percentage of the cost of operation and maintenance of city governments. However, since 1906 the general trend has been slightly downward. The cost of operating and maintaining city police departments actually formed a smaller percentage of municipal expenditures in 1927 than in 1903. These figures demonstrate that while

TABLE 6—COST OF POLICE WORK, AND OF PLANT FOR CITIES OF 30,000 AND OVER
1903 TO 1927 (a)

Year	Operation and Maintenance of Police Departments			Pensions and Gratuities for Policemen	Outlays for Land and Improvements for Use of Police Departments
	Amount	Per Capita	Per cent of Total		
1903...............	$38,248,924	$1.83	11.5	$1,908,949	(b)
1904...............	40,075,426	1.86	12.2	2,103,198	(b)
1905...............	40,975,197	1.85	12.0	2,364,883	(b)
1906...............	43,212,548	1.89	13.0	2,436,674	(b)
1907...............	46,468,153	1.98	12.5	2,778,559	1,525,988
1908...............	51,037,147	2.12	12.7	3,037,198	1,667,300
1909...............	55,069,791 (c)	(c) 2.15	(c) 13.4	(b)	1,319,361
1910...............	58,752,108 (c)	(c) 2.15	(c) 13.1	(b)	1,587,214
1911...............	56,773,059	1.99	12.0	(b)	1,761,220
1912...............	59,777,366	2.04	11.8	(b)	1,849,146
1913...............	60,454,804	2.00	11.6	(b)	(b)
1915...............	64,392,291	2.08	11.9	(b)	1,091,247
1916...............	67,647,508	2.10	11.2	4,950,038	1,073,759
1917...............	69,082,060	2.08	10.9	5,196,080	1,339,706
1918...............	75,143,407	2.19	10.9	5,599,944	1,604,807
1919...............	80,917,027	2.33	10.7	5,860,909	1,237,911
1923...............	135,838,430	3.47	10.2	9,655,813	3,576,243
1924...............	145,170,115	3.63	10.2	10,630,160	3,446,852
1925...............	157,194,635	3.86	10.3	11,185,952	6,136,654
1926...............	171,167,246	4.09	10.4	12,004,004	6,362,130
1927...............	184,501,599	4.32	10.5	12,702,560	5,874,280

(a) Data from census reports on financial statistics of cities.
(b) Not separately reported.
(c) Includes pensions and gratuities to Policemen.

city police expenditures have increased since 1903 much faster than the general population, the cost of other departments of municipal government have increased still more rapidly than police expenditures.

COST OF STATE POLICE WORK

The census statistics concerning the cost of police work of the state governments in 1927, for the United States and for each principal geographic division, are shown in Table Seven. This table also shows the estimated general population and the total state expenditures of each area covered. Since prohibition enforcement is ac-

tually a specialized type of police work, the reported cost of state prohibition enforcement is shown in Table Seven, and is combined with the cost of state police departments as the basis for per capita rates and percentages.

The figures in Table Seven show marked differences between the geographic divisions both in respect to the per capita cost of state police work and to the percentage of state governmental expenditures which was devoted to police work. The West North Central Division had the smallest per capita cost; while the New England Division had by far the largest per capita cost. Both the New England and the Middle

TABLE 7—COST OF POLICE WORK OF STATE GOVERNMENTS, BY GEOGRAPHIC DIVISION:

1927 (a)

Geographic Division	Estimated Population (b)	Grand Total for all Activities	Payments for Operation and Maintenance				
			Police and Prohibition Enforcement				
			Total			Police Departments	Prohibition Enforcement
			Amount	Per Capita cents	Per- cent of Total		
Grand Total....	117,305,534	$1,120,004,895	$8,116,313	6.9	0.72	$7,426,458	$689,855
New England......	8,160,428	89,225,092	1,220,750	14.9	1.36	1,183,263	37,487
Middle Atlantic.....	24,741,000	270,987,076	3,244,750	13.1	1.19	3,244,750	......
East North Central...	24,393,000	195,755,874	677,543	2.8	0.46	352,919	324,624
West North Central.	13,151,192	126,393,413	147,181	1.1	0.12	85,518	61,663
South Atlantic......	15,282,000	124,470,634	896,755	5.7	0.72	768,606	128,149
East South Central..	9,340,618	62,477,429	516,544	5.5	0.83	488,274	28,270
West South Central..	11,579,000	106,754,778	320,482	2.8	0.30	320,482	......
Mountain..........	3,830,296	48,632,243	88,278	2.3	0.18	35,987	52,291
Pacific............	6,828,000	95,308,356	1,004,030	1.5	0.10	946,659	57,371

(a) Data from annual census report on financial statistics of states for 1927, and cover the fiscal year of each state.

(b) Estimated population of each state at middle of the fiscal year of the state government.

Atlantic divisions had per capita costs more than ten times as large as the cost for the West North Central Division, and more than twice as large as the South Atlantic Division, which ranked third in the per capita cost of police work.

The percentage of state expenditures devoted to police work was larger for New England than for any other division, and was thirteen times as large as the percentage for the Pacific Division, which had the smallest percentage of all the nine divisions. The Middle Atlantic and the West South Central divisions had no expenditures for prohibition enforcement, and the cost of prohibition enforcement formed only a relatively small proportion of the total cost of police work in six of the nine divisions. But prohibition enforcement costs were nearly as large as the cost of police departments in the two North Central divisions, and in the Mountain Division prohibition enforcement cost considerably more than the state police department.

The cost of police work by the state governments is very much smaller than municipal police costs, as shown by comparing the figures in Tables Six and Seven. In 1927, the per capita cost of operation and maintenance of police departments in cities of thirty thousand and over was 4.32 dollars as compared with 1.3 cents per capita for police work of state governments. Thus, the municipal police work cost more than three hundred times as much per capita as the state police work. To a large extent, of course, state police activity is conducted outside of the cities and deals with such matters as highway patrol and the policing of rural districts. Probably the proportion of state police costs which should be considered as chargeable to the urban population is somewhat smaller than the percentage which the urban population forms of the total population. But there is no satisfactory basis for determining the true quota of state police costs which should be charged to the rural and urban populations.

TREND IN COST OF STATE POLICE WORK

Financial statistics of states have been published since 1915 by the United States Bureau of the Census. The figures concerning annual costs of state police work, including prohibition enforcement, for each year for which statistics are available, are summarized in Table Eight. No data can be shown for 1916, 1918, and 1920, since no census was taken covering these years. Data for 1921 were collected, but covered only part of the states. The 1922 report showed no separate figures concerning the cost of police work.

The figures in Table Eight show a striking increase in the annual cost of state police work during the twelve years from 1915 to 1927. The amount spent in 1927 was nearly seven times as large as the amount spent in 1915. The per capita cost was over five times as large in 1927 as in 1915, and the percentage of state governmental costs which was devoted to police work was more than twice as large in 1927 as in 1915. This striking increase cannot be explained by the increased expenditures for prohibition enforcement. It is true that these expenditures were over fifty per cent higher in 1927 than in 1915, but there was a much more rapid increase in the regular "police department" expenditures, which were over nine times as large in 1927 as in 1915.

It is apparent that the state governments are rapidly increasing the scope

TABLE 8—COMPARATIVE COST OF POLICE WORK OF STATE GOVERNMENTS 1915 TO 1927 (a)

Year	Estimated Population (b)	Grand Total for All Activities	Payments for Operation and Maintenance					
			Police and Prohibition Enforcement					
			Total			Police Departments	Prohibition Enforcement
			Amount	Per Capita cents	Per Cent of Total		
1915.......	98,396,733	$379,030,094	$1,231,355	1.3	0.31	$792,275	$439,080
1917.......	101,809,990	426,329,432	1,189,490	1.2	0.28	864,365	325,125
1919.......	105,082,600	542,661,141	2,038,114	1.9	0.38	1,664,327	373,787
1923.......	109,638,713	895,953,782	4,679,488	4.3	0.52	4,130,859	548,629
1924.......	111,231,649	1,001,465,258	5,220,192	4.7	0.52	4,540,095	680,097
1925.......	112,641,877	1,035,478,035	6,754,988	6.0	0.65	6,053,631	701,357
1926.......	115,856,645	1,040,234,452	7,422,064	6.3	0.71	6,754,419	667,645
1927.......	117,305,534	1,120,004,895	8,116,313	6.9	0.72	7,426,458	689,855

(a) Data from census report on financial statistics of states.
(b) Estimated population of each state at middle of the states fiscal year.

of their police work, and may eventually assume as large a responsibility in the field of law enforcement as the cities now exercise. If, for example, the per capita costs of both state and city police work should continue to accelerate as rapidly as they did between 1915 and 1927, by about 1950 the state police work would cost as much per capita as the city work. Probably the chief factors responsible for this trend are the growing number of automobiles, the accompanying spread of the network of good roads, and the consequent extension of state highway patrols during recent years. Of course, it cannot safely be predicted how much longer such rapid growth will continue, but it is quite possible that the further development of other phases of state police activity, such as the policing of rural districts, the patrolling of airways, and the tracing and apprehension of criminals who escape from the locality of their crimes, will result in a further acceleration in the rate of growth of the cost of state police work.

TABLE 9—NUMBER OF OFFENSES KNOWN TO THE POLICE, AND TOTAL ESTIMATED POPULATION, FOR SELECTED CITIES IN THE UNITED STATES, CANADA AND ENGLAND: 1928 OR 1927 (a)

City	Estimated Population (b)	Total (c)	Homicide	Robbery	Burglary	Larceny (c)	Automobile Theft
United States (1928):							
Detroit, Michigan.........	1,378,900	16,397	177	777	548	13,992	11,259
Cleveland, Ohio (d)........	1,010,300	5,664	132	1,185	2,105	517	5,640
Los Angeles, California.....	(e)	19,547	52	1,736	7,921	8,611	10,813
Baltimore, Maryland.......	830,400	9,276	223	337	2,246	5,466	2,610
Buffalo, New York.........	555,800	2,981	137	242	856	1,360	2,296
Rochester, New York......	328,200	(f) 3,095	17	43	684	1,693	868
Canada (1927):							
Montreal, Quebec..........	618,506	23,576	(g)	100	1,491	5,562	(g)
Toronto, Ontario..........	521,893	72,915	(g)	72	731	4,665	(g)
Winnipeg, Manitoba.......	191,998	22,540	(g)	57	713	4,026	(g)
Vancouver, British Columbia	117,217	27,995	(g)	59	495	2,188	(g)
Hamilton, Ontario.........	114,151	8,806	(g)	30	94	389	(g)
Ottawa, Ontario...........	107,843	3,821	(g)	7	178	1,248	(g)
Quebec, Quebec...........	95,193	4,517	(g)	..	25	94	(g)
England (1928):							
London..................	7,783,062	15,886	50	34	3,494	8,450	1,844

(a) Data taken from 1928 annual reports of police departments of cities in the United States, and 1927 annual report, "Criminal Statistics," issued by Dominion Bureau of Statistics.

(b) Estimates for United States by Bureau of the Census, as of July 1, 1928. Estimates for Canada as given in annual report, "Criminal Statistics."

(c) Exclusive of automobile theft in the United States, but includes automobile theft in Canada. Total also includes offenses not separately shown in this table.

(d) Data cover felonies only.

(e) No census estimate available.

(f) Clearances reported for offense classes of which total was 2,437.

(g) Figures not available.

TABLE 10—NUMBER OF OFFENSES CLEARED BY ARREST FOR SELECTED CITIES IN THE
UNITED STATES: 1928 (a)

City	Total (b)	Homicide	Robbery	Burglary	Larceny (b)	Automobile Theft
Detroit, Michigan............	4,871	136	387	301	3,350	670
Cleveland, Ohio..............	2,566	121	350	499	173	639
Los Angeles, California.......	2,161	38	332	844	518	(d)
Baltimore, Maryland.........	3,673	210	190	710	1,839	(d)
Buffalo, New York...........	1,911	32	109	479	920	379
Rochester, New York........	312	15	16	106	81	94

(a) See Table 9, note (a) for sources of data.
(b) Exclusive of automobile theft in the United States, but includes automobile theft in Canada.
Total also includes offenses not separately shown in this table.
(c) Data cover felonies only.
(d) Figures not available.

TABLE 11—CRIMES AND CRIME CLEARANCES IN BALTIMORE, MARYLAND 1924 TO 1928 (a)

Offense	Total Number of Offenses Known to the Police					Number of Offenses Cleared (b)				
	1924	1925	1926	1927	1928	1924	1925	1926	1927	1928
Total (c)..........	11,088	10,203	9,098	9,510	9,276	3,651	3,533	3,500	3,640	3,673
Homicide..........	160	190	174	199	223	151	180	169	185	210
Robbery............	388	339	296	329	337	212	203	167	164	190
Burglary............	2,455	2,277	1,886	1,912	2,246	625	639	577	644	710
Larceny (c).........	7,135	6,405	5,700	6,147	5,466	2,070	1,938	1,982	2,053	1,839
Fraud..............	687	729	795	695	763	383	343	480	393	505
Embezzlement.......	94	97	113	103	111	79	83	102	90	100
Other (d)...........	169	100	134	125	130	131	147	113	111	119
Automobile Theft (e)..	1,703	2,206	2,447	2,949	2,690	1,647	2,141	2,356	2,883	2,010

(a) Data from annual reports of the police commissioner for the city of Baltimore.
(b) Figures represent clearances by arrest, except in the case of automobile theft. See note (e).
(c) Exclusive of automobile theft.
(d) Includes assault to kill, rape, and forgery.
(e) Figures given for automobile theft represent total number of automobiles stolen in the city
during the year, and the number both stolen and recovered during the year.

The Annual Police Report

By L. S. TIMMERMAN

National Institute of Public Administration, New York City

TO most police administrators, preparing and publishing the annual report has been a burdensome duty required by law. In the past, and to a large extent at the present time, these officials have been content to follow traditional lines, modeling their reports after those of their predecessors and paying no particular attention to the quality or the usefulness of the product.

As a direct and unfortunate result of this apathy, the annual report of police departments has fallen into disrepute. It has become an edition of little or no importance to be filed away in the archives of public offices, to be read by some citizens only in case of direct personal interest and by most citizens not at all.

Official disregard for the annual police report has grown to such an extent that approximately fifty per cent of the cities of over thirty thousand inhabitants do not now print a report for distribution. The reports of such departments find their way, in abbreviated form only, into the municipal report of the city in question and consequently reach the eyes of an extremely limited number of people. Some other police departments fail to report promptly so that when their report is published, it is of historical value only.

GOOD REPORTS LACKING

Any examination of existing annual police reports will suffice to prove their inadequacy and lack of real value. They range all the way from an elaborate inventory of personnel and equipment to a cumbersome and detailed cost statement of departmental activity. Usually they are quite uninforming, or present in hesitating fashion a story that should be of vital interest and importance to all citizens of the community and to police departments throughout the country. But resigned as the annual report is to official habit, little or no thought has been given to what use it may serve as an informative document or how it affects the general scheme of police administration. Existing reports run to extremes. They are either so long that they are filled with a jumbled mass of irrelevant matter which serves only to confuse the reader, or so brief that the content is of no real value. Some employ an alphabetical classification of offenses so inclusive that it is hard to condense, while others abbreviate it to such an extent that it is stripped of meaning. Nearly all, with a few notable exceptions, use poorly constructed tables with confusing tabular headings, changed enough from year to year to destroy the possibility of comparison between different periods or with other cities. So far as can be determined from the review of many such reports, no standard method of scoring offenses has ever been attempted. As for physical make-up, the reports have been all sizes and shapes; some printed, others typed or mimeographed and none—with rare exceptions—entirely satisfactory.

Behind the annual police reports lie a great mass of records which serve as the official memory of the department.

96

If the chief or some other administrative officer is to meet with success in the conduct of the affairs of his department, the prevention and the detection of crime and the protection of life and property, he must be fortified with accurate daily reports. He must know how much and what kind of crime there is, the location and the time of occurrence and the success of the department in combatting it. These periodic reports can only be secured from a well-developed system of records devised to serve as the department's memory and to be a live library of facts for ready reference.

The daily report serves to reveal unusual and abnormal conditions or to give evidence to the contrary. The monthly report is a summarization of the work of the department over a longer period of time and the annual report, presented in uniform fashion, serves as the grand accounting to the public for comparative purposes. Intelligent police officers find the annual report of primary importance in drawing a comparison between the effectiveness of their own department and that of some other. The interpretation of the statistics is all important but can only be accomplished well when all departments report in the same manner.

ESSENTIAL FEATURES

Having such a uniformly comparable system of records, it should be a simple matter at the end of the year to compile the data required for the annual report in such a manner that it will be of value to all concerned. Not all of the work of the department should be included in the year's report because such a procedure would merely confuse the reader by obscuring important matters with petty details. The report should be brief and to the point and combine such characteristics as the following: (1) promptness; (2) completeness (as to

essentials); (3) accuracy; (4) classification of materials; (5) uniform classification of offenses; (6) intelligent summarization; and, (7) comparability.

(1) *Promptness.*—Reports that are delayed will never receive the attention that prompt reports do. The annual police report should be published and distributed as soon after the close of the period covered as practical considerations will permit. (It should preferably cover the calendar year.) The prompt report is an indication of the alertness of the department's head and has a direct bearing on the impression the public will receive concerning the alertness of the department itself. It has the power of engaging the attention of the general public and of other police administrators, while the six-month old report will be reviewed only by a select few and the year old report will usually be filed away without so much as being opened.

(2) *Completeness.*—As has been previously pointed out, the annual report should not be cluttered with every detail of departmental activity. But, such matters as are deemed of essential value should be set forth in all necessary completeness.

(3) *Accuracy.*—If such reports are to be of any value and if they are to form a basis for conclusions concerning offenses, offenders and the work of law enforcement agencies, particularly the police department, then they must be accurate. In the past, attempts to combat crime have been crippled by the lack of dependable information concerning it. Integrity in reporting by the members of the department itself is essential and will, in a large measure, determine the accuracy and, in turn, the real worth of the annual report.

(4) *Classification of Materials.*—The facts contained in the annual report should be separated into such groups as will assure clarity. If department

records are kept in an orderly, well-defined manner, statistical reports are easily obtainable and will be neither confusing nor ambiguous to the reader.

(5) *Uniform Classification of Offenses.*—Differences in the statutory definitions of crime have made comparisons between jurisdictions extremely difficult. While it is necessary for a given jurisdiction to list the offenses according to the definitions of the statutes governing it, these offenses can be grouped in such a manner as not to destroy comparability. This can be accomplished by the use of a uniform classification of offenses.

(6) *Summarization.*—Tabular presentation of materials and data which lend themselves to such treatment should be summarized in a manner making comparisons possible over a period of years.

(7) *Comparability.*—Much has already been said about comparability. One additional item is important. The general form of the annual police report should remain the same from year to year. Some definite outline with specific table numbers and arrangement should be employed. This practice will assure the permanence of the value of the report and, for the student of public affairs, preserve its importance for many years.

COMMITTEE ON UNIFORM CRIME RECORDS

The International Association of Chiefs of Police, realizing the necessity for accurate records of crime and recognizing the present lack of uniformity in the compilation of criminal statistics, appointed a Committee on Uniform Crime Records at the 1927 convention. This committee of police officials was drawn from all parts of the country and was authorized to study and report on the question. As stated by the chairman, Commissioner William P. Rutledge of Detroit, "We are in the absurd position of endeavoring to diagnose and cure a social disease with little knowledge of its causes, its nature and its prevalence."

The major program of the Committee on Uniform Crime Records dealt with the preparation of a manual entitled "Uniform Crime Reporting." This document describes the manner in which returns concerning crime and criminals are to be made to a national bureau and suggests forms and procedure for current crime accounting by police departments.

There was, however, a natural by-product of the work of the committee. In December, 1928, it published and distributed to two thousand police departments throughout the United States and Canada a tentative draft of "A Guide for Preparing Annual Police Reports." This guide represented the first real attempt to standardize the information essential for the annual police report. After editing and revision, it was presented to the 1929 convention of the association for adoption.

The guide pretends only to point out the essential facts that should be contained in every annual report of a police department and the method of presenting them. It devotes part of its contents to other subjects which, if also included, would make a well-rounded statement of departmental activity but the tabulation of which cannot be expected of all police departments at the present time. The guide received the unanimous approval of the convention and even at this early date several departments have followed it meticulously, notably those of Detroit and of Buffalo. Initiated as it was by police authorities and conducted under police auspices, there should be no logical reason in the future why departments should continue in their present igno-

rance of actual conditions. A method
has been suggested whereby the widespread feeling of uncertainty, expressed
in the daily and the periodical press concerning the effectiveness of the police,
can be combatted. It is up to the individual department to give the public
authentic and comparable records of
the extent and incidence of crime in
the community and make it possible
to demonstrate with integrity what
changes, if any, should be adopted
for the improvement of the administration of criminal justice.

In preparing the annual police report
it is well to bear in mind for whom the
report is written. Two classes of people are usually interested: (1) the
general public, and (2) other police administrators. Both of these classes are
essentially interested in the same type
of information, viz., the amount and the
kind of crime in the community and the
success of the department in combatting it, the type of offenders with certain
social facts about them and the cost to
the city for police protection. These
are the essentials which may be elaborated upon considerably in presenting
a complete story of the department's
yearly activity.

CONTENTS AND MAKE-UP OF GOOD REPORT

Every annual police report should
contain an introductory statement.
Rather than merely a letter of transmit-
tal from the executive head of the department to the Mayor or the Common
Council, it should be a concise summary of the year's accomplishments
showing, briefly, the outstanding de-
velopments, progress and changes in
the police department during the year;
an interpretation of the facts contained
in tables, graphs and charts, together with significant generalizations
drawn from the figures to safeguard the
public from erroneous conclusions; and

recommendations concerning the needs
of the department and a proposed
program for the coming year.

Facts concerning the personnel of the
department are intended to inform the
public as to the authorized and the actual strength of the force, the amount of
remuneration received by the various
ranks and grades of officers and civilian
employees, gains from the addition of
new men, and losses through death,
pension, dismissal, resignation, and so
forth, and, finally, the distribution of
the force throughout the city under the
several commands. The distribution
should show not only assignments to
the various precincts or districts but
also the number attached to the several
bureaus, sections or divisions, such as
headquarters, traffic, detective, records, and so forth.

In addition to the above, the chief
surgeon's report complements and
rounds out the matter of department
personnel. Depletions of the force
through illness and injury in line of
duty run to a much higher figure than
is generally supposed and this report
should show in accurate detail the
number so afflicted and the total
amount of time lost by them. Because of its direct bearing on the patrol
strength of the police force, the above
is extremely important. There are
other matters, such as the number of
professional calls made, the number of
applicants examined, the number of
applicants rejected, the number of civilians cared for, and the like, which
might well be included. Any such additional information may be left entirely to the discretion of the police
surgeon.

Next, and unquestionably the most
important feature of the annual report
from the standpoint of the student of
crime conditions, are facts concerning
"offenses known to the police." Offenses known to have been committed

serve as the one logical basis for determining the amount and the incidence of crime in a community. This should not be confused with the accepted meaning of the word "complaint" so widely used in police circles. Ordinarily, "complaint" is taken to mean a complaint from a citizen while "offenses known to the police" should

and "otherwise," and to divide burglary in such a manner as to show the different kinds of property attacked.

A suggested table with pertinent information concerning offenses known to the police, designed to show the success of the department in dealing with these more important crimes of the classification, appears herewith.

Nature of Offense	Offenses Known to the Police (Current Year)	Un-founded	Actual Number of Offenses Known to the Police	Cleared by Arrest	Not Cleared	Offenses Reported Not Cleared Other Years; Cleared by Arrest
(1)	(2)	(3)	(4)	(5)	(6)	(7)
1. Murder..............						
2. Manslaughter						
(a) By auto........						
(b) Otherwise......						
3. Aggravated assault....						
4. Rape................						
5. Robbery............						
6. Burglary—Breaking and Entering						
7. Larceny—Theft (except auto-theft)........						
8. Auto-theft..........						
Totals............						

include all crimes brought to the attention of the department from whatever source, such as citizens' complaints, reports by police officers, "on-view" arrests and otherwise.

Because it is necessary to record data concerning offenses known to the police, the classification of offenses divides itself naturally into two parts. The first part includes only such serious offenses as are generally reported to the police, such as murder, manslaughter, aggravated assault, rape, robbery, burglary, larceny, and auto-theft. Further sub-divisions may be made when advisable; for instance, it is well to divide manslaughter into "by auto"

Here we have in column 1 the offenses about which the information is to be recorded. Column 2 records all offenses reported to the police from whatever source during the current year. By substracting the number of offenses which investigation proved to be unfounded (column 3) from those known to the police, the actual number of offenses known to have been committed can be recorded in column 4. The number of offenses cleared by arrest should appear in column 5. This does not mean the number of arrests made but the number of cases cleared by such arrests. As an example, the arrest of one hold-up man who has been victimizing a community for a considerable length of time might clear a dozen or more cases upon his confession. Likewise, the arrest of four auto bandits who have held up but one man would constitute four arrests but only one clearance by arrest. If exceptional clearances, such as suicide, arrest in other jurisdictions, death-bed confession, and the like, appear in column 5, a footnote to that effect may be inserted showing the actual number of such clearances. In column 6 are entered the number of offenses not cleared in any manner. The last column is designed to care for cases that have been reported not cleared in previous years but which have been cleared by arrest during the current year.

The second part of the classification of offenses is used, in conjunction with the first part, in recording facts about persons charged. It contains all offenses not listed in Part I and while some of these offenses are serious in nature and carry heavy penalties, they are not universally reported to the police and hence cannot be used as an index of crime.

The complete classification should be used in a table presenting facts about persons charged and taken into custody. The number of persons apprehended by any means and dismissed by the police should be recorded there, as well as the number of these apprehensions resulting in prosecution and the number of convictions either of the offense charged or of a lesser offense. A lesser offense is accepted to mean one which carries a less severe penalty. Violations of traffic and motor vehicle laws can be set forth in an additional table dealing solely with this subject and showing particularly the large number of violators whose charges are dismissed by the police without action, a growing practice which should be discouraged. Tables showing motor vehicle accidents may be included and should preferably follow the recommendations of the National Safety Council.

Social facts concerning persons taken into custody, dealing with such familiar subjects as nativity, color, age, and sex, can be shown for all offenses for which they have value, in tables designed for that purpose.

Two tables should suffice to show all necessary facts about lost, stolen and recovered property. Because of the increasing number of auto-thefts from year to year, these should be the subject of a separate table. Another table should include all types of property and deal with *values* rather than *numbers*. The value of property reported recovered should always coincide with the original estimate of the property when reported stolen, even though that estimate proves to be inaccurate.

Many miscellaneous services rendered by the police department and consuming much of its time, which are not directly concerned with the prevention and the detection of crime, should be separately treated and tabulated. In such a table can be entered items like aided cases, lodgers cared for, missing persons found, lamp outages, licenses issued and revoked, and so forth. This list does not have to be held to any bounds but can be expanded to include all similar services rendered by the department during the year.

Police departments, generally, function as a part of the city government. Because the people whose duty it is to pay the bills are interested in how their money is spent, it devolves upon all departments to include in the annual report such financial information as will enable the citizen and the student of public affairs to ascertain the facts concerning these matters of public trust. Together with the financial statement there should be a table showing, in as much detail as possible, the distribution and the cost of all plant and equipment.

The report of the work of the Bureau of Identification deserves place among the essentials in the annual police report. It should indicate not only the activity of the bureau in the city in question, but also to what extent it has been coöperating with the Bureau of Investigation of the United States Department of Justice, the State Bureau of Identification, in states where there is one, and other police departments.

ADDITIONAL FACTS

The above may be considered essential material for the annual police report. No matter how much else is recorded, if facts concerning the above are included in every police report, comparability of salient information will be assured.

There are, however, additional facts for the annual report which help to round out and expand the story of police service. While these additional facts are important and should be included whenever possible, not all departments are at the present time able to report on them. Hence it remains for the individual department to select and record such of these facts as will make a well-balanced and business-like account of the year's work.

All departments should be able to report on the daily average strength of the patrol force. Contrary to general belief, depletions in the patrol force of a city, due to special and permanent assignments and details, sickness, leave of absence, days off, furlough, and the like, run very high. It is a comparatively simple task for departments to determine from their daily attendance record and record of details and assignments how many of the existing patrol force are available for patrol duty. A tabular summary of these facts for the year is of inestimable value.

The distribution of certain major offenses by month and hour of day has great administrative value and is of general interest to the public at large.

Comparative rates per one hundred thousand population for the offenses of Part I of the classification will serve to correct the crude figures of the actual number of offenses known to the police. A city may labor under the impression that crime is rising to unprecedented levels within its boundaries although, when figured by rates, it may be proven that it is actually on the decrease. In order to figure rates properly, the annual population estimates for the city should be procured from an unquestionably reliable source.

There are innumerable other subjects which might well be treated in the annual police report in order to make a complete picture of departmental activity. The choice of these subjects will be left to the discretion of the departments themselves. Such information as is uniformly desirable has been outlined above. It is believed that the publication and the general distribution of a report containing these essentials will merit the approval and appreciation of the public and the municipal officials and be an important contributory factor in the general improvement of police service.

There has been, in the past, a regretful reluctance on the part of police officials to show the actual number of crimes committed. This attitude was an outgrowth of the public's willingness to charge the crime rate *against the police* rather than *against the community*. But this same public has never been known to blame the health department for the visitation of an epidemic of influenza. Crime, like epidemics of disease, is a social misfortune and if police departments are to meet with success in combatting it, they must receive the fullest coöperation from the public and the press. The sooner all facts concerning offenses and offenders are conscientiously collected and published, the sooner departments will receive that helpful coöperation required by them and the less apt the public will be to use statistics concerning the prevalence of crime as a measure of the efficiency of the police.

The Policewoman

By Eleonore L. Hutzel

Deputy Commissioner of Police, Detroit, Michigan

THE interest which eventually resulted in the appointment of women police officers was first expressed by certain groups of women who felt the need for protective work with girls in their communities. These women realized that changing conditions were bringing a large group of women and girls to the attention of the police, and that these women and girls presented problems which could perhaps be handled better by women officers than by men officers.

The continued efforts of these women's organizations are largely responsible for the rapid increase in the number of cities employing women officers. Police officials have questioned the wisdom of such a change in their organizations and there is still no general agreement among them in favor of the idea. In those cities where competent women officers are doing satisfactory work, the officials consider them as necessary members of the police force and would not wish to do without them. In other cities where the women have not been wisely chosen, they have failed at tasks which they were unfitted to perform. This has caused the officials in those cities to question the value of any women officers as a factor in police work.

Those who have studied the situation feel that there is need for women officers in every police department. It is agreed that while most of the problems coming to the attention of the police can be handled best by men officers, there are some cases where this is not true. Those problems which have to do with women and children can, without question, be better taken care of by women officers.

In order that the women officers may do their work well and make their contribution to an improved police service, it is important that they should be very carefully selected. It is necessary that they be qualified by personality, training and experience to carry out the very specialized work which will be required of them in the police department. It is equally important that these women have the sympathetic coöperation of the police officials in all their efforts.

GROWTH OF MOVEMENT IN THE UNITED STATES

In general, two groups of women have been employed in police departments in the United States. The one group consists of civilian employees designated as matrons who are employed to supervise and attend women held in custody. The other group consists of those sworn in as police officers, assigned to regular police duties.[1] Theoretically, the functions of these two groups are very distinct and in the larger cities, where the work is well organized, the division of duties is clear. In smaller cities there is much less distinction and consequent overlapping. One finds many examples to indicate that women sworn in as

[1] New York City presents an exception to this terminology—women elsewhere designated as matrons are there called "policewomen," while women doing police work are designated as "patrolwomen."

104

officers are occupied with administering
to the physical well-being of women
prisoners, and other examples of women
employed as matrons functioning as
police officers. This situation makes it
difficult to obtain accurate information
in regard to the number of cities employing women officers and in regard
to the number of women officers employed.

Matrons were first appointed in the
United States in 1845 in New York
City. Since then the plan of appointing matrons to be responsible for
women who are held in custody by
public departments has become a part
of established procedure. The first
appointment of a woman officer functioning at regular police duties was in
1905 in Portland, Oregon. The appointment of women officers, as we
have already stated, is not so generally
accepted. Information in regard to
the progress which has been made in
the appointment of women officers is
offered from facts obtained through
three questionnaires. The first questionnaire on this subject, which is a
matter of record, was sent out in 1919
and in 1920 by Lieutenant Mina C.
Van Winkle, Director of the Woman's
Bureau, Washington, District of Columbia. A later one, giving partially
comparable information, was sent out
by the Bureau of Social Hygiene of
New York City in 1924. This particular questionnaire was sent out to obtain information for the book "Women
Police" under preparation by the
Bureau at that time. The third was
sent out in March of 1929 by Commissioner William P. Rutledge of the Detroit Police Department.[2]

One hundred and forty-six cities replied to Lieutenant Van Winkle's questionnaire.

56 cities reported that they em-
      ployed 175 women in their po-
      lice departments;
26 states are represented by these
      56 cities.

Two hundred and sixty-eight cities
replied to the Bureau of Social Hygiene
questionnaire.

210 employ women in the follow-
      ing capacities:
   71 employ both matrons and
         women police;
   65 employ matrons only;
   52 employ women police only;
   22 employ one person as both
         matron and policewoman;
   58 employ no women in their police
         departments.

Of the one hundred largest cities in
the United States, ninety-two employ
women in their police departments:

   56 employ both matrons and
         women police;
   24 employ matrons only;
   10 employ women police only;
    2 employ one person as matron
         and policewoman.

Two hundred and two cities replied
to Commissioner Rutledge's questionnaire.[3]

164 employ women in the following
      capacities:
   77 employ women police only;
   48 employ both matrons and
         women police;
   39 employ matrons only;
   38 employ no women in their police
         departments.

These cities employ four hundred
and sixty-five women officers and two
hundred and ninety-four matrons.

Eighty-nine cities replied to the question regarding date of appointment:
    4 appointed women officers before
         1910;

---

[2] Information from the first two questionnaires
abridged from Chapter VIII of "Women Police"
by Cloe Owings.

[3] Information from this questionnaire is
offered, although the replies were in many cases
incomplete. A further effort is being made at
this time to complete the facts.

37 appointed women officers between 1910 and 1920;

48 appointed women officers after
1920.

The best information available indicates that we have today about two
hundred cities in the United States
employing women officers. The work
which is being done by these women
officers naturally varies greatly in different cities. The reason for this is
clear when we realize that out of forty
cities replying to Commissioner Rutledge's questionnaire as employing
just one officer:

7 cities gave population as under
25,000;

14 cities gave population from
25,000 to 50,000;

8 cities gave population from
50,000 to 100,000;

11 cities gave population from 100,-
000 to 500,000.

THE POLICEWOMAN'S TASKS

Since the earliest appointments, it
has been the practice for women officers
to work almost entirely on complaints
made to the police department having
to do with women and children. In
some cities there are enough women
officers to take care of all of such complaints. In other cities, because of
lack of women officers, many of these
complaints must be taken care of by
men. In certain cities, in addition to
the work on complaints which come to
the department, the women officers
are occupied with investigating community conditions that make for delinquency, supervising commercial recreation open to women and children and
seeking to make contact with girls who
may need protection. This work is
designated as protective patrol and in
cities where it is being done it is considered a very important part of the
work of the women officers.

We have several times referred to the
complaints received concerning women
and children and will therefore go on to
give some details of the different problems represented by these complaints.
First, there are complaints on lost children, children who are problems because of bad family situations, dependent and neglected children and
little girls who by truancy from home
or school, petty larceny or wayward-
ness, come to the attention of the police. There are also complaints made
about adolescent girls, leaders of gangs,
girls who take what does not belong to
them and those who are immoral; complaints made about older girls who present the same problems intensified by
longer experience, less parental influence and greater economic independence. Other complaints have to do
with adults. These present problems
of domestic difficulty, dependency and
immorality, complicated because these
women are often the mothers of little
children.

Complaints are also received in regard to missing persons of any age, distinguished from runaways by the fact
that there is no evidence of premedita-
tion. The runaways are either children, young girls or women. The
children run away because of maladjustment in the home, lack of sympathy and understanding, poverty,
very strict or abusive parents, or school
problems. The young girl runs away
for the same reasons that children run
away but in addition there may be in-
fatuation for some man or the desire
for adventure. Women run away because of difficulties with their husbands,
interest in another man or, sometimes,
just to get away from the overwhelming problems caused by many children
and little money.

There are also complaints in regard
to community conditions—suspected
blind-pigs, suspected disorderly houses,
unlicensed places of amusement, gang

dezvous, or complaints of unlawful ctices in certain apartment houses hotels. Another group of comints has to do with cases in which es have been committed against is or little children. Most often nese crimes have been committed by strangers but sometimes they are committed by a member of the household which complicates the problem. Still other complaints are of crimes committed by women and girls. Many of these cases are store larcenies. The individuals involved in these cases range from the young girls or even children who are found stealing trinkets in the five- and ten-cent stores to the cases of confirmed shoplifters and pickpockets. Other cases involving women are those concerned with the violation of prohibition and drug laws.

Consideration of the facts underlying these various complaints brings one into agreement with those individuals who, after studying the situation, are of the opinion that an adequate number of women officers should be provided in each police department to handle these complaints.

PROTECTIVE PATROL WORK

We have said that in certain cities women officers, in addition to the work which they do on complaints which come to the police department, are engaged in what is known as protective patrol.[4]

[4] In Detroit, Michigan, sixteen of the forty-two women officers are engaged in this work, four officers working during the day and twelve at night. In 1928, these officers interested themselves in and made investigations of 1553 suspicious places. They made 1079 supervision visits to dance halls; contact was made with 472 children and 1642 girls who presented serious problems. Four hundred and seventeen men found with these girls were taken into custody. No record was made of the large number of individuals who were questioned or advised without any specific action being taken.

The patrol work of women officers had its origin in the war-time work of the Commission on Training Camp Activities of the Interdepartmental Social Hygiene Board. The representatives of this organization, working in the camp towns, demonstrated very clearly that real protection could be afforded boys and girls by providing decent recreation and by eliminating vicious individuals and undesirable places. They also proved the value of making early contact with girls who were in need of counsel and assistance by going out into the streets and public places to look for them.

As a basis for estimating the field of service, we may consider that the woman patrol officer will concern herself with any situation arising in a place open to the public which might be considered as potentially harmful to women and children. She will give attention to downtown streets, depots, docks, parks, public restrooms, burlesque theaters, moving picture houses, amusement parks, tourists camps, employment agencies for unskilled and semi-skilled workers, questionable hotels, rooming houses, dance halls, cabarets, barbecues, suspected beer-flats, suspected blind-pigs and suspected disorderly houses. She will look for truants from home and school, unemployed girls, men looking for pick-ups, girls soliciting for prostitution, drug peddlers, procurers, other underworld characters, obscene posters and salacious literature. The officers are also looking for intoxicated girls, children engaged in street trades, and disorderly conduct in parked cars. Generally speaking, these are the duties as outlined for the woman officer on patrol work. Specifically, however, she studies the district in which she is working and develops a plan of work which meets the need of that particular district.

Recently there has been some experimentation in assigning women officers to work which has to do with women but which is not protective in its nature. I refer to the assigning of women officers to work in the detective bureau, the narcotic squad, the homicide squad and other crime detection divisions. These efforts are still very experimental. There is little doubt that in the future women officers will be placed at work in many squads of the crime detection divisions of the police department, but at present the few efforts that have been made do not justify any general conclusions as to their usefulness or as to the peculiar qualifications required for success in such work.

POLICEWOMEN AND POLICE MATRONS

A discussion of the duties of women officers is not complete without mention of their work, in some cities, with women held in custody by the police and of their relation to police matrons. We have previously mentioned the difficulty in obtaining information which differentiates between the policewomen and the police matrons, and called attention to the fact that especially in the smaller cities there is overlapping of duties. There is an ever increasing feeling in favor of the centralization of women held in custody by the police in so far as the local conditions permit. Where there are well organized woman's bureaus, the plan of making the administration of the detention quarters for women an activity of the woman's bureau has been successfully worked out over a period of years. In these cities the matrons are made responsible to a woman officer who is in charge of the detention quarters. The general opinion is that matrons are not fitted by training or experience to do the work or to take the responsibilities which are

required of policewomen either in the detention quarters or in other police work. They are usually women of good character with limited educational background, often having no experience outside of their own homes before appointment. The work of matrons, in ministering to the well-being of the women held in custody and of accompanying them when it is necessary for a prisoner to leave the detention quarters while held there, is a necessary and important part of the work of the police department. It is, however, quite distinct from the work of the policewoman. Since the matrons in many cities were the first women appointed in the police department there has been a tendency to promote them by appointing them as women officers when such positions have been created, or of combining the duties. It is this situation which has brought about the confusion between policewomen and police matrons, and which has in many cities been responsible for the fact that expected results have not been obtained after the appointment of women officers.

ORGANIZATION OF WORK

There is much variation in the form of organization under which women police operate in different cities. Three general forms of organization have been followed. Under the first form, women officers are placed at work under precinct commanders, heads of detective bureaus, or chief inspectors. The women are assigned to do whatever work is detailed to them by the commanding officer. There are no special records under this form of organization, the reports of the women officers being absorbed into the general records of the police department. In the second form of organization, certain of the women officers are assigned to work in a woman's bureau, while other women officers are assigned to work as in the first plan, that is, under men officers in detective bureaus or precinct stations. The third plan is designated as the "Unit Plan." Under this form of organization the women officers operate in a separate bureau with a commanding officer who is responsible to the chief of police for the work of the officers and for the accomplishment of the bureau.

The appointment of women officers is in most police departments a first step in crime prevention work. The type of service introduced by these officers is therefore not familiar to the men officers. A large percentage of the cases coming to the attention of women officers will present problems which they will themselves adjust.[5] This situation carries with it a great responsibility. The fact that the women officers are the only social workers making contact with such a large number of individuals makes it very important that their disposition be based on correct diagnosis. It is not to be expected that men officers will be able to direct this work which requires not only that the individual be a good police officer but that he be an experienced worker with problem girls. For this reason, it is advocated by those having given close study to the problem, that women executives be appointed as directors of women's bureaus. These women should be given rank in the police department and be made responsible directly to the chief of police.

Where there are enough women officers the work of the bureau has been divided so that different officers are occupied at patrol, at making search for missing girls or at investigation of

[5] The 1928 report of the Woman's Bureau of the Detroit Police Department shows for example 1735 complaints received that have to do with girls under seventeen years—of which 643 were adjusted by the women officers.

crimes. These different activities are supervised by officers who have rank in the department lower than that of the director. In cities where there are not enough officers so that there can be specialization, the women are required to work on any complaints assigned to them.

Even where there are only a few officers the unit form of organization is considered desirable—one officer being given rank in the department and made responsible for the work of the other officers. Where there is only one officer it has still been found advantageous to consider her a special bureau, and, even when she does not have rank in the department, make her directly responsible to the chief of police.

THE WOMAN'S BUREAU

Those who advocate the unit form of organization for women officers argue that it assures that all complaints will be dealt with in a uniform way, that the special record system of the woman's bureau will build up a fund of information in regard to problem girls in the community, that duplication will be avoided and that by pooling information in regard to trouble girls, valuable data are obtained in regard to community problems and needs which point the way to an improved service. As far as is known, the women officers in cities where there are women's bureaus operate, with one exception, from a central office. In this one city[6] a branch office has been established in connection with the offices of the Juvenile Court where complaints which have to do with boys under ten years and with girls under seventeen years are received. In several cities there are indications that, from point of time, it is considered disadvantageous for the officers of the women's bureaus to work out of a central office. Plans

[6] Detroit, Michigan.

are now under way in one city[6] to have certain of the officers of the woman's bureau stationed at precincts. These women would remain a part of the woman's bureau, the supervision of their work would be from the central office through reports which would be filed as part of the records of the woman's bureau. The officers would, however, receive their assignments from and report on cases to the officer in charge of the precinct. All problems of discipline and responsibility for accomplishment would remain with the central office. This plan is similar to that under which detectives in some cities are assigned to precinct work.

STANDARDS OF APPOINTMENT

Students of police problems are everywhere giving consideration to ways and means of improving the personnel of the departments. It is recognized that if police officers are to meet adequately the problems with which they are required to deal, it is necessary that applicants for appointment be very carefully considered and that minimum standards be adopted which will tend to assure the appointment of competent candidates. This is especially true in the case of women officers who have been brought into the police department to do a special service. In 1916, the International Association of Policewomen first advocated certain minimum standards for policewomen. These early educational requirements were further defined and standardized at the Twenty-ninth Annual Convention of the Chiefs of Police in San Francisco in 1922, where they were unanimously adopted as a basis for the appointment of women officers.[7] Unfortunately the

adoption of these minimum standards by the chiefs of police has not resulted in appointments actually being made on this basis. Instead, there is the greatest lack of uniformity in the methods used to select women officers. It is estimated that about half of the cities of the United States have civil service examinations for their police officers. In many cities, women officers take the same examination that is given to men officers. There are certain exceptions to this procedure and in several cities much time and thought have been given to working out suitable examinations for women applicants.[8] Even though the emphasis in civil service examinations is on physical qualifications, general information, principally of a local type, and problems of simple police duty, it may be said that the situation in cities where there is civil service is relatively better than in cities where there are no minimum requirements. Here and there one encounters cities where, without the help of civil service, efforts are being made to standardize minimum requirements and where, in addition to this, individuals considered for appointment are carefully selected with regard to their

---

[7] Standards established by the chiefs of police:
(1) Graduation from a four-year course in a standard high school or the completion of at least fourteen college entrance units of study and not less than two years experience, recent and responsible, in social service or educational work;
(2) Graduation from a recognized school for trained nurses requiring a residence of at least two years; or,
(3) Completion of at least seven college entrance units of study or two years in a standard high school and not less than two years of responsible commercial work involving public contacts and responsibilities, tending to qualify the applicant to perform the duties or possessing the equivalent of a college education through experience such as secretarial work.

[8] Washington, District of Columbia; Cleveland, Ohio; and Minneapolis, Minnesota, have special examinations for women officers which are the best available examples of their kind.

possible adaptability to police work.[9] As a part of the applicant's examination in one of these cities,[10] women officers are required to take a psychiatric examination. This examination includes an extensive inquiry into family and personal history, a neurological examination and a standard psychometric test. The latter gives the intelligence rating—a definite limit is set below which an applicant is not considered—auditory and visual memory, powers of observation, comprehension and judgment and ability to make simple and complex associations. They are also tested for ability to detect absurdities, capacity for reasoning, academic achievement, ability to adjust to new situations and emotional stability.[11] The opinion of the psychia-

[9] Information in regard to educational background and experience of forty-two officers in the Woman's Bureau, Detroit Police Department, shows—
Education:
    Less than High School—4
    Graduation from High School—10
    High School and University Extension Courses or Business College—5
    High School and Nurses Training—6
    Two years in University or Normal School—4
    University Graduate—10
    Graduate of Law School—3
Previous occupation:
    Teaching—2
    Nursing—6
    Social Service—13
    Commercial—16
    No previous occupation—5
[10] Detroit, Michigan.
[11] It is of interest to note that the reports on mental age and intelligence quotient of twenty-seven officers, who have taken the examination and who are still on the staff of the Detroit Police Department, show—
    Mental age:
        12 to 14 years—2;
        14 to 16 " —6;
        16 to 18 " —14;
        Over 18   " —5.
    Intelligence Quotient:
        80–100—8;
        100–110—14;
        Over 110—5.
(Tests Made by the Stanford Abbreviated Scale.)

trist, with the report of the examining physician, is considered by the director of the bureau in recommending appointments.

So far as can be determined, no promotional examinations have been developed for women officers. Few women officers other than directors of bureaus have rank and in those few cases promotion has been made on the recommendation of the director. Several cities are now endeavoring to develop promotional examinations and, as an aid in selection, monthly rating sheets for all officers are being considered.

EXPERIENCE AND TRAINING

We have said that certain minimum requirements were approved by the chiefs of police. In addition to educational requirements there are certain experience qualifications. It is felt that experience in social case work is most desirable for a woman police officer. Teaching and public health nursing are next in order of desirability. Women whose only experience has been in the commercial field may prove very valuable, especially if they show a high mental age and other exceptional personal qualifications, but ordinarily this field of experience is considered as being least desirable. It is the general practice in the United States to require that police officers be residents of the city and of the state in which they are employed. For this reason it is difficult, even with an increasingly large number of trained experienced women officers available, to secure the appointment in a particular locality of women who have had actual experience in police work. This is most unfortunate, because, however well fitted by training and experience in a related field a woman may be, it takes actual experience in a police department to make a good officer. Few police departments have schools in which their officers receive instruction before being sent out to work. Where there are such schools it is considered necessary that women officers attend as well as men officers. In police departments where there are no training schools, instruction of women officers is administered in a haphazard way by superiors or fellow officers, unless there is a woman's bureau in which case instruction for the new officers is provided by the director of the bureau. In addition to instruction in police procedure, interdepartmental relations, and legislation, which should be obtained in class work with men officers if possible, the new woman officer should be taught the principles of interviewing and of investigation, special psychology and professional ethics. She should also be instructed in the local program of protective work with girls and be made familiar with the work of coöperating social agencies. Class instruction should be followed by a period of training on duty during which the new officer will work under the direction of a more experienced member of the staff.

Salaries and Legal Status

Women officers are regular officers in the police department and it is expected that whatever may be required of an officer in the performance of his duty will be rendered by the woman officer on the cases which are assigned to her. In no city are requirements for appointment as a woman officer lower than the requirements for appointment as a man officer, and in many cities the requirements for the women officers are very much higher. This being the case it is the general opinion that the salaries of women officers should be the same as the salaries of men officers and that the woman officer should be entitled to privileges of pension on retirement on

the same basis as men officers. No actual statistics have been obtained, but the best available information indicates that about one half of the cities in the United States employing women officers are paying them the same salaries as those of their men officers and that, in most other cities, they are paid less. A few cities having only one policewoman are known to be paying her a larger salary than is paid the men officers in the department.

The appointment of women officers in many cities is provided for by some legislative measure. This provision is considered necessary because there are records of cities where a well-organized service of policewomen has been entirely wiped out, or at least rendered impotent, by a changing city administration. The measures adopted providing for women officers take the form of city ordinances, city charter amendments or state laws. The form is sometimes very simple, being nothing more than a provision that there be a minimum number of women police officers in the police department. In other cases very detailed measures have been enacted providing for the organization and functioning of the women officers. It is not possible to say at this time which, if any, of the present plans of procedure is most desirable.[12]

Position in Police Department

The appointment of women officers creates many problems in police departments. These problems are due, first, to the fact that it has been difficult to fit women into a well-organized mili-

[12] Of eighty-five cities answering the question of legal status in Mr. Rutledge's questionnaire, thirty-six report provision for women officers made by city ordinance, four by state law and two by city charter; forty-three report no provision. Cleveland, Ohio, is an example of the use of a city ordinance. Washington, District of Columbia, has made no legal provision, but an elaborately worked out bill is pending. ·

tary system developed for and by men, and second, to the fact that the appointment of women officers in a police department has, in almost every case, been a first step in preventive protective work. Thus the difficulty of bringing women into a men's organization has been aggravated by the new type of service which they have introduced. The chief of police as the commanding officer of the police department holds the key to the situation. In cities where the chief has an understanding of the new service and is sympathetic toward it, the other members of the department quickly follow his example. In cities where the chief is not favorably disposed to preventive protective work and is antagonistic toward women officers, the opposite is the case and the efforts which very capable women have made have not succeeded in changing this attitude. In cities where a satisfactory relationship has been established, the men and the women have learned from each other. From an appreciation, on the part of each group, of the contribution which the other group offers has come mutual respect and an improved police service.

RELATIONS WITH SOCIAL SERVICE AGENCIES

Having discussed the position of women officers in the police department, it is essential, in view of the protective nature of their work, to discuss their relationship with other social protective agencies. In their relationship with these organizations the situation again differs greatly in different cities. In those cities where there are well organized women's bureaus, functioning under a woman director, who is an experienced worker with problems of girls, the woman's bureau takes an important place in the community program of protection work. This is also

the case in cities where one or more women who have been appointed as officers are by training and experience qualified to work out plans for coöperative procedure with other agencies. In other cities, partially trained or untrained women appointed as officers have failed to make a place for themselves in the program of work of protective agencies. In these cities there is lack of coöperation and overlapping of services. Where this situation exists there is general dissatisfaction with the work of women officers on the part of other social workers. In those cities where the work of women officers has been most satisfactorily developed they are considered as agents of contact and diagnosis. In their relation to other social agencies working with girls, they serve as the largest single source of cases referred for treatment. At the same time, by their supervision of commercial recreation, their general community patrol work and their prosecution of individuals who commit crimes against girls and women, they make the rehabilitation efforts of the treatment worker easier.[13] In cities where there are well-organized social agencies it is not considered necessary for the women officers to do treatment work. In other cities where there are no such agencies the women officers find it necessary to do the work themselves. In

[13] The Juvenile Court of Wayne County, in a comparative report of one hundred cases of white girls charged with immoral conduct, issued in 1926, shows that in 1920 the majority of the girls had been associating with older men and that fifty-six had prostituted, while in 1925 the majority of the girls had been associating with boys from sixteen to twenty-one years and only six had prostituted. This decrease in prostitution among juveniles is attributed by the Juvenile Court officials to the fact that officers of the Woman's Division of the Detroit Police Department have since 1921 been carefully watching for young girls and that they have been persistent in the prosecution of adults who have committed crimes against them.

order that the woman officer may be free to do the work which we have outlined as being logically the work of a police officer, it is considered desirable that, whenever possible, she avoid making herself responsible for treatment work.

LACK OF DATA FOR EVALUATING WORK

Although much progress has been made in the number of cities employing women officers, it is evident that little has been done to estimate their usefulness, either in the police department or in the general plan of protective work. Little study has been made of the results of the efforts of the women officers in any city. The women themselves are so busy with the problems which come to them each day that they have not had time for research. It is hoped that in the next few years studies will be made from the cases on which women officers are working and that much helpful information will be brought out. It is also expected that police departments, in which the women officers are now accepted as useful members of the force will employ more women each year. The increased number of women in these cities will make it possible to extend the work into other branches of service. Those who are desirous of having every city offer its citizens the service of women officers will watch these studies and these experiments with much interest.

It has been most difficult to cover the various aspects of the work of women police officers in so short an article and the result must seem unsatisfactory to those who are interested in obtaining detailed information in regard to the methods by which the women officers do their work. For the benefit of such persons, the writer wishes to say that, through the courtesy of the Bureau of Social Hygiene, Commissioner William P. Rutledge of the Detroit Police Department is now having prepared a manual on the work of policewomen. This manual will give complete information about the work of women officers and will be available through the Bureau of Social Hygiene some time during the coming winter.

The Police, Crime and Politics

By CHARLES E. MERRIAM

Professor of Political Science, University of Chicago, Chicago, Illinois

THE alliance between police, crime and politics in American and other communities is no new thing in history, but recent events have focused attention on certain aspects of it more sharply than before. The Rothstein case in New York and the St. Valentine's day massacre in Chicago are familiar examples of outcroppings which indicate the presence of intimate combinations between criminals and the organized forces of the government. In some places and at certain times the organization against the government is stronger than the organization of the government itself, and in some ways the underworld is better prepared for protection than is the state for defence of persons and property in society. The evidence of this has been so frequently presented in the most conclusive form in so many cities within the last quarter of a century that there is no need to relate the familiar details, varying in communities, but essentially the same sort of phenomenon.[1] The automobile, the machine gun, the bomb, the bootlegger and racketeering may present new and interesting variations, but after all they do not represent any fundamental change in the basic situation depicted in the report of the Chicago Council Committee on Crime of which I was chairman in 1914. Even

judicial collusion with politics and crime is by no means new, for brazen examples of this distressing situation are found in the Tweed exposé of the early 70's.

What we really find in some of these situations seems to be two competing types of organizations and two competing types of cultures struggling for mastery in the community, and it is evident to any experienced student of social and political conditions that the causes of this are not superficial but fundamental. The control of the case requires not merely salve but specifics, not merely punishment but preventive measures of a thoroughgoing kind. "For this effect defective comes by cause." For this reason man hunts and crusades, necessary as they may be, do not reach the goal sought, and often leave a trail of disappointment in their wake. There are not jails enough to punish everybody involved in these combinations from whose operation we recoil, and the choice of the victims marked for sacrifice may not be happy. This is not to say that integrity, competence and energy on the part of prosecuting officers is not both necessary and desirable, nor that community revolution against gangs of corruptionists is to be disparaged. It is merely intended to indicate that this is not enough.

At the outset, allow me to register a protest against the attitude that makes of vice and crime and graft a thing apart from our own human life, as if they were not an integral cross-section of the life of our community and our society. There would not be bribe-takers, if there were no bribe-givers; there could not be collections from

[1] The fullest and most recent exposition of this type of situation is found in the *Report of The Illinois Association for Criminal Justice* (1929), a mine of material on the most recent practices and tactics.

See also my discussion of the "Big Fix" in Chapter Two, of *Chicago: A More Intimate View of Urban Politics*.

prostitutes if there were not a wide market for prostitution; nor from gambling if there were not many gamblers, great and small; nor from bootlegging if there were not patrons of the industry; nor grafters in government if there were none in business or labor.

It is too simple, and often too hypocritical, to assume that all graft and crime are the acts of wilful and wicked persons entirely set apart from the superior rest of us, and by the same logic that the simple remedy is the rigorous application of the criminal law. Upon this very attitude, unreal as it is, the underworld has thriven. Vivid pictures may be drawn of the breakdown of the law under certain urban conditions, and they may be truthful, but the real picture must be that of a world in reconstruction, under new conditions; and not merely that of the old lines fading in the new surroundings.[2]

THE SPOILS SYSTEM IN GOVERNMENT

It may be useful to examine briefly some of these more fundamental situations, realizing that in the limits of a few pages such consideration must be very sketchy and inadequate. One of the prime difficulties is the general public toleration of the spoils system in government. Party, factional or personal, favoritism and advantage as a basis for appointment, promotion and dismissal are ruinous to the morale and effectiveness of any group of men and devastating in their effects upon officials whose duty it is to administer the community's standards of justice. It is true that in many instances the merit system has been established, and, where applied as well as enacted, the effects have been very beneficial. But in many other cases the merit system has been nominal rather than real, and so many exceptions have been made that its full effects have not been felt. It is well known in the police field that local lords struggle for the control of the captain of their district

[2] Quoted from my *Chicago: A More Intimate View of Urban Politics.* (Courtesy of the Macmillan Company.)

and regard him as their man, and that assignments and promotions are difficult to obtain without strong political influence. It has come to such a pass under these conditions that the honest and effective officer may be penalized while the dishonest and slothful may be rewarded—with the inevitable effect. In gang terminology the "wrong guy" is the honest man and the "right guy" is the dishonest man. The honest man cannot be trusted and the dishonest man is reliable. And this is not Alice in Wonderland but modern policing in many sad cases.

The city does not vote this, one may say. No, but the community is likely, from time to time, to select its mayors and councils frankly on a spoils basis, with the clear understanding that they will play the spoils game as and where they will. And they will not be so shortsighted or forgetful as to omit from their careful calculations the police department, once defined by Goodnow as the greatest get-rich-quick institution in the country. They have too many hungry mouths to feed.

Under these conditions, to ask the individual or the officer to maintain other and higher standards than the community itself has is wholly naïve. Nor can we expect to hold the police in line by the penalties and threats of the law under such conditions. In short, and this perhaps seems elementary, the standards of the police force will not rise higher than their source, and if the city plays with spoils politics in the office of mayor and alderman, it will not escape the disastrous workings of this ancient system in the protection of persons and property. If this seems too simple, so also was the old command to "Go wash in Jordan."

NEED FOR SCIENCE IN POLICE WORK

Related to the police situation is the lack of scientific study of police in the

United States. Until the last ten years this important field was wholly neglected in this country and even now it is only beginning to develop. Men like Commissioner Woods in New York City and Chief Vollmer of Berkeley have made notable steps in this direction, but they are in a small minority. Likewise, the Bureau of Social Hygiene is now making progress in this direction, the National Institute of Public Administration is busy, and men like Bruce Smith, Lawrence Dunham and Harrison are doing valiant service. The studies of Fosdick in this field are epoch making. Only this year a chair of research in police administration has been established at the University of Chicago with Chief Vollmer as its first incumbent. Telford's studies of police tests, in connection with the Bureau of Public Personnel Administration, are also of great importance and point the way to important advances in the recruitment and the promotion of police officials.

In European countries, notably in France and in Germany, very important studies have been made in scientific policing, to say nothing of enormous strides in the science of criminology. The scientific section of the Paris *Institut de Criminologie*, for example, carries on work of the highest type, and we are making a beginning here.

In a changing world, such as that in which we live, the neglect of technical studies of crime is itself almost criminal. New types of crimes in a high-powered scientific and mechanical age require the most careful analysis and the most diligent and assiduous attention on the part of the most competent workers. Even the most ingenious of fiction detective stories have difficulty in keeping their imagination apace with the possibilities of the modern age, and to suppose that a spoils gang will not follow these new situations is absurd. The gang may itself appropriate the results of modern science more rapidly and effectively than the custodian of public order and safety. The race between the safe crackers and the safe owners is only an illustration of what is going on in the whole field of modern police and crime. Professional standards of policing are yet to be developed, and are the indispensable instruments of the new order. With them will come research, invention and adaptability to a shifting set of social conditions in the matrix of which modern crime is developed.

LARGER ASPECTS OF CRIME

A step beyond this brings us to the larger aspects of the crime problem, which after all concerns more persons than police and prosecutors and politicians. The sources of crime are as important as its manifestations. The world of human beings is full of social deviates and deviations, and the question of how to deal with the more extreme forms of deviation or those which at the moment seem to require curbing is not merely a matter of punishment but a problem of prevention. Here we may find the hospital as useful as the jail, the nurse more effective than the warden. Years ago, Butler in his fascinating volume, "Erewhon," depicted a situation in which those who committed crime were regarded as diseased and received the sympathy of their friends and their comforting care, but the diseased were looked upon as criminals and suffered social reprobation. A fanciful sketch this, but not without an element of truth, well worth considering in the days of man hunts.

We have scarcely begun to tap the resources of medicine and psychiatry and social science at this point, and the possibilities in this direction are difficult to overestimate. Likewise, we must deal with housing, with recreation and the use of leisure time, with basic economic situations—all of these are closely related to the solution of the problem of politics and police and crime, for it is out of these maladjustments that the criminal cases spring in large number. The social deviations that become troublesome maladjustments of which the community must take cognizance—these are the fundamental materials with which we are dealing, and to cope with them successfully we must use the analyses and the controls that are appropriate to newly discovered relations.

The attack upon the crime problem, the liquor problem, the prostitution problem must go far deeper down than the surface of repressive police activity into the levels of human nature affected by the new urban environment. Unattractive living conditions, the stress of an intensive mechanical age, the lack of sufficient attention to recreation facilities and the use of leisure time; all these are of prime importance in any study of social maladjustments and of social deviates and deviations. In many ways, the place of the old-time policeman is being taken by the modern technician in various forms of social service, and there is good reason to believe that this process will continue for some time to come. Schools, housing, recreation, medicine, and social science on its preventive side will loom larger and larger as we go along.

PUBLIC OPINION AND LAW OBSERVANCE

A factor of very great importance in the police and crime problem is the public attitude toward the making and the enforcement of law. At present it is difficult to say just what laws the community takes seriously and which it is inclined to regard more lightly.

It is plain that many different types of offenses are jumbled together, and while the law is in each case venerable, it is not in all cases equally venerated. There are offenses which have been condemned from time immemorial, such as murder, assault, and robbery; there are offenses which have been contrary to law for many years, but not contrary to widespread custom, such as gambling and prostitution and drunkenness; there are other offenses freshly created under the stress of new urban conditions, as by speeding ordinances, health regulations, and building laws; there are offenses arising out of the industrial conflict of the time, as anti-trust laws, tax laws, types of labor laws on which struggling classes hold divergent views. These are all Laws, but they are differently regarded by the community or by large groups of it, although in theory all are administered upon exactly the same basis. Practically the result is confusing when the red-handed murderer, the citizen taken in a game of stoss, the automobilist who forgot his tail-light, the merchant guilty of a technical violation of the anti-trust law, are all taken in the wagon or put in the bull-pen, or at least held up to public scorn and put, so to speak, in the stocks at the same time.

In the whole field of municipal relation with the morals of the community, I have been struck with what may be characterized as the unreality or the hollowness of the general attitude. In the field of crime, except as it touches the industrial conflict on one side or the other, the public is in deadly earnest. There is no mistaking the determination to deal with ordinary crimes against persons and property. But in dealing with vice, gambling, Sunday laws, and liquor laws, tax and trust laws, the community clearly sets up a double standard of morality which is puzzling for the administration and the government. In the abstract, every city is against gambling, and would vote strongly against the repeal of existing statutes forbidding it, but in the concrete, the citizens are not deeply interested in strict enforcement of the law against games of chance. In low dives and in splendid clubs, in little stores and in private houses, in churches even, games of chance are constantly going on, and if the law were drastically enforced, an army of inspectors would be necessary, and additional judges in the local courts. No one has ever taken a census of the number of persons gambling on a given day or a given week, but I do not doubt that the figure would be generous.[3]

In the actual policing of a city, this confusion regarding the law is demoralizing in the extreme. District Attorney Jerome of New York referred years ago to the "administrative lie," which obliges the police officer to swear to enforce the law and punishes him if he does. No system can survive this fundamental confusion in public attitude, and it is necessary to develop a much more definite public understanding before rapid progress can be made. It is precisely in this twilight that the so-called Underworld flourishes. Its denizens may be lawbreakers, but they find themselves in excellent company, and do not feel themselves in any sense outlawed by the rest of society. Not all the finest legal mechanism man can invent will save a community that does not know its own mind. Judges, juries, police will not enforce law, if they do not know what the law is, for the basis of government is common understanding of the bases of order and justice.

INDUSTRIAL RELATIONS

A part of the problem of police and crime arises from the fact that the struggle between employer and employees cuts across the whole situation again and again. Both are struggling for the control of and the most favorable use of the law-enforcing agencies of the state, and this applies with especial pertinence to the control of the operating police force. Both tend to forgive or forget anything else that may be done if the police support their side of the industrial controversy. The

[3] Quoted from my *Chicago, op. cit.*

officer who helps to break up the strike or who is friendly to the strikers is likely to be popular with one side, no matter what else he may do. In this sense the police force may become the scape goat of the industrial controversy, and all else in the way of honesty, efficiency or broad social purpose be subordinated to this consideration, which becomes paramount in the opinion of the representatives of labor or of the employers.

Furthermore, there is a well defined tendency for both sides to use violence and to ignore the law in desperate situations. They may even be found to have enlisted on either side professional gunmen and clubbers. It is fortunately true that the more reputable and responsible leaders on both sides attempt to repress this tendency, but it is also true that the irresponsible, greedy and crooked representatives on both sides, and they are not wanting, are willing to ignore these remonstrances and practically become a law unto themselves. These leaders are not outlaws or criminals in the ordinary usage of the term, but men of the highest standing and ability in their respective groups, and in the society as a whole. Social and political control can scarcely be organized without them.

If there were not weak and venal representatives of labor and of employers, and if there were not interlocking arrangements between them, the way toward order and justice would be much smoother and more direct. In the discussion of the police problem, these situations are often neglected or minimized, but in the realistic world of events they cannot be glossed over or their importance wished away. Again and again the best laid plans of reformers in this field are swept aside, because they are built in ignorance or neglect of these foundation considerations without which no enduring structure of order may be securely built.

Business organizations have often been most active in the study of police and crime conditions, but their inquiries have often failed to touch these challenging situations, or to deal with them in a thorough and satisfactory manner. In great industrial communities it is not possible, however, to ignore the basic industrial conditions, and the most earnest effort must be made to seek out the facts and to organize not merely new mechanisms but also those common understandings without which the best political arrangements amount to little.

THE FUTURE OUTLOOK

Is the situation growing better or worse? This question no one can answer definitely because the necessary facts are lacking. Is the public growing less tolerant of the spoils system and less or more insistent on professional standards in policing? Are we digging deeper down into the roots of social maladjustment and excess deviation? Are we tending to clear up the clouds regarding the public attitude toward law and regarding the relation of the industrial conflict toward police and crime?

Questions one and two may be answered in the affirmative. The old system and the old bosses are slowly dying in the country as a whole, faster than most of us realize, spectacular as are the living examples of the *ancien régime* in some of our cities and states. Professional standards of policing are slowly emerging, through the wonderful work of men like Woods and Vollmer, the studies inaugurated by groups like the Bureau of Social Hygiene, the National Institute of Public Administration, and more recently by the estab-

lishment of research work in police administration in universities.

Unfortunately, as much cannot be said regarding the reorganization of the prosecuting machinery, the constitution of the courts, and the reformation of the criminal procedure. The new era in the study of law may affect this situation profoundly, but thus far has not done so.

It may also be said that we are digging deeper into the social bases of the problem through scientific study of crime and its social concomitants, through medicine, social science, studies of leisure time, and analyses of civic education. We have not arrived here, but we are on our way and if present trends continue will make substantial progress in the next generation. It may be said that we have advanced in the direction of a better understanding of the relations of employer and employees through the development of a more coöperative spirit in industry. In a period of great prosperity this has relaxed the tension of harder times, and but for the rise of racketeering, notable progress would be recorded in this direction. But on the whole it may be said, without undue optimism, that the rapport between property and persons has favorably affected the basic crime and police situation in the United States.

But there remains a most serious state of confusion in the public attitude toward the law and in the general understanding as to rigidity of law enforcement. Not even the most optimistic would say that progress has been made at this point during the last ten years. Thousands of laws and ordinances are hastily and carelessly enacted and their enforcement is not taken more seriously than their enactment.

The International Association of Chiefs of Police and Other American Police Organizations

By LENT D. UPSON

Director, Detroit Bureau of Governmental Research; Chairman, Advisory Committee, Committee on Uniform Crime Records, International Association of Chiefs of Police

IN view of the huge number of peace officers in the United States and of the technical character of their work, it might be expected that they would be associated in one or more strong professional organizations to further cooperation among members, to study technical police problems, and to disseminate information to both the police and the public.

However, such is not the case. Not that there is a dearth of police organizations—they number a legion—international, national, state and local, embracing municipal police chiefs, members of specialized branches of the municipal police, state police superintendents, United States marshals and other Federal law enforcement officers, county sheriffs and their deputies, constables, and private police and detectives. Yet, apparently, the variety of police offices and of police activities and the absence of professionalization within the groups combine to prevent the establishment of an all embracing and powerful organization to promote this important public service.

Perhaps the greatest deterrent to effective organization by police officers is insecure tenure in higher offices. There are, of course, some municipalities in which the chief of police is in every sense out of politics and holds his position year after year. However, in many cities the office is the plaything of politics and each change in administration sees the chief of police, and sometimes his principal subordinates, relegated to minor positions and new men elevated in their stead. It is obviously difficult for the head of a department, selected and dismissed through political influences and sure of his position for only a limited period, to interest himself in the building up of a professional spirit among police departments or to contribute actively to the work of a police organization of which he may not long be a part. This periodic rotation in membership, combined with what may be termed a practical in place of a scientific attitude toward police problems, has perhaps done most to prevent existing police organizations from undertaking the aggressive programs that have characterized, for example, such groups as the National Education Association or the National Conference of Social Work.

Little effort has been made to weld the rank and file of police departments into a professional organization. Existing groups are almost entirely limited to chiefs of police and the technical heads of divisions within departments, the more important examples being the International Association of Chiefs of Police, the International Association for Identification, the International Association of Policewomen, and state and local organizations of these same offices. There is, however, the Sheriffs' and Police Officers' Association of America whose membership consists of sheriffs, policemen, wardens, detectives, marshals, and so forth, and the Fraternal Order of Police, whose membership is recruited from the police ranks in larger cities. The chiefs of private police forces frequently take membership in the International Association of Chiefs of Police, while private detectives are found in the World Association of Detectives.

INTERNATIONAL ASSOCIATION OF CHIEFS OF POLICE

The most important police organization, in which is combined the possibilities and, in recent years, the promise of aggressive action in police matters, is the International Association of Chiefs of Police. This group had its inception as far back as 1871, in the National Police Convention called by James McDonough, chief of police of St. Louis. It considered uniform crime records, juvenile delinquency, alcoholism, prostitution, and the effects of the Civil War upon the increase in crime—problems that half a century of discussion have not solved.

This early convention was short lived, and in 1893, the chief of police of Omaha communicated with several police departments pointing out the rather obvious fact that there was no sort of coöperation between municipal departments in the supression of crime and the apprehension of criminals. He suggested that this might be remedied by a voluntary association of police executives, meeting occasionally to discuss police problems and arranging for much desired coöperation between departments.

The World's Fair was then being held in Chicago; the first meeting was called in that city on May 28. Fifty-one chiefs were in attendance, and after the customary addresses of welcome and liberal entertainment they organized the National Chiefs of Police Union. It is interesting to note that at this meeting a visit was paid to the Chicago Bertillon Bureau to examine what was probably the first effort on this continent to establish a scientific method of criminal identification. That the chiefs at that time were think-

ing about the interchange of identification material is indicated by the remark that there was little hope that either the state or the Federal governments would soon consider the possibility of a central clearing house, and that any exchange of information would have to be through voluntary efforts. By 1897, however, the Union was assessing cities from ten to one hundred dollars each, to maintain at Washington a central clearing house of criminal identification.

Annual conventions were held thereafter. At the meeting in New York City, in 1901, the name of the Union was changed to the International Association of Chiefs of Police, and Major Richard Sylvester, then superintendent of police of Washington, District of Columbia, was elected president. He retained this office for fifteen years and is often spoken of as the father of the association, since under his direction and leadership it came through its struggling years and reached its present importance among police organizations. The purposes of the organization are:

To secure a closer official and personal relationship among police officials at home and abroad; to secure unity of action in police matters; to elevate the standards of police institutions by urging the elimination of politics from their conduct; to extend the tenure of office for those employed in the service; the maintenance of honorable men engaged in the transaction of police business; the general adoption of pension and relief laws; the adoption of humane efforts in the enforcement of law; the provision of temporary relief for its worthy members and their families in certain emergencies; the advancement along all lines pertaining to the prevention and the detection of crime and the identification and the treatment of prisoners.

Membership in the association is of three classes: active membership, consisting of superintendents and chiefs of police of municipal corporations in the United States and Canada, and chiefs of detectives, upon recommendation of the chief of police; honorary membership, consisting of civilian police commissioners and directors of public safety and other officials having police departments in their charge; active membership, consisting of men who may have been retired from service or have failed of reappointment or election to their position; and, associate membership, consisting of executives of municipalities, together with a few individuals who are especially interested in police matters. Apparently, the requirements of membership are not strictly enforced since the roster contains the names of a number of ex-chiefs of police, as well as chiefs of private police departments, notably those of railroads.

Membership in the organization involves the payment of ten dollars a year, which does not furnish a budget sufficiently large to undertake any particularly constructive work in the field of police research, or to enable the association to publish anything but an annual year book and occasional reports. The programs of the association have had to do largely with specific police problems, and occasional committees have been appointed to carry on lines of inquiries in definite fields.

The most outstanding example of accomplishment by the association has been the establishment of the Bureau of Criminal Identification in the Department of Justice at Washington. Police authorities throughout the country are presumed to provide this central clearing house with fingerprints and other criteria of identification of all persons suspected of serious offenses who may be identified by them. The bureau now has on file more than 1,400,000 fingerprints and receives more than 200,000 separate prints each year. The principal difficulty arises from its coöperative character. The bureau can only furnish data upon request and can only possess in its archives such information as it receives voluntarily from its correspondents. However, the State of New York requires enforcement officers to file the fingerprints of criminals coming into their jurisdiction with the bureau at Washington, and it is hoped that other states will follow this precedent. The bureau receives a substantial appropriation each year from Congress, but it has never been formally authorized by legislative enactment, an omission which it is hoped will be remedied shortly.

Approximately two years ago, the Committee on Uniform Crime Records of the association received an adequate appropriation from one of the Foundations to carry out the work of preparing a system of uniform crime records, uniform definitions of offenses known to the police, and suggestions regarding the contents of a uniform report. The recommendations of this committee have been adopted by the national association and the state associations of Ohio, Michigan, California and New Jersey, and it is hoped that they will be carried out by individual members. Steps are also being taken to secure the reporting of the resulting data to the Department of Justice, in order that some accurate information may be had as to the amount of crime existing in the United States.

Other important activities include the exchange of standardized information concerning automobile thefts, the development of minor violation bureaus, the furtherance of the use of radio-equipped scout cars, and so forth.

STATE AND LOCAL ORGANIZATIONS OF CHIEFS

There are numerous state and local organizations of chiefs of police which have ostensibly the same purpose as the International Association, although they are less formally organized. The local groups are concerned primarily with the highly essential coöperation among chiefs operating in any large urban area, in which uniformity in traffic regulations, use of traffic lights, use of radio, protection of banks and payrolls, and so forth, must come through voluntary effort. Informal and frequent meetings of chiefs are exceedingly helpful to secure these ends.

The larger state associations are concerned with proposed state legislation and similar matters. These groups meet annually rather than monthly or quarterly, and ordinarily they have a considerable list of proposals to place before their law makers. Usually, coöperative relationships with the state police must be arranged, and in New York, at the instance of the Conference of Mayors, district schools for the training of police officers have been established. This successful experiment offers a field of fruitful opportunity to other state associations. State organizations are known to exist in Arkansas, Alabama, Colorado, Kansas, Louisiana, New Jersey, Missouri, Minnesota, Mississippi, Nebraska, New York, Oklahoma, Pennsylvania, Tennessee, Texas and Wyoming; they probably exist in other states. Printed proceedings of their conventions are seldom issued.

The commanding officers of state police also have an informal organization, naturally of limited membership.

INTERNATIONAL POLICE CONFERENCE

The International Police Conference has practically the same purposes and membership requirements as the International Association of Chiefs of Police. It was organized, in 1920, by Mr. Richard E. Enright, then com-

missioner of police of New York City, who continues as its president and mentor, although he is no longer in public police work. Conferences were held in New York in 1921, 1922, 1923 and 1925, and one is planned in Paris, in 1929. At the last meeting, forty-four nations were represented by their highest police executives. The numerous officers of the organization include a distinguished group of police officials from the entire world. The conference is evidently liberally financed from private sources and its occasional meetings are imposing spectacles, no doubt stimulating international good will and coöperation. The organization does not undertake the continuous activities of the International Association of Chiefs of Police.

INTERNATIONAL ASSOCIATION FOR IDENTIFICATION

The use of fingerprints as a means of identification has naturally created a technical staff in practically every large police department, concerned particularly with the technique of fingerprinting and its development as an exact science. These officers are technicians of a high order, dealing with a limited phase of police activity. Policing may or may not be a science, but fingerprinting is. It was only natural that these technicians should very early create an association for the discussion of the problems and the development of fingerprint identification. The organization was established in 1914, for the purpose of inducing coöperation between the several states, and between the United States and foreign countries; to make the profession of fingerprint identification more distinctive; to "employ the collective wisdom of the profession to advance the scientific technique of identification by research and the dissemination of knowledge . . . and to induce all bureaus of identification and investigation to adopt modern methods."

Active membership in the Association is limited to police executives and others actually engaged in the business of personal identification and investigation.

The papers presented at the annual convention are printed in the Proceedings and are of a decidedly technical character, dealing not only with fingerprinting but also with other scientific methods of criminal detection.

INTERNATIONAL ASSOCIATION OF POLICEWOMEN

Policewomen, both in executive positions and in the ranks, are often recruited from the ranks of social workers. It was, therefore, only natural that the National Conference of Social Work should have given the impetus to the initial organization of this group of peace officers. In 1915, the program of the National Conference of Social Work found space for a discussion of the work of women officers in police departments, and the women police in attendance organized the International Association of Policewomen.

The constitutional aims of the association are: to insist that the work of women police officers should be largely preventive and protective; to urge the need of trained women for this office; to support courses of instruction in social work, with field work in police departments, for candidates; to secure proper legislation for the appointment of women police; to insist that separate divisions be created in police departments, to be officered by women with a rank not lower than that of captain; to insure that careful records and reports of work be made; to require that simple civilian clothes be worn, except when on special duty; and to coöperate in the exchange of officers between cities in order to provide for enlarged experience.

Membership in the organization is limited to regularly appointed women police and does not include officers of private protective associations with police powers.

POLICE UNIONS AND RANK AND FILE ORGANIZATIONS

Beginning about 1918, the police commenced to feel the unrest that swept over labor groups as a result of the war. Salaries often failed to keep pace with the increased cost of living and the scarcity of men for public employment made recruiting difficult. The result was attempts at unionization and affiliation with the American Federation of Labor, by the rank and file of the police in several cities.

However, the unionization and the strike of police officers in Boston, which was beaten only by utilization of state militia and the dismissal of all members of the department associated with the union, brought the question of police unions and strikes vividly to the minds of police executives. In practically every city the movement was nipped in the bud by the prompt dismissal of the ring leaders and others actively associated with the movement. On the whole, municipal officials have not tolerated the unionization of police officers, on the grounds that it is entirely incompatible with the semimilitary character of the police and the corresponding need for the maintenance of discipline.

In how far the Fraternal Order of Police may be considered a union is problematical and no doubt depends upon the attitude of the leaders of local lodges. The order was organized in Pittsburgh, in 1915. It has grown slowly until now there are sixty lodges in Pennsylvania, New York, Ohio, West Virginia, Florida and Michigan. A national organizer has recently been employed.

This order has the usual fraternal purposes. It

believes that legislation is the honorable and surest means of promoting the occupation of policemen to a higher plane by improving their status on such vital subjects that affect their daily social and economic life, as laws governing pensions, uniform working hours, minimum wage, civil service, and so forth.

In spite of the fact that strikes are denounced by its officers, the order has been viewed with suspicion by some police officers, who have forbidden its establishment in their departments.

Benevolent associations exist in many departments. These are usually operated under the guidance of the police executives and are kept entirely within the bounds of charitable agencies. Ordinarily, assessments are levied upon members to provide a specific fund that will be paid to the dependents of deceased policemen. There is little social activity, and their objects and organization are very similar to those of assessment insurance associations.

Police officers, with other municipal employees, are eligible to membership in the Metropolitan Clubs, to be found in many cities. These organizations maintain club houses and are primarily of a social nature, although occasionally they do take part in political activities.

THE FUTURE OF POLICE ORGANIZATIONS

Although a principal purpose of the International Association of Chiefs of Police is to emphasize the professional character of policing to the public and secure the benefits that would naturally follow such recognition, the police have made far less progress in this direction than have other groups less deserving. Perhaps the cause of this failure lies in a vicious circle, whereby the present lack of professionalization prevents the continuous leadership that would eventually build up a professional attitude on the part of the police themselves.

It may be gross presumption for a layman to volunteer suggestions as to how the organized efforts of the police may be improved. Yet, the experience of the engineering, educational and other professional groups may offer something of value. The modern policeman is, perhaps, much more likely to profit from the experience of others than was his immediate predecessor who felt that policing was one activity closed to laymen. The use that modern police departments are compelled to make of statisticians, penologists, psychologists, psychiatrists, social workers, toxicologists and electricians compels an admission that policing is not an independent science, to the advancement of which those outside the department have nothing to contribute.

Perhaps a step forward in attaining the ends outlined by the International Association of Chiefs of Police would be the consolidation into a single organization of the several, now distinct, police groups which meet and operate separately, and the formation of additional groups within the larger unit. In such an organization, sections might easily be arranged for chiefs of police and other police executives, identification experts, policewomen, detectives, heads of traffic divisions, heads of scientific laboratories, county peace officers, and perhaps other individual groups, each with their own identity and program, yet merging their collective activities into a single effort for the raising of police standards and the promotion of public recognition of police activities. The very magnitude of such an organization would impress the public with the importance of police protection in their daily lives, the necessity that it be given every facility for carrying on its work and, particularly—that it be divorced from political interference. Annual conventions, attracting several thousand instead of several hundred individuals, including perhaps a substantial sprinkling of laymen, would perhaps focus newspaper and public attention upon police problems in a way it is now focused on the meetings of the National Education Association and the National Conference of Social Work.

The combined membership of such a group, even with nominal dues, would of itself guarantee sufficient funds to employ one or more full time executives whose purposes it would be to stimulate membership; to arrange really worth while programs for the several sections; to undertake adequate research into a number of unsolved police problems, possibly with the aid of private benefactions, which have so liberally contributed to other social progress; and, to publish an informing police journal of high standard, comparable and similar in quality and dignity to the English *Police Journal*, if not similar in actual content.

On this point of research and publicity, it is a rather interesting commentary on professionalization that the police do not have a single consolidated journal that may be said to represent them in a non-commercial way. There are numerous police publications, notably the *Police Journal*, the *Police Magazine*, the *Sheriffs', Police and Peace Officers' Review*, the *Peace Officer*, as well as local journals. Several of these journals are designated as the "official publications" of certain groups. Few, if any, however, are official in the sense of being issued by any particular group itself. On the contrary, they are usually commercial ventures. Their content is largely devoted to "write-ups" of particular police departments or of police individuals

interspersed with occasional articles of interest on police matters. A number of their pages are devoted to photographs and fingerprints of persons wanted. They carry a large amount of advertising, only a limited amount of which is of particular interest to the police.[1]

Presumably, the large number of peace officers in the United States, together with a considerable group of citizens, libraries and other organizations interested in police matters, would furnish adequate support for a non-commercial police journal which could, through the professional character of its content, serve as a source of helpful information to police officers, and by its very character impress the public with the importance of the police profession. Such a journal would doubtless supply a medium for legitimate advertising which would more than pay for its cost of preparation and publication. It appears unfortunate that the peace officers of the United States are so disorganized that no concerted effort can be made in this direction.

From time to time, the International Association of Chiefs of Police has discussed the question of a full time secretary who could guide, in some measure, the destinies of the organization, undertake the detail work of the annual meeting, and be responsible for the presentation of really helpful programs, representing not only the police but associated activities. The limited membership and dues that can be collected from members, have up to this time rendered such a desirable step impossible. Unfortunately, the work of the association must be carried on entirely by the private contributions it receives, some cities being even so parsimonious as to deny traveling expenses to chiefs for attending these conventions.

[1] See article on police journalism, in this volume, by Dr. Donald Young.—Editor.

Police Journalism in the United States

Assistant Professor of Sociology, University of Pennsylvania, Philadelphia, Pennsylvania

MAGAZINES devoted to the work and the interests of the police are catalogued by public opinion under the headings of "lowbrow" fiction, morbid curiosity, cheap adventure, crude pictures and the exploitation of sex interest. This attitude is due in large measure to the wide circulation of a number of well-known detective story and police periodicals filled with sensational fiction and advertising of doubtful ethics. Such trash appeals to a great number of what, for the want of a better term, may be called the handicapped classes while the true police journals contain so little material of either popular or scientific interest that they remain almost unknown. Police journals, properly so called, have as a result failed to impress themselves on either the general public or on the more specialized students of crime.[1]

In spite of this lack of interest in police publications, their significance in connection with a restricted clientele is such that they may not be brushed aside as without sufficient merit to

justify analysis. There are literally dozens of them in Europe and America, published by individuals for private profit or by or under the supervision of police departments as a means for increasing efficiency. Some, though without official sanction, seem to have no other motive than the promotion of public welfare. Their total circulation—much of it unpaid—compares favorably with that of some respectable trade journals if one may judge from the statements of business managers and from the advertising they secure.

It is reasonable to assume that these journals reflect and to a degree influence the attitudes of their readers towards crime, the criminal and his treatment. They are factors in the education and training of police officers and officials. Copies fall into the hands of individuals not directly connected with the administration of justice. What part, then, do they play in the lives of the people they reach and in the more general field of criminology?

Any attempt to generalize about all police journals must necessarily fail. They are of different types, their editors and management vary considerably in calibre and intent, their financial support comes from all kinds of sources and the subscription lists of some of them probably overlap little more than do those of *Harper's* and a motion picture magazine. Possibly the simplest means of evaluation would be to consider seriatim the purposes which might be served by a police journal, to discover which are emphasized and which neglected.

[1] *The Journal of the American Institute of Criminal Law and Criminology*, while in a sense a police journal, is not considered in this article because, by virtue of its academic control, it differs fundamentally from the types selected for discussion.

The Chief, a weekly newspaper devoted to the particular interests of New York state, city and Federal employees, is also not included, although it naturally gives much space to police affairs. It is interesting to note that this paper, not properly a police journal, was the only one so listed, on p. 626, in the admirable study of *Principles of Judicial Administration*, by W. F. Willoughby, recently published by the Brookings Institution, Washington.

Praising the Police

With few exceptions, editors of police journals in the United States apparently believe that one of their primary functions is that of establishing a high status for policemen. To their way of thinking, policemen are guardians of the law who can do no wrong. They are the bravest people in the land. They are the admiration of all little boys and girls, and adults might do well to follow the example of their children. Policemen solve all crimes; they always get their man, and people they arrest should be convicted. Policemen are underpaid but they never take graft. They have all the virtues, such as loyalty, honesty and courage, but no vices. No doubt it is good for the mental health of the police officer to be reassured of his intellectual, moral and physical superiority. Possibly it is good that the people he protects should be told about it and it is undoubtedly good— for the circulation department.

While it is the small local publication that excels in this respect, practically all indulge to some extent in unwarranted exaltation of police personnel. Used with reason, such a practice seems of real value but it is difficult to understand how anything but unjustified vanity, with some consequent inefficiency, could grow out of the empty boasting so commonly encountered. The monotony of story after story of dime novel heroism, often recounted by the hero himself directly or modestly through a none too modest mouthpiece, may inspire a few fellow officers to similar deeds but does not afford the ordinary patrolman a realistic, usable concept of his duties. Personal notices of trifling events in a man's life may give him a psychologically necessary opportunity to see his name in print

once in a while, but when columns of such forced news take the place of, rather than supplement, more valuable articles their comparative wisdom may be questioned. A policy of condemning every criticism of the police is also all too common.

What is needed in this respect is a better balance and a finer discrimination in judgment. Occasional notices, in the *Canadian Police Gazette*, of convictions for inefficiency or corruption are a relief from this overemphasis on the power of the police but journals south of the Canadian border make no mention of such things. One wonders why it is necessary to publish so many reminiscences of the "scarlet coated guardians of the western plains" who always "got their man" and whose successors, the Royal Canadian Mounted Police, still always get theirs, in a periodical dealing primarily with modern police problems. In the United States, it is the less romantic, but equally efficient "long arm of the law" which is glorified in the past, present and future. It is regrettable that the present apparent childlike editorial faith in an omnipotent, omniscient and unassailable law enforcement staff can not be replaced by a policy of giving credit where credit is due, placing at least part of the blame for failures where it belongs, and realizing that there are still other uses for police journals than to act as media for bragging.

Profits for Management

There are, of course, some journals whose sole function is private profit for the management. One of these has made its money out of selling detective books, fingerprint paraphernalia and the enrollment of gullible students in a school which they are assured will make them experts in crime detection. This publication naturally exists only as an advertising medium in disguise, is easily detected as such and need not concern us further. A number of others of the money making class make their profits from advertising which is secured under what amounts to false pretenses. Advertisers may be assured that they will get better police protection in proportion to the size of their checks. Sometimes there are suggestions that non-advertisers may find peculiar difficulty in obtaining justice. Again, the inducement to spend money on a medium which has practically no advertising value may be a direct or implied promise of special privileges for offenders, such as the remission of the fines of traffic violators. This type of journal makes little attempt to appear to be anything more than it really is, a hold-up scheme.

Printers' bills must be paid and sometimes profits are desirable. Out of these two simple facts grows one of the most important problems in connection with the publication of police journals. It is not likely that an editor will be able to free himself entirely from bias in discussing the work of police during a strike when his magazine contains page after page of advertising by local manufacturers—lumber companies, railroads, mills of various sorts, and so forth—as is the case with the *State Police Magazine*, for instance. One even wonders why these concerns spend money advertising their products in such a publication. Other journals also have extraordinary amounts of advertising, which seems peculiar considering the type of subscriber they are likely to have. In most cases there is no suspicion of conscious corruption but even with the best of intentions of all concerned the business office interests help sway editorial policies. The type of advertising may sometimes suggest the real reason for a journal's existence.

The June, 1927, copy of the *State Police Magazine* (98 pages in length), selected at random, was found to contain the following kinds of advertising.[2]

Coal, coke, gas and coal products corporations...... 7¾ pages (14 advertisers)
Lumber and furniture manufacturers............ 2 " (8 ")
Power, glass, oil, transportation, automobile, iron and steel companies......... 9¾ " (18 ")
Other advertisements included banks, hotels, pie bakers, milk dealers, glove and hosiery manufacturers, garages and a cemetery.

A similar count for the *Peace Officer*, Oklahoma City, Oklahoma (74 pages in length), for March 1929, gave the following figures:

Gas and oil companies......... 12¼ pages (25 advertisers)
Oil machinery..... 3¼ " (8 ")
Contractors...... 1¾ " (4 ")
Other advertisements included automobile dealers, airships, plumbers, night clubs and restaurants, hotels, theatres, laundries, jewelers, banks, cemeteries and undertakers.

---

[2] These were rough counts which did not include advertisements of less than a quarter page in reaching the totals listed. In view of the frequent charge that state police and sometimes other law enforcement officers have exaggerated ideas of their duties in protecting large corporations this advertising has its suspicious aspects. At the least it is an attempt to buy the good will of public officials rather than an effort to sell petroleum, drilling machinery, coke, lumber, and so forth, to policemen and their acquaintances. The point of view of the accompanying reading matter supports this contention.

The less pretentious journals have similarly misplaced advertisements from smaller fry, prominent among which are lawyers, restaurants, hotels, theatres, stores, banks, dentists, contractors, and so forth. For many of these, a direct return in increased business can be granted for the sake of argument but other expectations of profit are also evident.

AMUSEMENT

There are no police journals which admit their major reason for existence to be the amusement of their readers. It is understandable that they all insist that their one grand passion is the enforcement of law and order. With but few exceptions the reading matter is made up largely of stories, reminiscences, personal notes and jokes, designed to entertain rather than to instruct. In the mass, this type of material probably ranks second only to status-establishing efforts previously discussed. Quantitative comparisons are difficult because of overlapping. For example, the reminiscences of an old time sheriff, detective, "mountie" or patrolman may be boasting, as well as entertaining and slightly educational. *The Police Journal* (New York), *The State Police Magazine* and *Police "13-13"* are three publications which have cut the amount of space devoted to straight entertainment to a minimum, with good results. Readers, however, must be secured and the mediocre editor, frequently of the paste pot and scissors variety, finds the amusement features his most easily obtained drawing cards.

THE "HOUSE ORGAN"

There are a number of small journals published for the benefit of local police departments. Examples of this type are *The Vigilant*, of Norfolk, Virginia, and the *Police News*, of Detroit, Michigan. Their purpose seems to be to aid departmental morale and efficiency through the printing of local police news, notices and weak humor. As a rule they bear a family resemblance to a college weekly, with the advantage slightly in favor of the college paper. *Police "13-13,"* which calls itself the official publication of the Chicago police department and

"the greatest police magazine in America," is so far superior to the ordinary run of this class as to be above comparison. Another type of publication which is similar to the police department journal is that which serves a geographical section of the country, such as the *Northwest Police Journal*, the "official publication of the sheriffs and police departments of the Northwest." This monthly is, of course, more pretentious than city publications, such as *The Vigilant*, but the contents and purposes differ only slightly.

There is no doubt that publications such as these can and do accomplish much in the way of improving staff morale, in the same way that a college paper develops college spirit and coöperation, or an industrial plant's printed propaganda for employees aids production. House organs have been found useful in the business world and professional journals in the scientific fields. There is no reason to believe that police departments might not profit in a similar manner.

POLICE TECHNIQUE AND TRAINING

Police journals can aid in the apprehension of criminals both directly and indirectly. Directly, they can publish photographs and descriptions of fugitives and thus keep police throughout the country informed about wanted criminals. *The Detective*, an eight-page, twenty-cent Chicago monthly, self-styled the "only official publication of its class in the world," and claiming to be "on file in practically every police headquarters in the world," contains little more than a page or two of advertising, a few columns of inconsequential reading matter and criminals' pictures and descriptions. While some other journals publish a few requests for the arrest of, or information concerning criminals the practice is rare and photographs are much more likely to be of police officers than of "jailbirds." This is probably as it should be, for it seems not unreasonable to hold that such activity is the function of governmental police agencies rather than of private or even "official" magazines.

Indirectly, these journals can and should be of great aid in the solution of crimes through the training it is possible for them to give to police officers both in specific techniques and in social attitudes. Articles by specialists on firearms, wounds, fingerprints, self-protection, microscopic work, traffic control, evidence, legal rights and duties, life saving, and so forth, appear in all of the better types of magazines and in some of the others as well. Unfortunately, all too frequently the "experts" are not so well qualified as might be desired. This is possibly due in part to the notorious lack of well-trained specialists in criminal detection in this country as well as to the ignorance of the editors. It is in this field, however, that the chances appear to be best for a marked improvement in the quality of American police journals. Editors are generally willing to take such material if they can get it and there is some likelihood that they will be able to get it with greater ease and frequency in the comparatively near future.

The social attitudes fostered by the journals naturally are the same as those of the people who are responsible for their publication. Editorials and articles alike reflect the same prejudices regarding radicals, prostitutes, murderers, thieves, Negroes, Chinese, South Europeans, strikers and other minority groups as those held by the mass of people in the communities they serve. It is too much to expect it to be otherwise. What reason have we to hope that a detached, open-minded and scientific attitude will be taken in their pages toward people who are nationally the subjects of prejudices. It is probably enough that one may find occasional, and only occasional, reference to the less controversial attitudes towards loyalty, fitness for the job, honesty and courtesy. One magazine insists that rewards should not be the main incentive to good work and that the number of arrests is no measure of efficiency. Another goes so far as to discourage unnecessary gun play. On the other hand, the advice that illegal "beating up" is the proper method of controlling gangsters when the courts are too lenient, found in a journal "devoted to police work and better law enforcement," is perhaps a bit surprising to the uninitiated. The warning of a magazine of the house organ type that one should not drink booze while driving an automobile is perhaps amusing after a decade of prohibition, but it is also indicative of a police department's attitude regarding the illegal sale of alcohol. On the whole, it can hardly be said that the average police journal does much, if anything, to improve the general social outlook of its readers or to change their attitudes towards their jobs and the work they have to do.

Educating the Public

There remain to be mentioned two functions which might help to justify the existence of these numerous and varied publications. They might help to educate the public in criminal matters and they might also, in a number of ways, help prevent at least a small proportion of our crimes. They do little to help educate the public because the public at large does not read them, and the public does not read them because, considering the present tables of contents, there is little reason why it should, even for amusement.

There is one common practice which might be listed under public education although it also smacks of police education, departmental morale building and private profit. This is the almost universal custom of publishing propaganda for higher wages, better uniforms and equipment, pension funds, staff increases and other means for spending more public money. In some instances, the editors have, no doubt, only the welfare of police and public at heart but more often than not the real purpose is to curry favor with the readers. One is reminded of certain politicians who fight hardest for the full dinner pail when the votes are most needed.

CRIME PREVENTION

Preventive work receives almost no attention even in the better class of journal, unless one considers an attempt to spread a fear of police and prisons the essence of prevention. There is much effort to prove the police infallible, relentless and hard boiled. A composite picture of our law enforcement agents taken from the pages of these journals might well strike terror into the hearts of all malefactors while inspiring confidence in the breasts of honest men. Somehow one is reminded of the small boy who whistles courageously, if breathlessly, as he walks through the woods after dark. Anyway, it is probable that only few prospective prisoners ever read these journals so that any attempt to cure criminality through fear is bound to fail except in so far as it may spur hardy policemen on to sterner action.

We thus have at least eight functions which may be served by police journals. They may be: (1) a status establishing device; (2) a means of profit; (3) a medium of amusement; (4) an efficiency measure for improving staff morale; (5) an aid in the apprehension of criminals; (6) a supplement to the almost non-existent police training school; (7) an instrument for public education in criminal matters; and, (8) a preventive agency. Their present relative efficiency in serving each of these purposes has been suggested.[3] The picture resulting from our survey is discouraging.

It is easy, of course, to blame the editors for the deficiencies of their publications but it is also, in more ways than one, unfair to do so. However, since in accepting editorships they have definitely assumed at least the public responsibility for the calibre of their journals, it is probably an appropriate procedure to inquire into the reasons for their failure to meet standards reasonably conceived.

A SUGGESTED PROGRAM

Theoretically, a police journal should pay attention to at least three fields of criminology, unless in a particular case there is some good reason for specialization. In performing the functions suggested above, it should ordinarily cover subjects relating to: (a) the solution of crimes and the apprehension of criminals; (b) the treatment of criminals and suspects by the police, the courts and the prisons; and, (c) the general field of crime prevention.

At the present time, the solution of crimes and the apprehension of criminals receive practically all of the attention given these three fields. Incidentally, it should be remembered that most of the material printed has

[3] The study of a number of foreign police journals, too few, however, to constitute a fair sample, indicates an editorial view of police problems which is infinitely more scientific than the average for this country. This might be partly explained by the greater emphasis on careful selection and training of staff and the possibility of a respected professional career.

no direct bearing whatever on any one of the three fields. With few exceptions, articles on criminal causation do not appear. There is no real attempt on the part of any American police journal to understand the criminal. An occasional article of unadulterated praise for the perfect architecture and the flawless management of a state prison or county jail, including photographs of the sheriff or the warden, deputies and stenographers, disposes of the subject of incarceration. Capital punishment is valiantly defended although once in a while an editor lets an opponent have his say, apparently as a means of adding to his supply of straw men to be knocked down and jumped upon in the next issue. Lawyers and judges get their share of admiration although reading between the lines there can be detected a pervasive undercurrent of suspicion that if only these people would not be so soft hearted, especially towards the wealthy, the police would not be so handicapped in their work. The trouble with juries is, apparently, that they do not always believe the policeman. The juvenile delinquent deserves some—not too much—special consideration because of his youth, which decreases his responsibility for his conduct. Of course, if he is very, very bad and annoying and over, say, sixteen years of age his responsibility increases tremendously. Boiled down, all this means that so far as the police journal is usually concerned the problems of criminal treatment and prevention are simple if only the fool sentimentalists, juries, lawyers, judges,

reformers and public will not interfere with the prisoner's getting what is coming to him. The main job is held to be to catch him. Given a free hand, the rest is assumed to be easy.

Of course, the rest is not easy. Only, the editors do not know it, or do not bother to mention it. Their lack of complete understanding of police functions, like their attitudes towards crime and criminals, is the result of their training, and readily forgiven. Those who know better, and some no doubt do, must remember the subscribers, the advertisers, the available contributors and the public in general. So they continue to take what they can get and to please as many readers and financial backers as possible. If their own prejudices fit in with the rest of the picture, so much the better.

It may be that the fundamental difficulty is that the police personnel of the United States is not yet ready for scientific police journalism. Pay is not remarkable. Promotion, even at the bottom of the scale, so often depends on politics, friendship and other things. A police career is uncertain and, at the best, does not lead to social heights. Why should intelligent, educated and ambitious men join the force? Unless they do, who is there to read a well-edited, professional police magazine? Newspapers emphasize every known kind of printed and pictorial matter to increase their circulation, except important news. What are police journals that they should be above the practices of their powerful cousins?

The Policeman's Hire

By William C. Beyer

Director

and

Helen C. Toerring

Staff member, Bureau of Municipal Research, Philadelphia, Pennsylvania.

GOOD pay and attractive conditions of employment do not guarantee a high type of personnel in the public service, but they are a great help to the administrator in securing and holding such a personnel. Conversely, if pay is low and conditions of employment are unattractive, no administrator, however well-intentioned he may be, can build up and maintain a first class working organization. Since good police administration is so vitally dependent upon the quality of the men who compose the police force, it is no idle undertaking to inquire into the arrangements under which the policeman is required to perform his duties.

In this inquiry an effort has been made to get a rather broad view of the realm of the American policeman. Both state and municipal police forces are brought into the picture. Of the nine state police forces in the United States, information for 1929 has been obtained from eight, those of Massachusetts, Michigan, New Jersey, New York, Pennsylvania, Rhode Island, Texas and West Virginia.[1] Of municipal police forces those of seventy-eight cities have been included in our study. For thirty-six of these the information is for 1928; for the remaining forty-two, it is for 1929. The first group is composed of the larger cities, ranging in population from 114,000 to 5,900,000; the second group consists of smaller cities ranging in population from 30,000 to 105,000.[2]

All the more important facts relating to the policeman's compensation and working conditions were sought from these states and cities. From the states we endeavored to learn about the policeman's pay; his clothing allowances; whether he is reimbursed for clothing ruined in the course of duty; to what extent he is provided with meals and quarters; what sick-leave he is allowed; how much vacation with pay he is granted; whether or not he is protected by a pension fund; and the

[2] The first group of cities is composed of New York, Chicago, Philadelphia, Detroit, Cleveland, St. Louis, Baltimore, Boston, Los Angeles, Pittsburgh, San Francisco, Buffalo, Washington, (District of Columbia), Milwaukee, Newark, Minneapolis, New Orleans, Cincinnati, Kansas City (Missouri), Seattle, Indianapolis, Rochester, Jersey City, Akron, Toledo, Portland (Oregon), Columbus, St. Paul, Syracuse, Dayton, Des Moines, Trenton, Fall River, Wilmington (Delaware), New Bedford and Duluth.

The second group is composed of Knoxville, Schenectady, Sioux City, Winston-Salem, Portland (Maine), Sacramento, Racine, Chester, Springfield (Ohio), Lincoln, Berkeley, Niagara Falls, Quincy, Pasadena, Pontiac, Lancaster, Cedar Rapids, Oak Park, Kenosha, Atlantic City, Mount Vernon (New York), Columbia, Madison, Elmira, Bay City, New Rochelle, Jamestown (New York), Brookline, San Jose, Austin, Hamilton, Stamford, Rock Island, Dubuque, Wilmington (North Carolina), Lynchburg, Waterloo, Moline, Sheboygan, Oshkosh, Superior and La Crosse.

[1] After this article was set up in type information was received from the Connecticut state police. So far as feasible, this information has been embodied in the article.

stability of his employment. The same information was sought about municipal policemen, except that the item of meals and quarters was omitted in this part of the inquiry.

It should be mentioned that all the information from cities, except that about turnover, has been obtained from the Municipal Administration Service, New York City. The authors feel especially indebted to that organization for permission to use the data relating to the forty-two smaller cities, for these had not yet been published. The data relating to the thirty-six larger cities appeared in a pamphlet published by Municipal Administration Service. All the information about state police forces and the information about the tenure of municipal policemen was obtained by the Bureau of Municipal Research of Philadelphia directly from the police officials themselves.

RATES OF PAY

Without doubt the rate of pay is the most important single factor in making the police service attractive or otherwise. What are the rates of pay of policemen in state and municipal employ? Let us turn first to the state police services.

State Police. There is little uniformity in the compensation of state policemen.[3] Table One shows the salaries paid to each of the various grades from trooper to superintendent. The base pay of *troopers*, it will be observed, ranges from $900 a year in New York to $1,900 in Rhode Island. Since all the states except Michigan, Rhode Island and West Virginia, pay their troopers on a sliding scale, it is necessary to take into account also the maximum salaries. These vary from $1,200 a year in Michigan and West

[3] In this discussion Connecticut salaries are not included.

Virginia to $2,200 in New Jersey. The base pay of *corporals*, who rank just above troopers, is as low as $950 a year in New York and as high as $2,100 in Rhode Island; their maximum pay ranges from $1,320 in West Virginia to $2,400 in New Jersey. For *sergeants*, the base rates run from $1,100 a year in New York to $2,220 in Rhode Island; and the maximum rates run from $1,380 in West Virginia to $2,500 in New Jersey. The grade of *first sergeant* appears in only four of the eight states and carries slightly higher compensation than that of sergeant. *Lieutenants'* base salaries vary from $2,040 in Massachusetts to $2,400 in New Jersey and New York; and their maximum salaries vary from $2,100 in Michigan and West Virginia, where the minimum rates are also the maximum rates, to $3,000 in New Jersey and New York. *Captains* are paid the lowest base salary, $2,400 a year, in West Virginia and the highest, $3,400, in New York. Their maximum salaries range from $2,400 in West Virginia to $4,000 in New York. *Deputy superintendents* are on a flat salary basis in all the four states in which such officials were on the payroll at the time of our inquiry. There is a variation of $2,000 a year in their pay, the lowest salary being $3,500 in Michigan, and the highest $5,500 in New York. *Superintendents* receive all the way from $5,000 a year, in Michigan, Rhode Island and West Virginia, to $10,000 in New York. It may be remarked that state policemen begin rather modestly in New York but have before them greater prizes in salary than in any other state.

Municipal Police. In the pay of municipal policemen there is, if anything, even greater diversity than in that of state policemen. It is not possible in the space here available to present a tabulation of all the rates of pay in the seventy-eight cities included in

TABLE 1.—SALARIES OF STATE POLICEMEN, 1929

States	Trooper	Corporal	Sergeant	First Sergeant	Lieutenant	Captain	Deputy Superintendent	Superintendent
Massachusetts........	$1,200–1,500	$1,320–1,620	$1,440–1,860	....	$2,040–2,400	$3,180–3,720 [1]	......	$6,000
Michigan.............	1,200	1,500	1,800	....	2,100	2,500	3,500	5,000
New Jersey [2]........	1,600–2,200	1,800–2,400	1,900–2,500	$2,000–2,600 [3]	2,400–3,000	3,000–3,600	5,000	9,000
New York [4].........	900–1,500	950–1,550	1,100–1,700	1,200–1,800	2,400–3,000	3,400–4,000 [5]	5,500	10,000
Pennsylvania........	1,400–2,000 [6]	1,500	1,700	2,000	2,200	3,000	5,500	7,500
Rhode Island........	1,900	2,100	2,220	none	2,300	3,200	4,500	5,000
Texas...............	1,800–2,160 [7]	none	2,100–2,920 [7]	none	none	2,700–3,250 [7]	none	none
West Virginia........	1,200	1,320	1,380	1,500	2,100	2,400	vacant	5,000

[1] Executive officer.

[2] Paid for nine months period. The pay of each member, other than the superintendent and the deputy superintendent, is increased $200 each two years for a six-year period, so that, beginning the seventh year of service, each one of the grades receives $600 plus the base pay.

[3] Also a supply sergeant and a sergeant-major who receives $2,200 per annum.

[4] One hundred dollars a year, for six years, added to the salaries of all members, except the superintendent and the deputy superintendent.

[5] Also an inspector-captain who receives $3,400 a year.

[6] Enlisted men receive increases yearly after the first year of $120 for a period of four years and $60 yearly for the following two years.

[7] The pay of all grades increases five per cent after two years, and five per cent every year thereafter until twenty per cent is reached.

NOTE.—Information about Connecticut salaries was received too late to be presented in comparable form in this table. The annual salaries in the police force in that state are as follows: State policemen, maximum, $1,800; sergeants, $2,300; lieutenants, $2,600; first lieutenant, $2,900; captain, $3,600 and major, $5,000.

this inquiry. Instead, a number of tables are given, one for each grade, showing the distribution of cities by maximum salaries. So long as the presentation of complete information about salary ranges is unfeasible, it seems better to show the highest rates that policemen have in prospect than to give the starting rates or average rates. The majority of cities, it might be added, pay patrolmen on a sliding scale and some cities extend the sliding scale plan also to higher grades.

But the modal group, containing thirteen cities, runs from $2,000 to $2,099. In it are Philadelphia, Boston, Pittsburgh and Buffalo.

Table Three shows the distribution of cities by maximum rates of *sergeants*, both house sergeants and street sergeants. Although sergeants rank above patrolmen, it is interesting to note that both their lowest and highest maximum rates fall in the same salary groups as those of patrolmen. Both grades span the range from $1,500 to $3,000.

TABLE 2—MAXIMUM SALARIES OF PATROLMEN IN CITIES, 1928-29

Maximum Salaries	Cities
$1,500–1,599	7: New Orleans, Lancaster, Columbia, Austin, Rock Island, Wilmington (North Carolina) and Moline.
1,600–1,699	6: Chester, Springfield (Ohio), Lincoln, Bay City, Dubuque and Waterloo.
1,700–1,799	8: Wilmington (Delaware), Sioux City, Winston-Salem, Cedar Rapids, Lynchburg, Sheboygan, Oshkosh and La Crosse.
1,800–1,899	8: Baltimore, Cincinnati, Kansas City (Missouri), Knoxville, Portland (Maine), Madison, Elmira and Hamilton.
1,900–1,999	9: Indianapolis, Columbus, Dayton, Des Moines, Duluth, Racine, Kenosha, Jamestown (New York) and Superior.
2,000–2,099	13: Philadelphia, Boston, Pittsburgh, Buffalo, Milwaukee, Minneapolis, Akron, Syracuse, Fall River, New Bedford, Schenectady, Niagara Falls and Pontiac.
2,100–2,199	8: St. Louis, Washington (District of Columbia), Seattle, Rochester, Oak Park, Quincy, Brookline and San Jose.
2,200–2,299	4: St. Paul, Trenton, Berkeley and Stamford.
2,300–2,399	1: Portland (Oregon).
2,400–2,499	5: Cleveland, Los Angeles, Toledo, Sacramento and Pasadena.
2,500–3,000	9: New York, Chicago, Detroit, San Francisco, Newark, Jersey City, Atlantic City, Mt. Vernon (New York) and New Rochelle.

Table Two relates to the compensation of *patrolmen*. The lowest maximum salary group, it will be noted, is from $1,500 to $1,599 a year and includes seven cities, most of them small in population. The highest maximum salary is paid in Atlantic City where patrolmen may reach the comfortable figure of $3,000. In the range from $2,500 to $3,000 are nine cities, among them New York, Chicago, Detroit and San Francisco, all quite populous.

There is, however, only one city, Rock Island, instead of seven, in the lowest salary group; and there are twenty cities, instead of only nine, in the range from $2,500 to $3,000. The modal group, moreover, is one step above that of patrolmen — $2,100 to $2,199, instead of $2,000 to $2,099. It contains nine cities, among them Philadelphia, Baltimore and Pittsburgh.

Table Four relates to *lieutenants*. Only three of the sixty-two cities from

TABLE 3—MAXIMUM SALARIES OF SERGEANTS (HOUSE AND STREET) IN CITIES, 1928–29

Maximum Salaries	Cities
$1,500–1,599	1: Rock Island.
1,600–1,699	5: Lancaster, Columbia, Austin, Wilmington, (North Carolina) and Moline.
1,700–1,799	3: New Orleans, Dubuque and Waterloo.
1,800–1,899	6: St. Paul, Chester, Lincoln, Cedar Rapids, Elmira and Hamilton.
1,900–1,999	8: Knoxville, Sioux City, Winston-Salem, Racine, Springfield (Ohio), Lynchburg, Sheboygan and La Crosse.
2,000–2,099	3: Des Moines, Portland (Maine) and Superior.
2,100–2,199	9: Philadelphia, Baltimore, Pittsburgh, Minneapolis, Indianapolis, Syracuse, Wilmington (Delaware), Duluth and Kenosha.
2,200–2,299	8: Cincinnati, Akron, Columbus, Dayton, Fall River, New Bedford, Schenectady and Niagara Falls.
2,300–2,399	4: Boston, Milwaukee, Quincy and Oak Park.
2,400–2,499	6: Washington (District of Columbia), Kansas City (Missouri), Seattle, Rochester, Portland (Oregon) and Trenton.
2,500–2,599	3: Berkeley, Brookline and Stamford.
2,600–2,699	5: Cleveland, St. Louis, San Francisco, Sacramento and Pontiac.
2,700–2,799	5: Detroit, Los Angeles, Buffalo, Toledo and Pasadena.
2,800–2,899	None.
2,900–3,000	7: New York, Chicago, Newark, Jersey City, Atlantic City, Mt. Vernon (New York) and New Rochelle.

TABLE 4—MAXIMUM SALARIES OF LIEUTENANTS IN CITIES, 1928–29

Maximum Salaries	Cities
$1,700–1,799	2: Bay City and Oshkosh.
1,800–1,899	4: Lancaster, Columbia, Rock Island and Wilmington (North Carolina.)
1,900–1,999	4: Winston-Salem, Elmira, Lynchburg and La Crosse.
2,000–2,099	6: St. Paul, Knoxville, Portland (Maine), Madison, Jamestown (New York) and Sheboygan.
2,100–2,199	2: Des Moines and Springfield (Ohio.)
2,200–2,299	3: Minneapolis, Syracuse and Duluth.
2,300–2,399	6: Buffalo, Indianapolis, Akron, Columbus, Wilmington (Delaware) and Kenosha.
2,400–2,499	7: Philadelphia, Pittsburgh, Cincinnati, Kansas City (Missouri), Fall River, Quincy and Pontiac.
2,500–2,599	3: Baltimore, Boston and New Bedford.
2,600–2,699	6: Milwaukee, Seattle, Rochester, Portland (Oregon), Trenton and Superior.
2,700–2,799	4: Cleveland, Washington (District of Columbia), Oak Park and Stamford.
2,800–2,899	2: Toledo and Brookline.
2,900–2,999	1: Detroit.
3,000–3,099	5: St. Louis, Los Angeles, San Francisco, Dayton and Pasadena.
3,100–3,199	1: Atlantic City.
3,200–3,299	3: Chicago, Newark and Jersey City.
3,300–3,500	3: New York, Mt. Vernon (New York) and New Rochelle.

which we have information about lieutenants pay these officials on a sliding scale. These are Buffalo, Newark and Columbus. Hence a classification of cities by minimum salaries of lieutenants would not be materially different from the classification shown in this table. That these officials receive a real differential in pay over the grades just below them is indicated by the fact that their lowest salary group is $200 higher than that of patrolmen and sergeants and that their highest salary group is $500 higher. In the lowest group are only two cities, Bay City and Oshkosh, both small in population; and in the range from $3,000 to $3,500 there are twelve cities, including centers of population like New York, Chicago and St. Louis. The modal group of

lieutenants is $2,400 to $2,499, also a distinct advance over patrolmen and sergeants. Among the seven cities in this group, we again find Philadelphia and Pittsburgh.

Table Five is for *captains*. While these officials class with lieutenants in starting in the $1,700 to $1,799 group they show their superior rank by reaching a much higher maximum pay than their immediate subordinates, the highest pay of captains being $4,500 a year —the rate paid in New York. They show their superiority also in their modal salary group of $2,700 to $2,799, which is $300 higher than the modal group of lieutenants. For the first time in our comparison thus far we find that neither Philadelphia nor Pittsburgh conforms to the mode,

TABLE 5—MAXIMUM SALARIES OF CAPTAINS IN CITIES, 1928–29

Maximum Salaries	Cities
$1,700–1,799	1: Moline.
1,800–1,899	4: Rock Island, Dubuque, Wilmington (North Carolina) and Oshkosh.
1,900–1,999	5: Cedar Rapids, Austin, Hamilton, Waterloo and La Crosse.
2,000–2,099	2: Chester and Lancaster.
2,100–2,199	3: Sioux City, Lynchburg and Sheboygan.
2,200–2,299	7: New Orleans, Des Moines, Knoxville, Winston-Salem, Madison, Bay City and Jamestown (New York).
2,300–2,399	2: Portland (Maine) and Elmira.
2,400–2,499	5: Minneapolis, St. Paul, Schenectady, Racine and San Jose.
2,500–2,599	3: Indianapolis, Columbus and Dayton.
2,600–2,699	2: Philadelphia and Wilmington (Delaware).
2,700–2,799	8: Buffalo, Akron, Syracuse, Fall River, Duluth, Quincy, Pontiac and Kenosha.
2,800–2,899	2: Milwaukee and Rochester.
2,900–2,999	1: New Bedford.
3,000–3,099	7: Pittsburgh, Washington (District of Columbia), Kansas City (Missouri), Seattle, Toledo, Portland (Oregon) and Sacramento.
3,100–3,199	1: Baltimore.
3,200–3,299	None.
3,300–3,399	3: Cincinnati, Berkeley and Pasadena.
3,400–3,499	3: Detroit, St. Louis and Trenton.
3,500–3,599	2: Cleveland and Boston.
3,600–3,699	2: Los Angeles and San Francisco.
3,700–3,799	2: New Rochelle and Stamford.
3,800–3,899	1: Atlantic City.
3,900–3,999	None.
4,000–4,500	5: New York, Chicago, Newark, Jersey City and Mount Vernon (New York).

Buffalo being the only city with a population of 500,000 or more that does. Captains, like lieutenants, are usually paid a flat rate.

Table Six is devoted to *assistant superintendents*. The thirty-nine cities from which we have information about these officials pay them all the way from $1,920 a year, in Oshkosh, to $8,000 a year, in Chicago. All but ten of these cities pay $3,000 or more.

The modal group is $3,500 to $3,999 and includes nine cities, all of them with populations over 100,000 and most of them with at least 500,000 inhabitants, the largest being Pittsburgh. While cities having more than one assistant superintendent frequently pay them at different rates, the rule is to pay a flat salary rather than to provide a sliding scale.

Table Seven, relating to *superintend-*

TABLE 6—Maximum Salaries of Assistant Superintendents in Cities, 1928–29

Maximum Salaries	Cities
$1,920	1: Oshkosh.
2,000–2,499	4: Sioux City, Cedar Rapids, Elmira and Lynchburg.
2,500–2,999	5: Akron, Columbus, Schenectady, Niagara Falls and Superior.
3,000–3,499	6: Toledo, St. Paul, Syracuse, Fall River, Wilmington (Delaware) and Sacramento.
3,500–3,999	9: Pittsburgh, San Francisco, Washington (District of Columbia), Milwaukee, Minneapolis, Indianapolis, Rochester, Portland (Oregon) and New Bedford.
4,000–4,499	8: Philadelphia, Cleveland, Baltimore, Boston, Buffalo, Cincinnati, Kansas City (Missouri) and Atlantic City.
4,500–4,999	1: St. Louis.
5,000–5,499	2: Los Angeles and Newark.
5,500–5,999	1: New York.
6,000–8,000	2: Chicago and Detroit.

TABLE 7—Maximum Salaries of Superintendents in Cities, 1928–29

Maximum Salaries	Cities
$2,000–2,499	6: Springfield (Ohio), Cedar Rapids, Bay City, Rock Island, Wilmington (North Carolina) and Moline.
2,500–2,999	7: Elmira, Jamestown (New York), Lynchburg, Waterloo, Sheboygan, Oshkosh and La Crosse.
3,000–3,499	11: Des Moines, Knoxville, Sioux City, Lincoln, Niagara Falls, Columbia, Madison, Austin, Hamilton, Dubuque and Superior.
3,500–3,999	7: Columbus, New Bedford, Duluth, Winston-Salem, Racine, Quincy and Pontiac.
4,000–4,499	11: Akron, Toledo, St. Paul, Dayton, Trenton, Fall River, Schenectady, Sacramento, Oak Park, Kenosha and Brookline.
4,500–4,999	12: Baltimore, Indianapolis, Rochester, Jersey City, Portland (Oregon), Syracuse, Wilmington (Delaware), Berkeley, Pasadena, New Rochelle, San Jose and Stamford.
5,000–5,999	9: Philadelphia, Pittsburgh, Buffalo, Washington (District of Columbia), Minneapolis, New Orleans, Kansas City (Missouri), Atlantic City and Mount Vernon (New York).
6,000–6,999	7: Cleveland, St. Louis, Los Angeles, Milwaukee, Newark, Cincinnati and Seattle.
7,000–7,999	3: Detroit, Boston and San Francisco.
8,000–10,000	2: New York and Chicago.

ents, concludes the series on municipal policemen. Superintendents, or chiefs of police as they are frequently called, receive a wide range of compensation. Of the seventy-five cities included in this table, six pay from $2,000 to $2,499 a year to their police executives and two pay from $8,000 to $10,000 a year. In the former group are only the less populous places, like Springfield, Ohio, and Cedar Rapids; and, as might be expected, the latter group is composed of our two largest cities, New York and Chicago. The modal group, cities paying from $4,500 to $4,999, contains twelve populous urban communities, among them Baltimore, Indianapolis and Rochester. With only two exceptions, Newark and Columbus, the cities listed in this table pay flat salaries to their superintendents.

CLOTHING ALLOWANCES

Closely related to the policeman's salary is his clothing allowance, for it forms a part of his compensation. Not everywhere are clothing allowances granted to policemen, nor are they the same wherever they are granted. In some jurisdictions uniforms are furnished free to members of the force, in others a cash allowance is substituted, and in still others policemen are obliged to purchase uniforms at their own expense. What the practice is in different police forces will be described briefly.

State Police. All the states having state police forces, except Rhode Island and Texas, furnish uniforms to all ranks of the force and all except Texas replace uniforms ruined in the course of duty. Texas, it should be explained, does not have the members of its police force wear uniforms.

Municipal Police. In cities the practice also varies. Forty-one or more than half of the seventy-six cities from which information on the subject was ob-

tained, make no provision whatever for uniforms but permit the men themselves to shoulder the cost. This group includes Chicago, Los Angeles, San Francisco and Buffalo. Of the remaining thirty-five cities, ten, including Philadelphia and Washington, furnish all or part of the required uniforms and bear the cost of repairing or replacing clothing ruined in the course of duty; two cities, Hamilton and Columbia, furnish uniforms but do not bear the cost of replacement of ruined clothing; two cities, Lancaster and Duluth, provide a cash allowance and also bear the cost of replacement of ruined clothing; four cities, Rock Island, Atlantic City, Moline and Lynchburg, provide a cash allowance but do not bear the cost of replacing or repairing ruined clothing; and seventeen cities, among them New York, Detroit, St. Louis and Pittsburgh, neither furnish uniforms nor provide a cash allowance but bear the cost of replacing or repairing ruined clothing.

MEALS AND QUARTERS

Another item closely related to compensation is the allowance for meals and quarters in state jurisdiction. All the states, except Pennsylvania, bear the cost of meals of the men in the field. In Pennsylvania where the men bear the cost themselves they have formed "troop mess associations" and pay monthly assessments to the associations sufficient to meet the expense of providing the food. Lodging is provided at state expense in every state except Texas. Usually the state maintains barracks in which the men are housed.

There is no occasion for similar provisions in municipal police forces, for policemen in cities are able to live at home.

SICK-LEAVE WITH PAY

In both states and cities it is a fairly general practice to allow sick-leave with pay, but there are variations in the details of this practice, especially in the cities.

State Police. Every one of the eight states from which information was obtained allows sick-leave with full pay. In Pennsylvania there is a limit of fifteen days on the length of such leave but this may be extended by the executive board of the state. The other states have no fixed limit but leave it to the discretion of the appropriate officials to determine how long sick or injured policemen are to be kept on the payroll.

Municipal Police. Of the seventy-three cities from which information about sick-leave is at hand all but eight continue all or part of the pay of men for varying periods during illness. These eight cities are Pittsburgh, Cincinnati, Indianapolis, Portland, New Bedford, Knoxville, Lynchburg and Sheboygan. Three cities, Springfield, Pasadena and Dubuque, are reported as allowing only half pay. In most of the cities the length of sick-leave allowed with pay seems to be left to the discretion of the administrative officials, but thirteen cities are reported as having fixed limits ranging all the way from ten days, as in Berkeley and Lancaster, to six months, as in Buffalo, Rochester, Toledo and Columbus. In Berkeley, it should be explained, the ten-day limit applies only to men in the service less than one year; under a sliding scale based on length of service men who have been in the service over fifteen years receive ninety days leave with pay.

VACATIONS

Annual vacations with pay, too, obtain practically everywhere in police circles, but they vary in length.

State Police. With the exception of Pennsylvania, all of the nine states grant about two weeks' vacation with pay. In Pennsylvania the length of vacation ranges from fifteen to twenty-one days, depending on length of service. No distinction seems to be made in any of these states between the upper and lower grades in the length of vacation allowed members of the force.

Municipal Police. All except one of the seventy-eight cities included in this inquiry grant a vacation to their policemen. The single exception is St. Louis. In that city members of the force are limited to two days off duty each month. Of the other seventy-seven cities, fifty-seven are reported as allowing about two weeks' vacation with pay. The word "about" is used because the reports read variously, as "two weeks," "fourteen days," and "fifteen days." Among the cities in this group are Chicago, Philadelphia, Boston, Los Angeles, Pittsburgh and San Francisco. Baltimore ranks as the most generous city, with a vacation of thirty days; Kansas City ranks next, with twenty-four days; and Atlantic City holds third place, with twenty-one days. At the other end of the scale are Wilmington (Delaware) and Lancaster, with only seven days of vacation for their policemen. The other cities grant vacations varying from ten to eighteen days. In nine cities men in the grades above patrolmen are allowed longer vacations than patrolmen. For example, New York grants eighteen days to patrolmen, twenty days to sergeants, twenty-two days to lieutenants, twenty-four days to captains, twenty-six days to inspectors, twenty-eight days to deputy chief inspectors, and thirty days to the chief inspector. The other cities that differentiate between grades in the length of vacation allowed are Los Angeles, Schenectady, Milwaukee, Jersey City, Trenton, Mount Vernon, Dayton and Atlantic City.

PENSIONS

To what extent are policemen protected by pension funds? The answer is: In the states, only partially; in cities, quite generally. But let us inquire more specifically.

State Police. Only four of the nine states having state police forces provide pensions for their policemen. They are Massachusetts, New Jersey, New York and Pennsylvania. In all these states the men are required to pay dues to the pension fund.

Municipal Police. All but seven of the seventy-eight cities reporting information about pensions, have pension funds of one kind or another for their guardians of life and property. The seven exceptions are Kansas City (Missouri), Winston-Salem, Chester, Lincoln, Pontiac, Columbia and Austin. How these funds are provided cannot be described in this brief article, but it may be noted that in all except sixteen of the seventy-one cities with police pension systems the members of the force make contributions to the fund. The larger of these sixteen cities are Cincinnati, Toledo, Columbus, Dayton, Fall River, New Bedford, Knoxville and Portland.

STABILITY OF EMPLOYMENT

Are policemen birds of passage or men engaged in life careers? In reference to this question state and municipal police forces present something of a contrast.

State Police. In his book *The State Police*, published in 1925, Bruce Smith comments as follows on the terms of employment in state police forces:

Instead of surrounding the rank and file with safeguards assuring undisturbed tenure of office, the state forces take steps to protect themselves against sudden resignations which would be detrimental to the service. The contract of employment therefore usu-

ally takes the form of an enlistment paper in which the recruit engages and undertakes to remain in the service of the state for a period of two years unless sooner released.

That this arrangement is much more than a mere copy of army practice and has real practical significance is shown by the fact that a turnover in state police forces as high as thirty per cent of the membership of the force was not unusual at the time of Mr. Smith's study. Since that time conditions probably have improved somewhat. In 1928, the police turnover in Rhode Island was slightly over twenty-six per cent; in Pennsylvania it was about twenty-two per cent; in Connecticut it was about twenty-one per cent in West Virginia it was about seventeen per cent; in New Jersey it was slightly less than fourteen per cent; and in Massachusetts it was only 2.63 per cent. The superintendent of the state police of Rhode Island, it is worth noting, regards the 1928 turnover in his force as higher than normally because "nineteen enlistments expired during 1928 which were three-year term enlistments made in 1925." No information about turnover was obtained from the other states.

Municipal Police. Far greater stability of employment appears to obtain in municipal police forces. In Table Eight is shown the 1928 police turnover in fifty-one cities of the United States. It will be observed that the average turnover in all these cities was only 4.17 per cent. The eight cities having police forces of one thousand members or more had an average turnover of only 3.91 per cent and the forty-three cities having forces of less than one thousand members had an average turnover of 5.36 per cent. While there are a number of cities with a turnover of about fifteen per cent, they are decidedly in the mi-

TABLE 8—SEPARATIONS FROM POLICE FORCES IN CITIES, 1928

Cities	Average on force in 1928	Separations from Force	
		Number	Per Cent of Average on Force
ALL OTHER CITIES................................	47,782.5	1,991	4.17
Cities having force of 1,000 or more.................	39,411.5	1,542	3.91
New York....................................	17,770.5	579	3.26
Chicago.....................................	6,079.5	248	4.08
Philadelphia.................................	4,944.0	231	4.67
St. Louis....................................	1,836.0	92	5.01
Baltimore...................................	1,681.0	65	3.87
Boston......................................	2,287.5	83	3.63
Los Angeles.................................	2,348.5	129	5.49
Washington.................................	1,273.5	76	5.97
Newark.....................................	1,191.0	39	3.27
Cities having force of less than 1,000..............	8,371.0	449	5.36
Milwaukee..................................	995.5	71	7.10
Minneapolis.................................	542.0	33	6.09
Cincinnati..................................	626.5	61	9.74
Kansas City, Missouri........................	705.0	63	8.94
Seattle.....................................	624.0	32	5.13
Rochester...................................	457.0	12	2.63
Portland, Oregon............................	376.0	6	1.60
Columbus...................................	359.0	25	6.96
St. Paul....................................	334.0	4	1.20
Dayton.....................................	201.0	12	5.97
Trenton....................................	247.5	9	3.64
Fall River..................................	228.0	5	2.19
Wilmington, Delaware........................	150.0	9	6.00
New Bedford................................	272.5	9	3.30
Schenectady................................	168.0	1	0.60
Sioux City..................................	82.0	1	1.22
Winston-Salem..............................	86.5	11	12.72
Sacramento.................................	110.0	1	0.91
Racine.....................................	60.5	0	0.00
Springfield, Ohio............................	49.0	2	4.08
Berkeley....................................	51.5	7	13.59
Niagara Falls...............................	99.5	4	4.02
Quincy.....................................	109.0	1	0.92
Pasadena...................................	95.0	4	4.21
Pontiac.....................................	67.5	11	16.30
Lancaster...................................	52.0	0	0.00
Oak Park...................................	61.0	7	11.48
Kenosha....................................	60.0	0	0.00
Atlantic City...............................	302.5	5	1.65
Mount Vernon, New York.....................	108.0	6	5.56
Madison....................................	61.5	7	11.38
Elmira......................................	57.5	5	8.70
Bay City...................................	51.0	0	0.00
Jamestown..................................	48.0	8	16.67
Brookline...................................	114.5	1	0.87
San Jose....................................	44.0	3	6.82
Austin......................................	47.5	0	0.00
Hamilton...................................	44.0	0	0.00
Stanford....................................	74.5	5	6.71
Rock Island.................................	20.0	3	15.00
Wilmington, North Carolina...................	45.0	0	0.00
Waterloo....................................	31.5	5	15.87
Sheboygan..................................	39.0	0	0.00

nority. Generally speaking, it may be said that the municipal policeman is in a life occupation. Compared with him, the state policeman is a bird of passage.

BY WAY OF CONCLUSION

This article is not intended primarily as a comparison of the state policeman's lot with that of his brother in municipal service, but differences between the two nevertheless force themselves upon one's attention. On the whole the municipal policeman seems to be better provided for than the state policeman and to have a happier, though perhaps a less romantic, existence. He can live in his own home; his compensation is probably as attractive as that of the state policeman or more attractive; his sick-leave and vacation privileges are at least as favorable as those of the state policeman; and he is better protected in old age. That he stays in his job longer than his compeer in state employ is not surprising.

No doubt time will gradually work a change in all this. State police forces are quite new in the United States, whereas municipal police forces have a history as old as the cities in which they serve. It is only natural that more provisions should have been made for the welfare of the long-standing municipal policeman than for the new-comer who has been welcomed thus far by only nine of our forty-eight states. But as the new-comer becomes more firmly established he, too, will doubtless be more adequately protected against the hazards of life.

The Use of Scientific Tests in the Selection and Promotion of Police

By L. J. O'ROURKE

Director of Personnel Research, United States Civil Service Commission, Washington, District of Columbia

THE increasing prevalence of crime has laid a heavy burden upon the personnel of police and investigative services. As the problem of frustrating criminal practices and apprehending lawbreakers presents new difficulties, the demand for men with the special qualifications and the intelligence necessary to cope with the situation becomes increasingly urgent.

To show the extent to which scientific selection methods are employed in securing police in the United States, I shall present a brief summary of reports submitted by thirty of the sixty largest cities of this country, with a few critical remarks based on findings of research which we have conducted for the purpose of improving police selection. I shall then confine the rest of this discussion to the work which we have done and are doing in the United States Civil Service Commission to bring about more scientific and practical police selection methods.

Federal and municipal civil service commissions, as well as police departments, realize the limitations of present selection methods. The necessity for a large number of alternative forms of the tests used for selection greatly increases the time, the difficulty and the expense of constructing standardized tests; hence, even when the examiners have adequate experience and training in the technique of test construction, a serious problem confronts them. The obtaining of an accurate criterion of a policeman's efficiency in actual service presents marked difficulties. It is not surprising then that little has been done in the way of statistical analysis and standardizing of measurements.

METHODS OF POLICE SELECTION

A study of the police selection methods in these representative cities shows a wide difference in the requirements, the types of measurements and the weights given to the factors considered. Physical requirements vary from the simple absence of physical defect to rather high standards in a series of tests of strength and agility. Educational requirements vary from "ability to read and write" to high-school graduation. Tests, mental or educational, which are used by eighty-seven per cent of the cities studied, also show marked differences. Twenty per cent of the cities use the Army Alpha test in whole or in part as a test of intelligence. Ten per cent more use other standardized intelligence tests, and fifty-seven per cent use unstandardized tests, some intended to indicate degree of general intelligence, others to measure extent of knowledge acquired. The most frequently used written tests are based upon laws, regulations and rules of evidence, or they relate to duties of police, police procedure and first aid. They require competitors to identify and classify crimes and to interpret commonly used legal terms. In most cases the questions in these tests are presented in such form as to permit objective scoring.

Some of the cities have tests designed to measure various qualifications that it is believed police should possess. Many of these tests look interesting. Reports show that, for reasons already stated, their validity and reliability have not been established. What is needed is less emphasis on originating a variety in forms and more knowledge about the validity and the reliability of a battery of selective tests which can be readily duplicated.

Aside from the information concerning the nature of tests, the data secured from the cities surveyed may be summarized as follows:

Selection standards. Standards of selection have been, with few exceptions, too low to insure the securing of men with sufficient intelligence to perform police work with the highest degree of effectiveness. This fact is strikingly indicated by the report of a study of the police department of Kansas City, Missouri, made under the direction of Mr. Vollmer. Twenty-five per cent of the police force of that city made scores of forty-five points or below on the Army Alpha test. The report also shows similar results in Los Angeles and Cleveland. Twenty-one per cent of the Cleveland police, and fourteen per cent of the Los Angeles police fell within the low average, the inferior, and the very inferior classes, as indicated by scores of forty-five or below.

To secure men of the proper calibre for police work, Mr. Vollmer suggests that the standard for entrance be raised until the equivalent of a score of seventy-five points on Army Alpha is required of men who qualify for appointment. Such a standard would have eliminated fifty-eight per cent of the Kansas City police force, fifty-five per cent of the Cleveland force, and forty-three per cent of the Los Angeles force.

The test developed, as a result of our research studies, to measure general adaptability of applicants for the Washington police force is so focused as to set an entrance standard equivalent to a score of seventy-five points on the Army Alpha test. The practical value of this test is indicated elsewhere in this paper.

The adaptability test is designed to show ability to adapt to new situations. Experience on the police force may enable men to perform police duties more effectively than could new men of a somewhat higher intelligence. It must not, therefore, be assumed that experienced men on the force should be dropped because their intelligence ratings are somewhat below the new entrance requirements. A higher entrance requirement on a test of adaptability to perform police work, plus experience, will tend to improve the efficiency of the force as a whole. Experienced men on the force who make the higher scores are men more efficient as a group than the men who make lower scores. There are always notable exceptions, however; correlation between test scores and efficiency in police work is far from perfect. For this reason the efficient man on the force should be thought of in terms of his efficiency, not in terms of his test score.

Raising entrance standards will eliminate some men who would make good policemen. The problem, however, is to insure increased efficiency in the force as a whole. Below a certain degree of adaptability, men as a group will not profit by experience, as will men of higher adaptability. Above a certain degree of adaptability higher scores on such a test are not significant. Viewed in the light of increasing the effectiveness of the police department as a whole, the adaptability test can be used as one important aid in selection.

Origin of selection standards. In

forty-one per cent of the cities studied, selection standards are fixed by municipal civil service commissions. In twenty-five per cent, standards are set by the police department. The two agencies unite in setting selection standards in thirty-four per cent of the cities submitting data.

Basis for promotion. Seniority is the common basis for promotion, although tests are very generally used. Fifty per cent of the cities surveyed base promotion on a combination of seniority, efficiency ratings and tests.

Promotion tests are based largely upon laws, regulations and principles of administration with which only the experienced policeman can be expected to be familiar. The tests which any given city uses for promotion to the positions of sergeant, lieutenant, and captain vary in difficulty rather than in form.

Efficiency ratings. Efficiency ratings are made in seventy-two per cent of the cities surveyed. Only two of these cities report the use of a graphic rating scale. Some determine efficiency by means of special tests, others on the basis of the men's monthly records of merits and demerits.

Character investigation. Each of the cities whose selection methods were examined investigates the character of applicants before making appointments. Thirty-eight per cent state that they use vouchers; twenty-one per cent use interviews; seven per cent use both. Police and court records are searched by twenty-eight per cent.

In the case of another twenty-eight per cent, character investigation is limited to securing statements from references. These statements either are filed by the applicant when he makes application, or are submitted by letter.

The interview as a means of selection.[1]

The interview or oral examination is used as a selection device in seventy-two per cent of the cities included in our study. In some cases, a committee of police officers interviews each candidate, to determine record, character and habits. In other instances, the interviewing is done by the civil service commission. At least one city uses the interview prior to the written tests, as a means of determining whether the applicant shall be admitted to the written examination.

Experience. More than thirty-five per cent of the cities give experience a weight in determining eligibility for appointment. Many of these give special credit for army service and for "work relating to police work."

None of the cities included in the survey has a required minimum of experience, though one or two state that "general experience" is required. A number require records of the applicant's experience during the years immediately preceding his application. Such records may be used as a basis both for investigating the applicant and for rating him.

Educational requirements. Of the cities surveyed, forty-one per cent demand at least a common-school education as an entrance requirement. In one instance a high-school education is the minimum. Other cities state that persons with a common-school education are preferred, or that a common-school education is necessary to pass the tests. One city "prefers high-school graduates," but does not make a high-school education a requisite for entrance. In one large city the only educational requirement is that the candidate be "able to read and write."

There is, however, a marked trend

[1] See *United States Civil Service Commissions Annual Report,* 1928, pp. 36–50, or *Personnel Journal,* Vol. 7, pp. 427–440, April, 1929, for discussion of a new technique for conducting oral examinations.

toward higher educational requirements. One commission states that
lack of an educational requirement in
the city in question is due only to
legislative opposition. Another municipality, while making no fixed requirement, gives a rating of seventy-five
for common-school education, and adds
or deducts three points for each year
over or under that standard.

In very few cities is education given
a definite weight. Some give a weight
for the combination of education and
experience.

ANALYSIS OF DUTIES AS BASIS OF SELECTION

The first step toward the scientific
solution of any problem of selecting
personnel is a critical and comprehensive analysis of the duties of the
position in question. In attacking the
problem of police selection we sought
to determine not merely which duties
are being performed by present police
employees, but also the abilities that
should be required in order to attain
the highest efficiency.

The attention of the public is called
to the work of a policeman only when
he makes an arrest or performs some
act of conspicuous heroism. Such
duties, however, form but a small part
of his daily work. He should be constantly alert and should patrol his post
so thoroughly and intelligently that he
prevents the occurrence of crime and
disorder. When an arrest is to be
made, apprehending the individual is
but one step; the policeman should also
be able to secure all evidence necessary
to convict the man arrested, if he is
guilty. The officer should be quick
and accurate in observation, able to
judge what facts ordinarily will be
valuable and admissible as evidence,
and capable of remembering faces as
well as of making and remembering
associations between facts and people.

The detective often acts alone and
confronts situations which require him
to rely upon his own judgment more
frequently than does the patrolman.
He should be able to make important
decisions quickly and accurately and to
interpret the facts of a situation or the
actions of human beings. He should
have the insight necessary to see to
what facts a given clue might lead, and
he should be wary enough not to be
led off the track by valueless clues or
those purposely "planted." He is
required not only to discover clues
and build his case, but to do so in the
face of constant effort, on the part of
those being apprehended, to place every
obstacle in his way and to have misleading information reach him.

SECURING A CRITERION OF EFFICIENCY

Before the effectiveness of any tests
designed to aid in selection can be
evaluated, it is necessary to have, as a
criterion, a measure of the efficiency
of the men selected by those tests.
No research findings can be more
reliable than is the criterion on which
they are based.

To obtain an accurate measure of
the extent to which a policeman performs his duties satisfactorily is difficult. There is no way of accurately
recording instances of crime prevention
or of the exercise of unusual skill.
Therefore, when a rating of a policeman's efficiency is desired, it is necessary to depend, at least in part, upon
the combined judgment of superior
officers. If the superior officers merely
classify the men as "good," "fairly
good," or "poor," it is impossible to
make accurate comparisons of the
men and to decide on the relative
merit of each. Yet is it desirable to
make such comparisons for purposes
of taking inventory of the force in
connection with training, assigning and
promoting its members. The graphic

rating scale assists a commanding officer in avoiding the rough classification spoken of, and in expressing in numerical terms a fair rating of the efficiency of each of his men.

One of the difficulties encountered in rating efficiency arises from the fact that no man is equally good in all traits—the one who excels in loyalty may be the poorest in knowledge of duties, and one who is familiar with his duties may be entirely lacking in loyalty. In order to obtain an accurate rating, then, it is necessary to consider and rate separately each of the several essential traits. By this means the rater is encouraged to give due credit to each quality rather than to allow his impression on one factor to determine the entire rating. The values of the ratings on the separate traits can later be combined into a total rating.

Before a decision was made as to what traits are of sufficient importance to be included in the rating scale which we were developing, the captains of all police precincts in Washington, District of Columbia, were asked to make independent judgments as to the qualities to be rated. They listed: (1) the qualities they considered absolutely essential for a policeman; (2) those they considered important, but not absolutely essential; (3) those they considered detrimental in the police service; and, (4) those they believed should absolutely bar a man from a position on the police force. Their statements indicated the traits which, at that time, largely influenced their opinions of the men. Their combined judgments were compared with the list of qualifications made as a result of the analysis of the actual work, and ten traits were finally included in the scale.

Each trait was defined as accurately as possible, since exact definitions tend to make the different raters think in the same terms. Wherever practi-

cable, the wording of the police captains was used in order to put the scales in terms familiar to the officers and actually used by them in describing the men.

The description of each point in the scale was made as specific as possible. Terms like "Somewhat below average" or "Far excels average" would have a different meaning for each rater, because each would have his own conception of the ability of the "average" policeman. Such general terms were replaced by phrases like "Frequently must be told what is meant," or "Always understands orders correctly."

The graphic rating scale is of value, not only as a means of securing a criterion for our tests, but as an aid in selecting men for promotion. When no device is available for rating and recording the relative ability of policemen, there is a tendency to use seniority alone, without regard to merit, as the basis for insuring fairness in making promotions. Some superior officers base promotions upon their general opinions of the men. This practice is inaccurate because, even when favoritism plays no part, the judgment is unconsciously influenced by some special quality or deficiency in the person rated. The use of the rating scale will aid in making it possible to recognize and reward hard work and real ability.

Since the rating scale discloses the strong and the weak points of each man, it will assist the commanding officer in considering the specific abilities of each man when assigning him to duty.

The scale also may serve as an incentive to the men and an aid in instruction and training. If policemen or detectives are shown the specific qualities which are considered the most important by their superiors, and if they are shown in which of these points they, individually, are weak, their attention can be focused on overcoming their deficiencies.

CONSTRUCTION OF TESTS

Many tests, designed to measure the qualifications which the study of duties had shown to be important, were prepared for trial.

Test of ability to reason. One test was designed to measure ability to reason in the specific situation which it presented. In the trial of this test, each policeman was directed to give briefly one, two, or three of what seemed to him to be the most reasonable explanations of the situation. He was told that the explanation could contain no facts nor implications contrary to the conditions set forth in the paragraph. A sample with possible answers was presented, to insure understanding of the requirements. The research study indicated that more progress can be made with controlled problems than with problems of the free-association type such as this test contained.

Test of ability to interpret situations (murder picture). Since a policeman or detective should be able to interpret evidence, and to reconstruct a crime, a test was devised to measure this ability. This test consists of a picture showing the scene of a murder a moment after the crime has been committed (see Figure One), and a paragraph of details concerning the happenings of a few seconds before and after the time shown in the picture.

The test measures, not the extent of factual information, but the candidate's ability to recreate a scene in his imagination, to weigh a number of factors in relation to each other and to arrive at logical conclusions.

The paragraph used with the picture reads as follows:

The facts are these: As you are patrolling your beat by motorcycle, you round a sharp curve and see the situation shown in the picture. A wrecked touring car is partly off the road, against the fence. A man, hereafter referred to as G, is lying on the road. A second man, hereafter called X, is hurrying toward a second car standing at the side of the road, ahead. As you appear, this man, X, fires at you. The front tire of your motorcycle is blown out and you are thrown from your machine. You see X get into the waiting car and drive straight ahead. You observe a bullet hole in the rear window of his car.

You find two letters, dropped by X as he ran. The letters are addressed to "Jas. Gunther," and signed "B. K." They contain the appeal, "For God's sake don't give me away," and the statement, "Everything will be made good." An automobile driver's permit and a club-membership card, found in G's pocket, bear the name of James Hadley Gunther. Only one bullet has been fired from G's revolver. His car has one bullet embedded in it.

With the picture[2] and the paragraph before him, the competitor is required to determine what events led up to the situation, and to answer such questions as:

1. The position and condition of the wallet most probably indicate that: (1) it fell from G's pocket as he fell; (2) it slipped out of X's pocket as he stooped over G; (3) X, fearing detection, ran away without taking it; (4) X and G had struggled over its possession; (5) X discarded it after searching it............... 5
2. Where was G when he received his fatal wound? Write the number of the answer: (1) running toward X; (2) trying to reënter his own car; (3) running away from X; (4) standing in front of his car; (5) standing beside his car; (6) in his car........................ 5
3. X may claim to have shot G during an argument and struggle, while crazed with anger. Which would indicate that his claim was false? (1) Apparent fear of G shown in letters; (2) G's position outside the

[2] Each competitor is given a large copy of the picture, on which all details are clearly shown.

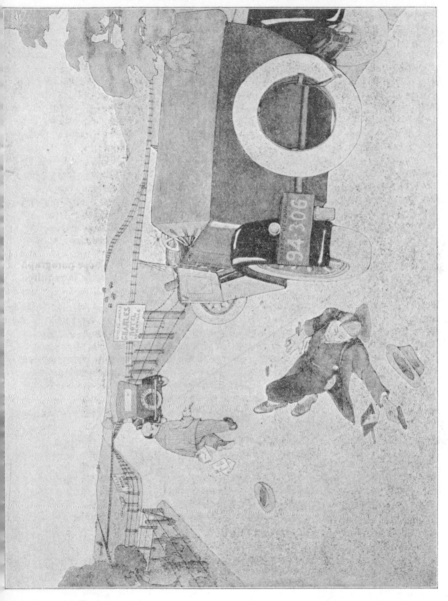

Figure 1

car; (3) the fact that G was prepared to shoot; (4) position of bullet holes in the cars; (5) the fact that one man held evidence against the other...................... 4

Judgment test. A test was designed to determine the significance which the prospective policeman attaches to different acts, thus determining his standards and his judgment with regard to the acts of others. Another test serves to determine his judgment as to the action which a policeman should take under certain specific conditions. The conditions set forth are practical; the situations involved in the problems are of the type which do not require sudden decisions or judgment based upon a few seconds of deliberation under emotional stress. Hence, in dealing with the problems during the examination, the applicant deliberates in much the same manner as he would in meeting such problems in actual work.

Other tests of specific abilities. There is not sufficient space here to discuss and illustrate all the tests developed, such as the test of ability to interpret clues, or the tests of ability to interpret the report of a crime. These tests are discussed in some detail in the Commission's annual report for 1926.

General adaptability. With the tests mentioned we tried a test of general adaptability, made up of items of different types, arranged in order of increasing difficulty and rotated so that persons unable to finish the entire test would try items of each type. The nature of these items is shown in the following samples. The actual test items are more difficult than these samples.

1. Which of the following is the *chief* reason why a police force is necessary? (1) To enforce law and order; (2) to control traffic; (3) to prevent criminals escaping from jail; (4) to record fingerprints; (5) to direct strangers.......... 1

2. Your superior officer assigns you to duty at a large public reception where you are expected to watch for pickpockets. "Remember," he tells you, "you can not always judge a man by his clothes." Which of the following most nearly expresses his meaning? (1) Look at all men with suspicion; (2) a detective should wear civilian clothes; (3) crimes are usually carefully planned; (4) a well-dressed man inspires confidence; (5) appearances may be deceiving.......... 5

3. The next question is based on the following statement: "The nature of police duty requires a policeman to be alert concerning persons, places, and happenings, in order to prevent crime and protect life and property." Which of the following does this statement show that a policeman on duty should be? (1) Obedient; (2) watchful; (3) ambitious; (4) systematic; (5) thrifty 2

4. A person who is *released on condition of good behavior* is said to be (1) pardoned; (2) restricted; (3) acquitted; (4) paroled; (5) discharged........................ 4

The test of general adaptability for police work is used in place of the Army Alpha test for the following reasons:

1. It is more easily administered than is the Army Alpha test. To give it, one needs only distribute the papers, instruct the competitors to read and follow the directions carefully, give the final signal for stopping, and collect the papers. The Army Alpha test, on the other hand, requires the examiner to read many detailed directions; the results of the test are, therefore, influenced by the training and the experience of the examiner and the speed and clearness of his speech; the size of the room in which the test is given, and the position of the

competitor in the room become administrative problems.

2. It can be more accurately administered than the Army Alpha test, for it requires only one timing. A record is kept of the time at which the competitor starts, and he is stopped at the end of one hour. In Army Alpha, eight tests are separately timed; in some of the tests an error of one minute is an error of fifty per cent; since these tests are variously weighted, an excess of time on one test will not make up for a shortage on another.

3. It measures qualifications more directly than does the Army Alpha test. That is, in order to determine whether or not a man can interpret directions intelligently, we require him to interpret paragraphs of directions. Likewise, to measure judgment and ability to solve problems of the type that arise in police work, such problems are presented.

4. It causes less nervous strain than the Army Alpha, among adults who are not used to taking tests. This is due to the absence of frequent timing and rapidly given verbal directions.

5. It is less unusual in appearance than the Army Alpha test. Since the subject matter of questions is definitely related to police work, competitors are inclined to regard it as a practical device. Furthermore, they are prepared for the form of the test by the sample test which is mailed to them with the examination announcements, and given to them again just prior to the regular examination.

6. It is constructed more as a "power" test than as a speed test.[3] It is designed to measure the extent of the competitors' judgment and adaptabil-

[3] The correlation between scores made when the test was given as a speed test, and when it was given with time for completion, was .912. (See *United States Civil Service Commission's Annual Report* for 1926, p. lix.)

ity. Their accomplishment on the test depends more upon their judgment and ability to reason than upon the amount of time allowed for taking the test.

TRIAL OF THE TESTS

By means of the rating scale already discussed we secured three separate efficiency ratings for each of the Washington policemen used in the trial group. These ratings were made independently by the captains, the lieutenants, and the sergeants in direct command of the men. No man concerning whom the three raters differed widely was included in the group used in testing the tests. Some men who were rated high in efficiency and some who were rated very low were included in the group.

The battery of experimental police tests was given to these men. A comparison of their efficiency ratings with their scores on these tests shows the extent to which the test scores indicate efficiency. As a result of a statistical comparison of scores on the different tests with each other, as well as with efficiency ratings, a number of the tests were selected for further consideration. The combination of tests which produced scores correlating highest with efficiency was then determined.

The most valuable one of a battery of tests is that which arranges the members of the trial group, by scores, in a relative order most nearly the same as that in which they are ranked on the basis of actual ability. Such a test is said to have the highest correlation with the criterion, and should be given the greatest weight when final scores are computed. In determining the test which should receive the next highest weight, we consider first, the extent to which the test measures efficiency as indicated by ratings, and second, the extent to which its use, in combination with the first test, adds to the selective value of the first test.

Each of a battery of tests is chosen according to the extent to which it measures an important factor that is not measured by other tests included in the battery. Statistical study of any test must, therefore, indicate: (1) the relation of scores on that test to proficiency in the position for which the test is to be used; (2) the relation, to proficiency, of scores on other tests; and, (3) the relation of the test to all the other tests to be used for the position in question.

If two tests are equally satisfactory in arranging members of the trial group in order of their known proficiency, nothing is gained by using both for purposes of selection. This does not mean that there is no choice between the two tests, or that they are necessarily equally desirable. There are many additional points which must be considered, such as difficulty of duplication, time required for administration, difficulties of giving the tests at various times and in various places with equal fairness, and difficulty of accurate scoring.

While tests which appear to be practical and related to the duties of the position are more likely to secure the coöperation of competitors and appointing officers, this appearance of practicability does not indicate the worth of the test. The selective value of a test can not be determined by inspection, even if such inspection is made by experts in the work for which the test is designed.[4] The only way to be sure of the value of any test is to test it and study results in the manner outlined above.

The reliability of the tests must also

be considered—that is, the extent to which similar results can be insured when alternative forms of a test are taken at different times by the same competitor. The reliability of our tests is increased by the fact that samples of the tests are printed on the announcements sent to each applicant. As a further precaution, sample tests are given to competitors just prior to the regular examination. Thus, we prevent test scores being influenced by the competitors' familiarity, or lack of familiarity, with the test form. These samples have an additional value in that they act as a shock-absorber and, since they are very simple, they tend to relieve nervous tension.

By using a battery including the general adaptability test and four of the special tests described or mentioned above, we obtained a coefficient of correlation with efficiency ratings of .666. The addition of two other tests produced only a slight increase in predictive value, the coefficient of correlation becoming .686. The criterion here was general efficiency in police work.

A comparison of efficiency ratings with scores made on our tests by detectives in Washington and other cities is not yet complete enough to justify our reporting coefficients of correlation. The indications are, however, that the battery will show still higher correlation with detective efficiency.

PROBATION AND PROMOTION TESTS

There is certain knowledge which a man must have before he is qualified to serve as a policeman, but which he can not be expected to possess at the time he enters police service. For example, he must have a thorough knowledge of city ordinances and state laws which he will be required to enforce. He must also understand all police regulations. He must have some knowledge of rules of evidence. He must know the poli-

[4] See *United States Civil Service Commission's Annual Report* for 1925, for discussion of subjective and objective evaluation of tests.

cies of the police department. He must be familiar with the geography of his city, and with the locations and the functions of civic institutions.

The majority of cities conduct training courses of various lengths to prepare new policemen for efficient duty. In most instances it is assumed that, at the end of the training period, the men will have absorbed the necessary information. The policy of deferring actual selection until after the training period is gaining favor, however, and this increases the demand for tests which will determine whether the men tentatively selected are fit to be employed permanently.

The following items are typical of those included in the probation-promotion tests developed for the Commission:

1. Members of the police force of Washington, D. C., should (1) refuse to give their names or numbers to inquirers whom they do not know: (2) require reasons for inquiries as to their names or numbers; (3) refuse to tell their names to suspicious-looking persons; (4) give their names or numbers only to duly authorized persons; (5) give their names or numbers to whoever asks for them.   5

2. A citizen tells you that the person who turned in a false fire alarm two hours ago is a certain 19-year-old boy. You can not arrest the boy without a warrant, because (1) he is under age; (2) the offense is serious; (3) you did not see the offense committed; (4) the citizen did not make the statement to your commanding officer; (5) the citizen may be mistaken.   3

3. John Marshall Place (1) is near the White House; (2) is in the Mall near Fourteenth Street; (3) is south of the Capitol; (4) meets Pennsylvania Avenue near Sixth Street;

(5) is between Center Market and Pennsylvania Avenue.   4

Another type of promotion test consists of a list of cases such as might come to the attention of a police officer. He is required to indicate which of the following procedures he would take in each case, his answers requiring comprehensive knowledge of the police manual: "(1) arrest; (2) communicate with headquarters at once; (3) report it the next time you telephone or go to police headquarters; (4) warn; (5) take no official action."

This is very much like the judgment test for applicants, but it demands specific knowledge of laws, regulations and police procedure.

The use of probation and promotion tests has been found to serve as an incentive for men to apply themselves to the task of learning the duties of their positions. In most departments, however, such tests are at present given much less consideration than they deserve.

Character Investigation

The Research Division of the United States Civil Service Commission is now making a study of character investigation methods. Results obtained by letters, vouchers and oral interviews are being compared and further analyzed with a view to developing the best practicable means of getting facts about each applicant's character. In the course of this study a new technique for interviewing has been developed.

The twenty-seven most important questions about an applicant are presented on a single sheet of paper. The possible answers to each of the essential questions used in interviewing are anticipated, and are printed under their respective questions on the interview form. (See Figure Two.) These answers

SECTIONS FROM
FORM FOR INVESTIGATING APPLICANTS FOR POSITION OF CLERK OR CARRIER IN POST OFFICES

....
(Name of applicant)

	First Inter-view	Second Inter-view	Third Inter-view
1. For how many years have you known him?			
2. When were you last in touch with him?			
3. How did you gain your knowledge of him? (a) through personal contact (b) through your friends (c) through his friends (d) through his enemies. If "(a)," ask "How well do you know him?" (1) only slightly (2) well (3) very well			
* * *			
5. If you have employed him, for how long, and how long ago?			
6. What is his attitude toward his work? (a) shows keen interest and wholehearted effort (b) shows interest and effort (x) is unconcerned, makes no voluntary effort.			
* * *			
7. Has he ever been discharged? (If "Yes," write "x," and ask "Why?").			
* * *			
9. Has he ever been accused of stealing? (If "Yes," write "x," and ask "What? When? By whom?" If he can not give details, ask 'R,' below).			

	First Inter-view	Second Inter-view	Third Inter-view
10. Might he take money from mails if he thought that no one would ever suspect him? (If "Yes," write "x," and ask "E," below).			
11. Has he ever been arrested? (If "Yes," write "x," and ask "For what offense? Where?" If he can not give details, ask "R," below).			
* * *			
13. Does he pay his debts to stores, landlord, friends, etc.? (a) always (b) good pay most of the time (x) will never pay if he can avoid it.			
* * *			
15. Is there any reason why he should not be employed in the post office? (If "Yes," write "x," and ask "E," below).			
* * *			
17. Is he related to you in any way? (If "Yes," write "x," and ask "How?").			
* * *			

(E) Can you give me any specific example or reason for your answer?
(R) Can you give me the name of anyone from whom I can secure more information regarding this point?

FIGURE 2

are coded: All information that is derogatory or that requires consideration for any other reason is coded x, y, or z; all information not derogatory and not requiring further consideration is coded a, b, or c. In most cases, the interviewer records merely a code letter, which fully conveys the information secured. Three interviews regarding one man are recorded in parallel columns on the same form, and thus all information secured in prior interviews is placed before the interviewer. There is no copying required, no time consumed in writing lengthy reports or in briefing reports and later interpreting the briefs.

Non-Political Police Appointments

In addition to providing means for selecting men of good character, capable of serving efficiently, there is a further step that is important if police selection is to be most effective.

To permit efficient police administration, the position of chief of police must be taken out of politics and this officer must be given an opportunity to select, promote, and discharge men on the basis of personnel records rather than as a result of political intervention. The best basis a chief of police can have for making appointments and removals is a scientifically organized system of selection and rating.

Psychological Methods in the Selection of Policemen in Europe

By Morris S. Viteles, Ph.D.

Assistant Professor of Psychology, University of Pennsylvania, Philadelphia, Pennsylvania

ALTHOUGH the United States is to be credited with the earliest experiment involving the use of psychological methods in the selection of policemen (7),[1] Europe, and more particularly Germany, has contributed most toward the comprehensive analysis of the mental qualifications necessary for police service and to the development of scientific techniques for determining whether applicants for the position of policeman possess such qualifications. The satisfactory use of a battery of tests for the selection of police officers for the criminal service in Stuttgart (4), in 1919, was followed by investigations in Munich, Berlin, Danzig, Austria, Russia, and so forth, leading to the establishment, in a number of the larger European cities, of centers at which applicants for police jobs are required to undergo psychological examination to determine their fitness for police work. It is not the purpose of this article to describe in detail the methods employed at these various centers. It is, however, proposed to outline the features which they have in common, and to refer in detail to the most extensive of these projects as a means of indicating the specific characteristics of the psychological approach in the selection of competent policemen and the progress which has been made in this direction in Europe.

In illustration of the specialized techniques, reference will be most frequently made to the methods employed in the selection of policemen in Berlin. These methods, devised by Schulte (6)

[1] Numbers in parentheses refer to the bibliography at the end of the article.

in coöperation with police officials in a series of investigations dating from 1922, were first employed in a testing center established under the immediate direction of the commanding officer of police in Berlin. In addition, they are at present being used in the examination of applicants for appointment to the police forces in a number of other German cities, as well as in cities outside of Germany.

The Analysis of Mental Qualifications for Police Service

The development of scientific methods by European psychologists for the selection of policemen has proceeded from an analysis of the specific traits necessary in performing police duties. So, for example, memory, judgment, complexity, analysis, presence of mind and moral judgment are assumed by Moll and Piorkowski (2) to be the most essential qualifications for police work, and tests for their measurement are provided. As the result of a more detailed and more comprehensive investigation, Schulte (6) extends as follows the number of "individual, temperamental and moral traits which are of prime importance in efficient service."

I. *Sensory Capacities*, including such specific qualities as visual discrimination, spatial perception, auditory discrimination, and so forth.

II. *Ideational Qualities*, including various types of attention, memory, and allied traits.

III. *Emotional Characteristics*, such as emotional sensitivity, emotional stability, self-confidence, reaction to monotony, and so forth.

IV. *Volitional Responses.* Under this heading are included reaction time, various types of motor activity, the capacity for carrying out complex motor reactions, courage, and so forth.

V. *Bodily Efficiency*, referring to the amount and the rate of energy discharge, endurance, and similar traits.

The Character of the Tests

The analysis of mental qualifications represents only a preliminary step in the development of scientific methods for the selection of competent policemen. The chief objective is that of supplying valid tests and other techniques for the objective measurements of these traits. The tendency in American investigations has been to use tests of a paper and pencil type, suitable for group administration, to predict success as a policeman. In general, these tests have been in the nature of tests of "general intelligence." As a matter of fact, in certain instances standard tests of general intelligence have been employed (1, 3, 7, 9). In other instances special items have been assembled into an examination in which performance has, however, been measured in terms of a single score without any attempt to arrive at an index of the applicant's memory, judgment, and so forth, as measured by the specific items included in this type of examination (8). In contrast, European investigators have emphasized the importance of measuring specialized traits, on the assumption that fitness for police work can only be predicted through a determination of the extent to which the applicant possesses each of the mental abilities and temperamental traits considered necessary to success as a policeman. They have been interested primarily in the profile of personality, in the depressions and the peaks of the pattern of a man's mental makeup, and not in a summa-

tion in which important, specialized defects and abilities are completely concealed.

As a result of this emphasis on specific traits the psychological examination of police applicants in Europe has tended to take the form of an individual examination, requiring in some instances as much as half a day, in the course of which the examiner has the opportunity not only of obtaining objective scores on standard tests, but of making detailed observations on the traits exhibited during such an examination.

So, for example, in Berlin, in an examination lasting about four hours, applicants, after filling in a personal data sheet, are required to take two series of tests. The first includes a number of tests of the pencil and paper type, given to forty or fifty applicants at one time, which make it possible to arrive at a preliminary classification on the basis of intellectual capacity. The second series includes a variety of individual, performance tests, designed to measure such highly specialized traits as reaction to fear, complexity of motor response, suggestibility, and so forth, of importance in general police service, and also those which are of particular significance in the more specialized services of traffic officer, river police service, police patrol operation, and so forth. A description of a few of these tests will serve to make clear the methods which are employed in the quest for efficient police officers.

The ability to reproduce visual images involving spatial relations, considered by Schulte (6) to be of extreme importance in police work, is measured by a test in which the following instructions are given:

It is reported that suspicious noises are coming from a house, the residents of which are away. The lay-out of the house is as follows. It is a long, narrow dwelling, the length stretching from north to south. On the northern, narrow side of the house a tradesmen's door leads directly into the kitchen, which stretches across the entire width of the house. Extending from the center of the kitchen wall is a long, narrow corridor leading to a reception room. On each side of the corridor are a small room and a large room, lying in the order given with respect to the kitchen. The main entrance to the house is by steps leading into the west side of the reception room. Leading from the south side of the reception room (on the west side of the house) is the music room; on the east side is the dining room. There is a glass door between the dining and the music rooms. On the south side of the dining room is an outside balcony.

This description is read once and the applicant is then required to draw a ground plan of the house. The sketch is scored for errors.

As a measure of his memory for places the applicant is handed a copy of the diagram shown in Figure One, and required, after viewing it for about three minutes, to reproduce it. The reproduction is scored for errors and omissions.

The ability to distinguish right from wrong is measured by tests of the Fernald type, in which subjects are required to rate in order of seriousness delinquencies as varied as the theft of a small sum of money from a mother's pocket book, for the purchase of chocolate, and forgery. Resourcefulness, ingenuity in difficult situations and allied traits are, according to those who designed the tests, measured by putting to the applicant such questions as the following:

In the course of a visit made with the purpose of arresting one of a band of criminals, you are knocked down and dragged into a cellar, where two thugs with drawn revolvers stand guard over you. You overhear them saying that the leader of the band is planning to cross the border

after a big haul, and that he is to be followed, within a few hours, by those who are guarding you. The guards are quite talkative, and willing to chat with you, but, at the same time, are very watchful. It is impossible to consider getting them druuk. What would you do to outwit them?

Other tests of the same type are provided for the measurement of temperamental traits, such as sense of humor, reaction to fear, courage, and so forth. Quantitative scoring methods are provided in the case of practically all of the tests. In addition, certain of the investigators, notably Schulte (6), emphasize the importance of qualitative observations made in the course of the examination. So, for example, in Berlin, a definite observation rating is assigned at the close of the testing period and this rating is employed, as well as the objective test scores, in determining suitability for employment.

VALIDATING THE TESTS

The validity of every test to be used in the selection of policemen, as in the case of every other occupation, must be established by a comparison of test results with performance in the occupation. Thus, a test designed to eliminate applicants unsuited for street car operation must be compared with accidents, or with some other criterion of satisfactory street car operation, in order to determine whether the test results can actually be used in predicting success or failure in this occupation. In the same way, tests for policemen cannot be said to be valid unless a positive relationship between test results and efficient service has been definitely shown to exist. In this respect the policeman selection tests which have been suggested for use and which are being employed in Europe cannot be said to be very satisfactory. So, for example, in the case of the Stuttgart tests the conclusion is drawn that the police administration in Stuttgart has succeeded, through the use of the tests, in selecting highly capable and efficient police officers (4). However, very necessary details concerning the criterion of efficiency with which the test results were compared are not given. Other important facts which must be considered in making a judgment on the scientific validity of the tests are also missing. Likewise, in the case of the tests employed by Schneickert (5), the description

FIGURE 1—DIAGRAM USED IN TESTING MEMORY FOR PLACES

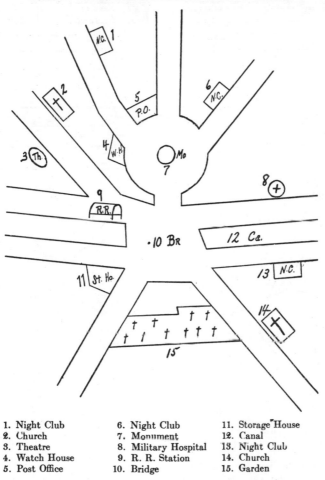

1. Night Club	6. Night Club	11. Storage House
2. Church	7. Monument	12. Canal
3. Theatre	8. Military Hospital	13. Night Club
4. Watch House	9. R. R. Station	14. Church
5. Post Office	10. Bridge	15. Garden

From R. W. Schulte, *Psychotechnik und Polizei.*

ever, very necessary details concerning the criterion of efficiency with which the test results were compared are not given. Other important facts which must be considered in making a judgment on the evaluation procedure is incomplete.

In a description of the Berlin tests recently published by Schulte (6), figures on a comparison of test results with performance on the job are given. The general character of the comparison is shown in Figure Two. In scription of the standards used in arriving at the performance rating in the station is given, although the nature of

FIGURE 2—COMPARISON OF TEST RESULTS AND PERFORMANCE RATINGS (Berlin)

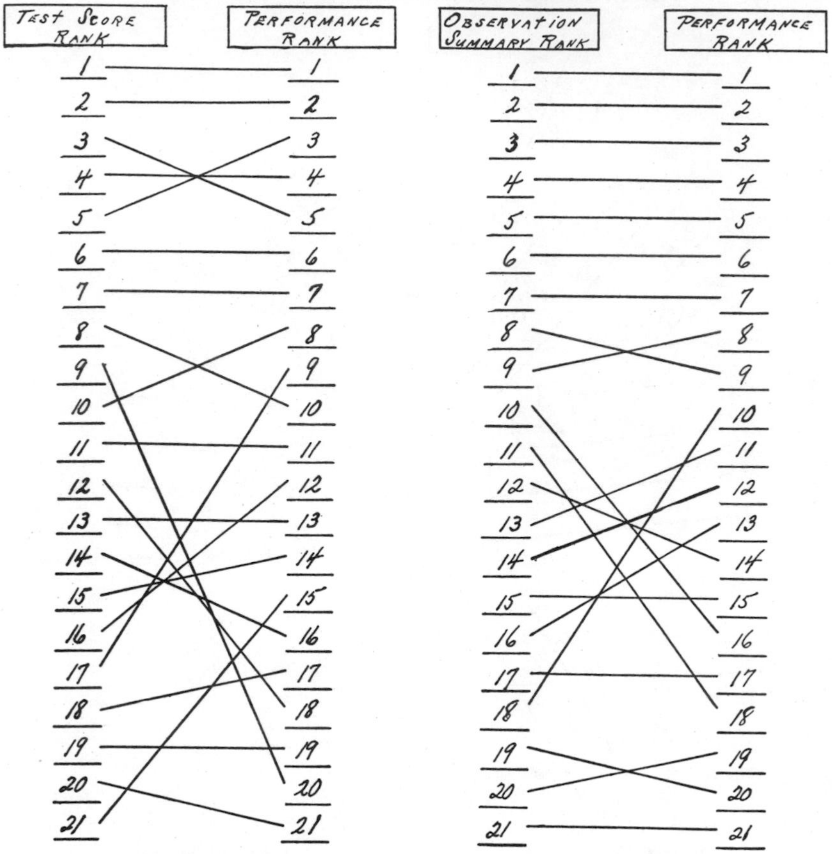

R= +0.81   R= +0.89

From R. W. Schulte, *Psychotechnik und Polizei*

this chart the vertical rows of figures indicate rank order ratings. The direction of the line indicates the extent of agreement in such ratings. The chart shows a very satisfactory agreement between rank order ratings made in the laboratory prior to employment and those made in the police stations after employment. No complete de-

it is perhaps illustrated in the sample case studies reported by the author, one of which is reproduced below.

POLICEMAN X

Laboratory Report: Exhibits sound, fast judgment. Very suitable from point of view of intelligence. Thoughtful, no signs of anxiety, sure, in general a sympathetic, unassuming, composed individual, with a point of view of his own.

Performance Report After Employment: Policeman X is a quiet, earnest officer with an unassuming disposition and a trustworthy, mellowed personality. He shows assurance in his work, which he handles thoughtfully and thoroughly. His deliberate, sympathetic manner is pleasing to his comrades, with whom he is very popular. Policeman X is a very satisfactory officer. The characteristics named above, as well as his skill in traffic are very useful in service on the street. The public gladly does as he desires.

However, the validation data presented by Schulte (6) in the case of the Berlin tests are also unsatisfactory in many respects. In the first place, an altogether inadequate number of cases is included in his report. In addition, the statistical methods he employs are of doubtful validity. Of perhaps greater importance is the failure to set up a standard, objective criterion or standard of accomplishment as a policeman with which to compare the test results.

In the opinion of the writer the development of such a criterion represents, at the present moment, the most important step to be taken in the development of objective and scientifically valid methods for the selection of policemen. New tests are certainly not needed. The reliability and validity of those which have already been prepared and are actually in use, as well as of other selection techniques, remain to be established. They cannot be established until police administrators, in coöperation with trained personnel investigators, have provided suitable standards by means of which the efficiency of police service can be measured. This involves a more thorough analysis of police training

school records, ratings by superior officers, of such objective data as number of observation reports, number of arrests, complaints by the public, and so forth, than has yet been made. Until it has been made, and a number of related problems resolved, final judgment on the suitability of selection tests now employed in Europe must be reserved. However, the progress which has been made in the use of objective selection methods in other occupations, and the wealth of material already available in the case of policemen, can awaken only a feeling of optimism with reference to the results which will follow from further work in the direction of providing objective techniques for the selection of competent policemen.

REFERENCES

(1) Martin, E. M., *New Methods of Selecting Policemen* Nat. Mun. Rev. 12: 671–81, 1923.

(2) Moll, A. and Piorkowski, C., *Psychotechnische Prüfung von Kriminalbeamten.* Prak. Psy. 1: 309–20, 1920.

(3) Ostrander, J., *Some Observations upon 150 Probationary Policemen of Detroit Police Department.* Ment. Hyg. 9: 60–74, 1925.

(4) Roemer, *Prüfung von Kriminalanwärten.* Z. ang. Psy. 18: 107–10, 1921.

(5) Schneickert, H., *Die psychotechnische Methode bei der Auswahl der Tüchtigsten, inbesondere im Kriminaldienste.* D. St. Z. 7–8: 221–25, 1920.

(6) Schulte, R. W., *Psychotechnik und Polizei.* Pp. 214. Oldenbourg: Gerhard Stalling, 1926.

(7) Terman, Lewis, *et al., A Trial of Mental and Pedagogical Tests in a Civil Service Examination for Policemen and Firemen.* J. App. Psy. 1, 1917.

(8) Telford, F. and Moss, F. A., *Suggested Tests for Patrolmen.* Pub. Pers. Stud. 2: 226–34, 1924.

(9) Thurstone, L. L., *The Intelligence of Policemen.* J. Pers. Res. 1: 64–74, 1922.

(10) Thurstone, L. L., *The Civil Service Test for Patrolmen in Philadelphia.* Pub. Pers. Stud. 2: 1–5, 1924.

Police Training

By Cornelius F. Cahalane
Police Consultant, New York City

A CENTURY ago, in a campaign to reorganize the London Metropolitan Police, Sir Robert Peel laid great stress upon the necessity of police training. He recognized the need of establishing, so far as possible, definite procedures in police work. He contended that a police force working in a haphazard manner, each man having no definite purpose, meant chaos, and as a result of his contention some system of police training has been established in most police departments.

POLICE DUTIES

No public servant is more dependent upon his own initiative than the policeman on patrol. In every other branch of public service a new man can either be assigned to an unimportant duty or to one in which he can be readily checked, so that if he makes a mistake it will be of slight importance; or, as in the fire department, he is almost constantly supervised and placed under the immediate control of a superior officer. When a policeman leaves the station house on his first tour of patrol duty, no one, regardless of his police experience, can foresee the intricate and exacting problems that are likely to confront him. To the average citizen he is a policeman, vested with authority and responsiblity to preserve the peace, enforce the law, protect life and property, prevent and detect crime, and arrest violators of the law. On his first tour, full duty is expected of him by the public. They consider it a lame excuse for him or for his superiors to claim that he failed because he was untrained or inexperienced.

On his first tour he may be called on to handle a serious accident wherein several persons are injured and he is required to extricate them, summon medical and police assistance, arrest the person or persons criminally responsible, procure witnesses and, like a revolving camera, take a mental photograph of the scene, assist the injured, render first aid, get the data for his report and keep traffic moving. All of this is no mean job. He may have to cope with a holdup or the commission of some other serious crime when he will have to bring into play his power of observation, his knowledge of human nature and all of his native cunning. On that same tour the policeman may be called upon to make an arrest or serve a legal paper, over which the Appellate Court may possibly have to spend hours to determine whether he did, or did not, take the proper action.

Police work has been revolutionized in the last few decades. The motor vehicle, in addition to increasing the policeman's duty on the street in directing traffic and safeguarding the life and limb of the motorist and the pedestrian, has also opened up every city and town to the law violator, has greatly increased his opportunity of getting to and from the scene of a crime and has lessened the chances of his detection. While scientific discoveries and inventions have been helpful to other departments in carrying out their functions, the improved means of transportation and communication have been in many instances a hindrance to the police in the exercise of their functions.

MEETING THE NEED FOR TRAINING

How to meet the need of training policemen, particularly those of a small force, has been for years a perplexing problem to persons responsible for the administration of police service in cities and towns throughout the country. Much has been written on the need of training. Police officials have recognized the need, but they have been helpless in establishing any systematic method. Text books have been written on this important subject but it has been difficult to get them into the hands of the average policeman.

In many of the larger departments, police training schools are maintained where the recruit is given some training before going on duty. In many of the smaller departments, the chief or some other official may be interested and does his best to give the new man some instructions in his duties while in many departments a policeman is appointed, uniformed and equipped with a baton and a revolver and sent out on duty, told to watch the older men, use good judgment, obey the Ten Commandments, not be too officious and never look for trouble, all of which is excellent advice if it can be applied in a crisis.

When such a man is confronted with a problem he is generally alone, with no one to advise or assist him. In most instances he must act quickly and must depend entirely upon his horse sense. Sometimes, he is right. Very often he is wrong and is censured for a failure for which he is not directly responsible, as he has had no way of learning what action to take under a given set of circumstances. From his experience and contact with other policemen and from appearances in court, he learns a part of his duty, but often he has passed many years in police service before experience ripens him.

In some instances a man is sent from a small city to a larger city which maintains a police training school, where he is supposed to observe the methods of training in order to install the system and teach his own force. In most of such instances, if he obtains any knowledge, he keeps it to himself and uses it to secure promotion or preferment rather than to arm a possible competitor within his own department. Men so selected are usually holding details and special assignments and are not particularly interested in the ordinary tasks of the man on patrol duty.

THE ZONE SYSTEM OF NEW YORK STATE

For years the New York State Conference of Mayors and the New York State Police Chief's Association have recognized the need of systematic training for their policemen. A committee from each organization was appointed to discuss this need and to formulate a plan. It was agreed that, at the time, it would be impossible to get support from the legislature and the city officials to establish one or several police schools where the new policemen could attend before being assigned to patrol duty, and that an effort to get the older men to attend would result in serious objections from them. The committee tried to devise a plan whereby the younger policemen of the State would be given an opportunity to attend a police school. They wanted to bring the school to the policeman and to make the instruction practical and interesting. No subject would be taught in the school during the first season unless it was one that would be likely to be useful to the average policeman the first five minutes he was on patrol. The committee unanimously agreed that police problems were similar in every city and town; that if a policeman was efficient in one town he likewise would be efficient in another as soon as he became familiar with the local situation; that there was very little difference in the methods of the law violator; that the same crime preventive methods could be made effective in every community; that the same procedure was required to catch the perpetrator and practically the same type of evidence to convict him; and, that the respectable element of every community wanted the best possible kind of police service. They further agreed that a state-wide plan of instruction, regardless of size of population or class of industry, would contribute toward uniform methods of police procedure throughout the State. With these fundamentals as a basis, a comprehensive plan was prepared, in substance as follows:

The state was divided into eleven zones, each zone embracing about twelve departments, each having a force of from four hundred to six hundred men. The chiefs of police of each zone held a conference and agreed upon a central city or town where classes were to be held. They also selected the instructors from within the forces of the zone. A syllabus was prepared containing ten subjects, namely: Fire and Accidents, Patrol Duty, Street Conditions, Traffic, Methods of Thieves, Homicide, Larceny, Court Procedure, Law and Procedure of Arrest and Summonses, and Investigations. The instructors were then brought to a central point and thoroughly drilled in the syllabus and the ordinary rules of pedagogy; they then returned to their respective zone centers. A schedule was prepared requiring each lecture to be delivered at three sessions to be held at ten A.M. on Monday, seven thirty P.M. on Wednesday, and four P.M. on Friday. In this way it was found that the men could attend one of the three weekly sessions without depleting the patrol force at any one time and it did not work a

hardship on the men by requiring them to attend all the sessions on their off time. A period of ten weeks was required to complete the course. The committee was particularly anxious to have the younger men attend and on an average force, with a total of twenty men, the official would have about twelve men whom he was desirous of having attend the school. The men were grouped in three squads and each squad attended one session each week, the session selected being the one most convenient to the men and the department.

Each zone committee also supplemented the zone instructors by invited officials whose duties brought them in direct contact with the police, such as court officials, district attorneys, coroners, and fire and health department officials, who lectured on such subjects as the coöperation and the relationship of the police with their departments.

It was the hope of the committee that outside of the New York City and the New York State Police, possibly one thousand men might attend. They were agreeably surprised to find that thirty-four hundred men of all ranks attended. The sacrifices made and the intense interest shown by these men confirmed their belief that the great majority of policemen are very anxious to embrace any reasonable opportunity that is offered, to fit themselves to render efficient service. This zone system, as explained, is not, of course, the best possible system, but it has gone farther than any other system yet devised in our country.

Many commissions, organizations and persons have petitioned the State Legislature, and laws have been drafted creating standards for appointments and promotions in police departments, even going so far as to entrust the supervision of such standards to the State Board of Education. This, of course, would be a simple method of getting rid of the problem temporarily. No thought or consideration has been given to means of establishing schools where municipalities might send their new appointees for a course of instruction. Persons who have given police training serious thought are of the opinion that the time has arrived when it is necessary for the State to establish recruit training schools where departments which do not, or cannot, maintain efficient training schools would be required to send their new recruits for a course of training, the expense to be borne by the municipality. There is no doubt that the municipality would be reimbursed a hundredfold by the increased efficiency of a man who has received such training. It might be contended that under our present political system this would not work, but it should be remembered that the local appointing power would still retain its control over appointments. A town has, let us say, ten men and intends to increase its force by one man to be ready for patrol on August 1. Appoint him on July 1 and send him to school for one month. The cost might be $500, including his salary and board. The schools could be placed under a State Board, which would supervise the syllabus and curriculum, and which might select instructors from among policemen throughout the State, who are in sympathy with the plan and whose adaptability fits them for the work of teaching.

The Police Training School

By GEORGE T. RAGSDALE

Director, Police School, Louisville, Kentucky

IN securing material for this article, the author sent a questionnaire to ninety-four cities having a population of one hundred thousand inhabitants or over. This was done in order to ascertain the approximate extent to which these cities possessed training schools for police. Forty-seven cities responded and thirty-one of these reported schools. The examination of the curriculum and the methods of these thirty-one schools warrants the statement that only sixteen can be regarded as real schools by any reasonable standard of judgment.

These schools have made their appearance chiefly during the last ten years, although some of them have been in existence for several decades. As a rule they have owed their existence to some zealous chief of police who recognized the need for organized training.

At the present time the usual method in establishing a school is to send some officer to a recognized police school, in New York or Detroit, for instance, and have him follow the lines of organization and methods learned in the school attended. Some cities have sought outside aid in solving their training problems; others have blazed their own trail.

THE NEW YORK POLICE ACADEMY

The Police Academy of New York City has the most elaborate organization of any police school in this country. It has eight departments: recruits, horsemanship, traffic, safety, special service, criminal identification, detectives, officer training and instructor training.

Recruits.—In this department four courses of instruction are given. Course One includes discipline, deportment, civics, rules and regulations, elements in classification of crime, *modus operandi* of criminals, ordinances, code of criminal procedure, arrest, summonses, court procedure and evidence, assemblages, parades and strikes, fires, accidents, patrol, coöperation with the Federal government, reports, forms and records. One hundred and forty-eight hours of instruction are devoted to this course.

Course Two is devoted to physical instruction and consists of setting-up exercises, work on all kinds of gymnasium apparatus, jumping, swimming, military drill, boxing, struggling exercises and games. One hundred and thirty hours are devoted to this course.

Course Three is a course in firearms, including the care and the use of weapons, aiming, firing and shooting for record. To this course six hours of instruction and practice are devoted.

Course Four is devoted to first-aid and personal hygiene. Ten hours are given in hygiene and sanitation, anatomy, first-aid and personal hygiene.

Horsemanship.—This department teaches the recruit the grooming, the exercise, and the care of horses, drill practice, clearing of obstacles and mounted target practice. Six days are required to complete this course.

Traffic and Safety.—Members of the uniformed forces who are assigned to this course must be at least five feet and eleven inches in height and must have had six months of experience in police work. For a period of fourteen days these men are instructed in the

170

following subjects: street congestion, deportment, traffic regulations, statistics, analysis of traffic accidents, systems for preventing accidents, and public education in safety measures.

Special Service.—In this department, three courses are given for as many types of service. One course is devised for policewomen and contains lectures on discipline, deportment, civics, observation, rules and regulations, juvenile and delinquent cases, crime, arrest, evidence, laws relating to amusement places, playgrounds, medical practitioners, dance halls, fortune tellers, schools and playgrounds, missing persons and unidentified dead, runaways, abandoned children, parents of wayward and disorderly children, health ordinances and patrol.

Another course is provided for the police clerk. Stenography, typing, grammar, communications, filing, penmanship and the care of typewriters, are the subjects treated in this course in an attempt to establish a standard of efficiency to be required of each clerk.

The course in motor transportation includes a study of the internal combustion engine and other parts of police transportation equipment. Training in the driving of all kinds of vehicles is also given and the student is taught the rules of the shop and the rules of the road.

Criminal Identification.—This department presents two courses. One of these covers the theoretical aspects of the work and calls for seventy-eight hours of instruction during a session lasting two weeks. The other course is practical in nature and is conducted at the Criminal Identification Bureau, for seventy-eight hours, covering a period of two weeks.

Detectives.—The department of detectives admits to its course any member of the police force who has had not less than one year and not more than ten years of experience in uniform and whose record justifies an assignment to the detective department. The four courses given require sixty days for their completion.

Course One includes instruction in the following subjects: organization of the detective department, rules and regulations, observation, reports, records, systems of criminal identification, descriptions, courts and their procedure, evidence, criminology, criminal methods, and criminal pathological psychology. This course requires one hundred and fifty-one hours of classroom work.

Course Two consists of physical instruction for one hour a day, mainly in calisthenics and drill.

Course Three is devoted to firearms and covers the same ground as that given to the recruits.

Course Four consists of field work done in the bureaus to which the members are assigned, and under the supervision of their commanding officer. Eighty-four hours are required for this work.

Officer Training.—This department gives courses in leadership, morale, current police problems, military drill, physical training, pistol practice and practical field work in the nature of surveys of police conditions.

Instructor Training.—This department aims to develop instructors by giving to properly qualified men courses in teaching methods, supplemented by attendance in a class in the School of Education of the College of the City of New York, where teaching methods are specially emphasized. So far as methods of instruction are concerned, lectures and demonstrations are used, as well as quizzes and discussions. At the close of each week the material covered is reviewed and an examination is given. A final examination is held during the closing week.

The Academy is in charge of an inspector, who is assisted by five lieutenants, nine sergeants and five patrolmen. The school is housed in a separate building fully adequate for its needs. It is equipped with every facility to make the teaching effective and interesting to both faculty and students.

THE POLICE SCHOOL, LOUISVILLE, KENTUCKY

The Police School of Louisville, Kentucky, was organized in 1919, and has since that time passed through several stages of growth. To begin with, members were called together while off active duty for attendance on lectures given by men outside the department who knew little about policing. The next step was to make all recruits attend three hours of school per day for a period of four weeks while they performed regular duty during the remaining seven hours each day. Then came the establishing of a full time school for six weeks, designed for recruits. An important division was next added for men in uniform who are required to attend school one hour a week for forty weeks a year. Still later, one division was added for the detective department and one for policewomen. The sixth division, recently ordered established by the chief of police, is for officers and others who want to know more about advanced police work or who are studying for promotion.

Recruits.—The division for recruits gives a number of courses, requiring for their completion a minimum of six weeks, seven days each, each class running from eight o'clock A.M. to six o'clock P.M. One and a half hours are taken for lunch and two hours of homework are required daily.

Course One. LAW.—As an introduction to this course, a general study is made of the legislative, judicial and executive branches of the city, county, state, and national governments. The Bill of Rights, the common law, Federal and state criminal statutes, city ordinances, evidence and court procedure, are studied. The work requires one hundred hours for its completion.

Course Two. GEOGRAPHY.—The history and the topography of Louisville introduce the student to this course. Each participant must draw a map of the city, showing its boundaries, districts and beats. Upon this map he must locate all station houses, posts, public buildings, hospitals, and so forth. A map of all street car lines is also drawn and the institutions near each line located. This map must also show the county roads. Thirty-six hours are required for this work.

Course Three. RECORDS AND REPORTS.—In this course all records are explained and each recruit taught to use every form required for the making of reports in the police system. Penmanship and spelling are stressed and drill is required in sentence construction and police terminology. Thirty-hours are spent on this work.

Course Four. ORGANIZATION AND DUTIES, RULES AND REGULATIONS.—This course includes a study of the duties of all officials connected with the police department, from the mayor to the corporal, and the general rules and regulations of the department. Twenty hours.

Course Five. TRAFFIC.—This course studies the traffic statutes and ordinances, traffic problems and signal systems. Each student is drilled in the handling of traffic at intersections and in congested areas.

Course Six. FIRST-AID AND RESCUE WORK.—The foundation of this course is laid by lectures on anatomy by a physician. The first-aid work is taught by a nurse and the rescue work

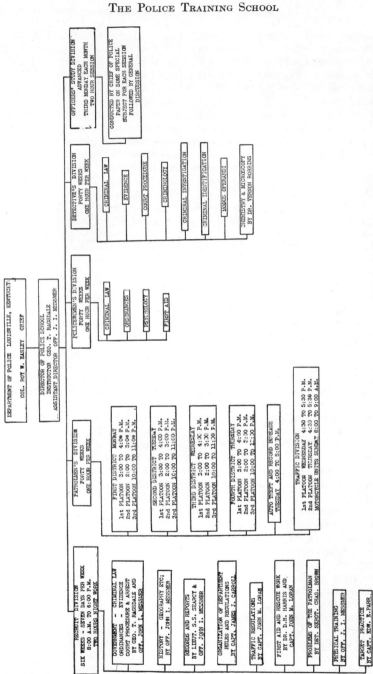

ORGANIZATION CHART OF THE LOUISVILLE, KENTUCKY, POLICE SCHOOL (Prepared by Officer J. I. Messmer)

by the captain of the first-aid squad. Each student is drilled in the Schaeffer method of resuscitation and in the use of the inhalator. Eighteen hours are devoted to the lectures and the drills.

Course Seven. The Problems of the Patrolman.—This course is given by an officer who has had experience in every line of police work. Its purpose is to give the recruit a practical knowledge of the right thing to do in every conceivable situation which may confront him on his beat. Thirty hours.

Course Eight. Investigation, Identification Systems, and so forth.— This course aims to give the recruit a general knowledge of these subjects so that he will know when to call for expert assistance and how to give such aid as his knowledge and limited experience may warrant. About twenty hours are given to this course.

Course Nine. Physical Culture. —This course is intended to put the recruit in the best physical condition possible. The work includes calisthenics, running, boxing, wrestling, swimming, drill and jiu-jitsu. The work is given twice per day, excepting Sunday, in the middle of the morning and the afternoon sessions. One hundred and eight hours are required of each student.

Course Ten. Firearms.—General experience is given in the construction and the use of firearms, and each student is required to spend eighteen hours at the target range in practice. There are thirty-six instruction and practice periods in this course.

Many other subjects, such as police morale, have not been included in the above summary; they require from one to four hours of instruction each and are sandwiched in at convenient times. The entire course for recruits is rarely finished in six weeks; sometimes it runs into eight weeks.

Textbooks are followed in a general way by the instructors in their lectures. Practical demonstrations are employed and the instructor illustrates his talks from his own experience. The blackboard is always used. The recruits are required to take notes on yellow paper and each night they must rewrite their notes on white lined paper. These notes are placed in a permanent book after they have been corrected by the instructor. Into this book all maps, charts and forms are also bound, making it into a manual for the recruit. With the exception of the director of the school all the instructors are members of the department, experienced in their work and possessed of personalities which command the respect of the recruit.

Patrolmen.—This division is a continuation school which constantly reviews the material presented in the police school curriculum and studies current problems and methods. Every member of the department is required to attend. The classes are conducted at the station houses and continue for forty weeks each year, one hour a week.

Policewomen.—Attendance in this division is required one hour a week for forty weeks. The following subjects are taught: criminal law, social service, psychology, problems of women and children, methods of investigation, coöperation with the juvenile court, court procedure, arrest and health ordinances.

Detectives —The members of the detective force must attend the course given in this division, one hour a week for forty weeks. Criminal law, criminal investigation, systems of identification, evidence, court procedure, criminal psychology, and so forth, are the subjects taught.

Officers' Study.—This division is planned for the purpose of assisting officers, patrolmen who are regarded as worthy of promotion, and all other

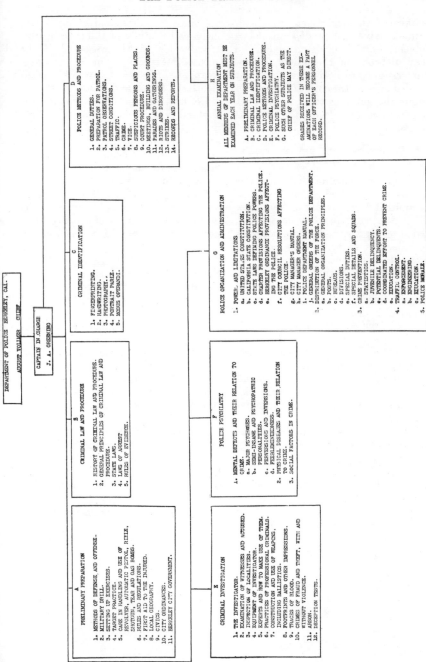

ORGANIZATION CHART OF THE BERKELEY, CALIFORNIA, POLICE TRAINING SCHOOL

members of the department who wish to make advanced studies in police problems not thoroughly treated in the other divisions of the school. Two-hour sessions are held once a month, presided over by the chief of police who assigns the subjects to be treated at each session and leads the general discussion.

THE POLICE SCHOOL OF BERKELEY, CALIFORNIA

The Police School of Berkeley owes its existence to Chief August Vollmer. It is quite different from the New York Police Academy, in that its work is carried on for a period of two years on the officers' own time, after hours of duty. The sessions are two hours in length and are held three times a week, a total of three hundred and twelve hours of work. The school gives seven courses of instruction for its recruits.

Course One consists of physical culture, military drill, use of firearms, rules and regulations, ordinances, first-aid, geography and civics.

Course Two is devoted to criminal law and procedure and covers the history and the principles of the criminal law, statutes and evidence.

Course Three on criminal identification includes fingerprints, handwriting, photography, *modus operandi* and the *portrait parlé*.

Course Four is devoted to police methods and procedure and aims to acquaint the recruit with every problem which he will meet on his beat.

Course Five, criminal investigation, includes the study of the investigator, examination of witnesses and of the accused, experts, criminal practice, weapons, ballistics, footprints, deception tests, fraud, and so forth.

Course Six, police psychiatry, is devoted to the study of mental defects in their relation to crime, semi-insane and psychopathic personalities, perversion and inverson, feeble-mindedness, physical diseases and crime, and social factors in crime.

Course Seven, police organization and administration. This course is introduced by a study of constitutional and statutory provisions relating to police work. It includes the study of the police manual, the general orders of the department, the organization of the department, the function of the jury, statistics, traffic problems and morale.

The instructors are selected from the members of the department and from the faculty of the University of California. The lecture method is used and at the conclusion of each course examinations are conducted and the grades entered on the recruit's personnel card.

For members of the force who are not recruits, an annual examination is held covering the course provided for recruits and such other subjects as the chief of police may designate. The grades secured in this examination are recorded on the personnel cards of those examined.

The English Police System

By A. L. DIXON, C.B., C.B.E.

Assistant Secretary at the Home Office, London, England

THE primary purpose of this article is to give an account of the system of selection and training of police personnel in the police forces of England and Wales, as part of a conspectus of police organisation and method in the investigation of crime which it is the object of this volume of the ANNALS to present. Undoubtedly, the method of selection and training of police personnel has an important bearing on the efficiency of the efforts of the police in crime detection, but so have many other features of the system to which the police belong, and if any valid conclusions are to be drawn from English police experience the main features of the English system of police must be kept in view. For this reason, as well as for the better understanding of the matters dealt with later in this article, it seems desirable first of all to give some brief description of the English [1] police system as a whole, its blending of local organisation and central supervision, the conditions of service (as respects pay, pensions and so forth) under which the police carry on their work, and the relationships of the police forces with one another and with the public at large.

HISTORICAL GROWTH AND ORGANIZATION

In the first place, it is essential to bear in mind that the English police system is not an institution of recent manufacture but a growth of centuries, traceable back without any real break to Anglo-Saxon times, when the responsibility for arresting felons and preserving the peace rested, not merely in theory but in actual practice, with the general body of freemen in each township or parish. The constable was of Norman introduction but he absorbed or became identified with the Anglo-Saxon tithingman, who was a sort of village peaceman, and he gradually developed into the local officer responsible in practice for the maintenance of law and order, notwithstanding that the office was unpaid and was filled, or supposed to be filled, by the parishioners in rotation. Alongside the constable there developed the office of the Justice of the Peace, who was during the first part of his history merely a superior form of constable but later became a magistrate as well as a police officer, until, in the nineteenth century, the County Justices developed into the police authority responsible for the control of a paid police force in every county,[2] while many boroughs, including all the larger ones, had organized paid police forces, separate from the county forces, controlled by the local authorities mainly through committees of the Town Councils, called the Watch Committees. It is unnecessary to dwell on the process of development, which will be found

---

[1] The police system in Scotland is in all essentials similar to that in England and Wales except that in Scotland the Secretary of State for Scotland takes the place of the Secretary of State for the Home Department, and there is no force in a position corresponding to that occupied by the Metropolitan Police in England.

[2] Since 1888, the county police authority has been a special *ad hoc* Committee, constituted from representatives of the County Justices and the County Council, in equal numbers.

set out elsewhere;[3] all that can be done is to give a brief description of the system as it exists today.

The English police system is essentially local in character, that is to say, it consists, not of a single police force with nation-wide jurisdiction, but of a number—actually one hundred and eighty-one—of separate police forces with separate territorial jurisdictions, separate police authorities, separate disciplinary powers and, as a rule, separate arrangements for the recruiting and training of personnel. In the fact that it consists of a number of separate police units, the English system has thus some resemblance to the police system in the United States of America, apart from the State police forces, but in other respects it is markedly different, more particularly in the fact that the separate police forces in England and Wales are closely linked together by various statutory provisions and regulations which bind all alike and have no counterpart in the American system. They are, moreover, subject to the supervision of the Central Government, which is exercised through the Home Office, the Secretary of State for the Home Department (commonly called, for short, the Home Secretary) being himself the police authority for the Metropolitan Police and exercising wide supervisory powers over all the local police forces in England and Wales. There are, besides, other agencies, such as a system of periodical Conferences between Chief Officers of Police, centred on the Home Office, which contribute to this linkage between all the separate forces. Taken together, these forces cover the whole

[3] See, for example, *A History of Police in England*, by W. L. Melville Lee, published by Methuen, 1901. *Scotland Yard and the Metropolitan Police*, by J. F. Moylan, C.B., C.B.E., published by Messrs. G. P. Putnam's Sons, Ltd., 1929.

country and leave no gaps, nor any sort of limbo or No Man's Land, outside their jurisdiction, but form a complete, linked and coördinated system for the preservation of order and the prevention and detection of crime. Finally, it may be mentioned that the members of the lower ranks in all forces have a common representative body, known as the Police Federation, established under Act of Parliament in 1919, which is further referred to below. The police system of England and Wales, therefore, though consisting of one hundred and eighty-one separate police forces, is in a real sense a system with a coördinated organisation and some, at any rate, of the characteristics and common features which would be found if the police throughout the country were under a single central control.

THE METROPOLITAN POLICE

Among the one hundred and eighty-one separate police forces, the Metropolitan Police Force holds a distinctive position for several reasons. It is by far the largest force, numbering about twenty thousand men (including some six hundred men who are employed outside the Metropolitan Police District policing dockyards or other Government establishments) and thus comprises over one third of the total police strength of England and Wales. Its jurisdiction extends over the whole of Greater London, comprising an area roughly thirty miles in diameter, with a population of about seven and a half million, but excluding the ancient City of London, with an area of approximately one square mile, which has a separate force of its own. The force, moreover, is unique in the fact, already alluded to, that the police authority, ultimately responsible for the control of the force and for all decisions as to its strength and for all expenditure, is not, as in the case of all other forces, any local authority, but the Home Secretary himself. The executive head of the Metropolitan Police is the Commissioner of Police of the Metropolis, to give him his full title. He is responsible for the executive direction of the force, for all appointments and promotions and for discipline. The Headquarters Office of the Metropolitan Police, as everyone knows, is at New Scotland Yard. It seems often to be supposed that Scotland Yard is the headquarters of a national detective service employed in unravelling mysteries and outwitting crooks throughout the country; but that is not the

OTHER POLICE FORCES

Outside Greater London there is in every county a police force which exercises jurisdiction over the whole of the county except in those boroughs, if any, which have separate police forces of their own. In England and Wales there are fifty-eight county forces and one hundred and twenty-one borough forces.[4] The forces vary very much in size, the authorised establishments ranging from over two thousand downwards, the smallest force having a total strength of only ten, all ranks. The general distribution is indicated by the following figures:

Strength of Force	Number of Forces		
	County	Borough	Total
1,000 and upwards............................	4	3	7
500–1,000....................................	5	3	8
250–500.....................................	18	10	28
100–250.....................................	15	36	51
50–100......................................	9	36	45
Under 50....................................	7	33	40
Total.....................................	58	121	179

case. The Scotland Yard detectives normally deal only with cases arising within the jurisdiction of the Metropolitan Police Force, and it is only in a few special cases, generally cases of murder, that they take charge of a difficult investigation elsewhere at the request of the Chief Officer of Police within whose jurisdiction the crime has taken place.

THE CITY OF LONDON POLICE

The City of London Police Force, which, as already mentioned, is quite separate from the Metropolitan Police, has a strength of about eleven hundred men under the direction of a Commissioner—the Commissioner of the City of London Police.

It will be seen that there are nearly one hundred forces with a strength of under one hundred men, and the existence of so large a number of comparatively small forces is undoubtedly a source of weakness in the system, however efficient in themselves such individual forces may be.

In the following table will be found some figures for a few typical forces and for the forces as a whole, showing the relations between the police strengths and the populations of the

[4] There are 58 police forces in Scotland, with a total strength of 6,607, more than one third of this number (2,284) belonging to the Glasgow City Police Force. Of these 58 forces, 45 have a total strength under 100 and 35 a strength under 50.

police districts over which the forces exercise jurisdiction, and the expenditure on the police:

normal maximum of the scale for constables is accordingly 95/- weekly. The sergeant's scale starts at £5 weekly

Police Force	Population of Police District (1921 Census)	Total Authorised Strength * (Sept. 1928)	Average Daily Strength (1927–28)	Population per Constable	Net Annual Expenditure ‡ (1926–27)
Metropolitan.............	7,466,492	19,379	19,234	385	£6,976,807
City of London...........	13,709†	1,162	1,110	†	428,922
Three County Forces—					
Lancashire.............	1,631,546	2,014	2,001	810	789,893
Kent.................	623,192	621	621	1,004	216,375
Northumberland	407,317	325	324	1,253	115,291
All County Forces........	17,296,029	18,156	17,694	953	6,426,711
Five Borough Forces—					
Liverpool.............	805,046	1,725	1,722	467	633,491
Manchester...........	730,307	1,395	1,389	524	437,073
Leeds.................	463,122	694	663	667	238,976
Brighton.............	147,373	213	205	692	74,980
York.................	84,039	102	102	824	36,213
All Borough Forces.......	13,108,720	18,739	18,044	700	6,251,162
Total (All Forces)	37,884,950	57,436	56,082	660	£20,083,602

* These figures represent the numbers authorised for regular police duty in the police district, excluding "additional" constables recruited for the protection of particular properties or for fire duty, etc.

† The figures in the second column represent the census or resident population.   In the case of the City of London, the resident population is so small and the day population so large that it is impossible to give comparable figures under the head "population per constable."

‡ 1926–27 is the latest financial year for which full audited figures are available.

POLICE SALARIES

The main conditions of service of all these forces are in substance the same and most are laid down by Act of Parliament or by regulations made by the Secretary of State which are binding on all police authorities.   Under the present regulations, the lower ranks (constable and sergeant) in all forces have the same scales of pay.   The constable's pay on appointment is £3.10.0d weekly, rising by annual increments of 2/- weekly to £4.10.0d weekly after 10 years' service; and by continued good conduct and efficiency a constable can thereafter qualify for additional increments of 2/6d weekly after 17 and 22 years' service respectively.   The

and rises by annual increments of 2/6d weekly to £5.12.6d after 5 years' service in the rank.   As respects this fundamental condition of service, the lower ranks in all forces are thus on exactly the same footing whatever the force or locality in which they serve, whether in London, in a provincial city or town, or on a rural beat in any county force.

The scales of pay for the higher ranks, Inspector, Superintendent and Chief Constable—with intermediate ranks in some of the larger forces—are subject to the Secretary of State's approval and are graded according to the work and responsibilities of the rank in the particular force concerned, the Metropolitan scale being, of course, the highest for all corresponding ranks. In this force the Inspector's scale is £325 rising to £375 per annum in five years and the Superintendent's £550 rising to £700 per annum in six years. In other forces the Superintendent's pay ranges in most cases between £400 and £500 per annum. The scales of pay for the Chief Officers in County and Borough Forces range from about £400 per annum in the smallest forces up to a maximum of £2,000 in the two largest provincial forces, Lancashire County and Liverpool. All ranks are provided with quarters or a house rent-free, or an allowance in lieu. Generally speaking, the men in county forces occupy quarters or houses owned or rented by the police authority, while in borough forces the single men and some officers are provided with quarters, and most of the married men find their own houses and draw the allowance. The Commissioner of Metropolitan Police receives a salary of £3,000 per annum, without rent allowance.

PENSIONS

Another fundamental condition of service, superannuation, is regulated by a general statute. The Police Pensions Act, 1921 (11 & 12 Geo. V, Ch. 31), introduced a standard scale of pensions applicable to men in all forces who have joined the service since July 1, 1919. Prior to that date the pension scales were fixed by the local police authorities at their discretion within limits laid down by an earlier statute, and the men whose scales under that Act were more favourable than the standard scale introduced in 1921 for new entrants were given the option of retaining the scale under which they previously served. Under the present standard scale a member of any force is entitled to retire after twenty-five years' service with a pension at the rate of half pay, and after thirty years' service with a pension at the rate of two thirds of his pay. In addition, men who are incapacitated by illness or injury are entitled to pensions on various scales according to the circumstances of their case, such as the degree of incapacity, whether the injury was accidental or non-accidental and whether it was received in the execution of duty or otherwise, the pensions applicable to cases where men are incapacitated by injury received in the execution of their duty being particularly generous.

CENTRAL CONTROL

Reference has been made to the element of central control exercised over all forces by the Home Office, mainly in matters of conditions of service through the medium of the Police Regulations, and so forth. In addition, every force —excepting the Metropolitan Police, which, as already mentioned, is under direct Home Office control—is inspected annually on behalf of the Home Office by an Inspector of Constabulary, of whom there are three, appointed by the Crown on the recommendation of the Home Secretary. They visit every force at least once in each year and report to the Home Office, and in this and other ways form a most important link between the several forces and that Department.

Another important feature of the system is the financial control exercised by the Home Office under the conditions which regulate the contribution from the national Exchequer towards the expenditure of the local forces. Under the present arrangements, half the cost of all police forces is borne by local funds and half by Government subventions which are based on the net expenditure of the force as approved for the purpose by the Home Office. This is not the place for any detailed discussion of the proper scope of a central supervisory authority in a local police system;[5] it is sufficient here to say that the object has been, and under present policy still is, to secure and maintain close unification of the conditions of service in the several police forces, to exercise sufficiently close supervision of the work, equipment, buildings, and so forth, of all forces to ensure a proper standard of efficiency and prevent wasteful expenditure, but, subject to these considerations, to leave full scope to the local authorities for the exercise of their discretion in matters of local import, e.g. as to appointments, promotions, discipline and administration generally, and to interfere as little as possible with local executive action in the prevention and detection of crime and other day to day work of the police.

THE POLICE FEDERATION

It may be interesting to add a few words as to the Police Federation, which has already been mentioned and has no counterpart in the police system of the United States. The Police Federation is a national representative body for the lower ranks of the police, established under the authority of section 1 of the Police Act, 1919,

for the purpose of enabling members of the police forces in England and Wales to consider and to bring to the notice of the police authorities and the Secretary of State all matters affecting their welfare and efficiency, other than questions of discipline and promotion affecting individuals.

Under this Act the members of all forces, Metropolitan, County and Borough, below the rank of Superintendent, are members of the Police Federation

[5] The subject is briefly discussed by the author in the course of a Memorandum prepared for the Royal Commission on Local Government: see Volume II of the evidence, published by H. M. Stationery Office.

by virtue of their office. In every force there is a local representative body, called the Branch Board, for each of the three ranks, Inspector, Sergeant and Constable. Central Conferences attended by delegates from each force are held annually in London and appoint a Central Committee, consisting of six men—two from the Metropolitan and City of London forces, two from the County forces and two from the Borough forces—for each of the three ranks. These Central Committees have the right to submit representations to the Secretary of State in writing or by way of deputation, and they are consulted from time to time by the Home Office on matters affecting their ranks. For an admirable exposition of the methods and ideals of the Police Federation readers may refer to an article by Constable J. M. Branthwaite of the Metropolitan Police, Chairman of the Joint Central Committee of the Police Federation, printed in the first number of the Police Journal.[6] The formation of the Police Federation rendered possible another institution mentioned in the Police Act, 1919, namely, the Police Council, which consists of representatives of County and Borough Police Authorities, Chief Officers of Police, the Superintendents and the Police Federation, and meets when required at the Home Office, under the presidency of the Home Secretary or an officer of the Department. The Council thus serves the purpose of a central representative and consultative body on matters affecting the conditions of service of the police as a whole, and it is provided in section four of the Police Act, 1919, that a draft of any regulation which the Home Secretary proposes to make in pursuance of the wide powers conferred upon him by that section shall be laid before

[6] Police Journal, Volume I, No. 1; published by Messrs. Philip Allan & Co., London.

the Police Council, and that before making any such regulation he shall consider any representations the Police Council may submit. The present code of regulations was accordingly laid in draft before the Police Council at its first meetings in July, 1920, and it is perhaps of interest to record that in the course of the discussions on the draft code, which occupied the whole of four days, there emerged fewer than a dozen points on which the representatives of all parties were unable to reach unanimous agreement.

SELECTION AND TRAINING

Turning now to the arrangements for the selection and training of police personnel, it may be stated at once that they are in keeping with the police system itself, in the sense that they are in the main made locally by the several police authorities and Chief Officers of Police, but are subject to an element of central control which, however, is in these matters exercised at present only to a very slight extent. Signs, however, are not wanting that the present arrangements are in some respects transitional: in a few years' time considerable changes may have taken place and the following remarks should be read with this proviso in mind.

SELECTION OF PERSONNEL

The responsibility for the actual choice of the candidates for appointment is in all forces in the hands of the local police authorities and Chief Officers of Police; there is for this purpose no central machinery for the Police Service as a whole. In the Metropolitan Police the Commissioner, and in the county forces the Chief Constable, is the appointing authority; in the borough forces all appointments require the authority of the Watch Committee but the actual selection of the recruits is left to the Chief Officer of Police and all arrangements for their examination are in his hands.

Candidates for appointment are in the first instance required to fill up an application form, which will vary in points of detail from force to force but as a rule requires the candidate to give not only full particulars of his age, height and other measurements, his educational qualifications, and so forth, but also a more or less complete account of his employment and associations since he left school. Limits of height, age, and so forth, vary to some extent, but all forces must comply with the requirements laid down in the following Police Regulations:

7. A candidate for appointment to a police force—

(1) must produce satisfactory references as to character, and, if he has served in any branch of His Majesty's Naval, Military or Air Forces, or in the Civil Service, or in any Police Force, produce satisfactory proof of his good conduct while in such Service or Force. A person dismissed from any such Service or Force shall not be eligible for appointment.

(2) must be under 30 years of age or, in case of an appointment as Chief Officer of Police, 40 years of age.

Provided that a candidate over the specified age limit may be appointed—

(a) if he has had previous service in a police force or is otherwise entitled to reckon previous service as approved service for purposes of pension, or

(b) in other special circumstances approved by the Secretary of State upon the recommendation of the appointing authority, that is to say, the Chief

Constable or the Police Authority, as the case may be.

(3) must, save for special reasons approved by the Secretary of State, be not less in height than 5 feet 8 inches or such higher standard as may have been prescribed by the Police Authority.

Provided that where a standard higher than 5 feet 8 inches has been prescribed, a candidate whose height is less than that standard, but not less than 5 feet 8 inches, may be appointed provided that he possesses special qualifications for service in the Police.

(4) must be certified by the Medical Officer of the Force to be in good health, of sound constitution and fitted both physically and mentally to perform the duties of his office.

(5) must satisfy the Chief Officer of Police that he is sufficiently educated by passing a written or oral examination in reading, writing and arithmetic (addition, subtraction, multiplication and division).

8. No person shall be eligible for appointment to, or shall be retained in, a police force to which these Regulations apply, if—

(a) he holds any other office or employment or carries on any business for hire or gain, or

(b) he resides, without the consent of the Chief Officer of Police, at any premises where his wife or any member of his family keeps a shop or carries on any like business, or

(c) he holds, or his wife or any member of his family living with him holds, any licence granted in pursuance of the Liquor Licensing laws or the laws regulating places of public entertainment in the district of the police force in which he seeks appointment or to which he has been ap-

pointed, as the case may be, or has any pecuniary interest in any such licence, or

(d) his wife, without the consent of the Chief Officer of Police, keeps a shop or carries on any like business in the district of the police force in which he seeks appointment or to which he has been appointed, as the case may be.

Provided that, in case of refusal of consent, there shall, in a Borough Police Force, be an appeal to the Watch Committee, whose decision shall be final.

For the purpose of this Regulation, the expression "member of his family" shall include parent, son or daughter, brother or sister.

9. Every appointment to the post of Chief Officer of Police in any County or Borough Police Force shall be subject to the approval of the Secretary of State, and no person without previous police experience shall be appointed to any such post unless he possesses some exceptional qualification or experience which specially fits him for the post, or there is no candidate from the Police Service who is considered sufficiently well qualified.

TYPE OF POLICE PERSONNEL

There is thus considerable room for local variations as to the physical standards favoured by the various forces. The City of London, for instance, still aims at getting recruits not far short of six feet in height: in other forces the usual limit of height is five feet and ten inches, but some take men slightly below that height if well qualified in other respects. All forces, of course, seek to get men of good physique, but there is a tendency, especially in county forces, to favour men who are closely knit and muscular but less brawny and bulky—and less likely to add to their bulk as time goes on— than the traditional type of policeman, the former being not only more active but "wearing" better under exposure and the other rigours incidental to police life. All applications are carefully sifted and likely candidates called up to be medically examined and seen by the Chief Officer of Police or officers acting on his behalf.

Taken altogether, the present conditions of service as regards pay, superannuation, and so forth, are distinctly attractive, and in most forces the number of applicants is vastly greater than the number of vacancies to be filled. The recruits are drawn from the population at large—not, as in some European police forces, mainly from the Army—and most come from the ranks of semi-skilled or unskilled labour. Today, an increasing number of men of superior education are joining the police as constables, but their numbers are still relatively insignificant. There is, of course, no limitation as to the locality from which candidates may come. Most forces, and all the large ones, receive applications from many parts of the country, and many of the borough forces, in particular, prefer to recruit in the main from candidates who come from other districts and have no particular connection with the place in which they are to serve.

The uniformity of the conditions of service is also an important factor in widening the field of choice of candidates for appointment, and nowadays employment in the police is undoubtedly viewed not as a matter of casual or temporary employment so much as an entry to a profession. As remarked by Mr. Cecil Moriarty, the Assistant Chief Constable of Birmingham, in a recent article in the *Police Journal*,[7]

In bye-gone days, when a constable's pay was about 25/—a week he had little hesitation about leaving the force and taking up a more lucrative occupation. Nowadays, the recruit intends to become and to remain a policeman, as he is satisfied that the

[7] "The Police Recruit", *Police Journal*, July, 1929, Volume II, No. 7.

remuneration is adequate and that the conditions of service are reasonable.

There can be no doubt that, in a number of ways which will be readily appreciated, English experience points quite definitely to the importance of uniform and generally satisfactory conditions of service as a means of securing a proper standard of police personnel and the right attitude on the part of the police towards their work and responsibilities.

Many of the applicants, of course, are found on investigation to be quite ineligible for police work on one ground or another, but most forces have an ample supply of well-qualified candidates from whom to choose, and are thus in a position to accept only those who seem to have really good all-round qualifications. To this rule there are still some exceptions, and the Metropolitan Police, in particular, are experiencing some difficulty in obtaining a sufficient number of recruits of the right stamp.

The following figures will serve to illustrate the experience of one large city force, namely, Birmingham, for which detailed figures are available. Taking the last five years, the number of applicants for appointment as constable averaged 3,020 annually, as against eighty-four recruits appointed, on the average, in each year. Of the 3,020 applicants, more than one third dropped out for one reason or another; a similar number were "weeded out" on preliminary investigation of their papers, and an average of one hundred and seventy-four were picked out and called up for examination. Of these, an average of eighteen failed to attend, thirty-nine were rejected by the Medical Officer of the force on physical grounds, thirty-three were rejected by the Chief Constable on other grounds, and eventually eighty-four joined the force. After their appointment, eight men, on the average, were discharged or left the force before completing their twelve months' probationary period, giving a net recruitment at the rate of seventy-six per annum, as against more than three thousand applications for appointment.

In the selection of candidates for appointment, regard will be paid to the applicant's education, physique, character, previous employment and associations, personal address and temperament, and the candidate whose record or qualifications in any of these respects is at all below the mark will have little or no chance of entering the police service under present conditions.

PERSONALITY TESTS

As regards personality, temperament, vocational fitness, and so forth, the method of selection followed in almost every case is that of "sizing up" the candidate by personal observation. Hardly any use has as yet been made of the various intelligence and other specific personality tests which have been devised for this and other occupations. One Chief Constable, at any rate, has used the Otis and other intelligence tests for a number of years, not as a substitute for but as a supplementary check upon personal ratings made by his officers, with results which, in his opinion, have been of definite value. For the most part these tests are unknown in the English service, and most Chief Officers would probably prefer to trust their own judgment than any "new fangled" methods of any kind. Undoubtedly the present methods of selection are successful in the sense that they secure for the police service recruits who are on the whole excellently qualified for the work, and no specific tests would take the place of the "sizing up" of the men by the trained eyes of experienced policemen. But whether such tests could not be used with great advantage to check the personal ratings and bring to light defects or abilities which would not otherwise be observed at the right time, is quite another question; probably they could, but a good deal of correlation work, for the purpose of comparing results attained by the two methods, still remains to be done. In this, as in other respects, it is not to be expected that methods in the English service will always remain exactly as they are, and this is perhaps one of the matters in which it is not too much to look for an interchange of experience between the United States and the English Police Services, to the mutual advantage of both.

POLICE TRAINING

The arrangements for the training of the selected candidates, like the arrangements for their selection from those who have applied for appointment, vary very much from force to force. They are, however, invariably planned with some regard to certain of the Police Regulations relating to the conditions for promotion, which may be quoted as follows:

27. Promotion up to the rank of Inspector shall, subject to qualifying examinations in police duties and educational subjects, be by selection.

28. No member of a Police Force shall be promoted to the rank of Sergeant or Inspector, unless—

(1) if a constable, he has completed five years' service and has for the last two years been free from punishment other than reprimand or caution, and if a sergeant, he has completed two years in that rank free from punishment other than reprimand or caution.

(2) he has passed, after having completed not less than 4 years' service, an examination in

educational subjects and an examination in police duties.

(3) he has had not less than one year's service. in the performance of ordinary outside police duty.

Provided that a member of a police force may be promoted before he has completed 5 years' service, or may be permitted to take the qualifying examinations before he has completed 4 years' service, if the Chief Officer of Police, or, in the case of a Borough Police Force, the Watch Committee, is satisfied that he possesses special qualifications for the performance of the particular duties on which he is to be employed. The requirement of paragraph (3) of this Regulation may be dispensed with in the case of a man who was serving on 20th August, 1920; and the expression "outside police duty" shall include detective duty.

29. The examinations shall be conducted by means of written papers and/or oral examinations upon the following subjects:

(1) Examination in Educational Subjects, including

(a) Reading aloud.

(b) Writing, including handwriting, spelling, punctuation, and the writing and composition of reports.

(c) Arithmetic, for promotion to Sergeant, first four rules, simple and compound, including Imperial Weights and Measures, and simple fractions; for promotion to Inspector, first four rules, simple and compound, including Imperial Weights and Measures, reduction, vulgar fractions and decimals (excluding recurring decimals), ratio and proportion, averages and percentages.

(d) Geography, especially the geography of the British Isles.

(e) General knowledge and intelligence.

(f) Any special subject or subjects which may be required in the circumstances of a particular force or forces.

(2) Examination in Police duties, including

(a) Criminal Law.

(b) Evidence and Procedure.

(c) General statutes, regulations and orders.

(d) Local Regulations and Bye-laws.

(e) Extra duties performed by the particular force concerned.

(f) Principles of Local Government.

(3) The papers on the educational subjects (b), (c), (d) and (e) shall be set and marked by a central examining authority approved by the Secretary of State, or such other competent examining body as the Police Authority of the force may adopt. The examinations in police duties, and, where necessary, the educational subjects (a) and (f), shall be conducted by the Chief Officer of Police, or, where the size of the force permits, a Board of officers acting under his directions.

(4) The examinations shall be held in large forces periodically, at least once in each year, and in smaller forces as often as may be required, and, subject to the provisions of Regulation 32, any sergeant or constable who has completed 4 years' service and has given due notice to the Chief Officer of Police, shall be entitled to sit for the respective examinations for these ranks.

30. The object of the required examinations is to test the educational and theoretical knowledge of the candidate, and the fact that he has passed them shall not entitle him to promotion, or to promotion before another member of the force who has passed the examination at a later date.

Training arrangements will accordingly provide for: (1) educational work (improvement of writing, composition, and, in particular, writing of reports); (2) instruction in police duties (this instruction being generally given on the basis of a manual of police duty called an Instruction Book); (3) physical training and drill; and, (4) first-aid work, to which may be added some instruction in jiu-jitsu or swimming, and so forth. In most forces, the accepted candidate is at once appointed a constable, being thus clothed with the powers attaching to his office, and is drafted to a training class, where class instruction will be alternated with attendance at a Police Court to study procedure, or duty in the streets under the eye of an experienced officer. In such forces the period of instruction thus forms part of the recruit's twelve months' probationary period. In the Metropolitan Police, however, the accepted candidate is drafted first to the Training School, and only if he successfully passes his Training School examination is he appointed a constable, when he is posted to a police station and undergoes further training combined with actual duty in the streets under the eye of a senior officer.

Some forces use as Instruction Book published works like Vincent's *Police Code*, Gregg and McGrath's *Police Constables' Guide*, Hastings Lees' *Constables' Pocket Guide* and Moriarty's *Police Law*, but many, including the Metropolitan Police, have books specially prepared for their own use. These vary considerably in the tone and treatment of their subject. In all cases their primary aim is to give the constable a general idea of his powers, duties and responsibilities and to instruct him with some precision as to the nature and essential characteristics of the offences with which he may have to deal and the method he should adopt in handling this, that or the other situation. They differ, however, in the fact that some emphasise the legal side of the work and use mainly legal, or quasi-legal, language, while others are couched in a more direct and "every day" tone and concentrate more on the practical side of the work than its merely legal aspects. At present a standard Instruction Book is in course of preparation by Sir Leonard Dunning, formerly Chief Constable of Liverpool and now one of the three Inspectors of Constabulary already referred to, with a view to its being issued by the Home Office for use in all forces as recommended by the Royal Commission on Police Powers and Procedure,[8] subject, of course, to the decision of the Secretary of State.

COÖPERATIVE TRAINING

It is impossible in an article of this kind to give any account, even in summary form, of the various arrangements for the training of recruits in operation in the several forces. They vary considerably in every respect, and, though great advances have been made in recent years, and many are excellent, some undoubtedly still fall definitely short of a proper standard, especially in the small forces where facilities are limited and the number of recruits is so small and the occasions for their appointment so irregular as almost to preclude anything in the nature of a regular training class. The needs of these forces are, however, being met to some extent by an interesting development in the shape of a sort of coöperative system by which some of the small forces, and indeed some of the larger ones, send their recruits for the major part of their training to one of the large forces where there are proper facilities for the conduct of regular classes for recruits and the Chief Officer is willing to undertake the training of recruits for forces other than his own. Of these arrangements the most notable illustration is that afforded by the Birmingham Police Training School. Since 1920, when a beginning was made by training fifteen recruits for two neighbouring forces, seven hundred and sixty-three outside recruits have been trained for forty-six different forces (sixteen county forces and thirty borough forces). The

[8] Report dated 16th March, 1929 (Cmd. 3297); published by H. M. Stationery Office.

numbers taken, which were at first comparatively small, increased till in 1927, when definite classes were formed specially for men from other forces, one hundred and thirty-seven of these "outside" recruits were trained for twenty-seven forces in all parts of the country; one hundred and ninety-eight were trained for thirty-three forces in 1928, and already this year, up to August 20, thirty-three forces had sent one hundred and forty-six recruits to the Training School.

In several other forces similar arrangements are made but on a smaller scale, and there is every likelihood of their further extension. Some particulars of the course of instruction given at the Birmingham Training School, with some general observations on the training of police recruits, are given in the article by Mr. Cecil Moriarty, Assistant Chief Constable of Birmingham, to which reference has just been made.[9]

THE METROPOLITAN POLICE TRAINING SCHOOL

Much the largest Police Training School in the country is, of course, that of the Metropolitan Police, and some particulars of the instruction given at this Training School must be included in an article of this kind. The Training School is housed in a building set apart for the purpose with the necessary class and lecture room accommodation, and messing and sleeping accommodation for one hundred and eighty-five men. The time allowed for the course is from ten to seventeen weeks, according to the aptitude of the individual men, especially the time which has to be devoted to educational instruction as distinct from specific instruction in police duties, first aid and self-defence, physical training and foot drill. During the normal ten weeks' course under the present syllabus, as

designed for those who require the minimum educational instruction, the time devoted in classes, lectures, and so forth, to these several subjects is allocated as follows:

Police Duty	63½ per cent
Foot Drill	10½ " "
Education	9 " "
First Aid	6 " "
Self Defence	5½ " "
Physical Training	5½ " "

The class arrangements are run on the weekly principle, to ensure that each week's work is properly mastered before the candidate proceeds to the next, and in connection with every lesson arrangements are made, so far as possible, for the development of the practical as well as the theoretical side of the work. For example, a mock Police Court is held and the candidates are not only accustomed to Court procedure but are subjected to rigorous cross-examination in the witness box and other practical tests. During the last week of the course, examination papers are set and a candidate must obtain two thirds marks to qualify for appointment.

The classes cover all branches of a constable's work, as will be seen from the following heads of the system of lectures on police duties, which are quoted in condensed form, omitting references to practical demonstrations, recapitulation classes, and so forth, which form an essential part of the instruction throughout the course:[10]

Junior Stage

(1) General outline of a constable's duties. Appointments issued.

(2) Duties of constables on beats, fixed points, patrols. Measures for prevention of crime; attention to premises, etc.

---

[9] *Police Journal*, Volume II, No. 7.

[10] The numbers do not represent the number of lectures. Some of the headings quoted are covered by a single lecture while others occupy a whole series of lectures with practical demonstrations.

(3) Pocket Book: taking of notes. Compilation of reports.

(4) Collisions: information required in various classes of cases.

(5) Accidents: illness in streets. Ambulances.

(6) Dangerous structures. Gas and water mains. Telegraph and telephone plant. Letter boxes. Condition of roadways.

(7) Games in streets. Runaway horses. Dogs. Coffee stalls. Railways.

(8) Property lost and found.

(9) Destitute persons. Lunatics. Mental defectives. Cases of loss of memory.

(10) Dead bodies: sudden deaths: suicides and attempted suicides.

(11) Royal personages: carriage passes, etc.

(12) Traffic regulations, rules, etc. Regulation of traffic.

(13) Fires: false alarms; chimneys on fire.

(14) Trespass: civil disputes: bailiffs. Factory inspectors. Public libraries.

(15) Sale and exposure of unfit food. Pedlars and hawkers. Old metal dealers and marine store dealers.

(16) Children Act.

(17) Assaults. Damage to property.

(18) Naval and Military.

(19) Protection of animals: cruelty to animals. Diseases of animals.

(20) Gun licences: Firearms Act. Fireworks. Explosives.

(21) Aliens. Air Navigation.

(22) Dangerous Drugs.

(23) Meetings: processions: strikes: riots.

Intermediate Stage

(24) Motor Car Acts. Roads Act. Orders and regulations. Lights on vehicles. Highway Act.

(25) Public carriages.

(26) Special offences under Metropolitan Police Act, 1839.

(27) London Traffic Act.

(28) Traffic regulation.

(29) Premises licensed for sale of intoxicating liquor: drunkenness. Clubs. Betting and gambling.

(30) Costermongers. Street collections. Street advertisements.

(31) Vagrancy. Prostitutes: brothels.

(32) Prevention of crime: suspected persons: unlawful possession. Pawnbrokers.

(33) Powers of arrest: mode of arrest: procedure by summons and legal process and Court procedure generally.

These stages are followed by a Final Stage, comprising further instruction in various of the subjects mentioned above, with classes for recapitulation, practical demonstrations, visits to Court, and so forth, and at the end the examination already mentioned, which candidates must pass in order to qualify for appointment to the force.

After being posted to the force the recruit's instruction is continued for a further period of six months, or more if necessary, under the guidance of a senior officer, by way of weekly classes recapitulating and developing the subjects on which the recruit has already had preliminary instruction at the Training School, with further attendance at Police Courts, and so forth. There is a further examination after three months, and a final examination after a further period, normally three months, and those who fail to pass the required examinations at the stated times, or at latest within the currency of their probationary period, are discharged from the force. The probationer's work is not, of course, judged merely on the basis of these examinations. In addition, the officer under whom he serves reports periodically on his practical ability and progress, and to be retained in the force the probationer must show practical ability as well as possess a sound knowledge of the law and regulations with which he will be concerned.

POST-PROBATIONARY TRAINING

The arrangements for post-probationary training are in most forces rather rudimentary, consisting of the circulation of orders and occasional explanatory memoranda, with perhaps classes or lectures arranged from time to time with special reference to the examinations for promotion. For a policeman it is undoubtedly true that experience is the best school, but more might be done to stimulate and develop the abilities of the average constable. This purpose could be served in part by the more frequent issue of suitable instructions designed to bring a constable's knowledge up to date and to correlate and if necessary correct impressions he is forming; but such instruction needs to be supplemented by personal instruction and guidance given by picked senior officers, and "refresher courses," such as those given in some forces in first aid work, to ensure that in matters of technical training the constable does not get "rusty."

As to detective training in particular, there is not much to be said. Detectives are chosen from the uniform constables who show special aptitude for detective work. They will already have received a measure of training and in many forces will have gained a good deal of detective experience in the course of their everyday work; for it is to be remembered that where the men are spread thinly over the ground as they are in the rural districts—one or two in a village or small township, primarily responsible for attending (at any rate in the first instance) to everything which occurs there and in a stretch of country round—every constable must be his own detective, and there is not the same high degree of specialisation as between the uniform and detective work that there is in some of the large city forces. The constable, however, who is picked for detective duties should be and generally is given a certain amount of special instruction in the principles and practice of criminal investigation, finger prints, foot prints, and so forth, and in the Metropolitan Police, in particular,

the constable's retention on detective duties is dependent on his passing a special examination as well as satisfying his superior officers as to his ability in this class of work.

Apart from the Police Regulations as to promotion which have been quoted above, no special requirements have been laid down by the Regulations or otherwise as to the nature and scope of the post-probationary training for uniform constables or detectives and all arrangements are in the hands of the individual Chief Officers of Police.

PROMOTIONS

In the earlier stages of a constable's career he is naturally thinking of "getting on," and if he has any enterprise at all soon takes stock of his chances of promotion and begins to prepare to qualify. Promotion is by selection, subject to qualifying examinations in educational subjects and police duties. Selection on the basis of proved merit in practical work should be the foundation of any promotion system. Qualifying examinations are desirable, even necessary nowadays when a larger measure of "polish" is required on a policeman than in days gone by, but in the operation of any such system great care must, of course, be exercised to prevent any relaxation or, still worse, suppression of the element of selection in favour of the mere answering of questions in examination papers. If a course cannot be steered between Scylla and Charybdis it would be wiser, at all costs, to steer away from the Scylla of mere theory, even at the risk of some trouble in the opposite direction.

It remains to say a few words on the subject of appointments to the higher ranks. These include the Superintendents of Divisions in the Metropolitan, the City of London, and the county and borough forces: the Chief Officers of the county and borough forces (with a few Assistant Chief Constables), the Commissioner and Assistant Commissioner of the City of London Police, and the Chief Constables, Assistant and Deputy Assistant Commissioners and the Commissioner of the Metropolitan Police. From what has been said already as to the size and characteristics of the various forces it will be apparent that the work and responsibilities of the Chief Officers vary within very wide limits indeed, and even the post of Superintendent of a division is far from carrying any uniform responsibility. Thus, in spite of the merging of a number of the smallest divisions, a good many county divisions still have only twenty or thirty men and a population of twenty to thirty thousand; others have over one hundred (in one case over two hundred) men with a population ranging from one hundred to two hundred thousand; some of the larger city divisions are still busier, while a division in the Metropolitan Police will have from five hundred to twelve hundred men and a population up to several hundreds of thousands.

In some county forces, appointments to the post of Superintendent were formerly made from outside the service, but promotion from within the service is now the invariable rule in all forces. Formerly, the Chief Constableships of counties were often filled by the appointment of retired Army officers who had no previous police experience, but appointments of this kind are now restricted by the regulation (Number Nine of the Police Regulations) already quoted,[11] and at the present time most appointments of Chief Constables of county and borough forces are made from officers serving in the county and borough forces themselves or, in some cases, from persons who have had previous police experience in India or the Colonies or elsewhere.

In the Metropolitan Police, in recent years, officers who have risen through the ranks have been promoted to the post of Chief Constable and even Assistant Commissioner, but generally these posts have been filled by appointments from outside. In this matter there have been, and still are, two schools of thought, or it may be two different standpoints from which the requirements are viewed, one emphasising the need for previous police experience and urging that all appointments to the higher ranks should be made by promotion from the lower, while the other would rather stress the need for a wider outlook and experience than mere passage through the lower ranks of a police force to the higher can possibly afford.

Experience certainly confirms the view, which theory would suggest, that appointments from outside the service may, whatever the handicaps, lead to the happiest results, and that promotion from the ranks cannot, under the present system, be regarded as capable of ensuring a constant and sufficient supply of the right type of personnel for the higher posts. It is a matter partly of personality, partly of experience and partly of organisation. The problem how best to meet the requirements and reconcile the various points of view is undoubtedly one of the most important problems of the English police service at the present time, and possibly of other police services elsewhere. It is not within the scope of the present article to enter into any discussion of ways and means, but some solution must certainly be sought and will, it is to be hoped, be found at no very distant date.

---

[11] The corresponding Scottish regulation differs from the English regulation in that it definitely requires five years' previous police experience as a condition for appointment to the post of Chief Constable.

The School of Criminology and of Scientific Police of Belgium

By Dr. Gustave De Rechter

Director, School of Criminology and of Scientific Police of Belgium, Brussels, Belgium

SINCE the time when Alphonse Bertillon in France (1878) and Hans Gross, Councillor of Justice at Graz, Austria (1890), each took the initiative of introducing scientific methods and procedure into criminal investigations, scientific police, in the sense of police technique or, still better, in the sense of science of identification—identification being taken in its broadest meaning and referring to the identification of objects as well as that of individuals—has made great strides.

The Bureau of Identification (*Service de l'Identité*) of the late Bertillon in France; Locard's Institute of Police Technique in Lyons; the Institute of Scientific Police in Lausanne, founded by Reiss and developed by him and by his pupils and successors; and, the Division of Police Technique of Ottolenghi's Institute in Rome mark stages in the progressive evolution made in this field.

In Germany—in Berlin, Dresden, Munich, and elsewhere—great institutes have been founded and since the War they have been greatly enlarged. In Czechoslovakia, university schools of criminology and of scientific police have been established in Prague and at Bratislava. In South America, notably in Argentine, vast scientific organizations have been created, which have enlarged our field of science by including forensic medicine within its scope. We notice here the growth of an interesting phenomenon. The rudiments of scientific police, which were concerned exclusively with the identi-

fication of persons, were born of forensic medicine, and today a marked tendency in certain quarters indicates that the child may devour its mother. The term scientific police may, as a matter of fact, include all the applications of science to criminal investigation and from that point of view forensic medicine can be regarded as one of the parts of the whole on the same basis as toxicology, ballistics, and so forth. Nevertheless, it is wise to consider custom and tradition. One must respect acquired rights. Let us leave then to forensic medicine her autonomy —she is a dowerage of old lineage and has a right to command respect. Let us reserve the term of scientific police, called police technique by many, for that vast domain which the science of identification opens up to the investigator—the term identification being understood in its widest sense as noted above.

POLICE LABORATORIES ABROAD

The concept governing the organization of police laboratories naturally differs according to the country and especially according to the variation of the legislation governing criminal investigation (*les expertises judiciaires*). Thus it is that in Germany, Italy, Austria, and Czechoslovakia, the investigations are generally made by public officials, doctors of science or of medicine—and even doctors of laws— police officials of high rank. In these countries the laboratories—or rather the institutes—are organized as institutes for research and its practical application. They are admirably equipped moreover but are not especially adapted to organized instruction.

If such instruction is more or less organized it is, as a rule, in connection with universities; such is the case at Lausanne, Prague, Bratislava, and particularly at Rome. The number of organized laboratories may be large or small for a given institute. In South America, in particular, we find the institutes of legal medicine absorbed by the institutes of police technique, in spite of the restrictions we have already noted.

In France where in principle the experts are "free," having no official rank as such—just as in Belgium—the custom prevails of confiding to persons attached to the organized official laboratories the special work falling within the domain of scientific police; but this is not obligatory and the judges retain the right to appeal for assistance to anyone whom they regard as competent.

So far as instruction is concerned, its organization differs fundamentally according to the country. The concept governing it is quite different in France from that in Belgium.

In Paris, in the *Service de l'Identité*, instruction is systematized only in so far as it concerns the descriptive signalment; but since 1924 a school or rather an institute of criminology, the curriculum of which includes police technique, has been established in that city by the university. Admission to this course is open to anyone, although, as a matter of fact, the plan of the organizers, headed by Dr. Balthazard, is particularly designed for police officials and magistrates.

In Italy, Ottolenghi's School at Rome, with no university affiliation, is above all designed to give the policeman a broad cultural education, and at Lausanne the institute, connected with the university, is especially designed for the training of experts.[1]

TRAINING THE POLICE IN BELGIUM

The idea governing the establishment of the School of Criminology and of Scientific Police of Belgium, with headquarters at Brussels, is quite different. This school is a state institution and therefore has the advantage of being able to define exactly the requirements for admission to its courses. Only in exceptional cases is any effort made to train future experts. The permanent and principal aim of our teaching in the elementary course is to train policemen, forced by their function to participate in or to begin investigations which imply criminal prosecution, by acquainting them with the new concepts of criminology and with the possibility of applying science to criminal investigation.

It is absolutely necessary that these splendid auxiliaries of Justice should know something about the individual and the social causes of crime, and that they should know what one may expect from the intervention of experts. Above all, their attention should be constantly on the alert concerning useful data and documents to be collected in the course of their investigation. The investigations and the searches which the police undertake cannot produce the best results unless the police have received a liberal education, placing them in the position of appreciating the full value of evidence (*les preuves indiciales*). This suggests the need for an institution where students may gather for an elementary course of instruction.

Our School accepts students from the following five groups:

[1] See my reports on the Institutes of Rome, Lausanne, Lyons and Paris in the *Revue de droit pénal et de criminologie*, 1921.

1. The investigating officers and agents of the prosecuting attorney's office (*les agents et les officiers de la police judiciaire des Parquets*), who must attend our courses;

2. Municipal agents and officers of similar category (*les agents et les officiers judiciaire des Communes*) who have been selected by the local authorities having jurisdiction over them;

3. Such non-commissioned officers of the state police (*gendarmerie*) as are designated by their commanding general;

4. The enforcement agents of the bureaus of control of the various state departments;

5. The chiefs of police at the railway stations.

Every year we complete three sessions of courses; two in French and one in Flemish. Each session lasts from six to seven weeks. Three or four lectures a day are given three days a week, and from forty to eighty pupils register for each session.

Our advanced courses are designed especially for young magistrates—assistant district attorneys and examining magistrates (*Juges d'instruction*)—the former being almost compelled to attend by order of their superiors, the latter exercising their free choice; for officers of the state police selected by their commanding general; for some of the higher police officers of the prosecuting attorney's office, selected by the chief prosecutors of the courts of appeal (*procureurs generaux*); and for attorneys who are recommended by the president of the bar association.

The aim of this course is to give, by instruction, advanced training to those who have a university education or its equivalent and who, therefore, can benefit from a special complementary course which aims to familiarize them with the new and modern concepts of criminology—particularly criminal anthropology—and to acquaint them with all the results already secured by the use of scientific methods and procedure in criminal investigation. Here they get glimpses of the hopes which the future may realize for us in this field—hopes which have no limits.

Here again we do not aim to make experts of our students. We only wish to define in their minds, by a study of past and present achievements, what they have a right to demand from experts and what they may expect from them in the future.

Only one session of the advanced course is held each year. It lasts three months and the lectures are given three or four hours a day, three days a week. On the whole, the curriculum of the advanced course closely follows that of the elementary course, but the material is more advanced and is treated in a more philosophical manner.

The programs of the two degrees of instruction offered in our schools, with the names and titles of the instructors, follow:

I. The Elementary Course: in French.[2]

1. *Scientific Police* (Eighteen lectures) —Prof. De Rechter, Director of the school, and formerly professor at the New University of Brussels.

2. *The Descriptive Signalment* (Fifteen lectures)—Mr. F. Louwage, chief officer of the police of the prosecuting attorney's office, Brussels. This course is of great importance to the police in their pursuit of criminals.

3. *Elements of Legal Medicine* (Nine lectures)—Professor Heger-Gilbert, Professor of Legal Medicine, University of Brussels.

4. *Criminal Anthropology* (Ten lectures)—Professor Louis Vervaeck, Direc-

[2] See *Syllabus des cours du degré inférieur de l'École belge de criminologie et de police scientifique.* 3ed. 131 pp. Impr. Typ. de l'Inst. Cartogr. Militaire, Brussels, 1928.

tor of the Penitentiary Anthropological Bureaus.

5. *Elements of Applied Criminal Law and Procedure* (Nine lectures)—Professor Charles Collard de Slovere, Advocate General, Court of Appeals, Brussels.

II. THE ELEMENTARY COURSE: IN FLEMISH.

1. *Scientific Police* (Fifteen lectures)— Professor Bessemans, Professor of Hygiene, University of Ghent.

2. *The Descriptive Signalment* (Fifteen lectures)—Mr. F. Louwage.

3. *Elements of Legal Medicine* (Nine lectures)—Professor Bruynooghe, Professor of Legal Medicine, University of Louvain.

4. *Criminal Anthropology* (Ten lectures)—Professor Louis Vervaeck.

5. *Elements of Applied Criminal Law and Procedure* (Nine lectures)—Professor de Wilde, Advocate General, Court of Appeals, Ghent.

III. THE ADVANCED COURSE

1. *Scientific Police*, including the elements of the descriptive signalment and the organization of bureaus of identification (Thirty lectures)—Professor De Rechter.

2. *Legal Medicine*, including the elements of toxicology and serology (Twentynine lectures).

Legal Medicine (Twenty lectures)— Professor Heger-Gilbert.

Toxicology (Four lectures)—Dr. De Laet, University of Brussels.

Serology (Five lectures)—Professor Bruynooghe.

3. *Physical Chemistry* (Three lectures) —Dr. De Laet.

4. *Criminal Anthropology* (Twenty lectures)—Professor Vervaeck.

5. *Elements of Psychiatry* (Nine lectures)—Professor Ley, Professor of Psychiatry, University of Brussels.

6. *Ballistics and Elementary Physics and Chemistry* (Nine lectures)—Colonel Mage, Professor, Military College, Brussels.

7. *Applied Criminal Law and Procedure* (Twenty lectures)—The Prosecuting Attorney, Brussels.

The results obtained deserve to be emphasized. The school is finishing its tenth year. The elementary course has been given to thirteen hundred and ninety-five students; the advanced course to two hundred and twenty-two, a total of sixteen hundred and seventeen students.

Perhaps it is to be recorded that our instruction is not recognized in any manner which would definitely register the assimilative efforts of our auditors. We do not as a matter of fact give any diploma, merely a certificate of good attendance. Only the police of the prosecuting attorney's office, working for the promotion to the grade of officer, are at the time of their promotion examination given detailed questions on the subjects taught in the elementary course. Nevertheless, the effectiveness of our efforts is marked by the practical results obtained. The police apply themselves with greater care and better methods to the accomplishments of their tasks. More and more do their investigations conform to modern usage.

The judges, who in great number have honored our courses by their presence, have become familiar not only with the modern doctrines which now dominate criminology but also with the principles and the methods which govern judicial proof. In Belgium today we hardly find, in contrast with a great neighboring country, judges who refuse to be convinced by the pertinence of fingerprint evidence, for instance. The judges, we repeat, are not transformed by the school into experts, but they know what they have a right to expect from such experts, having already become acquainted with the possibilities of scientific investigations.

It would perhaps be desirable to have our instruction sanctioned by a diploma. If we, subsequent to the examination, were permitted to grant the degree of graduate in criminology and in scientific police, the zeal and the attention of the students could not fail to be stimulated, resulting in a better administration of justice. This is a personal opinion which unfortunately is not shared by the majority of the administrative board of the school. This Administrative Board, presided over by the Minister of Justice, is composed of three prosecutors of the Courts of Appeal, two high functionaries of the Department of Justice, the prosecutor of the capital, the dean of the examining magistrates of the capital, the president of the bar association, a delegate of the instruction staff, and the director of the school.

RESEARCH ACTIVITIES

Outside its teaching, the activity of the School of Criminology and of Scientific Police is emphasized in the practical field by the researches and the examinations which are carried out by the professors in their laboratories. Our organization includes a laboratory of judicial photography, which is consolidated with the official laboratory of the prosecutor's office, a laboratory of police technique, and a physico-chemical laboratory. Among the researches made in these laboratories let us cite the following:

"Regarding a new method of identification of footprints cast in plaster"—Dr. De Rechter, 1924;

"The identification of cartridges and fired bullets"—Dr. De Rechter and Colonel Mage, 1923 and 1925;

"Control studies of Locard's graphometry"—Dr. DeRechter and Mr. Tihon;

"The identification of the impression of the handle of a tool on a leather glove"—Dr. De Rechter, 1926;

"Remarks on a method of identification of objects"—Dr. De Rechter and Colonel Mage;

"Researches on the permanence of written documents made by various commercial inks"—Dr. De Rechter and Dr. De Laet, 1927;

"Studies in dactyloscopy"—Dr. De Rechter, 1927;

"The application of micrography and of photo-micrography to the study of questioned documents."—Dr. De Rechter, 1927;

"The application of physical processes, ultra-violet rays, x-rays and ordinary light, to the examination of paintings"—Dr. De Rechter, 1928;

"The identification of a hatchet used to cut down young trees; act of vandalism"—Dr. De Rechter, 1929;

"Syllabus of the course in criminal anthropology" Dr. Louis Vervaeck, 1927.

Let us also call attention to the fine work of the anthropological prison laboratories, brilliantly directed by Dr. Vervaeck in the prison at Forest, near Brussels. Through the instruction given there, this organization, while administratively independent, may be considered as a supplement of the school, a supplement of capital value.

In establishing the School of Criminology and of Scientific Police of Belgium, we do not pretend to have built a perfect structure. The lack of financial means has not permitted us to realize our plan on the great scale we conceived it. The necessity for keeping down expenditures, imposed on us by the economic conditions of the postwar period, has handicapped us in many ways. Our personnel and our equipment could profitably be enlarged. But—such as it is, we believe that our school, a state institution without university connection, constitutes a progressive step of social value, particularly as it aims to reach not only the police but also the magistrates who in the exercise of their functions must proceed to the judicial investigation of crime.

In this age when all the civilized

countries of the world are occupied in reforming their penal law and procedure and when the repression of crime is being more and more guided by the new and basic principles of criminology, is it not desirable to see centers of study and research multiply themselves, inspired by the motives which produced our own program and its realization in concrete form?

Criminalistic Institutes and Laboratories [1]

By Dr. Siegfried Türkel

Vice-President, *Académie Internationale de Criminalistique;* Scientific Director, Criminalistic
Institute, Police Department, Vienna, Austria

IN the prospectus of the Criminalistic Institute of the police department of Vienna the observation was made that the problems of crime and criminals have in the last decades been considered from entirely new points of view and that the attention of the research student and the practitioner must turn not only to questions of criminal law but also to the data of science concerning types, causes, treatment, repression and prevention of crime. Side by side with the science of criminal law and procedure other criminalistic subjects were developing, such as the phenomenology, the etiology, the therapy and the prophylaxis of crime, and creating the necessity for giving all those persons professionally devoting themselves to the repression of crime a training corresponding to the levels reached by science. In many European states persons who entered upon careers in the higher police service or who became criminal judges or prosecuting attorneys were at the most asked to show proof of attendance at a university law school, while in others even this was not necessary.

Until recently the European universities, with rare exceptions, offered no opportunity for a detailed study of all the criminalistic fields and the applied sciences of criminalistic importance. In Austria the conditions were as follows.

Hans Gross had founded a criminological university institute in Graz (Steiermark) which after his death

[1] Translated from the author's German manuscript.

was continued and enlarged by Professor Hoepler and Professor Adol-Lenz. In Vienna no such university institute existed until the establishment of the Austrian Republic; in 1923 an institute for penal science and criminalistics was founded at the University of Vienna, in connection with the law school.

Considering the fact that the numerous branches of science needed by the criminalist in his work were taught not only in different colleges of the university but also to a considerable part by entirely different institutions—the Institute of Technology, for instance, the School for World Commerce and other professional schools, such as the Graphic School and Experimental Institute—the idea presented itself of founding a new institution, independent of the university institutes, in order that the future criminalist might study all fields of importance and value to him in one single institution. Guided by these considerations the police department of Vienna, as early as 1919, proposed to the government the establishment of a criminalistic institute. On the basis of permission granted by the State Department on October 19, 1919, steps were taken for the realization of this program.

THE CRIMINALISTIC INSTITUTE OF THE VIENNA POLICE DEPARTMENT

In this way the Criminalistic Institute of the Vienna police department originated. It is, consequently, a division of the police department and has its headquarters there. It aims to give to police officials with university training the necessary scientific professional training in order to bring these future criminalists to that level which is necessary so that they may fulfil their duties in accordance with the demands of the times. As a division of the police department, the institute is under the control of the Commissioner of Police (*Polizeipräsident*), who entrusts its administration to a high police official. The scientific leadership is entrusted to the professor who teaches the criminalistic sciences at the institute.

Those who attend the institute are either regular students, auditors or guests. Both the regular students and the auditors must be college graduates. As regular students Austrian citizens who are engaged in the service of the police, the gendarmerie or some "political" administrative department are accepted. Other public officials with university education, such as judicial and prosecuting officials, may also become regular students of the institute. As auditors such persons may be admitted who are not Austrian citizens or are not connected with the public services mentioned. Persons who are not attached to a police organization, the gendarmerie, a court, a prosecutor's office, and so forth, and who cannot show evidence of having finished college, may be accepted as guests when their educational level is such that they are prepared to follow instruction in a real university institute. The police department decides the question of the admission of auditors and guests.

The best survey of the curriculum and its division into four semesters' work is given by the roster of the school. As an example I shall give a list of the lectures for the summer and winter of 1929. The first and the third semesters fall in the winter months; the second and fourth semesters in the summer months.

	Hours a Week
FIRST SEMESTER	
Photographic Chemistry	1
Criminalistically Important Skin Changes Characteristic of Professional and Industrial Work	1
Industrial and Business Administration, with practical exercises in Accounting	2
Criminalistic Symptomatology and Diagnosis, Part One	2
Photographic Optics	1
Industrial Technology: Organic Raw Materials and their Microscopic Examination	2
SECOND SEMESTER	
Elementary Chemistry	2
Industrial Technology: (a) Textile Materials and their Preparation	1
(b) Metals and their Treatment	1
Industrial and Business Administration, with practical exercises in Accounting	2
Criminalistic Optics	1
Criminalistic Symptomatology and Diagnosis, Part Two	1
Science of Identification	1
General Phenomenology of Criminals Anthropology, with special reference to the Science of Identification and Heredity	1
	2
THIRD SEMESTER	
Criminalistically Important Phases of Technical Chemistry	2
Evidence Presented by Medical Experts	2
Special Phenomenology and Criminalistic Technology, Part One	1
Forensically Important Parts of Toxicology and Associated Fields (Examination of fibres, feces, and so forth)	2
FOURTH SEMESTER	
Criminal Biology	2
Elementary Forensic Psychiatry	2
Criminal Tactics	1
The Psychology of Police Work	1
Special Phenomenology and Criminalistic Technology, Part Two	1
Forensic Examination of Documents (limited number of students)	1

In addition to the regular lectures, special lectures are given every semester. For instance, during the winter semester of 1929 two hours a week were reserved for lectures on the modern technique of making casts (*Reproduktionstechnik*). In addition, a ten-hour course is held during the winter semester on the technique of making microscopic preparations and practical exercises in this procedure are given. During the summer semester of 1919, a series of lectures were given concerning the securing of evidence, and during the winter semester of 1929 Professor M. A. Bischoff, of the University of Lausanne, will lecture, as our guest, on "Selected Chapters in Criminalistics."

To the faculty of the Criminalistic Institute belong, either as permanently engaged or as guest lecturers, university professors both from Austria and from other countries, professors of technological institutes in and outside of Austria, professors of the School for World Commerce, professors from the Graphic School and Experimental Institute, and experienced and scientifically competent high police officials.

The regular students and the auditors of the institute may pass examinations on the lectures they have attended. These examinations, which are difficult, are regularly held every year in June. Those admitted are examined in the following subjects: (1) the purely criminalistic fields: criminalistics, forensic examination of handwriting, criminalistic optics, criminalistic microscopy and criminal tactics; (2) the anthropological fields: anthropology, the science of identification, criminal biology, psychology; (3) the medical fields: legal medicine, toxicology, legal psychiatry; (4) the technical fields: industrial technology, chemistry, photo-chemistry, photographic optics, photo-technique; and (5) accounting. Those taking the examination in criminalistics, the forensic examination of handwriting, criminalistic microscopy, the science of identification, industrial technology and photo-technique must also pass a practical test.

The Criminalistic Institute of the police department in Vienna is, as appears from the foregoing, not a school for higher police officials alone. Its curriculum guarantees, in addition, very adequate special training for all persons with a university education who wish to become judges of criminal courts or prosecuting attorneys.

CRIMINALISTIC TRAINING FOR JURISTS

For some years the Criminalistic Institute has been developing its activities. In the meanwhile similar institutes have been established at some German universities. Only recently, however, did the German Bar Association (*Juristentag*), at its thirty-fifth meeting, place this question on the program: "How should the personnel concerned with the administration of criminal law be trained?" First of all, it was to be decided *whether or not* future judges of criminal courts and prosecuting attorneys should be given a specialized criminalistic training; second, whether or not this training should be given *in the law school*, or later; and finally, *where* the courses should be given, if such specialized training were to be imparted after graduation from the law school, and *how long* these courses should last.

Professor Josef Heinberger, of the University of Frankfurt a.M., presented a report at the meeting which was held in Salzburg. He emphasized that a future criminal judge or prosecuting attorney should, without question, be given criminological training. Heinberger was quite naturally faced with the question of where this training should be given, that is, where these institutes should be established. He expressly stated in his report that universities are not the only suitable places for such courses. Where a criminalistic institute such as that of the Vienna police department already exists, courses for judges and prosecutors should obviously be given there.

I indicated, at the meeting in question, that the situation regarded as desirable was already a reality in the Vienna institute, and I formulated my opinions in the following theses.

Question: Should the specialized criminological training of the judge or the prosecutor be given while he is still purusing his legal studies in the university? *Thesis:* The university training of the law schools must from the juridical point of view be very broad. For that reason the student would not during this period have enough time to secure the profound knowledge in the criminological fields which is necessary for his career as a high police official, a criminal judge or a prosecutor.

Question: Could not the student during his stay at the university decide to which juridical branch he should like to devote himself? That is, could not those students who wish to become police officials, judges or prosecutors be given a juridical training at the university different in part from the training given the rest of the students? *Thesis:* It cannot be expected that students enrolled in the law school for the study of jurisprudence should during their period of training be able to decide which juridical profession to follow after their graduation.

Questions: Should the student of jurisprudence, no matter what profession he may enter in the future, be given an elementary criminological training? In addition to this elementary training which every law student at the university would receive, should a special course of training be developed which could be given in suitable institutes to the jurists who wish to enter a career in the penal sciences in the capacity of police officials, criminal judges or prosecutors? *Thesis:* Even if the law student during his university course were to attend criminalistic lectures or were to receive during that period an elementary criminological training, there must nevertheless be instituted specialized criminological instruction for those jurists who have already finished their university studies and wish to enter some branch of the penal sciences. This specialized instruction should follow upon the law school studies and could be given during that period of preparation which the jurist in Austria and Germany must pass through before he takes his examination for the judgeship. In order that the jurists may finish this period of preparatory service with the court and at the same time attend a criminological institute, the instruction in the latter should occupy only half of the day. The course should preferably be four semesters in length.

After considerable discussion, the third section of the German Bar Association reached the conclusion that the future criminal judge or prosecutor should be criminologically trained. It decided that the law school student might very properly be given an elementary criminological training, but it was unfavorable to the proposal that the *specialized* training of the future judge or prosecutor should be included in the work for the law degree. It was suggested that this training should not be given until after the passing of the first examination for the judgeship (*Assessorexamen*). The Bar Association consequently gave its sanction to the idea which was expressed in the 1919 prospectus of the Criminalistic Institute of the police department of Vienna:

Since criminalistics in its narrower sense has already secured a foot-hold in the curriculum of the universities this science, considering the wealth of other subject matter prescribed for legal study, cannot possibly be treated there in that detailed manner which is necessary for the well-rounded specialized training of the professional criminalist.

The conclusions referred to in the previous paragraph differentiate quite clearly between the elementary criminological instruction which every jurist should receive while in the law school and the specialized criminological training of those who wish to enter criminological professions. The Association was of the opinion that this specialized training of the future criminal jurist should not be directly joined with his university studies. The question of *where* it should be given was not answered.

WHERE SHOULD SUCH TRAINING BE GIVEN?

I wish to treat this matter in a rather detailed manner because several inquiries have been addressed to me from America as to whether criminalistic institutes for police officials and judges should be instituted at the universities or in connection with police departments. The question cannot be answered categorically. The University of Lausanne has a criminalistic institute which is, so to speak, made up from the different schools of that university. The student at this institute passes examinations in the schools of philosophy, medicine, and law, and also in criminalistic subjects, after which he is granted a diploma by the institute. A criminological institute can, therefore, be established at a university where the schools are not separated from each other as if they were "foreign states." If one considers, however, that the criminalist must also

master fields which are not all taught at the university but at other institutions and professional schools, one must favor the idea of a special criminalistic institute independent of the university where professors of the university, of the institutes of technology, of the School for World Commerce, and of other professional schools, will teach.

In answering the question of where the specialized criminalistic training should be given to future penal jurists, one must, then, keep in mind the conditions of a given country, the relationships between the schools of the universities there, and, finally, the goal toward which the criminalistic institute in question should strive in its instruction. Even the nature of the curriculum must depend upon this goal, which may be the elementary criminological training of the university student, the specialized criminological training of graduates who wish to become police officials, criminal judges or prosecutors, or, finally, the training of criminalistic experts. This will be discussed in somewhat greater detail.

It was stated at the meeting of the Bar Association that the study load of the law school student at the university is already so heavy that it should not be increased. Criminological instruction at the university falling within the law curriculum could therefore only mean instruction of an elementary kind.

A quite different goal of instruction must be reached by those institutes at which police officials with university training, criminal judges and prosecutors of the future wish to secure that criminological knowledge which is essential for their work. These men wish to acquire the widest possible information concerning criminalistics and the criminalistically useful sciences and techniques. They wish to know how the different scientific and technical fields of knowledge can be criminalistically applied; when they engage an expert they wish to make the right choice; and, finally, they want to read and evaluate the report of that expert with understanding.

Institutes in which criminalistic experts are to be trained must, on the other hand, pursue an entirely different aim in their instruction. The course for criminalistic experts is, so far as I know, six semesters in length at Lausanne. I should imagine, however, that an eight-semester course for experts would be desirable. The institutes which have been established for the specialized criminological training of future police officials, criminal judges and prosecutors may, of course, easily be enlarged so that experts may be trained there.

CRIMINALISTIC LABORATORIES

Lately, inquiries from America have touched the question of the relationship between the so-called criminalistic institutes and criminalistic laboratories. This question is easy to answer. A criminalistic institute is a school and requires student laboratories and laboratories for the scientists who are teaching and doing research at the institute. In a large criminalistic institute, therefore, research and other laboratories must be planned for the examination of industrial products and for chemical, microscopical, photographical, optical and crimino-technical work. Up to the present time there are very few such institutes.

The various university institutes must, of course, also be equipped with crimino-technical and photographic laboratories and it is quite obvious that a criminalistic laboratory should be found in every large police department. In a paper on criminalistic schools

and laboratories which I wrote for the meeting of the Bar Association already mentioned, I indicated that in addition to the laboratories of the great criminalistic institutes, the laboratories of the penal law departments of the universities and the laboratories of individual police departments, there should be erected in every large state a central laboratory which could test the methods and the results of all the laboratories of the country and thus be of service to research. I wrote as follows:

The ideal criminalistic laboratory would without doubt be a large establishment in which, under common direction, experts in all the scientific fields concerned could work together in the solution of all theoretical and practical questions of forensic importance. Such an ideal criminalistic laboratory should be so organized that in case of a stain or dust analysis, for instance, botanists, pharmacologists, mineralogists, industrial technologists, medico-legal experts, and so on, could work together through a mutual exchange of ideas; or that, for instance, the criminalistic, pharmacological, medical and zoölogical examination of fecal material could be performed in the same building by experts who are in close contact with one another. In most states, quite apart from the absence of financial means required, the construction of such a super-laboratory, with special workrooms for the representatives of the various applied sciences, could perhaps not be realized because sufficient material for research and study could not be secured.

These suggestions concerning a "central laboratory" have been taken up by the *Académie internationale de Criminalistique*, founded last summer in Lausanne, and preparatory work leading to the foundation of such an "international central laboratory" has been designated by this Academy as one of its many tasks.

Criminal Identification

By J. Edgar Hoover

Director, Bureau of Investigation, Department of Justice, Washington, District of Columbia

CRIMINAL identification is indispensable in the combatting of crime. It is not only the most potent factor in securing the apprehension of the criminal but its establishment enables the judiciary to sentence the guilty equitably. Severer penalties for the individual who repeatedly violates the law, or life imprisonment for the individual who has been convicted for his fourth felony, become significant only when it is possible to determine accurately the number of previous sentences served. Generally, the first offender can only be distinguished from the recidivist through the medium of scientific criminal identification.

Historical Background

From the earliest annals of society it would appear that personal identification of one kind or another has been in vogue. In the earlier civilizations, differences in the dress of various social classes were clearly defined, sometimes by law but more often with the sanction of custom. The branding of criminals and slaves was also resorted to at a time when no other method of identification was known, and various forms of tattooing were used by the ancient Romans to identify and to prevent the desertion of mercenaries employed to defend the empire. During the early part of the eighteenth century, the better organized police departments in Europe employed officers with good visual memories who attempted to record mentally the faces of criminals and the crimes connected with these individuals.

It was not until the advent of photography that law enforcement agencies began the development of modern methods of criminal identification. The science of photography resulted in the establishment by the more highly organized police departments of "rogues galleries" and bureaus containing the photographs of thousands of criminals. Although photography continues to be a very important aid in the detection and the prosecution of crime, its early use was hampered by the fact that photographs were not easily subdivided except on the basis of names, which constantly change.

Bertillon System

The first system of identification which made the photograph effective in large bureaus was the Bertillon system which derives its name from Alphonse M. Bertillon, a noted French anthropologist, who devised and perfected the system in 1882. The necessity for the classification of photographs was so urgent that the Bertillon system was adopted almost immediately by France and later by most of the other civilized countries of the world. The most important feature of the system, which was based upon the proposition that certain parts of the human anatomy remain unchanged during the adult life of the individual, consisted in the taking of measurements of certain bony structures of the body; i.e., height, the length of the outer arms, trunk, head, ear, left foot, left middle finger, left little finger, and left forearm and the width of the cheek and the head. After being subdivided into the three classes of small, medium and large, these measurements were listed in a designated sequence and formed the basis for the classification of the photographs to which they referred.

In addition to his anthropometrical system of identification, Mr. Bertillon established definite rules for recording the personal description of the criminal. Certain characteristics, such as weight, color of hair, eyes and complexion, as well as location, size and shape of all scars, marks, moles and tattooes, were designated as part of each individual record. A photograph showing the front and the right profile view of the head of the subject was attached to each record. At the present time this feature of the Bertillon system is an invaluable aid to all agencies and organizations that deal with offenders.

Although the Bertillon system of identification was established by law in many of the institutions of the United States, it was not long before its deficiency was discovered. The success of the system depended upon slight differences in measurements and it was soon realized that one operator would take them "loose" while another would take them "close." The Bertillon system, furthermore, was not an effective means of identifying persons under twenty-one or over sixty years of age, for in the excluded periods the measurements of the human body constantly change.

However, the Bertillon system continued to render valuable service to organized society in its fight against crime until the advent of scientific fingerprint identification. During the ages when man was seeking a method of personal identification, he carried on the inside of the nail joint of each finger thousands of ridge formations or patterns by which positive identifications could have been made. Physiologists have not definitely decided why nature provided these ridges and depressions on the hands and the feet. Some authorities contend that the ridges offset

and lessen wear, while others advance the theory that they assist the sense of touch, produce friction and elevate the pores, thus enabling the ducts to discharge perspiration more easily. Irrespective of the reason for their existence, the fact remains that the ridge formations remain unchanged during the entire life of an individual and until putrefaction sets in after death, and that the characteristics of these patterns are never identical in any two fingers.

EVOLUTION OF FINGERPRINT INDENTIFICATION

In attempting to trace the origin of the fingerprint science a distinction must be drawn between man's realization that the tips of his fingers bear a diversified ridge construction and the application of this phenomenon to the problem of personal identification; the first is a matter of idle observation, the second the result of development and study. History is replete with references to prove that even in ancient times man was aware of the peculiar permanent lineations described by the ridges of the fingertips. On the face of a cliff in Nova Scotia, for instance, can be found an Indian carving of the outline of a hand with ridges and patterns clearly but crudely marked. So also the Chinese had used the impression of the thumb as a counter-signature and, according to Sir William Herschel, had even applied the idea to bank notes by placing a thumb impression partly on the counterfoil and partly on the note itself so that its genuineness might be easily established. The imagination of the English wood engraver, Bewick, was apparently aroused by the same realization, for he resorted to the fanciful practice of engraving the impression of his own thumb on many of his works.

The first known scientific observation on finger ridges was made in 1686 by Malpighi, the father of the science of histology and a professor of anatomy at the University of Bologna, who tersely alluded to the ridges which "describe different patterns." In 1823, J. E. Purkinje, a professor of anatomy at the University of Breslau, read a Latin thesis, commenting upon the diversity of ridge patterns connected with the organs of touch and even evolving a vague differentiation of these patterns into nine varieties.

There is a diversity of opinion as to the first practical application of fingerprints as a means of positive identification. Certain it is, however, that the imperfect impressions left on cliffs and pottery and the Chinese counter-signature were not sufficiently clear for close comparison and were probably manifestations of the prehistoric belief, which to some extent pervades the law of sealed instruments today, that personal contact conveys some nebular essence from the thing touched to the person touching it, thereby elevating it in dignity and binding effect. Certain it is, also, that the comments of Malpighi and Purkinje were little more than scholarly physiological treatises on the mere phenomenon of ridge diversity from a factual basis and lacked the concluding conception of their practical value as media of identification.

It remained for Doctor Henry Faulds, an English authority on the subject of dactylography, to write the first article on the practical use of fingerprints for the identification of criminals. In 1880, Doctor Faulds, who was connected at that time with the Tsukiji Hospital at Tokyo, Japan, conducted experiments which definitely established that the varieties of individual fingerprint patterns were very great; that the patterns remained constant throughout life; and, that even after the removal of ridges by the use of pumice stone and acid the patterns invariably grew out again "with unimpeachable fidelity" to their originals. Doctor Faulds published the results of his experiments in a letter appearing in the magazine *Nature*, under date of October 28, 1880. Shortly after the appearance of Doctor Faulds' article, Sir William Herschel, chief administrative officer in the Hoogley district of Bengal, India, wrote an article for the same magazine commenting upon the success with which he had utilized fingerprints for seventeen years in identifying government pensioners and in preventing impersonation and repudiation. It is apparent, therefore, that Doctor Faulds was the first to write concerning the practical use of fingerprints and that Sir William Herschel was the first to make extensive use of them. However, neither developed a method of classification suitable for general use and the intensive application of fingerprint identification.

The next great name in the history of fingerprint identification is that of Sir Francis Galton, a noted English scientist, who became interested in the subject through his study of heredity. Sir Francis not only established by extended investigations that no two fingerprints were alike but he devised the first method of classification that was sufficiently scientific to subdivide large collections of fingerprint records. As a result of his work, a committee was appointed by the British Government to consider the advisability of employing the fingerprint system in the identification of criminals. His articles relating to fingerprints were published in 1892 and 1893, and shortly after, Juan Vucetich, noted Argentine dactyloscopist, claims to have made his first criminal identification through the medium of fingerprints. In order to lessen the difficulty of dealing with large collections, Sir E. R. Henry, Commissioner of Scotland Yard, London, England, devised a more simple, yet more comprehensive system of filing and classifying prints. His system was successfully introduced into England and Wales in July, 1901, and forms the basis of the present system employed by all identification bureaus in the United States.

According to the "Henry System" all fingerprint impressions are divided into the following types of patterns: Loops, Twinned Loops, Central Pocket Loops, Lateral Pocket Loops, Arches, Tented Arches, Whorls and Accidentals. By utilizing these patterns together with the ridges intervening and surrounding two fixed points, known as the core and the delta, a classification for the ten fingers is developed. This classification permits the filing of fingerprint records in sequence, without reference to name, description or crime specialty of the individual, and enables the fingerprint expert in a bureau containing millions of prints to establish an identification in less than five minutes. It has been necessary for the larger bureaus in the United States to amplify and extend the original Henry System in order to facilitate the searching of files.

FINGERPRINT IDENTIFICATION IN THE UNITED STATES

The first authentic record of the use of fingerprints in the United States reveals that Mr. Gilbert Thompson of the United States Geological Survey utilized fingerprints to prevent the forgery of commissary orders during his supervision of a survey in New Mexico in 1882, or just shortly after Tabor, an eminent San Francisco photographer, suggested the fingerprint method for the registration of the Chinese whose identification had always been difficult. The first practical introduction of

fingerprints for criminal identification in the United States is claimed by the prison system of New York State, based on the adoption of the system at Sing Sing Prison on June 5, 1903, although the files of the present Department of Correction at Albany contain fingerprints of state prisoners from the institutions at Sing Sing, Napanoch, Auburn and Clinton, which show that they were classified as early as March, 1903, by Captain James H. Parke of the office of the then Superintendent of Prisons, Cornelius V. Collins. Then, on September 24, 1904, Mr. R. W. McClaughry, Warden of the United States Penitentiary at Leavenworth, Kansas, requested authority of the Attorney General to undertake sufficient expenditures for equipment to take fingerprints of Federal prisoners, which authorization was granted him November 2, 1904, only five days after the system was introduced in the police department of St. Louis, Missouri, by Sergeant Ferrier of Scotland Yard, London, England, who was guarding the Queen's Jubilee presents, on exhibition at the St. Louis Exposition in that year.

Since this time the use of dactylography for the identification of criminals has rapidly increased until today it is the most important factor in the identification work in the United States. Police departments, sheriffs, state police organizations and penal institutions realized the benefits to be derived from this comparatively simple and positive method of identification and gradually discontinued the use of Bertillon's anthropometrical system. Local bureaus were established and employees instructed in the taking, classifying, searching and filing of fingerprint records. In order to cope with the problem presented by migratory criminals, state bureaus were established to act as clearing houses for the information submitted by their correspondents. At the present time, the following states maintain bureaus which contain large collections of fingerprint records and which render invaluable service to any peace officer requesting assistance: Arizona, California, Florida, Illinois, Indiana, Iowa, Kansas, Louisiana, Massachusetts, Michigan, Mississippi, Missouri, Minnesota, Nebraska, New York, North Carolina, North Dakota, Ohio, Oklahoma, Rhode Island, South Dakota, Utah, Vermont and Washington. The International Association of Chiefs of Police, which embraces in its membership the heads of police departments of all the principal cities of the United States and Canada, founded a bureau at Washington, D. C., in 1896, known as the National Bureau of Criminal Identification, for the purpose of compiling Bertillon records. As its members began adopting the fingerprint system, the National Bureau of Criminal Identification gradually acquired a valuable collection of fingerprint records. As previously mentioned, the United States Department of Justice established a fingerprint bureau at the Leavenworth Penitentiary, Leavenworth, Kansas, in 1904, which first contained the fingerprints of Federal prisoners only, but soon expanded the scope of its operations by maintaining a free exchange service whereby criminal records were received and circularized among a growing list of contributing peace officers.

THE NATIONAL DIVISION OF IDENTIFICATION AND INFORMATION

The growing and insistent demand by police officials throughout the country for one system of coöperation on a national scale finally resulted in the creation of the National Division of Identification and Information, which was placed under the jurisdiction of the Bureau of Investigation of the United States Department of Justice. In 1924, this newly organized division received and consolidated in Washington, D. C., the records of both the National Bureau of Criminal Identification and the Leavenworth Penitentiary Bureau, and since that time the National Division of Identification and Information has enjoyed a remarkable growth and development. On July 1, 1929, it possessed 1,744,483 fingerprint records of actual current value and 2,624,944 alphabetical record cards. The extent to which law enforcement officials utilize the services of the National Division of Identification and Information is indicated by the following statistics covering the activities of the division from July 1, 1928 to June 30, 1929:

Fingerprint records received	304,384
Fingerprint records classified	287,142
Fingerprint records searched	314,910
Fingerprint records answered	314,482
Fingerprint records filed	337,693
Alphabetical cards searched	318,134
Alphabetical cards made	310,231
Number of Identifications made	86,965

The procedure by which the National Division of Identification and Information handles the hundreds of fingerprint records received daily from the peace officers of the country is both accurate and expeditious. The first operation consists of recording the name of the contributor, the date upon which the print is received and the police number of the criminal. The prints then pass to the technical section where trained experts classify them and carefully search through the master files for records with fingerprint impressions that are identical with those appearing on the current prints. In order to eliminate the possibility of error, each print is again searched in the alphabetical files for similar names and aliases. When an identification has been established, the current print is sent to an assembly section where the complete record of the individual is assembled, rechecked and consolidated. The final operation is performed by the typing section which prepares letters and telegrams advising all interested officials of the information appearing in the consolidated record. Over twelve hundred fingerprint records are now received daily by the National Division of Identification and Information and each inquiry is answered by letter within forty-eight hours of its receipt.

All peace officials are invited to avail themselves of the information contained in the files of the National Division of Identification and Information. Its service is rendered to all legally constituted law enforcement agencies free of any cost; in fact, fingerprint cards and franked envelopes for the transmission of records to the National Division are furnished gratuitously.

Occasionally it is possible for police officers to secure fingerprint impressions at the scene of a crime. When these impressions are latent, various powders can be applied to develop and emphasize the characteristics and the comparison of such prints with the fingerprint impressions of suspects forms one of the most interesting and valuable branches of the science. The National Division of Identification and Information is often called upon to establish identifications from latent prints furnished by its contributors and in this way has been successful in solving many crimes where the only clues were the latent fingerprint impressions left by the criminals.

Identification by means of palm impressions and footprints has been experimented with to some extent in this country, and there is nothing to prevent the establishment of identification by such means. For obvious reasons, however, footprints have received very little consideration by the police organizations of the United States, their principal use being confined to the practice of taking foot impressions of children in maternity hospitals.

BULLET IDENTIFICATION

In recent years considerable study has been given to the subject of bullet identification, which is based upon the fact that when two metals are pressed together with sufficient force, the softer metal will conform to the surface irregularities of the harder metal. When this principle was applied to ballistic identification it was found that the lead bullet and the brass primer cap, being softer than the steel barrel or firing-pin, assumed the surface characteristics of the latter as a result of the pressure created by the explosion of the propelling charge or by the hammer. It is possible, therefore, for police officers to compare test bullets fired from the gun of the suspected criminal with the bullet found at the scene of the crime and to determine in many cases the identity of the gun which was employed in the commission of the crime. It is also possible for the ballistic expert to study the dimensional measurements of bore and bullet diameters, the number and the depth of grooves and thus to present very valuable evidence during trial.

MODUS OPERANDI AND HANDWRITING IDENTIFICATION

In addition to fingerprint records, many police organizations maintain *modus operandi* files to assist in the identification and the apprehension of criminals. These files contain records which are subdivided and filed according to the nature of the crime and the manner of its commission. By employing this system, police officers are able to select the records of individuals who have committed crimes similar to the crime under investigation. Photographs of the suspects are immediately submitted for identification to any persons who may have seen the offender. These photographs are generally attached to the *modus operandi* records, but occasionally independent cabinets and albums (Rogues Galleries) are utilized to supplement the *modus operandi* files.

Handwriting, as a means of establishing the identity of the individual, depends for its efficacy to a very great extent upon the ability of the expert to whom the matter is submitted. However, most police organizations employ personnel capable of arriving at an intelligent solution of the problem presented by questioned documents and forgeries. In this work, photography plays an important part. By means of an enlarged photographic reproduction of the handwriting, the general alignment, the spacing, the shading, the frequency of contact, the crossing of stems, the flourishes, the relation of letters to the base line and the muscular coördination which produces certain characteristics can be studied. It is also possible to determine whether the tissue of the paper has been disturbed, the gloss removed or a new gloss applied. Many of the elements which enter into the identification of handwriting are equally important in determining the identity of the typewriter by which questioned words or documents have been written.

Many of the metropolitan police organizations in the United States maintain scientific laboratories in which tests are made of blood, cloth, hair, drugs, metals, and other objects which may provide possible clues in criminal investigations.

CRIMINAL IDENTIFICATION ABROAD

Generally speaking, the methods of criminal identification employed in the United States are similar to those utilized by law enforcement agencies in foreign countries. Fingerprints, photography, *modus operandi* files, ballistics, handwriting, scientific laboratory analysis and anthropometry are used in various combinations to form the basis of criminal identification in all the civilized countries of the world.

Europe

In France, the *Service de l'Identité judiciaire*, which is maintained in Paris by the Department of Justice, employs practically all of these methods and acts as a central clearing house of information pertaining to criminals. The entire police organization of France coöperates with this bureau, forwarding the fingerprint records of all persons arrested. Upon being received by the *Service de l'Identité judiciaire*, these records are classified according to a system which combines features of the Galton, Henry and Bertillon methods. While a separate Bertillon file is not maintained by the Paris bureau, three of the first six Bertillon measurements are employed to amplify the fingerprint classifications of the larger groups. An alphabetical name and alias file, with cross references to fingerprints and photographs, is also maintained. The Paris bureau possesses well equipped chemical, physical, and photographic laboratories to assist in the scientific investigation of crime. In these laboratories, the subjects of ballistics and latent fingerprint impressions receive intensive study.

Fingerprints and photography form the basis of criminal identification in the British Empire. The following possessions: England, Scotland, Ireland, Canada, Australia, Bahamas, Barbados, British East Africa, Burma, Ceylon, India, South Africa and Zanzibar maintain independent bureaus of identification which coöperate with the

New Scotland Yard bureau in London. All these bureaus employ the Henry system, with certain modifications and extensions, to classify their fingerprint records. In addition to its fingerprint files, New Scotland Yard has devised a *modus operandi* file, known as the Crime Index. This system provides for the filing of a crime card: first, under the crime-specialty, then under the age and, finally, under the height of each subject. Photographs referring to the crime index are kept in albums for the purpose of inspection.

Since the Conference of the German States in 1912, anthropometry has been discontinued as a method of criminal identification in Germany and fingerprint identification has assumed a position of foremost importance with photography playing an important but subordinate part. The laws of Germany do not provide for a national bureau of identification. However, in practice, the headquarters of police at Berlin acts as a national bureau and furnishes information concerning professional offenders. Although a combination of the Galton and Henry systems predominates throughout the country, many cities in Germany, such as Bremen, Dresden, Karlsruhe, Leipzig, Munich and Stuttgart maintain independent bureaus and have their own method of fingerprint classification. In 1903, the State of Hamburg adopted a system of classification devised by Mr. Roscher, who was, at that time, president of the police of Hamburg. The Roscher system was later adopted by Japan and Russia.

Italy utilizes all the known methods of criminal identification, excepting anthropometry, and maintains a national bureau of criminal identification in Rome. All police departments are compelled by statute to submit to the national bureau the fingerprints and record of each convicted subject. The system of fingerprint classification employed throughout Italy is known as the "Gasti System," which derives its name from Professor Questore Gasti of the University of Milan, who devised and perfected it. To supplement its fingerprint work, the national bureau has devised the Dactyloscopic Register, which enables the bureau to establish identification when the fingerprint impressions of less than ten digits are submitted for search.

The Government of Holland maintains an identification bureau which coöperates with its Department of Justice. This bureau is located in The Hague and renders assistance only in certain cases to the police authorities of the country. Its usefulness is probably limited by the fact that the science of dactyloscopy was not adopted by many of the most important cities in Holland until 1928. At the present time all fingerprint records are classified according to the system of Sir E. R. Henry, but the national bureau is reported to be planning the adoption of the Smallegange system.

In 1900, the city of Copenhagen, Denmark, established a local bureau for handling Bertillon records and four years later introduced fingerprints to supplement its anthropometrical system. The Danish Government took over this bureau, in 1908, and united with all Danish police districts in adopting dactyloscopy for identification work. Coöperation with the national bureau is made compulsory by law and the fingerprint record of each individual arrested is forwarded immediately to the central bureau where it is classified and searched according to the Henry system.

Fingerprints, photography and anthropometry are the important methods of criminal identification in Norway. A national identification bureau has been established at Oslo by the Norwegian Government and while coöperation with the national bureau is not mandatory, the police organizations of the country promptly submit the records of all persons arrested. Fingerprint records are classified by the national bureau according to a modified form of the Vucetich system.

South America

In connection with the different methods of fingerprint classification employed in foreign countries, it is important to mention again the Vucetich system which was devised by Juan Vucetich, a noted Argentine dactyloscopist. This system has been adopted by the national bureaus of Argentine, Brazil, Columbia, Chile, Czechoslovakia, and, in combination with the Henry System, it constitutes the method of classification used in Belgium. Of those countries which utilize the Vucetich system, Argentine has by far the largest centralized bureau of identification, which is maintained under the jurisdiction of the police of the capital at Buenos Aires. With compulsory civilian fingerprinting prescribed only for passport applicants, members of regulated professions, government employees, chauffeurs, taxidrivers and certain minor occupations, the department of police has accumulated a collection of 2,197,000 fingerprint records, a figure representing approximately one fifth of the total population.

INTERNATIONAL COÖPERATION

In order to cope with the international criminal, a bureau has been established recently in Vienna, Austria. This bureau, which is known as the *Internationale Kriminalpolizeiliche Kommission,* includes among its correspondents practically all of the national identification bureaus of the world. Each correspondent is requested to submit to the *Kommission,* the fingerprints, photographs and descriptions of all criminals who operate internationally. This information is recorded by the *Kommission* and copies transmitted to all its correspondents.

Real progress has been made in the field of criminal identification both in this country and abroad. The benefits to be derived from scientific methods in this important branch of police work have been definitely established. However, both the fingerprint and the *modus operandi* systems depend upon the accumulation of large collections of criminal information for their efficacy. It is necessary, therefore, for law enforcement officials to exercise care and thoroughness in the preparation of criminal records in order that local, state, national and international bureaus of identification may acquire accurate and complete information concerning all criminals.

The Technique of the American Detective

By Duncan Matheson

Captain of Detectives, San Francisco, California

THE public usually has a wrong conception of the detective. They assume that he is a mysterious individual with occult and supernatural powers, having a complete knowledge of individuals and events, past, present and future. This assumption is entirely erroneous. A detective, after all, is only a peace officer possessed of sound judgment, with the ability to apply it along sound practical business lines, to the solution of a criminal case. Whatever success I have met with has been accomplished by strict attention to duty and hard work. There is no other formula for success.

Much has been said and written about scientific detectives. The unfortunate part of the situation is that they become so scientific that they have to put out their hands to find out if they are in bed. They talk about science and abstract theories, incapable of application only to their own individual selves, with the result that their services are valueless and they are unable to distinguish the difference between a first class crook and a canary bird.

However, that does not mean that science has no place in the investigation of crime. Quite the contrary is true. The scientist is called in many cases and renders invaluable service. In plain English, the scientist "knows his stuff" and the so-called scientific detective is a fool.

THE DETECTIVE AT WORK

Every crime tells a story capable of interpretation. A peace officer that cannot read the story has no value in its solution. That is where the detective comes in. He makes a survey of the premises, the scene of the crime, the neighborhood and all the intimate details connected therewith. If it is a homicide, he notes the location, paying attention to entrances and exits, the kind of premises, the location of the body, the arrangement or the disarrangement of the furniture, the exact location of everything at or near the body, the exact location of weapons, their identification and how used. These intimate details may seem valueless to the public, but they are vital in criminal prosecution. For instance, the clothing of the victim will tell a complete story. They may recite the history of a struggle and the number of persons involved.

Blood stains tell their own story. If on clothing, they indicate conclusively whether the victim was standing up, recumbent or prone. Blood stains or drops on shoes play an important part in the story. If drops are found, one has a right to assume that the victim was standing and that the wounds were in the upper portion of the body. In an important murder case, the person who committed the murder stepped into a pool of blood in making his escape. He took the precaution to wash his shoes, but in doing so he failed to find the blood that was located in the crack between the upper and the sole. It was found and conclusively proved that it was human blood.

That is where the scientist comes in. Only a few years ago no method of analysis was known for distinguishing human from animal blood, but science has proved its worth by overcoming many difficulties in analyzing blood stains. Clothing with blood stains to be used in evidence should never be folded, because the stains may be transferred, in folding, from one place to another. They should be kept on hangers until their use as evidence ceases.

Photography plays a very important part in solving crime problems. In homicide cases a photograph will show the exact conditions at the scene and it goes even further in many cases. If the weapon used was a firearm and the bullet and the empty shell were recovered, it can be demonstrated to an absolute certainty, whether or not the bullet was discharged from that particular weapon. That is important because it removes a doubt. Consequently, defense attorneys cannot cloud the issue by uncertainties.

Fingerprints are also important. If there is a suspect in the case and prints are found, comparison will immediately determine whether or not the suspect is involved. However, in cases where there are no suspects and the perpetrator has never been fingerprinted they are not, at that particular moment, of any great value. Sometimes a fingerprint impression of only one or two fingers is left on a job and it is very difficult to identify them, even when the prints are on file. Considerable time and study has been devoted to a single-print formula but the problem has not yet been solved. When it is, it will be of great value to all investigating officers.

OUTWITTING THE PROFESSIONAL CRIMINAL

However, criminals are practical and soon learn to use gloves while committing crimes, thus defeating the fingerprint experts. This is particularly true of organized gangs of burglars of all classes. Safe-blowers never attack a safe barehanded and rarely leave tools behind unless disturbed while working. It must not be assumed for a moment that criminals are, in the language of the streets, dumb-bells. Quite the contrary, they are experts in their particular lines. Expert safe-blowers know the mechanism of every make of safe. A safe-burglar was searched after arrest and a complete formula, accompanied by exact diagrams, for opening safes with explosives was found on his person. The measurements were worked out to one-sixteenth of an inch. There was nothing haphazard about his work. He is now serving a life sentence in Ohio for murder committed while blowing a safe.

But that is not all. Safe-burglars often know the effect certain brands of explosives will have on safes. If they use forty or sixty per cent dynamite, they know about the exact quantity and how to use it. If, on the other hand, they use nitro-glycerine, they know the dangers connected therewith and are rarely, if ever, injured by it. The detective detailed to investigate this class of burglary must be able to determine, in a few moments, the type of burglar committing the offense and the explosive used and proceed along logical lines to apprehend the criminals. A case once came to my attention, where a safe-door was supposedly opened by the use of explosives, but on investigation it developed that the explosives were used on the open door. This established the motive, making the solution easy.

Sometimes the question is asked: Have footprints any value? They have, when a plaster cast can be made. It is a very simple matter to make a plaster cast of a footprint, when the impression is such that it will hold liquid plaster of Paris until it hardens. Footprints are usually found in garden plots about private residences. However, in the large cities, with their dense populations and their paved streets and alleyways, they are very seldom found. This, of course, applies equally to automobile tracks. The tread of tires is important, particularly in the rural districts. Many cases have been solved by the tread mark of tires. In a case of safe-burglary, the car used on the job was parked in a lot while the burglary was being committed. The tire tread impressions were left. When the car was recovered the tread was identical with the impressions, even to a defect. It was an important link in the evidence.

All of this, however, is incidental. It is part of the job. Every up-to-date police department is equipped with all appliances for fingerprinting, photographing, microscopic and chemical development, and research.

We often hear and read of what they are doing in Europe by scientific methods. If they had in Europe today the problems that we have in this country, they would not know where to start, let alone reach the end of the trail. This is not a criticism of what they are doing or attempting to do but it is a criticism of the disgraceful condition in this country. There is an over-abundance of self-styled scientific detectives and crime experts in this country. They would have a gullible public believe that they are so scientific that the crooks would respond to engraved invitations to visit police headquarters and surrender and after surrendering be rejuvenated by a magic wand and made over into good and useful citizens. Just how long the public will stand for this rot is a question.

Perhaps the most difficult cases coming to the attention of the police are the so-called "Hit and Run" cases. But, even when there are no witnesses and the victim is either dead or unable to throw any light on the case, they are not impossible of solution. Skid marks, broken glass or other wreckage tell a story. Many cases have been cleared up by fragments of glass left on the road. Thorough searches in garages, repair shops, including paint shops, and private garages, reveal many such stories and incidents.

Pages could be written on how relatively unimportant things lead to the solution of apparently difficult cases. It simply demonstrates that a peace officer endowed with good common sense and an analytical mind can by following simple rules solve most any case assigned to him. It is also true that scientists are invaluable in determining what a practical detective brings to him for analysis and report.

Organizing Detective Work

Individual detective ability, as such, does not mean a great deal. It is organization that counts. An unorganized detective bureau is valueless and a burden on the taxpayers. Every successful business is organized, and the better the organization, the nearer it is to one hundred per cent efficiency. That is why real executives are always found in charge of large corporations and big businesses. It should be so in police detective bureaus. The question then is asked: Can they be so organized? The answer is in the affirmative. Then you may well ask how.

Every person knowing anything at all about criminals knows that criminality is their "game" or profession. They follow well defined lines and therefore can be classified. Bad check artists live off the change of bad checks. They are called "paper hangers." Bank hold-up men follow that "game." Store burglars are proud of their profession, and so on, down every line of criminal endeavor. Criminals usually stick to their own particular line, but there are exceptions to every rule. Bunco men are always bunco artists. Pickpockets specialize in their line.

The reason they do not change is that they would have to learn a new "game."

An efficient bureau must be organized in special groups or details to cope successfully with the situation. The members of these details become expert in their particular line and have a mental grasp of the situation. They can tell offhand, by reading a report, just what class of burglar is operating and, by the process of elimination, narrow the perpetrators to a limited few. Practical experience is what counts.

Much has been said and published about the educated college policeman and detective and it is all bunk. Give me the practical detective with actual experience in handling criminals and criminal cases and with ten such men I will do more work than any college professor or so-called expert can do with one hundred of his trained "nuts." Most of those that I have seen could not put a harness on a mule, let alone catch a crook.

The question may be asked: How shall a bureau be organized? It is a fair question and deserves an honest answer. Specialization in police work is part of the organization program. The bureau should contain the following details: Pawnshop detail, Retail Shopping detail, Burglary detail, Robbery detail, Homicide detail, Automobile detail, Bunco and Pickpocket detail, Banking detail, Bogus Check and Forgery detail, Hotel detail, Federal detail, cöoperating with all Federal agencies, Efficiency Bureau, Letters and Inquiry detail, Diagrams and Photograph Gallery and Bureau of Identification.

In selecting detectives for the various details, special attention should be given to natural aptitude for the work. It frequently happens that a detective suited for the Check detail would be a failure on the Automobile detail. Quarterly reports will show exactly what they are doing. Police departments should charge themselves with all property reported lost or stolen and credit themselves with all property recovered at the same value as reported. By striking a balance every three months, the department will know just how it stands. The San Francisco department has been doing this for years. Weak spots appear and proper action is taken to remedy the situation. The department simply applies business methods to police work. There is no technique to it, just plain common sense.

THE DETECTIVES AND THE COURT

Investigations follow the same line in all countries of the world, although local and social conditions are different. For instance, in Great Britain it is considered a patriotic duty to appear as a witness in criminal cases. Here it is almost impossible to obtain witnesses simply because they are terrorized by the crooks and their friends. Statutes prohibiting the intimidation of witnesses are a dead letter. Years ago, boys could be seen on the streets carrying sacks of gold. Now it is none too safe in armored cars, protected by guards. The public would rush to the assistance of the boy, if attacked; if the armored car is attacked, they would hear and see nothing.

Why the change? Simply because witnesses are tried instead of the defendants. They are bully-ragged while on the stand and are subjected to all kinds of abuse. The purpose of any trial or hearing is to arrive at the truth in the most direct manner. That is the very thing defense attorneys do not want to do and they resort to every trick known to the trade in order to prevent it. When there is no defense, they want to try the arresting officers, who simply perform an official duty in a lawful way.

They look toward high heaven and

cry out against the use of third degree methods by law enforcement officers and they weep and wail against man's inhumanity. to man, pure and unadulterated "bunk." Why? Simply because a few simple direct questions are asked the defendant, to ascertain the exact truth.

The questions are, in most cases, helpful to him when they are answered truthfully. If answered untruthfully, the responsibility is his. The reason defense attorneys wail so much is that it prevents them from building up a defense not in accord with the facts, and also because the prosecution is possessed of facts that can be used in rebuttal. In plain English, all this anti-third-degree nonsense is to prevent the introduction of rebuttal testimony in criminal cases.

Detectives should know how far hearsay testimony can be used in criminal cases and make notes accordingly. A dying declaration is hearsay, but it is admissible under certain rules of evidence. The difference between a conversation and an admission and confession must be thoroughly understood.

A real test of a detective's ability comes when he marshals his facts and his evidence in presenting his case to the jury through the prosecuting attorney. Then, weaknesses will show. Something may be missing in the sequence of the case or some of the evidence may be improperly marked for identification. The defense will always take advantage of this and use it to the discredit of the officer. He must also be able to determine in advance what the defense will be and be prepared to meet it. That is just as important as the prosecution.

But his duties do not end there. He must remember that his case is tried before a jury. It is his duty to see that there are no "plants" on the jury, that the prosecuting officer is fully informed of the qualifications of the members thereof and that the latter are not interfered with as jurors during the trial. Preserving the sanctity of the jury is in itself a problem.

The enforcement of law and the administration of justice is a national disgrace. Prisons are slowly and surely becoming comfortable clubs without a membership fee or annual dues. The reformers have had full swing in advancing new theories about crime, more laws to make scoundrels happy and probation and parole for almost every crime, no matter how diabolical it might be. These theories and laws have reached into the courts. Restitution is asked for and accepted in all cases where property loss occurs. Probation has grabbed the restitution theory, solely to make it popular. Restitution is proper in failure-to-provide cases, but in all other cases it makes a mockery of law by making the court a collection agency, while the crime still remains and is forgotten. Thus justice is crucified on the altar of the almighty dollar.

THE GREAT HANDICAP—POLITICS

When will this disgraceful condition be stopped, or can it be stopped? The answer is affirmative. Every peace officer, regardless of rank, knows that the enforcement of law and the administration of justice are in the realm of politics. It is quite common to see election literature and campaign banners placed over the doors of blind-pigs, gambling and so-called social clubs, thus explaining to the public their choice for the office. It is quite common for candidates to make open declarations of policy as to their conduct if elected. Any person accepting appointive office under a so-called liberal administration is writing the epitaph on his official tombstone. Our national sin is the sacrifice of principle for political expediency.

The Technique of Investigation of the English Detective

By F. J. CRAWLEY

Chief Constable of the City and County of Newcastle, England

THERE is an impression among the rank and file of American Police, that the remarkable success of the English detective is due to the fact that in England a prisoner is guilty until he proves himself innocent. Thoughtful Americans will of course realise that this is an absurdity. The confusion of thought doubtless arises by reason of the superior law enforcement system in England, although the law machinery in the two countries is practically identical.

In England there is no interference, and witnesses are afforded complete protection; the people are united in thought, action, race and historical background. It is therefore right to say that the success of the English Police is due to the unfailing coöperation of the public, a public which exposes vice and crime and gives no shelter to the criminal. On the other hand, this public, having performed its own policing from the time of the Saxon moot, is jealous of its liberties and privileges.

In the investigation of crime, the detective has to tread cautiously lest he incur castigation or an action for damages. His powers are but slightly greater than those of the ordinary citizen. Everything works to protect an arraigned person from policeman, lawyer, Magistrate and Judge right up to the time of being found guilty. Juries too are chary of accepting circumstantial evidence unless heavily streaked with direct testimony. Therefore, the English detective must see to it that his technique in crime investigation produces evidence of the kind and quality acceptable to a Court, obtained in accordance with legal rules and thus admissible. The quiet dignity of an English Court makes for restraint and mental discipline to which the detective subconsciously inclines.

The English detective's methods will not differ, except perhaps in degree, from those of his American colleague. Although not admitted, the degree is dependent on what the public will tolerate. The public's toleration will depend on its conceptions of personal liberty, racially, historically, culturally and politically arrived at, but it will invariably also be governed by the kind and the amount of crime prevalent at the time. When atrocious crime is rampant, the citizen is prepared to forego something in order to bring about its suppression. In America, the public attitude differs in almost every State and town; this is also reflected in the differing State laws, despite the same common law. The illegal rounding up and the temporary incarceration of mere suspects, tolerated in one Police area and not in another, is illustrative of varying methods of crime investigation which do not operate in England. Of course, the crime problem in America, on account of its enormity and variety, calls for entirely different handling and treatment than it does in England.

PRELIMINARY STEPS

The first line of investigation of the English detective is to collaborate with his public on the spot, and later elsewhere. It should be here stated, however, that whilst it is customary to regard the detective as the special investigator of crime, yet it must be realised that uniform Police on patrol duty are almost always first on the scene of a crime, and as much hinges on the early aspects of a crime, uniform Police are instructed and empowered to act on lines identical with those of their plainclothes colleagues. In the development of such cases the detective merely assists the uniform man and only supersedes him on special direction. A member of a Police Force being apprised of a crime is required speedily to take certain preliminary steps, such as: (a) responding to notification; (b) transmitting brief particulars to Headquarters by the readiest means, for dissemination to Police; (c) investigating; (d) transmitting further particulars for further dissemination to Police, if necessary.

It is clearly the first duty, where possible, to apprise Police Headquarters at the earliest moment in order that such steps may be taken inside and outside the Force as the case may warrant; yet to meet all cases, it is left to a Policeman's own judgment whether he shall proceed directly to the scene of a crime or first apprise Headquarters. The writing of reports other than the statements of dying persons and suspects are left till later. It is specially emphasised that the obligations of uniform Police do not cease on taking the preliminary steps and they are looked to to contribute their share to the solution of problems and the detection of offenders.

Headquarters will designate the type and the numbers of officers for dealing with the crime, and the organisation provides means for telephoning to the Force concerned and to other Forces; the pursuit by Police vehicles or the cutting off of roads and bridges; the search of railway stations, trains, hotels,

lodging houses, public houses and restaurants; the circulation of information to pawnbrokers, jewellers, automobile agents and so forth, as the case may require; the apprising of informants and the questioning of criminal associates and prostitutes; and if necessary, the notification of the Press and the wireless stations, as well as the wireless transmission of photographs, finger prints and other details.

To date, some fifty Police Areas have adopted the Decentralised System of Policing through Police Boxes, originated by the present writer; this means in brief that patrolling Police work on an extended organisation and thus never touch Headquarters except telephonically from their miniature Police Stations, popularly known as "Boxes." Apart from a host of other advantages, the System is particularly effective in countering automobile crime and will become more so as other Police Areas are linked up. In any case, the escape of criminals is more difficult in England than in America by reason of the absence of tracts of deserted country, on the one hand; and, on the other, on account of the effective town and county Police organisations coördinated through the Home Office, although autonomous.

THE INVESTIGATION OF CRIME

The investigating Police officer (who for the purpose of this article will be presumed to be a detective) naturally has to vary his line of investigation to meet each case, yet ordinarily he can be expected to proceed somewhat as follows: He will obtain all the information possible in respect to the crime, time, character of victim and his financial, commercial, social and family history; victim's friends, associates, servants; persons visiting or seen in vicinity; suspects; persons recently released from prison or known for violent acts or criminal tendencies of a kind similar to those shown in the crime; paramours; insane persons, epileptics, drunkards, drug addicts, and so forth.

If a person is suspected, his description, photograph, habits, associates and anything that will help to find him will be obtained. In obtaining a description, special attention will be paid to physical peculiarities, peculiarities of gait and manner, height, build, age, hair, eyes, clothes and occupation. In obtaining a description of missing property, attention will be paid to such points as shape, value, marks, makers' names, whether old or new, and so forth. The fact that articles and wearing apparel have been left, or certain articles specially taken whilst other articles of even greater value are left, may serve to indicate the type of offender. Photographs of the scene, of the victim, of tools or stolen property are freely taken to support a line of prosecution or defence or otherwise assist in the investigation.

In England, it must be understood that Police are free to interrogate anyone who voluntarily submits, including a person who may ultimately turn out to be the prisoner, but as soon as an interrogating Police Officer discovers that he is dealing with a person who may possibly become a prisoner he has to cease interrogation. Moreover, a recent Royal Commission not only endorses the practice of Police being required to give a caution to a person immediately he becomes suspect, but recommends that at the outset of any formal questioning, whether of a potential witness or of a suspected person, with regard to any crime or any circumstance connected therewith, the Police Officer must caution that person in the following words: "I am a Police officer. I am making inquiries (into so and so), and I want to know anything you can tell me about it. It is a serious matter, and I must warn you to be careful what you say."

Means and Methods of Identification

In certain circumstances, if finger prints are found, it may be advisable to take the finger prints of members of a household for comparison; there is no power to require this to be done. Since January 1926, Police have been forbidden to require any person in custody to be fingerprinted; Prison Governors, however, have the right. Still, it will be gathered that Police have been deprived of a valuable means of determining the antecedents of a detained person; thus the possibility arises of criminals being discharged through inability to present sufficient evidence at an early stage.

The detective particularly concentrates on tracks and marks. Physical traces left behind in the commission of a crime become items of circumstantial evidence or may give a clue to the identity of an offender. The type of weapon; marks which indicate the type of weapon used; blood marks on doors, windows, broken glass, tools, or showing line of retreat; blood marks indicating the nature of wounds for identification purposes; marks of bloody hands, clotted blood and hair, teeth and nails connected up to culprit or victim; marks showing mode of ingress and egress and those showing direction of blows and bullets on walls and furniture; marks of burglarious tools on doors, safes, cupboards, drawers, and so forth; footmarks on soil and other surfaces which may be expected to register imprints, with careful regard to deductions which may be drawn from the type, gait, and so forth, of the wearer; the nails, gaps, heels, and so forth, of footprints will be counted and paper patterns or plaster casts will be made if possible; handmarks left in the dust and marks with ink or on wet paint are of value.

Every effort is made to obtain fingerprints which may be of value not only for comparison and elimination of prints of persons in the household, but also with a view of tracing the person through the fingerprint bureau at Scotland Yard. If, as is well known, an offender's original fingerprints are filed in the bureau, the chances of identification increase according to the clearness and number of the finger impressions. The British Police, through Sir Edward Henry, a former Commissioner of Police of London, can be justly proud of being the creators of the system of classification and identification by fingerprints, a system which has completely superseded the Bertillon method.

Police have also another valuable innovation in the *Modus Operandi* System. This was originated by Sir L. W. Atcherley, a Home Office Inspector of Constabulary. It reduces to classification all the data obtainable about travelling criminals; from a few particulars received at a central bureau from one town, and a few more from another, a concrete presentation of the culprit's description, habits and *modus operandi* is ultimately possible.

DETECTIVE SPECIALISTS

There is no bureau of criminology in England such as is to be found in certain countries on the continent of Europe. Each large City and County Headquarters has, however, a department which specialises to some extent in the purely scientific study of criminal exhibits. For instance, firearms, bullets and poisons receive a good deal of attention. But in the case of most other exhibits which require that evidence be given thereon by the best experts in the country, it is usual to have recourse to such experts. As an illustration, an expert would be required to state the difference between human and animal blood. The Home Office, on application, provides expert pathologists.

Writers of fiction generally ascribe to detectives unusual capacity in the unravelling of crime. They ought to possess this to some extent, but their equally important duty and value lie in their capacity to handle a case. In England, by reason of the many legal restrictions existing, this is no mean task. The work requires much initiative and a certain amount of audacity. On the same set of facts, one detective can bring a case to a successful issue and another lose it. For this reason a case may demand the services of a detective who has specialised in the handling of such cases. Cases involving finance, cheque frauds and banking will demand one type, whilst murder will require another. The London Force, being a large one, can afford to develop and carry such detective specialists, and by reason of their specialisation they are often lent to provincial Forces. The provincial detective, however, has a much more general experience, and his greatest value lies in his local knowledge.

The Technique of Criminal Investigation in Germany

By Dr. Robert Heindl

Legation Councillor, German Foreign Office; formerly Commissioner of Police, Berlin, Germany [1]

WE begin with a few words anent the legal regulations governing the investigation of crime in Germany. So much by way of preface is necessary to a clear explanation of the technical aids and the methods of applying them used by the German criminal police.

DIVISION OF AUTHORITY

In accordance with the law of the German Reich (*Strafprozessordnung*), criminal investigation devolves upon three governmental agencies: the police, the Federal prosecutor (*Staatsanwalt*) and the investigating judge, to whom the police magistrate of Anglo-Saxon countries offers the closest analogy.

For our present purposes, we need not speak in detail of the investigating judge, for he acts only in exceptional cases defined by law. His entry cannot take place until a definite individual is named as the guilty person and until public accusation has already been made by the Federal prosecutor.

The Federal prosecutor must take the lead in criminal investigation, according to the letter of the law, while the third of the agencies named above, the police, is assigned a very modest part in criminal investigation. It is merely an auxiliary to the Federal prosecutor. The latter prescribes the course of the investigation to be followed in specific cases, and the police must carry out his orders obediently.[2] Only in urgent cases, when the awaital of orders from the Federal prosecutor would imperil the success of the investigation, may the police act independently.[3]

In practice, however, the situation is the reverse of what one might suppose from the text of the law. Inasmuch as criminal cases almost always require prompt attention, by far the greater number of all criminal investigations are carried on by the police, and indeed, are carried on independently. Not until the investigation has issued in what may for most purposes be regarded as a definite conclusion is the result of the investigation transmitted to the Federal prosecutor. Only when major crimes occur (murder, and so forth) is the office of the Federal prosecutor at once notified; in such cases representatives are frequently sent to the scene of the crime, but even then the police are usually left entire freedom of action. Only in small towns, villages and rural districts, where few police are available, does the Federal prosecutor, of necessity, personally conduct the first inquiries.

When we speak of the technique of criminal investigation in Germany, we are, therefore, almost exclusively concerned with police technique, for whenever the Federal prosecutor and the investigating judge take an active part in a case, such intervention is usually through the medium of the criminal police (*Kriminalpolizei*). Without the aid of the latter, the agencies just mentioned hardly do more than examine the accused, the witnesses and the forensic experts during the later stages of complicated criminal cases.

[1] Translated by Howard P. Becker, University of Pennsylvania.

[2] *Strafprozessordnung*, par. 161.

[3] *Op. cit.*, par. 163, section 1.

The technique of such proceedings is analogous to that used by the police.

ORGANIZATION OF GERMAN POLICE

Hence, we turn to the police in particular. In so doing, we must pay due regard to the following peculiarity of German constitutional law: the fact that although the division of authority among Federal prosecutor, investigating judge and police is based, as we have seen, upon a law of the Reich, the police as such is solely the affair of the *provinces* (*i.e.*, the separate units of the Reich—Prussia, Bavaria, Saxony, and so forth). There is no German police force; there are only Prussian, Bavarian and other provincial police forces. In the post-war, post-revolutionary period, attempts were made to establish one police force for the Reich as a whole, but they came to nothing, with minor exceptions negligible here, because of the opposition of the provinces. Foreign affairs, the railroads, the post office, the army, and so forth, are in the hands of the Reich, but not the police.

In spite of the fact that Germany has no unified police force, a strong similarity among the police organizations of the separate provinces has nevertheless developed in the course of time. In what follows, we shall consider only the criminal police.

THE "KRIMINALPOLIZEI"

By "criminal police" is usually understood, in practice, that division of the police which deals with felonies and misdemeanors exclusive of political crimes (high treason, and so forth) and those offenses against the moral code which in the United States are usually called "statutory." For these excepted classifications, special divisions are usually organized within the larger police forces. Infractions of the law are usually dealt with by the criminal police only when they involve felonies or misdemeanors which are not political or statutory. As a practical matter — contrast with this the theoretical standpoint of the literature — the criminal police are also concerned with the *prevention* of crime. Indeed, the task of prevention has recently assumed a place well in the foreground of police activity. For this reason alone, the demand for separation of the criminal police from all connection with the rest of the police force and for their subordination to the Federal prosecutor and the judiciary is, in the writer's estimation, a step backward, although this demand is frequently found in the German literature and is strongly backed by the German group within the *Internationale Kriminalistische Vereinigung.* In one German province, Baden, such subordination of the police indeed obtains (historically explicable as due to the influence of French law—*police judiciaire*); but the other German provinces have, up to the present day, rightly avoided this arrangement. The efforts of the criminal police are much more likely to be successful when they are closely coordinated with all the other divisions of the police force; this coördination can be guaranteed only by the executive authority of a common chief. One need only recall how frequently practical exigencies demand the coöperation of the criminal police with alien, moral and traffic police (*Fremden- Sitten- und Verkehrspolizei*). The provision of the Code of Criminal Procedure (§161) giving the Federal prosecutor power either to make inquiries himself or to do so with the help of the police, vouchsafes him sufficient and proper influence upon the course of the investigation without linking him with the police by any formal bond of organization.

The popular expression "secret police," when used to designate the criminal police, is based upon confused ideas, for the use of policemen in civilian clothing for the purpose of shadowing suspected persons is a practice found in all fields of police administration and is by no means peculiar to the criminal police.

"Confidential agents," a phrase to which the closest American analogy is "stool pigeons," may have given rise to the expression "secret police" (*police secrète*) during the period at the beginning of the nineteenth century when they were much too frequently used in France (Fouché: *Cohorte cythérique*). Such agents are at present used by the criminal police of the German provinces only in limited measure, being hired only temporarily and for specific cases. Their use is of course legally unobjectionable, and is frequently unavoidable when the clarification of serious crimes cannot be otherwise achieved. The use of *agents provocateurs*, however, is not permissible, being forbidden by paragraphs 47–49 of the criminal code of the Reich.

Private detectives are seldom concerned with criminal investigations in Germany—a marked contrast to England and other countries! Their activity is usually limited to privately financed investigations concerning reputation, manner of living and financial status.

We must consider another question which to my knowledge is especially important to American readers, or which at least formed the nucleus for many discussions during my sojourn in the United States: What is the relation of the state criminal police to the municipal? Since 1848 there has been a distinct tendency to remove the criminal police from the control of the larger municipalities and to place it in the hands of the provincial government. This is also true of the political police and in fact of all protective police with the exception of traffic police, sanitary police, and so forth. In the opinion of the writer, this tendency is quite justified.

In Prussia at the present time, the criminal police of sixty-seven cities are directly responsible to the provincial government.[4] The cost of maintaining the criminal police in such cases is borne by both the government and the municipality, and the proportion paid by each is legally fixed.

DUTIES AND POWERS OF THE CRIMINAL POLICE

The duties and the powers of the criminal police are as follows: punishable acts *may* be reported to the Federal prosecutor's office and to the court of first instance, as per paragraph 158 of the code of criminal procedure already cited. This paragraph also permits the lodging of such complaints with the police. In practice, by far the greater number of offenses are reported directly to the police because they are more readily accessible to the public. The criminal police are in duty bound to investigate these complaints. Furthermore, they must act on their own initiative if they learn of a punishable action in other ways. Neglect to follow up such cases makes the policeman himself liable to punishment (*Strafgesetzbuch*, par. 341). The criminal police must observe all regulations which forbid delay and postponement, in order that the true state of affairs may not be obscured by failure to act promptly.

---

[4] Berlin, with 2402 officials concerned only with criminal police activities, Cologne with 342, Elberfeld-Barmen with 236, and so forth. The smallest state criminal police departments are Schneidemühl with ten and Suhl with six investigators. In Berlin, therefore, there is about one criminal police official to every seventeen hundred inhabitants; in Cologne, about one to every two thousand; in Suhl about one to every thirty-three hundred.

According to §152 of the law of the Reich governing the judiciary (*Gerichtsverfassungsgesetz*), the officials of the criminal police *may* be placed at the disposal of the Federal prosecutor. In this auxiliary capacity, they are obliged to carry out in their territory his orders and regulations or those of his representatives. The police, therefore, are functionally subordinate to the Federal prosecutor and his officials, although so far as organization is concerned, no such subordination exists.[5] The particular officials of the provincial and the municipal police who may thus be placed at the disposal of the Federal prosecutor vary from province to province. High-ranking police officers are not as a rule required to serve as auxiliaries to the Federal prosecutor. The police departments *as such* are not as a matter of fact auxiliary organs (in the sense above indicated) of the Federal prosecutor. They and those of their officials not *specifically* placed at the disposal of the Federal prosecutor may be called upon by him and his aides only through a request for assistance. The same is true of the commissions and the requests of the investigating judge.[6] In case of danger arising from delay, the district judge has the same power to compel prompt action as does the investigating judge.

In carrying out their tasks, the criminal police, according to the code of criminal procedure of the Reich, may use measures of force—a provision which may not be extended by provincial legislation. (Par. 6 of Supplement to Code of Criminal Procedure.) These measures are search, seizure,

[5] In Prussia, censure, for disregard of regulations in carrying out official business, and disciplinary punishment, by fine not exceeding one thousand marks, may be imposed as a means of forcing the police to carry out the tasks entrusted to them by the Federal prosecutor (Judiciary Act, par. 81).

[6] *Strafprozessordnung*, par. 189:

arrest and examination. The right to take testimony under oath, however, is not vouchsafed to the criminal police. Further, they do not have the right, at least not according to the Code of Criminal Procedure, to force, by the infliction of punishment, suspected persons and witnesses to appear and give evidence. Nevertheless, they do have at their disposal the right to use the force which, in their capacity of preventive police, accrues to them under the provincial law. In addition, the right to summon eyewitnesses of a punishable action for the purpose of learning their identity and obtaining information is recognized. When engaged in official activity at the place where a crime has occurred, the official in charge has the right to arrest persons who wilfully interfere with him in his official capacity, or who violate regulations, the enforcement of which is the duty of such officials. The person or persons so arrested may be kept in custody not to exceed one day beyond the termination of said official activity (*Strafprozessordnung*, par. 164).

Further details, especially more exact citation of the laws, ministerial decrees and judicial decisions relevant to all of the above problems may be found in my article *Kriminalpolizei*, in the *Handwörterbuch der Rechtswissenschaft*, published in Berlin by de Gruyter.

TECHNICAL AIDS IN CRIMINAL INVESTIGATION

The technical aids used by the criminal police in Germany are somewhat similar to those used in the United States and in all other civilized countries. In recent decades practically every country has learned much from its fellows. A detailed description of all the technical aids in criminal investigations in Germany would therefore be only a tedious repetition of matters which are probably dealt with in other articles in the present volume. Furthermore, everything that I could say I have already said in a book,[7] which comprises over eight hundred pages with more than nine hundred illustrations and is, to the best of my knowledge, the most detailed work hitherto published on the questions here dealt with. In what follows, therefore, I shall be quite brief, and must refer those readers who are interested in further particulars to the book just mentioned.

In connection with the articles which my honored colleagues here present on the criminalistic technique of their respective countries, I believe that a very modest task remains for me, namely, the precise determination of a few dates in the historical development of criminalistic technique in Germany. Beyond this, I shall do no more than refer to a few points of general interest which may not have been mentioned in the other articles in this volume.

ANTHROPOMETRY

As early as 1860, Stevens had already measured the head, ears, feet, chest and body length of convicts. He justified his method of identification by these two principles: first, two human beings with the same measurements do not exist; and second, certain bony structures do not alter after a certain age has been reached.[8]

Bertillon appeared twenty years later (1879) with the same proposal. In the criminalistic literature, surprisingly enough, the name of Stevens does not occur; time and again Bertillon is called the "discoverer" of anthropometry.

[7] Robert Heindl, *System und Praxis der Daktyloskopie und der sonstigen technischen Methoden der Kriminalpolizei*, Berlin, de Gruyter, 14th ed., 1926.

[8] Heindl, *op. cit.*, p. 56.

In Germany, anthropometry was first made use of by the Dresden police in 1895. After September 26, 1896, measurements were regularly made throughout the whole Kingdom of Saxony. The central bureau or place of deposit for the card records was Dresden. Hamburg soon followed, and in December, 1896, Berlin. In June, 1897, on the initiative of the Dresden police, an agreement was entered into by all the provinces of the Reich in accordance with which anthropometry was introduced into all the provinces and an exchange of card records was instituted both within Germany and with foreign central bureaus. In December, 1912, largely on the writer's initiative, this agreement was annulled. Since that time, anthropometry has not been officially practised in Germany.

DACTYLOSCOPY

The recording of fingerprints at the scene of a crime for the purpose of identifying the criminal was now and again practised in Germany before the turn of the century (after 1896), but not systematically. The preparation of fingerprint records for the purpose of registering and identifying recidivists has been carried on in Germany since 1903. (Since this period we have also had systematic examination of fingerprints at the scene of crime!) After the writer had a short time previously made a fruitless attempt to institute a fingerprint bureau in Munich after the model of the Anglo-Indian example (Galton-Henry), a similar attempt was successfully made in Dresden on April 1, 1903. After October 24, 1903, fingerprints of all persons arrested throughout the whole Kingdom of Saxony were taken, and were classified in the central bureau at Dresden. In the same year Hamburg and Berlin followed suit. In Bavaria, in 1908, my proposal of 1902–1903 was revived and an identification service was instituted in Munich by Dr. Harster and myself; in 1911 this was given legal sanction throughout the whole province. Württemberg soon followed. As a result of an agreement among the provinces dating from December, 1912, the fingerprint method was finally introduced throughout all of Germany. Because of the peculiar relation of the police to the Reich, already mentioned in the first part of this article, there resulted the fact that a unitary identification service (like that found in England, for example) with one central bureau, a uniformly distributed network of recording stations, and uniform regulations could not arise. Instead, there remained the previously existing central bureaus of the various provinces with their widely differing systems of registration.[9] They were treated as independent units, and for the remaining German provinces a few additional central bureaus were instituted, leaving only the exchange of fingerprint records of professional interprovincial criminals for regulation by the Reich. This was arranged as follows. When the fingerprint method was instituted in 1912, as above mentioned, a voluntary agreement was made by all the provinces to the effect that all professional, presumably interprovincial criminals should be registered by depositing one or more fingerprint records in the central bureaus of the provinces concerned, with an additional record for the Berlin bureau. This method is still followed, by and large, throughout Germany. If the police department of an American city, for example, wishes to send a dactyloscopic inquiry to Germany, a fingerprint record must

[9] In Dresden, Munich and Stuttgart the Galton-Henry system was used; in Berlin, the Klatt (Bertillon) system; in Hamburg, the Roscher system.

be sent to the *Polizeipräsidium Berlin, Erkennungsdienst.* If the suspected individual is already known in Germany as a professional interprovincial or international criminal, a record bearing identical fingerprints will be found in the Berlin bureau. If, however, the individual has confined his activities to one province when in Germany, his fingerprints probably will not be found in Berlin but in Dresden, Munich or elsewhere. In very important cases, therefore, search must be made not only in Berlin but in all the central bureaus of the German provinces.

The method appears complicated, and at first glance one is likely to think that the constitutional structure of the Reich places the criminal police at a disadvantage. This opinion is frequently advanced in Germany by defenders of the "unified state." I personally think otherwise, for I believe that when dactyloscopy is conscientiously carried out in a given country or province, and all arrested persons are fingerprinted—as in my opinion they should be—a central fingerprint bureau should not serve a territory containing more than ten to fifteen million inhabitants. If all the records for the whole German Reich, with its sixty million inhabitants, were gathered at one central point there would result a mass of material which in my opinion would soon become unmanageable. I have only pronounced scepticism for central bureaus which amass very large quantities of fingerprint records. Of course, from the very nature of dactyloscopy, no erroneous identifications are to be feared; I think it quite likely, however, that important identifications frequently cannot be made although a sheet bearing identical fingerprints lies somewhere in the collection. In my estimation neither the Galton-Henry system nor any other can keep in surveyable order the enormous number of records which one central bureau for the whole Reich would contain.

THE CLASSIFICATION OF FINGERPRINTS

I know that there are a great many methods of classification, and every discoverer of a method asserts that his system can keep millions of records in order. Theoretically, all these gentlemen are right. When we study the problem thoroughly, however, and discount the natural pride of the discoverer, substituting for mere assertions a careful check on the mathematical fundamentals of the question, we arrive at the conclusion that all systems, regardless of their external appearance, must reckon with the same mathematical conditions, and all have, consequently, the same limits of practical efficiency. For more than thirty years I have seen new systems come and go and, I believe, have examined them all conscientiously, with the result that I have arrived at the conclusion that the beautiful optimism of the discoverer leads him to see the problem in too rosy a light. One should not be deceived by the very large number of identifications achieved in the large central bureau, for the larger the number of registrations, the larger the number of identifications. No one has up to the present time determined the number of identifications which, because of the swollen proportions of these large bureaus, have *not* been made.

Hence, for countries with very large populations, there are in my estimation only three possibilities: First, the fingerprints of professional criminals only may be taken. This method is not satisfactory, for its limitations make it impossible to identify *all* criminals in the continuum comprising both the occasional and the professional lawbreaker. Again, it is usually impossi-ble to identify the corpses of unknown individuals. Further, the success of dactyloscopy, even in the strictly criminalistic field, hinges upon the extent to which it has been found possible to register the population involved—a fact which every expert will confirm.

The second possibility is to divide the country into territories with about fifteen million inhabitants, to collect the fingerprints for each territory in a separate bureau, and when necessary—in the case of especially important identifications—to search in all of the bureaus in question. In cases where it is obvious that only local or territorial criminals are to be identified, a search in the bureau of the territory would be sufficient. This, as we have seen, is the situation in Germany.

A NEW METHOD PROPOSED

If we wish to provide for the ideal situation, however—that in which every citizen has his fingerprints taken—even the German method would be no longer practicable. In America, especially, the proposal has often been made to take the fingerprints of *all* citizens. I thoroughly agree with this idea. The small formality of registering one's fingerprints—certainly small in comparison with some of the tedious and at the time unprofitable formalities which must be submitted to under a highly organized government—would soon repay the effort. The whole matter of visas and passports, this *via crucis* of the traveller, hangs in thin air when the practice of general dactyloscopy is not followed. The registration of those convicted of penal offenses is frequently a farce, when we go to the root of the matter. And, if we wish to be candid, we must admit that the present police methods of identifying criminals leave much to be desired. What can we really find out in identification bureaus? The real name? By no means! Only the various aliases which the suspected person has given in his previous conflicts with the law. Only when all citizens have their fingerprints taken at an age when falsification of identity is more or less impossible, that is, during the elementary school period, can we learn the true name.

But how shall we classify the resulting mass of fingerprint records? I believe that I can propose a solution. In Germany at the present time, however, my proposal is not practicable because money is lacking. During the last ten years, the German police have suffered greatly from the terrible financial situation, and I believe it necessary to postpone the introduction of even simple and cheap innovations. But my American colleagues can, I think, consider my proposal more or less unhampered by such considerations. Every citizen is to have his fingerprints taken before leaving the elementary school; between the ages of thirteen and fifteen the ridges of the skin are sufficiently developed to yield clear and usable prints. The fingerprint sheets are to be deposited in small local bureaus; e.g., with some judicial or executive department which deals with the local registration of persons. Small localities can then be organized into larger units through some superior department, as is usual in the case of other administrative measures.

The collections of prints, in every case, are to be arranged in strictly alphabetical order, i.e., in accordance with the true names of those fingerprinted. This is the Archimedean point of my proposal, as we shall later see. Conjointly with this system is to be practised the usual dactyloscopy of apprehended criminals, just as at present carried on in the existing fingerprint bureaus of the various police departments. The collection of these fingerprints is to be made by the existing central bureaus and classified by the usual method (e.g., Galton-Henry). What will be the result?

Let us compare the present situation with that which would follow the adoption of my proposal!

Present situation: A criminal is apprehended. His fingerprints are taken and duplicates sought for among those previously classified. If a record bearing identical prints is found, we thereby obtain his name, but not necessarily his *real* name, merely the name given at the time of former offenses. If the person has not previously been convicted of any crime, or has not yet been convicted in the area served by the central bureau, nothing at all can be found.

My proposal: The arrested person is asked where his fingerprints have been registered. Inasmuch as all citizens have had their fingerprints registered somewhere in the country, he must, if he is a native, give the name of some local bureau. The identification bureau then requests from the place named the fingerprint sheet corresponding to the name given by the arrested person. If he has told the truth, it is confirmed with little trouble by comparison of the fingerprints, and the real name is now positively known. If he has given a false name, it is apparent that the identical fingerprint record cannot be found. Such failure constitutes proof of falsification of name, and the man *remains in custody* (given appropriate legislation) until he sees fit to tell his real name and the local bureau where his fingerprint sheet can be found. According to the laws of Germany, France, and so forth, such detention may go on *ad infinitum;* the American laws probably vary from state to state.

If the detained person, tired of imprisonment, finally gives true information, confirmed by a comparison of fingerprints, the fingerprint record obtained from the local alphabetically arranged collection goes back to the same collection, and the record taken from the files of the criminal police is marked to show that it now carries the real name and is then restored to its place in the Galton-Henry file. If the same man again commits a criminal act, it is not necessary to obtain the sheet from the local alphabetic collection; the identification takes place thereafter by means of the central fingerprint bureau.

Present situation: A non-criminal citizen disappears as the result of murder, accident, suicide or mental derangement. Not being a criminal, his fingerprints have never been taken. The only resources are more or less inexact bodily marks such as moles and scars, old photographs, samples of clothing material, markings on linen and, finally, the inconvenient, expensive and usually uncertain method of "recognition" by witnesses.

My proposal: As soon as a non-criminal disappears, his fingerprints are obtained from his local bureau, copies are made and distributed to all the other bureaus in question. In each one, the fingerprint record is classified and placed in the files so that as soon as the missing person appears, whether alive or as an unknown corpse, in the territory served by one of these bureaus, identification follows as a matter of course. A prerequisite, however, is that in America, as in Germany, every unknown corpse and every mentally deranged individual taken into custody has his fingerprints recorded.

In the foregoing, I said that the Archimedean point of the proposed system is that all citizens have their fingerprints taken at about the age of thirteen, and that the primary classifi-

cation of these fingerprints should be in simple alphabetical order. In this way, procedure is extraordinarily simplified. It is well known that very rapid and cheap reproduction of fingerprints is a marked advantage possessed by dactyloscopy. Specialized knowledge and a great deal of time, however, are necessary for the arrangement of sheets in accordance with dactyloscopic classification methods (Galton-Henry, and so forth), as well as the comparison of fingerprints for purposes of identification. The labor of identification and classification would not be greater, if my proposal were followed, than it is at present. The local fingerprint collections, in simple alphabetical order, would only require simple labor of a type which any local official or government clerk could readily perform.

OTHER TECHNICAL AIDS

Among the other more important technical aids of criminal investigation in Germany (more detailed information in my book mentioned above) are the following: photographic laboratory, handwriting collections, records of scars and other physical peculiarities, "rogues' gallery" and files of "wanted" bulletins (publicly posted notices describing criminals) extracted from the "fliers" distributed by the police, together with other special data assisting in the apprehension of professionals. These aids are comprised in the so-called "identification service," one of the special departments affiliated with the criminal police and found in almost every metropolitan police force in Germany. In addition to these aids, we must not forget the police dog, whose value as a watch and defense dog is generally recognized, but whose usefulness as a trailer or "bloodhound" is contested.

The legal right of the criminal police to practise dactyloscopy, photography, and so forth, flows from the general duty of the police to preserve public safety.[10] The right to copy photographs, distribute them and place them on public view is also granted.[11]

The instruction of the criminal police in the use of all these technical aids is carried out by means of police schools, post-graduate courses in criminalistics and criminalistic museums. A few police forces possess special laboratories in which chemical analyses and the development of new methods of police technique can be carried on. In Prussia at the present time, the criminal police are instructed in the Berlin Police Institute (*Polizeiinstitut Berlin*) which is directly in charge of the Ministry of the Interior and which has twenty-one officials. Further, we have the advanced police school in Eiche near Berlin which has fifty-six officials. There are ten provincial police schools.

SYSTEMATIC USE OF TECHNICAL AIDS

In the larger cities the local criminal police are usually divided into special divisions dealing with special categories of crime. There is usually a special "murder squad" in charge of murder cases. There are also special divisions for burglary, pickpockets, swindlers, blackmailers, and so forth. All these departments are presided over by specialists who have had wide experience in dealing with their particular field of crime. The coöperation of all the subdivisions, aside from the coöperation automatically secured by the leadership of a common chief, is insured by daily conferences (*Kriminalrapporte*) in which all the heads of specialized subdivisions participate. This

division of labor is usually supplemented by local decentralization made necessary in the larger cities by the justifiable demand of the population for rapid and effective aid. Thus we have on the one hand a division of labor based upon the different kinds of crime dealt with, and on the other, division or decentralization on a geographic basis. The proportion in which one or the other of these principles predominates varies from province to province. The most complete exposition, both for Germany and other countries, of the problem in organization here presented is to be found in the book by R. B. Fosdick, *European Police Systems* (New York, 1915); it is also studied from a more theoretical angle in Heindl, *Organizatie de Recherche* (Alphen Rijn, 1924. [In Dutch].) It should be remarked that in the case of the largest police force in Germany, that of Berlin, investigation of all the more important criminal offenses, such as murder and the crimes of professional criminals, is centralized in police headquarters (Section four of the *Polizeipräsidium*). In order to make possible expert investigation by specialists, a great number of local "special inspection centers" have been instituted; these are further subdivided into departments dealing with particular types of crime. There now exist in Berlin fifty-nine special inspection centers.

In addition to these criminal police centers, there are also precinct criminal police in every police precinct in Berlin. Thereby the principle of decentralization is applied still further. The duties of the precinct police are limited to accepting reports, making hurried arrests and searches and dealing with minor criminal cases. When more important cases occur, the precinct police must immediately notify the special inspection center and may only take abso-

---

[10] *Strafprozessordnung*, E 32, par. 199.

[11] *Reichsgesetz*, January 9, 1907, par. 24. Further citations from the laws dealing with identification methods may be found in Heindl, *op. cit.*, pp. 644 ff.

lutely unavoidable measures before the arrival of the specialists mentioned.

In addition to all this, there are also criminal departments in all of the twenty Berlin district offices. These district departments have precedence over the more numerous precinct stations and also have greater jurisdiction, but they must not deal with the more important criminal cases already mentioned, leaving these for the specialists noted above. The coöperation of these three categories of criminal police is furthered by frequent conferences of their chiefs, by police telegraph, special messengers and a daily police journal issued by headquarters. In addition to this local police journal, there are naturally the police journals of the separate German provinces and, further, a special circular which carries descriptions of important criminals and news of interprovincial interest. It is issued in editions of twenty thousand and distributed throughout the Reich.

The two essential points in organization, i.e., specialization of police officials and their equipment with technical aids, are practicable only in the larger police forces. In small towns and in the country, costs are prohibitive. In order effectively to combat crime in such places, mobile rural police were instituted, first in Saxony in 1911. The example was set by the French mobile brigades of criminal police created by Clémenceau in 1907.[12]

The fundamental idea of this type of organization is the creation of a brigade of experienced and well equipped criminal police not bound to any definite locality and always available when a criminal offense especially dangerous to the public safety occurs. These police range over whole administrative and judicial districts and even over whole provinces. Their officials and the local police always coöperate in dealing with criminal cases, and in this way the wide experience and technical aids of the specialized mobile police and the intimate knowledge of persons and locale possessed by the local police greatly further the investigation.

Recently the attempt has been made to extent this principle to the whole Reich.[13] Before the passage of the enabling act in 1922, Saxony and Württemberg already had mobile brigades; in 1925, Prussia instituted such a brigade.[14]

Special attention should be called to paragraph 8 of the 1922 enabling act, for it changes completely the jurisdictional scope held by the criminal police under previous laws. It runs as follows:

The executive officials . . . of the mobile criminal police force are permitted to carry out all official actions within their proper jurisdiction throughout the *entire area of the Reich;* such police officials have the right to function throughout the Reich as aides of the Federal prosecutor.

The general regulation, analyzed at the beginning of this article, to the effect that the police are an auxiliary organ of the Federal prosecutor and their action therefore limited to the local boundaries of one or another of the administrative areas into which the Reich is divided, is abrogated by the

[12] A comprehensive description of the Saxon police may be found in Heindl, *Die sächsische Landeskriminalpolizei,* in the *Archiv für Kriminologie,* vol. 72, pp. 71 ff.; a similar description of the French mobile brigades together with all the pertinent regulations and a survey of similar problems of organization in other countries may be found in Heindl's *Polizeiliche Bekämpfung des interlokalen Verbrechertums,* in the *Archiv für Kriminologie,* vol. 72, pp. 191 ff.

[13] *Reichskriminalpolizeigesetz,* July 21, 1922; see also *Reichs-Gesetzblatt,* 1922, p. 593.

[14] *Min. Blatt der inneren Verwaltung,* 1925, pp. 569, 638, 989; 1926, p. 450; *Erlass,* May 20, 1925, supplemented by *Erlass,* May 29, 1925, September 19, 1925, May 6, 1926.

act of 1922, whenever an *important* criminal case is to be dealt with. In such cases, the mobile criminal police may pass beyond the local boundaries of their districts and make arrests, searches, seizures, and so forth, in any part of Germany.

The 1922 act also contains, in my estimation, several more significant improvements which at the present time serve as the foundation for proposed reforms looking toward a uniform procedure for the criminal police of the several German provinces. I prefer to omit any further exposition or criticism of this law, inasmuch as I am its author.

A DOCUMENT PREVIOUSLY UNKNOWN IN THE HISTORY OF POLICE TECHNIQUE

In conclusion, I should like to call the attention of my American colleagues to a document of which literally nothing has been known until the present time, for the following lines constitute the first public notice since its discovery. It is a contribution to the question so often discussed, especially in England and South America: Who is the "inventor" of dactyloscopy?

Argentinians frequently assert that their countryman, Juan Vucetich, was the first to propose the fingerprint method for use by the police. He is, however, in no way entitled to priority, as may be conclusively demonstrated. His first publication on fingerprints appeared in the 1890's. Several decades before this, Englishmen and North Americans had written on this subject. Sir William Herschel began his dactyloscopic experiments in 1858, in India (Hooghli District, Calcutta); the English physician, Faulds, also experimented in the year 1880, in Japan (Tokio). This is proved by a series of documents which were published in my previously cited book on dactyloscopy.

In the years following these first attempts, experiments were made in North America which merely had to do with the problem of establishing identity, however, and which led to no results of any value (New Mexico, 1882; Cincinnati and San Francisco, 1885).

In England, Sir Francis Galton carried on experiments, beginning in 1888. In 1892, his first important book, *Finger Prints*, appeared. In 1889, the medico-legal institute of the University of Lyons began to work with fingerprints taken at the scene of crime.

In all these attempts, from Herschel to the Lyons experiments, effort was directed toward the use of fingerprints for purposes of identification, while the earlier labors of Purkinje (Breslau, Germany, 1823) and numerous other German authors (*e.g.*, Hintze in Göttingen, 1751; Albinus in Göttingen, 1764; Welker in Giessen, 1856; Kollmann in Hamburg, 1883, and so forth) were turned toward the purely anatomical and medical side of fingerprint patterns, without any thought of identification. This cannot be too plainly stated because in the literature —Gross, Locard, Fosdick, and others— the false assertion is frequently made that Purkinje was the discoverer of dactyloscopy.

There now comes to mind the further question: In what degree were these authors original and in what degree merely elaborators of ideas originating elsewhere?

Herschel expressly stated that the idea of using fingerprints for identification came to him without any outside stimulus. We know, however, that centuries before, the Chinese and Japanese used fingerprints as proofs of identity. Numerous citations from Chinese literature (the first in civil law, 650 A.D., the first in criminal law, 1160 A.D.) and from Japanese literature (the first, Law of Taiho, 702 A.D.) have been published in my book on dactyloscopy; these citations were gathered on my journeys in eastern Asia and India.

One can scarcely believe that Herschel originated the idea when it is known that for a number of years, in Calcutta, he was professionally busied with the identification papers and other documents of Chinese and Japanese servants, for fingerprint procedure plays a great rôle in the legitimation procedure of these orientals. A man who works for years on his discovery can easily forget whence his first impulse came.

Faulds himself gives evidence of Asiatic influence; one of his letters tells how the Japanese called his attention to their practice of taking fingerprints. The American experiments are traceable to Chinese immigrants: Galton, as he himself states, was inspired by Herschel. When Vucetich published his first papers, there already existed a considerable English and French literature on the problem.

From this evidence we would be forced to the conclusion that no white man independently "invented" dactyloscopy; it would appear to be a discovery of the Asiatics.

But now appears a new, or rather, long-lost document which compels a revision of this opinion.

In May, 1888, Wilhelm Eber, a veterinarian who later became a professor in the Veterinary College of Berlin, sent a detailed proposal to the Prussian Ministry of the Interior pointing out the value of fingerprints for the identification of criminals. The first draft of the ministry's reply to Eber was found by the writer in the official documents of the ministry in 1917. The original proposal was returned to Eber as unusable and up to this time could not be found. Further

search, however, has finally led to the goal; the proposal has been stumbled upon among old papers kept by Eber's heirs. A small box of instruments was also sent with the proposal, and in the ministerial documents of 1888 was noted as "Received and returned to the sender because useless." This box has also been discovered among the effects of the heirs. The voluminous exposé, now in my possession, explains not only the fundamental principles of dactyloscopy, but most remarkable of all, gives instructions for a number of dactyloscopic procedures which were not "discovered" until much later, i.e., during the twentieth century. He suggested, for example, the "folio method" which in 1910 was hailed in all countries as an important amplification of police technique. He proposed poroscopy, which was introduced into police technique in 1912 by the Frenchman Locard. He described the details which the Dane Jörgensen makes use of in his "distant identification method," so much discussed in recent years. To give complete details of this remarkable proposal would exceed our present space limitations. The text of the proposal will soon be published in Gross-Heindl's *Archiv für Kriminologie*, vol. 85, part 1, pp. 30 ff. Every expert will then be able to see the way in which Eber foresaw the most minute details.

Now, however, there remains for us this problem: Was Eber influenced by Chinese and Japanese examples? He was never in Asia. He cannot have been inspired by Galton, because the ministerial *answer* to Eber's proposal is dated May 26, 1888, and Galton announced the results of his experiments for the first time on May 25, 1888 in a lecture before the Royal Institution at London. Any influence by Herschel, Faulds, the American experiments or the Chinese and Japanese methods, in short, by any suggestions prior to 1888, also seem excluded. Why? Because the Chinese and Japanese, and consequently all authors influenced by them before 1888, used *black* coloring substance (India ink, printers' ink, rubber stamp ink, and so forth) for producing fingerprints. The impressions sent to the ministry by Eber, however, and which are now in my possession, were produced by fixated iodine vapor.

We cannot discuss the matter at greater length here, but every fingerprint expert will understand without further explanation why Eber would unquestionably have proposed the use of black coloring matter had he had any knowledge of it, *i.e.*, had he known of the work done by others before 1888. Further, if he had mentioned in his proposal that in eastern Asia the use of fingerprints had been practised for centuries, the ministry perhaps would not have been able forthwith to reject his proposal as fantastic nonsense. As it was, however, the Prussian Ministry of the Interior rendered a judgment in the amazingly short time of a few days, *i.e.*, without careful investigation, to the effect that Eber's proposal was "of no practical value" and that as a consequence it was "of no use to discuss it in all its details."

Eber, whom we may presume is the only *original* discoverer of dactyloscopy in recent times, threw his proposal angrily into a corner, the instrument box was turned into a sewing-box for Madame Eber, and the detailed instructions, covering all problems of dactyloscopy, passed into forgetfulness until now, after forty years, they have been rescued from the dust of an old storeroom.

Science and Criminal Investigation

By Harry Söderman, D.Sc.

Lecturer on Police Technique, Law School, University of Stockholm, Stockholm, Sweden

DURING the last decades there has gradually developed a new science which in Europe is ordinarily called *police scientifique* or *technique policière*. It is rather difficult to say which of these terms is preferable. The former refers to a given, definite science, the latter, to the practical application of that science. The term *technique policière* is no doubt best, since it refers to the eminently practical application of a large number of different sciences to the investigation of crime.

Modern Police Technicians

The founder of modern police technique is no doubt the Austrian Hans Gross (1847–1915), author of the famous *Handbuch für Untersuchungsrichter*. At the beginning of his career Gross was an examining magistrate (*Untersuchungsrichter*) and as such he had ample opportunity to witness the unreliability of human testimony. He therefore tried to supplant or strengthen such testimony by scientific means. Gross was a lawyer and made no great discoveries in police technique, but with inexhaustible energy he gathered, from all the different branches of science, everything that could be useful in his work. Thus he had a productive and animating effect upon the new art to which he gave rise.

Alphonse Bertillon (1853–1914), the famous chief of the *Service d'Identité judiciaire* in Paris, is of equally great importance although more within the field of identification technique. Bertillon created the anthropometric method of identification, the criminal photograph, the *portrait parlé* and the metric photograph of the scene of the crime. In the public mind he is erroneously credited with the discovery of fingerprints. On the contrary, Bertillon was for a long time opposed to the fingerprint method which displaced his own anthropometric system. The honor of having made fingerprints of use to the police falls to the Englishmen Sir Francis Galton and Sir Edward Henry and to the Argentine Juan Vucetich.

Following Gross and Bertillon, natural scientists became interested in police technique, and during the first decades of this century a number of new methods were perfected. Among the foremost representatives of modern police technique mention should be made of Edmond Locard at Lyons (poroscopy; questioned documents; dust and blood analysis), R. A. Reiss, formerly at Lausanne and now at Belgrade (criminal photographic methods), De Rechter at Brussels (identification of bullets, cartridges and traces of burglars' tools), Edmond Bayle in Paris (use of optical and photographic methods in police technique), Robert Heindl (metric photography and fingerprints) and Hans Schneickert (questioned documents; a number of classification methods), both in Berlin, Siegfried Türkel in Vienna (the examination of objects of art and antiques), and Van Ledden-Hulsebosch in Amsterdam (numerous chemical and optical methods of criminal investigation). The technique of identification alone presents a long list of prominent names, such as the late Jørgensen in Copenhagen (distant identification by means of a dactyloscopic code; single fingerprint classification), Wentworth at Dover, Maine (classification of palmprints and footprints; dactyloscopic code), Collins in London (distant identification by means of a dactyloscopic code), and others.

As mentioned, police technique has borrowed its methods from many sciences, but principally from three, i. e., biology, chemistry and physics. Under biology falls the fingerprints, certain examinations of blood and of hair, and strictly speaking the identification of disguised or imitated handwriting, in the sense that handwriting may be regarded as the self-registered expression of a biological process of mind and body. Under chemistry fall the examinations of stains and dust, poisons, counterfeit coins, and so forth; and under physics, all sorts of measurements and methods of comparison, as well as the more and more frequently used aids of a physical nature, such as spectrography, photometry, luminescence analysis, and so forth. In reality it is very difficult to draw any definite border line between the chemical and the physical methods used in police technique. On a reduced scale we see here the same phenomenon as in the relationship between the domains of physics and chemistry; the boundaries fade and disappear more and more. Besides this general tendency, there is something else in police technique that speaks in favor of physics, and that is the frequent necessity for working with very small quantities of material for investigation. Here spectrography and other physical methods offer the possibility of determining infinitely small quantities. Many modern criminalists maintain that the police laboratories of the future will almost entirely base their investigations on physics. Another advantage offered by the physical methods lies in their objectivity and in the relatively few sources of errors existing, in comparison with those in chemistry. This is to a certain extent true, particularly with reference to the sources of errors, but microchemical analysis still is in many cases decidedly superior to spectrography because it permits quantitative measurements. It is true that a quantitative spectro-analysis has been worked out through the researches of De Grammond, and others, but it does not give sufficiently exact results and, furthermore, is not always applicable.

In the following pages, besides a short description of some of the most important instruments used in a modern police laboratory, a brief survey will be made of the different fields of police technique in which the natural sciences or their applications play an important part. For the benefit of the reader I have made this survey from a critical point of view, at the same time emphasizing the most recent conquests of science, wherever made.

THE EQUIPMENT OF A POLICE LABORATORY

Some time ago I was asked to propose a plan for the equipment of the Copenhagen Police Laboratory. Copenhagen has a population of about one million. With its heavy traffic, its teeming business life and its large groups of foreigners, this city offers a wide variety of crimes, although their frequency is relatively low, as is the case in the other Scandinavian countries. The plan proposed included the following apparatus:

A microphotographic apparatus with complete optical equipment and a special arrangement for the illumination of objects by means of oblique light, as in the examination of intersecting ink lines or in the photography of bullets.

A *microscope*, equipped with dry objectives, magnifying from eight hundred to nine hundred times.

A *comparison microscope*, an apparatus consisting of two objectives from which the light is cast through a series of prisms to a common eye piece. It is used in the identification of bullets and cartridges and gives exceedingly rapid and accurate results.

A *thick, welded steel pipe* for use in the firing of trial bullets.

A *spectrophotometer* or else a Zeiss *Stufenphotometer*, for the determination of the absolute shade of color in the examination of ink, stamps, and so forth. This apparatus is indispensable in many investigations, primarily because it permits the construction of accurate filters in the photographic process when it is necessary to distinguish between or to remove colors.

An *ultraviolet ray lamp* for so-called luminescence analyses in filtered ultraviolet light. This apparatus consists of an ordinary quartz lamp, from the light of which all visible rays are removed by means of a special filter, through which only ultraviolet rays pass. Different articles show a fluorescence in different colors under exposure to ultraviolet rays. This lamp is therefore an excellent and speedily operating aid in the examination of counterfeit bills, the bringing forth of otherwise invisible spots on woven material, and so forth. The ultraviolet ray lamp is furthermore indispensable in certain photographic processes.

A *spectrograph* for the photography of both the visible and the ultraviolet spectrum. This apparatus, which is quite expensive, is not absolutely indispensable but of very great value in the analysis of dust and powder stains, as well as in certain examinations of objects of art.

A *polarizer* to be inserted, when needed, in the microscope. This small apparatus is of great help in the examination of hair, fibres, textile material, and so forth.

A *reproduction camera* for plates.

A *magnifying apparatus* with a condenser, magnifying negatives up to thirteen by eighteen.

A *complete set of filters*, for instance, Wratten's.

A *chemical balance*.

Chemical glass, such as test tubes, retorts, microfiltration apparatus, and so forth.

Various chemicals, such as reagents for ink testing, filters, and so forth.

Some of these apparatus presuppose for their correct usage considerable scientific training. We shall discuss them further in connection with the description of problems of police technique which require their use.

PHOTOGRAPHING THE SCENE OF THE CRIME

Although photographs of this kind are usually taken by a special police photographer, it is in many countries included in the work of the police laboratories. As mentioned above, Bertillon was the first to photograph systematically the scene of the crime, and he also devised the so-called metric photograph, which made it possible to compute all the measurements directly from the photograph. The camera for metric photography is equipped with a series of wide-angled objectives, the focal distances of which are exact multiples of ten. Each objective is fitted with a thread, which at each turn produces a change corresponding to one tenth of the focus. This arrangement makes a sharp focus possible for all levels of reduction from one tenth on.

The camera is a simple, square box without either bellows or pinions, and the plates are thirty by thirty centimeters. The depth of the box is thirty centimeters, and inside, it has five ridges for the insertion of the plate-holders. The distance between the ridges is five centimeters. The objectives are all in the same place, five millimeters in front of the first ridge. Thus nothing is movable in the apparatus, but, owing to the decimal focal distances and the regularly increasing distance between the ridges, one can obtain all sorts of combinations to meet the infinitely varying needs that the photographing of the scene of a crime may bring.

When a photograph is to be made, the apparatus is placed absolutely horizontally and at a "decimal" height, in practice usually fifty centimeters, one meter or one and a half meter. Bertillon also constructed a special base for this purpose.

With the aid of a simple geometrical process one can compute all measurements from the finished photograph. In order to simplify this, Bertillon had special cardboard mountings printed with scales varying according to the height of the apparatus and the focal width of the objective. Thus without any mathematical operations one could make all the measurements on the mounted photograph.

The metric photograph was a very important device but it has never been appreciated to its full value, due perhaps to the fact that it is more complicated to take than an ordinary photograph. In spite of the fact that several German, Austrian and Dutch students have tried to simplify it, it has fallen into disuse, and even in Bertillon's old laboratory in Paris it is probably used only in rare cases. This is deplorable, because it is often very important to be able to measure accurately the distances between different objects in a room as it appeared when the crime was committed.

In place of the metric photograph one nowadays uses two parallel methods: partly ordinary photographs of all interesting features, taking great care to retain the natural perspective, and partly sketched plans. As regards the latter it is noticeable that the so-called method of cross-projection in sketching interiors is used more and more. In such sketches the room is seen from above with walls and ceiling folded out so that they appear level with the floor.

Fingerprint Researches

We shall not deal here with the classification of fingerprints although this is often made by the police laboratories. The methods for taking fingerprints at the scene of the crime have not undergone any great changes during the last decades. Latent fingerprints are still being stained with the aid of a hair brush and a staining powder, white lead for prints on a dark background, for instance, and lampblack for those on a light background. Many bureaus of identification have their own special staining powder and since almost every pulverized, heavy metallic salt can be used, there are many opportunities for variation. Photographs of fingerprints are made with an ordinary camera or possibly with a so-called fingerprint camera (Kodak or Bermpohl). Other special apparatus constructed for the photographing of fingerprints have proved unsatisfactory. In many European cities, especially in Berlin and in Vienna, so-called fingerprint foils are now used instead of photographs. These are thin celluloid plates covered on one side with a sticky substance which is protected by a very thin leaf of celluloid. The leaf is removed when the foil is to be used. The fingerprint is stained in the usual way, in this case preferably with aluminum powder, whereupon a foil is carefully pressed against it. The pigment adheres to the foil and the whole fingerprint with its minutest details is transferred to it and can be brought to the laboratory for leisured study.

The researches so zealously carried on some decades ago by Stockis, Lecca-Marzo, and others, in order to discover a perfect staining powder for finger-prints, preferably one that would chemically affect the fat deposits of the print, have not brought remarkable results and have been discontinued. It may furthermore be mentioned that the above staining powders serve the purpose very well, so long as very old fingerprints or those on paper are not concerned.

Old fingerprints may sometimes be stained with ordinary methods—the author has, for instance, with normal results stained two-year-old finger-prints on glass with lead white—but in many cases one must use other means. Reiss and Stockis, and others, have developed staining fluids con-taining alcohol, for the staining of old fingerprints. These methods are, how-ever, complicated, often bring no re-sults, and can only be used in important cases when other methods fail. Paper with fingerprints becomes considerably soiled by the usual staining powders. Therefore one frequently makes use of pulverized metallic antimony, but this also soils the paper although to a less extent than the others. Hence in place of powders iodine fumes have long been used. The paper is held above a heated receptacle with iodine, whereupon the rising fumes from the iodine are sublimated on the cold paper so that the fingerprint appears in a dark brown color. This method has the advantage that the iodine evap-orates very quickly, leaving the paper white again. Although lately several apparatus have been constructed to spread the iodine fumes evenly over the surface of the paper, it is neverthe-less very difficult to get a uniform stain. Hence the problem of staining fingerprints in this way has not as yet been definitely solved.

As a novelty in the field of dactylos-copy one may designate Professor Kögel's method of taking fingerprints by making use of the reaction of p-phenylenediamine upon wood fibre. When this method is used, the fingers are moistened with a hydrochloric acid solution of p-phenylenediamine and then pressed against a wood-fibrous paper. Due no doubt to the forma-tion of azo-pigments, the fingerprints then appear in a blood-red color. The disadvantage of this method is of course the use of wood-fibrous paper which is not durable.

EXAMINATION OF STAINS

In the common term of stains we include bloodstains, those from semen, urine, feces, meconium, paint, fat, and so forth. The differential diagnosis of stains and their determination and individualization are among the most important tasks of police technique.

The discovery of stains, which presents very great difficulties in case they are on a background of the same color, as for instance bloodstains on rust-colored plush or those of semen on dark woollen material, has become an easy matter through the aid of ultraviolet rays. Van Ledden-Hulse-bosch relates for example a case in which he had to examine a large couch cover to ascertain the presence of spermatozoa. The couch cover had been removed from the office of a doctor accused of sex assault upon a woman patient. Formerly the search for a few spermatozoa by means of a microscope would, if carefully done, have taken several days. Now, how-ever, with the aid of the quartz lamp all the stains were localized in a few minutes.

BLOOD ANALYSIS

The problems arising in connection with blood analysis have been carefully studied during the last few years by several experts and although as yet one cannot say that all the questions have been answered, it can safely be asserted that within a relatively short time this will be the case. It has long been possible to determine whether a stain is blood or not. In doing this one makes use of Teichmann's or Stryzowsky's microchemical methods, by which, in case blood is present, one gets crystals of hematine-chlorhydrate and hematine-iodohydrate, respectively. Stryzowsky's method is particularly delicate but nowadays many laboratories make use of microspectroscopic methods by which the presence of blood is noted through the characteristic bands produced in the spectrum by the hemo-chromogene.

In determining whether blood is human or animal, the old methods of measuring and determining the form of the blood corpuscles have been generally displaced by serological methods, such as anaphylaxis, Uhlenhut's precipitation test, erytro-agglutination, and so forth. Uhlenhut's precipitation test is no doubt most commonly used nowadays, although anaphylaxis is, in spite of its complication and length, no doubt still used in some places. In the case of the precipitation test, the suspected bloodstain is dissolved in a small quantity of physiological salt solution, whereupon one tests if this solution is precipitated by animal anti-serum. If this reaction is controlled by a sufficient number of tests, one can consider it very reliable.

With the modern methods of blood determination it is also, owing to the discovery of the four blood groups, possible to individualize blood, although unfortunately in a negative way. The four blood groups are based upon two different characteristics in the red blood corpuscles—A and B—and two characteristics in the blood-serum—a and β. Serum a precipitates blood corpuscle A, and serum β precipitates blood corpuscle B, if mixed. This phenomenon, in which elements contained in certain sera precipitate or agglutinate certain blood corpuscles, is called iso-agglutination. In blood group One, the blood corpuscles are agglutinated by sera from all the other three groups, while serum from this group has no effect upon the blood corpuscles of the other groups. In blood group Two, the blood corpuscles are agglutinated by sera from groups Three and Four, and serum from this group agglutinates the blood corpuscles in groups Three and One. In group Three the blood corpuscles are agglutinated by sera from groups Two and Four and the serum from this group agglutinates the blood corpuscles from groups Two and One. The blood corpuscles from group Four remain unchanged in all sera and its serum agglutinates the blood corpuscles from all the other blood groups. By following the method of Moss one can, with a very simple reaction, in a few minutes determine the category of a blood group. Using only a drop of serum each from groups Two and Three one mixes each drop with a drop of the blood to be analyzed. The group can be determined at once by watching the reaction in the two drops of blood:

If agglutination occurs in test sera Two and Three, the blood belongs to group One;

If no agglutination occurs in test serum Two, but in Three, the blood belongs to group Two;

If agglutination occurs in test serum

Two, but not in Three, the blood is from group Three;

If no agglutination occurs in any test serum, the blood belongs to group Four.

As mentioned above, one cannot make a positive identification by using the blood groups, as each group includes a very large number of people. In the case of a murder, however, a blood analysis may offer grave evidence.

In determining the presence of *semen*, Florence's reaction is still chiefly used. The reagents consist of potassium iodide, iodine, and distilled water, and if spermatic fluid is present, brown crystals are formed, which are visible under slight magnification. Since, however, the reaction can also occur in connection with several other fluids of organic origin, it is regarded as conclusive evidence of the presence of semen only when spermatozoa have actually been found.

The development of the technique for the differential diagnosis of other stains has kept pace with that of microchemical analysis, and due to the great progress of the latter there nowadays scarcely exists any problem connected with stains that cannot be solved.

MISCELLANEOUS TRACES LEFT BY CRIMINALS

Under the heading of traces left by criminals we usually include footprints, marks of burglars' tools, hair, dust, and so forth.

Footprints.—The technique used in making a cast of footprints has undergone no great changes in late years. Plaster of Paris is still used, while the suggestions of older authors as to the use of wax, for instance, are not followed nowadays. It is moreover rather odd how very few policemen actually know the best way of making a cast, although theoretically almost all are acquainted with it. During the last decades it has become more and more common simply to photograph footprints, which of course was necessary previously in cases where the footprint was made in such soft material that it would be ruined if a cast were taken.

In the last mentioned case, a method invented by an Austrian gendarme, Johan Müller, is used which will save the minutest details of the print even if it is made in light dust. His method is to shake fine plaster of Paris in a very thin layer over the footprint, which is then moistened with a fine spray of alcohol from a suitable syringe. This is repeated three or four times, whereupon one reinforces the plaster with sticks and proceeds to make an ordinary cast.

Another novelty in the technique of making casts is the method devised by Poller of Vienna, who uses a special kind of paste, called *Negocoll*, in making casts of all sorts of objects. Poller's method gives surprisingly fine results with facial masks, and therefore it has been suggested that, for identification purposes, negocoll casts should be made of the faces of all unidentified corpses. When bodies that are in a more or less advanced state of decomposition are photographed, the face is discolored to such an extent that it can hardly be recognized from a photograph. The casts which are white may be painted flesh color, and according to Poller several corpses in Vienna have been identified by relatives with the aid of his method, when recognition from a photograph would have been difficult or impossible.

Traces of Tools.—Regarding casts of traces made by burglars' tools we shall notice only that the old principle has been followed: the simpler the better. Hence, all complicated methods suggested earlier, such as galvanic casts, Bertillon's effractometer, and others, have been replaced by the simple way of taking an impression with plasteline and from it make a plaster cast.

Hair.—The technique in examining hair, which in the case of so many crimes proves important, has not changed during the last decades unless one regards the studies in polarized light as having a place here. When hair is to be identified, its color, length, curliness, and so forth, are established macroscopically. The microscopic examination includes the examination of impurities attached to the hair, damages, which may have been inflicted upon it, the distribution of the pigment grains inside the hair, the position of the air cells in the canal, and the relation between the diameter of the canal and that of the hair itself.

During the last few years it is a noticeable fact that experts have become more careful in reaching conclusions in the identification of hair. There are very few cases nowadays in which an expert would grant to the identification of hair absolute and decisive value as evidence, although such identification may be of great subsidiary assistance.

Dust.—The examination of dust from the clothes of a suspected person may be of great significance in proving that he has been at a certain place where characteristic dust is found, or in ascertaining his occupation. The analysis of dust, which was first introduced by Sir Arthur Conan Doyle and used by him as a valuable ingredient in his Sherlock Holmes novels, has during the last few years been systematized and organized by Dr. Edmond Locard at Lyons. The technique is briefly as follows. With the aid of a specially constructed vacuum cleaner or else by beating the clothes of a suspect in a large paper bag, the dust is collected and examined under the microscope. Here all the most modern methods of microanalysis are used, and in many cases special experts must be employed to ascertain the origin of the extremely small vegetable particles, textile fibres, and so forth, that might be found. Numerous cases in which dust analysis has given good results could be related. A counterfeiter shows traces of antimony and other metals in his clothes; a man who has broken into a mill has flour dust, and so on. One might also include here cases in which the soil that may adhere to the shoes of the suspect is analyzed.

THE EXAMINATIONS OF FIREARMS

One branch of police technique that has made considerable progress in the last few years is the examination of firearms. Nowadays it is regarded as an axiom that every firearm gives each bullet and each cartridge discharged from it absolutely individual characteristics that cause them to differ from all other bullets and cartridges. This holds true not only with regard to weapons from different factories but also for those of the same make, and of the same series. A Browning barrel number 46647 is absolutely different from barrel number 46648. If these characteristics are sufficiently pronounced, one is able to distinguish between the bullets discharged from these barrels.

This is easy to explain. The final work upon the barrel is done by a groove-making tool, which is subjected to a microscopically measurable wear during each operation. The material in the barrel also varies a little as to hardness, and these factors so operate together that the grooves or rather their bottom never has the same appearance twice. When a bullet passes through the barrel and the grooves are stamped on it, it becomes the carrier of all the scratches and the irregularities that it meets. When the bullet leaves the barrel it bears evidence of all the obstructions it has met on its way.

Let us suppose that a murder has been committed and a bullet found in the body of the victim. A man is arrested for the murder and a pistol is found in his possession. It is now necessary to discover if the fatal bullet was discharged from this particular weapon. This is done in the following manner. A series of trial bullets are discharged from the suspected weapon. For this purpose one shoots into a heavy steel pipe which is three fourths filled with water. The resistance of the water is quite sufficient to check even a Mauser bullet within a distance of somewhat more than one meter; it drops quietly and undamaged to the bottom of the steel pipe where it can be collected with the aid of a sieve. This device was prepared by the author for the Lyons Police Laboratory and has proved decidedly superior to the older methods which employed cotton, wax cakes, earth, sawdust, and so forth, instead of water.

In order to compare the suspected bullet with the trial bullets, each groove is photographed according to De Rechter's method, under medium magnification in oblique light. To simplify the search for the corresponding grooves, the Americans Waite, Goddard and Graville have constructed a special comparison microscope in which one can examine two bullets at once and compare their characteristics. Each bullet is put into a holder, strongly illuminated, and then placed under the objective of a microscope. The light from each objective is cast towards a prism, deflected in a horizontal direction and, again, vertically

by means of another prism, in the middle of the apparatus, which deflects it upwards through a common eye-piece. In the eye-piece one now sees the two bullets side by side and can easily compare the microscopic scratches in the grooves. These comparison microscopes are now made in France in a form modified by the author and have spread to quite a few police departments in the Old World.

Regarding the value of these identifications as evidence, it must be pointed out that they do not always give full certainty as some experts declare, for the characteristic marks may be more or less pronounced. Contrary to earlier principles of the examinations of firearms, the idea is now held that a new weapon leaves more characteristic marks on its missiles than does an old one.

IDENTIFICATION OF GUNPOWDER

Closely connected with the examination of firearms there are many other problems, such as the identification of the gun powder used and the fixing of the distance from which the shot was fired. The identity of the gunpowder is determined through the deposits on the inside of the barrel or the powder stains on the clothes or on the skin of the victim. It is naturally very easy to ascertain if it is black gunpowder or smokeless gunpowder, but when it comes to determining the individual powder, its make, for instance, the difficulties are greater. If it is black powder the problem cannot be solved, for almost all gunpowder factories use the classical recipe. If it is smokeless powder, on the other hand, the whole matter looks more favorable, especially if one has been able to find unconsumed grains in the powder stains. A simple microscopical examination coupled with microchemical analysis often enables one in such a case to determine definitely the origin of the gunpowder. If, as is usually the case, the smokeless powder only occurs in the form of very small deposits inside the barrel, a spectrographic examination may give good results. In such a case one tries to determine the inorganic elements which might be found in the gunpowder in the form of stabilizers or oxygen-carriers. All smokeless gunpowder by no means contains such elements, and on the whole one may consider the close differential diagnosis of the powder deposits as rather difficult.

Through the researches of Chavigny, in particular, it has been established that one can approximately ascertain the distance from which a close shot has been fired. This determination is made through observing the distribution of the powder stains and necessitates a large number of verified trial shots.

COUNTERFEIT COINS AND BANK NOTES

During the years immediately after the War counterfeit coins disappeared from Europe, coins of precious metals being no longer in circulation on the continent. Recently they have appeared again and before long this industry will thrive as vigorously as it did before the War. All falsifications of this kind, however, are easily revealed through chemical analysis, no matter how skillfully they have been made. Besides, this industry would not be very lucrative if it were not based on the carelessness with which people generally accept money.

Another kind of counterfeit coins which probably soon will have become as common as they were before the War is the factory-made genuine coins, manufactured in Spain and in several other countries. The manufacturers stamp real coins of full weight from different countries and make their profit by the rather great difference existing between the value of the coin and that of the metal. It is, of course, quite impossible to discover these counterfeiters if they have carefully observed the composition of the real coins.

Bank notes and all sorts of easily-disposed-of bonds or paper securities are forged in great numbers and since the forgers keep up to date regarding the latest progress of the technique of forgery one may come across some very well-made counterfeits. The luminescence analysis mentioned earlier, as well as microchemical analysis and photography with the aid of filters, infallibly reveal all such forgeries. The luminescence analysis, in particular, has great practical value, for with its aid one can rapidly examine large quantities of bank notes with comparatively safe results. The examination is so easy that it can be made by any bank clerk.

POSTAL THEFTS—COUNTERFEIT STAMPS

Under the heading of postal crimes we usually find all sorts of tampering with letters, forgeries of seals, and so forth. Such a crime never fails to be discovered if it is handled by an expert. A microscopic examination and luminescence analysis reveal the addition of sealing wax in damaged seals, gummed edges that have been disturbed, forged seals, and so forth.

Postage stamps are forged both in order to profit from philatelists and to circulate them through the mails. There are two classes of forgeries to be distinguished here: copies of postage stamps, seals, and so forth, which must of course be made by real printers; and old stamps that have been washed with some bleaching fluid in order that the stamped date, and so forth, should disappear, or that have had a second print put over the first in imitation of an official second print. Here again luminescence analysis comes to the aid of the investigator. During late years it has become widely used among stamp dealers. When stamps that have been treated with a bleaching fluid or that have very faint traces of a second print are to be examined, the ordinary luminescence analysis cannot be used, but in its place we may employ some of the ingenious methods elaborated by Professor Kögel, such as kathode-fluorescence, direct ultraviolet photographs, spectrostatic methods, and so on. In order to understand these, however, one must have a rather thorough training in the natural sciences.

QUESTIONED DOCUMENTS

The examination of questioned documents may be divided into two groups, one of which may be suitably called the examination of *mechanical* forgeries and the other the identification of *imitated or disguised handwriting*. In the case of the former group one makes use of chemical and physical methods that allow a rather high degree of objectivity; in the latter, on the other hand, in spite of creditable attempts to introduce scientific and objective methods during the last years, one cannot to a certain extent avoid subjectivity.

The mechanical forgeries include erasures, uses of bleaching fluids, tracings, and so forth. To these belong also the problems connected with the determination of kind and age of ink, writing in pencil, intersections of lines and folds, investigations of paper, and so forth.

To distinguish between different kinds of ink there are several methods of which we might mention Miehte's photographic method, fluorescence photography, spectography and "touch" analysis. Due no doubt to its simplicity, the last mentioned is most frequently used. The principle of this analysis is as follows. With the fine point of a glass rod or a gold pen one places tiny drops of different reagents on the writing to be examined. The changes that occur make it possible to determine the nature of the ink. Naturally it is not possible fully to individualize ink in this way, for within each main group of ink there are a number of makes of similar composition. For closer individualization one makes use of photography with filters, examination with a so-called color-microscope using Lovibond's tintometer glass, or optic color analysis with the help of a photometer.

The determination of the age of ink is still a delicate chapter. Thanks to the researches of Osborn, Van Ledden-Hulsebosch, and others, there now exist methods that determine whether an ink is old or not, but when an iron-nutgall ink has become more than six months old there is scarcely any possibility of determining its age up to the time that it begins to turn yellow, which, depending on the way it is stored, does not begin until it is from six to ten years old.

As regards writing with lead pencil and indelible pencil there have been valuable researches made during the last few years by Michael Ainsworth, Locard, Türkel, Beroud, and others.

As is well-known, the identification of imitated or disguised handwriting is an old art; its ancestry goes back several hundred years. One might say that it is to the graphology of olden times what chemistry is to alchemy. Extensive researches by Locard, Schneickert, Osborn, and others, have led to systematization and to attempts to create an objective evaluation of the importance of the specific peculiarities of handwriting. As evidence of great progress we might note Locard's graphometry and Schneickert's division of the peculiarities in handwriting into primary and secondary groups. Briefly told, Locard's graphometry proposes to calculate and evaluate statistically a number of quantitative peculiarities in handwriting. It can only be applied, however, to long texts and the value of the investigation is in direct proportion to the number of measurements made.

The value of identifications of handwriting is still a much debated matter and is usually an apple of contention in the courts. A certain degree of subjectivity is unavoidable when the graphologist tries to find and build up a composite whole of those peculiarities of handwriting which characterize the writer. The handwriting expert must have a highly developed power of observation and a sense of form. The latter is not the least important, for many people are blind to form and cannot notice small differences in details. Furthermore, he must be able to evaluate the specific peculiarities in handwriting, an ability that calls for great experience and knowledge of modern methods of graphology. If all handwriting experts would realize their own limitations and, when formulating their conclusions, would try their very best to help the court by stressing the degree of probability that they consider as characteristic of the results of their investigations, and if they all had special training and were conscientious, the results of the identifications of imitated or disguised handwriting would be of the very greatest aid in the repression of crime.

Objects of Art and Antiques

Thanks to microchemical analyses, X-ray examinations, different applications of fluorescence photography, spectrography, and so forth, most forgeries can probably be revealed. However, since one can never tell how skillful a forger may be, the principle holds true that although the expert may be able to establish the fact that an object of art is forged, he may nevertheless be unable definitely to prove that it is genuine.

The above review of scientific methods in criminal investigations is naturally superficial and incomplete. I hope, however, that it will give the reader an idea of the importance of scientific methods in all kinds of criminal investigations. It is an old truth that criminals always take advantage of the latest progress within technique and science. Therefore, the police, fighting as it does an often uneven battle to protect society, has every reason in the world to keep in step with the development of science—at least to the same extent as do the criminals.

Medical Science in the Service of the State

With Especial Reference to the Investigation of Deaths

By George Burgess Magrath, A.M., M.D.

Instructor in Legal Medicine, Harvard University; Medical Examiner
for Suffolk County, Boston, Massachusetts

MEDICAL science is a factor in human affairs unsurpassed in importance by any of the agencies making for the welfare of mankind. The increase in knowledge in all branches of natural science, which has been so largely instrumental in man's control of his environment, is nowhere better illustrated than by the advance in those fields of inquiry which have yielded the knowledge of the nature and the causes of disease, which have enabled man to combat successfully many of his biological adversaries. Prominent among the causes of disability, suffering and death, are parasitic micro-organisms of various sorts, including those which are causative of communicable disease, the prevention and control of which is so largely a matter of state medicine. A function of the state of equal importance with the safeguarding of the public health, is the protecting of the community from avoidable hazard to health or to life due to causes other than disease, such hazards as are incidental to the conditions of modern life, to industrial activities and to unlawful acts.

Conditions unfavorable or dangerous to health by reason of disease are capable of regulation or control by the state through a department of public health, within the purview of which lie such matters as diseases dangerous to the public health, notably those which are communicable either from man to man, or from animal to man, the oversight of water supply, of food and of drugs, sanitation, housing, methods of disposition of the bodies of the dead, and the regulation of the conditions under which such disposition may be practiced. Many of the activities of public health officials involve the use of medical and biological science in various forms of laboratory work, and the modern health officer of first class capacity is one equipped by training in the medical sciences.

Hazards to health or to life, due to causes other than disease, are also matters subject to regulation and control by the state under general or special laws, instances of which are those relating to "common carriers," to the use of the highways by motor vehicles, to the construction of buildings, and to protection from conflagration. Acts of violence or other unlawful procedure resulting in death, are by their very nature subject to the provisions of common or of statute law. In the exercise of its function in this field of protective activity, circumstances arise wherein the need of the kind of service which medical science alone can render is no less urgent than it is in the protection of the public health. In the event of death from injury as a cause, injury of any sort, obvious or supposable, the responsibility of someone may be at issue. In every such death the state is inevitably interested, for the incidence of injury may involve some infraction of law, in which case the machinery for the administration of justice must be set in motion.

THE INVESTIGATION OF DEATHS

The official investigation of death when it occurs under certain circumstances, investigation by and in the name of the state, is a traditional and world-wide practice. The circumstances inviting such inquiry are primarily the agency of injury of any sort, and however sustained, as a factor; suddenness or abruptness in the onset of rapidly fatal symptoms; the circumstances of being "found dead"; and any vagueness regarding the cause of a death, whether from lack of clinical facts or otherwise, of a degree sufficient to make the nature of the death conjectural. The nature and the scope of such inquiry, the sort of official conducting it, and his relation to other public officials, the character of his work and his way of doing it, together with the use made of its results, all are matters varying widely with locality and with custom. In some parts of the world, a high type of professional skill is available through the relationship between academic institutions and the government, through medico-legal institutes or similar channels. In this country such inquiry is in the hands of officials ranging from the police surgeon to the coroner and his jury or, as he exists in a few of the states, an official known as the medical examiner. Not infrequently the person on whom the state depends for medical facts and opinion is one who possesses no especial qualifications or skill, and as a result the character and usefulness of his work varies widely.

The general purpose of medico-legal inquiry in the name of the state is the determining of the cause and the manner of a death occurring under circumstances such as to make investigation a matter of sound public policy. A more particular purpose is the establishing of all medical facts relating to death

from unlawful acts and to forfend against the passing of such unrecognized through failure of investigation.

The results of such inquiry enable primarily the classification of deaths into those due to disease of some sort, commonly known as "natural causes," and into those due wholly or in part to injury of some sort. In the case of deaths included in the second of these main classification groups, inquiry also tends to determine, in addition to the cause of the death, the manner in which the injury was sustained or became operative, on the basis of which a death due to injury may be assigned to one of three categories: (1) accidental; (2) suicidal; (3) homicidal; or if the facts are insufficient, to a fourth category, circumstances unknown.

In consequence of such inquiry, a death may either be dismissed from further attention by the state, or be referred to the judicial authorities having jurisdiction over deaths obviously or presumably the result of the act or negligence of another.

Under some systems of medico-legal inquiry, to the investigation as above outlined, is added the responsibility of determining who committed the act or was guilty of the negligence causing the death.

Such being in outline the purpose, the results, and the consequences of the investigation of deaths in the name of the state, by whom, under what auspices, and with what mode of procedure may such inquiry be most advantageously and acceptably conducted? It is not within the scope of this article, nor is it the intention of the writer to discuss the various methods and systems of medico-legal inquiry, or to comment on their merits or their defects. It is the purpose of the writer to present evidence of the value to the community of the investigation of deaths in the name of the state as a form of scientific research the object of which is the gathering and the recording of true facts from which may be drawn sound conclusions yielding trustworthy opinion.

METHODS OF MEDICO-LEGAL INQUIRY

In English-speaking countries medico-legal inquiry into the cause and the manner of a death is very generally conducted through the office of the *coroner*, an English institution of ancient origin, which together with other systems of procedure peculiar to English jurisprudence became a part of American colonial government.

In the United States the office of coroner is widely existent, and in some of the states is one established by constitution.

In Massachusetts this office has been replaced by a method of procedure under which the medical and the judicial functions of the coroner are separated and are assigned to officials especially qualified to perform them. All of the duties and responsibilities connected with the determining of the cause and the manner of a death appropriate for medico-legal inquiry are here incumbent on physicians designated as medical examiners, and all such as have to do with the determining of whether or not a death proven to have been caused by injury was the result of an unlawful act, and if so whose, devolve on magistrates, judges of courts of the first instance.

The law establishing this method of procedure, which at the time was quite new, was enacted in the year 1877 and contains the following general provisions:

(1) The division of the commonwealth into territorial districts determined by population, and consisting of counties or subdivisions of such.

(2) The creating in each such district of the offices of medical examiner and of associate medical examiner.

(3) The appointment to these offices by the governor for a term of seven years of physicians selected as "able and discreet men, learned in the science of medicine."

(4) The prescribing as the duties of the medical examiners and their associates the investigation of any death brought to their notice as that of a person "supposed to have come to his death by violence."

Further and more specific provisions of the law place in charge of the medical examiner the body of the person whose death he is investigating and indicate the general method of his procedure which is to include inquiry into the circumstances of the death or the discovery of the body, survey of the body itself, and whenever he considers such necessary, and with the authority of the district attorney, the making of an internal examination of the body, or autopsy. He is further directed to keep a record of each investigation, to file a copy thereof with the district attorney and, if in his opinion the death may have been due to the act or negligence of another, to file a similar report with the district court having jurisdiction. The law further provides that in case the disposition of the body by cremation is intended, authority therefor shall issue from the medical examiner. The law also specifies that if the services of a chemist are needed in the investigation of a death, these may be obtained by the medical examiner. In other respects the law is non-specific as to the duties of the medical examiner and the manner in which he shall perform them.

The office of medical examiner as thus briefly outlined is one subordinate to no other, and in affiliation with none save those of the district attorney and the courts. It is unrelated save by contact in instances such as to invoke their activities with either municipal or state police. It is administered very largely by physicians engaged in the practice of general medicine, who are appointed to office on the basis of general rather than of special qualifications, and who perform their official duties collaterally with those incidental to their profession. Every medical examiner approaches his duties with the instincts and the manners of a physician rather than as an officer of the commonwealth. Service thus rendered has proven acceptable, and during the years within which it has been available has developed no fundamental defects. That this is true is due to the increasing use by the medical examiners of consultation service whereby they secure the benefit of special knowledge and of special technical skill in the conduct of their more difficult and important investigations. Fifty years ago any physician was considered competent to make a satisfactory post mortem examination. Today such examinations are generally regarded as matters properly for the pathologist, whose services must be sought if the cause of death is to be determined with scientific accuracy. The last half century has witnessed the changes and advances in medicine which have made specialization inevitable and rendered individual proficiency in every branch impossible, and the general practitioner of today, whenever in need of knowledge or skill beyond his own, unhesitatingly calls to his aid a specialist.

In 1907, some thirty years after the office was instituted, the writer was appointed a medical examiner for the county of Suffolk, a district comprising the city of Boston and three other lesser municipalities, and containing a population of about one third of that of the commonwealth. Selected because of special qualifications derived from training under eminent masters, his were alike the privilege and the responsibility of introducing into this branch of public service the methods and the standards of modern scientific medicine as practiced in the pathological laboratory and governing medical research. Opportunity was ample, but facilities were meager, and time, persistent effort and special legislation were required to put into operation all of the activities deemed essential to the conduct of scientific medico-legal inquiry.

From the outset, every investigation was regarded as a research, and as such a matter entitled to all of the consideration called for by the nature of the case. Careful and complete history-taking; detailed objective description of the body under examination; and, in appropriate instances, of its surroundings; and the embodying of the results of these, together with all other material relating to the investigation, in properly edited and typewritten records permanently filed and indexed, were procedures practiced from the start.

Research in any field consists fundamentally in the gathering of facts, the arranging, coördinating and study of these facts, the interpretation of their significance, and the deducing from them of conclusions. Medico-legal inquiry as related to the investigation of deaths is concerned mainly with the gathering of facts, and on the completeness with which these are collected and on the use to which they are put depends in large measure its value.

Such inquiry, as conducted in the district served by the writer, is with a purview wide enough to bring into jurisdiction every death appropriate for investigation, a state of affairs made possible by a liberal interpretation of the statute, and by the coöperation, sought and obtained, of physicians, hospitals, health departments, the police, burial permit offices and undertakers. It is practiced with such facilities as are furnished by an office with accomplished and experienced secretarial and clerical assistants; a public mortuary for the conservation of the bodies of the dead and the making of post mortem examinations; an ambulance service for the transportation to the mortuary of the body of any person which for any reason is to be conveyed thither; a mortuary staff of lay assistants trained to a variety of duties; photographic service; laboratory equipment for histological, bacteriological and serological studies; and the services of a chemist skilled both as a pharmacologist and a toxicologist.

With these aids at his disposal, the writer although at some cost to his liberty, is enabled to perform his duties with the thoroughness and the completeness which his standards require.

Experience with the mode of procedure so outlined as the method of medico-legal inquiry developed and used by the writer within his official district, an experience prolonged over a period of twenty-two years, together with similar experience growing out of consultation practice as a medico-legal pathologist, in retrospect suggests certain generalizations regarding the value, in various ways, of the application of medical science to the investigation of deaths, in the name of the state.

OUTCOME OF INVESTIGATION

A significant result of the inquiry into deaths reported merely because they were sudden, or for the reason that a person was "found dead," deaths unattended by suspicion of violence or of the agency of causes other than natural, is the discovery, from time to time, of internal injuries or of poison of some sort as the true cause of death. Injuries thus disclosed by autopsy have been traced to as-

sault, and the poisonings thus brought to light, possibly with the aid of and always with the confirmatory researches of the toxicologist, while in many instances attributable to suicidal intent or to accident of some sort, in others have led to indictment for murder. Likewise significant, but for different reasons, is the occasional discovery as the cause of sudden death, death so abrupt as to suggest to the layman the possible action of poison, of a disease dangerous to the public health because communicable, such as epidemic cerebrospinal meningitis in its fulminating form. In this connection it may be noted that the investigation of deaths reported because of suddenness or of supposable relation to occupational activities has revealed laryngeal diphtheria, anthrax, and glanders as causes, diseases highly dangerous to the public health by reason of their communicability.

Equally significant are the results of investigations invoked by reason of the presence on the body of bruises, wounds, or other "marks of violence," which to the lay eye may appear impressive, but which assuming them to be actual traumatisms, sustained during life, and not the result of post mortem changes or of the action of marine or other forms of animal life, on internal examination of the body are found to be in no sense factors in the death, although perhaps explanatory of the manner in which it occurred. A man may walk about for days suffering from fracture of the skull, and finally die from its effects, and yet show no outward evidence of injury, while another, found lying on the sidewalk, dead, and showing an extensive lacerated wound of the back of his head, at autopsy is found to have died from disease of the arteries of his heart, a condition explanatory of instant death and of the backward fall creating the wound.

Value of Reconstruction

Considerations of this sort lead directly to the field of activity in which the medico-legal pathologist is pre-eminently useful, namely, the determining of the cause and the manner of death in instances where for any reason the *reconstruction* of the events leading up to the death is important. Responsibility for an accident, including degree of negligence as evidenced by the kind and the degree of bodily injury; the differentiation of suicide, on the one hand from accident, and on the other from homicide; these and other phases of medico-legal inquiry call for the gathering and the assembling of all available facts and the determining therefrom, if possible, of *what happened* to bring about the death, and whether or not, in the course of events, the agency of anyone other than the decedent was involved. Assistive to such "reconstruction" work is opportunity for the medical investigator himself to gather physical facts bearing on the circumstances of a death, himself to study the conditions disclosed by his examination of the body in the light of the surroundings under which the death occurred. Casualties incidental to the use of elevators or lifts, involving the question of responsibility, invite examination not only of the body but also of the scene of the accident, and on all of the facts disclosed by such investigation it may appear that a death was caused not by the fall through an incompletely closed doorway to the bottom of the shaft, alleged by the operator to have happened to a passenger, but to crushing injuries, disclosed by autopsy, for which in some manner the operator was responsible.

The interpretation of wounds or other bodily injuries, not only as to their significance as causes of death but also as to their mode of production, is of large importance, varying with the nature of the case. It plays an important part in "reconstruction" and is one of the most widely useful modes of the applying of medical science to the problems of medico-legal inquiry. Finger nail marks on the skin of the front of the neck, marks unmistakable to the eye of the trained observer, in themselves insignificant, considered in the light of damage to the underlying structures, and other conditions established by post mortem examination, are of high forensic value, for they may establish the fact that death was by manual strangulation. Teeth marks bitten into the skin of the forearm of a police officer by a thief whom he sought to arrest and by whom he was fatally shot during the scuffle, led to the identification of the assailant, when, long after his escape, a suspect was arrested, models of whose teeth accurately fitted the marks in the skin preserved as a specimen.

Injuries which by reason of their nature, their mode of production, the regions or parts of the body involved, their number, and their significance as causes of death, are such as to exclude casualty and to predicate suicide or homicide, constitute a most important field for objective study and medico-legal inquiry, the outcome of which may be such as to warrant the attention of the prosecuting authorities and the police.

It is in situations of this sort that the activities termed "reconstruction," procedures largely dependent on medical facts, are of great value. When, where and by what means the death occurred, by whose hand the fatal injury was inflicted, these and others similar are questions, the answer to which may be immediate and definite or involve prolonged study and careful analysis of facts. Important evidence concerning the *time* of the death may be gathered from physical examination of the body for the presence and the distribution of body heat or warmth, and for the presence and the character of the rigidity of the muscles consequent on death, known as *rigor mortis*. In this connection careful observation by the trained investigator may establish facts bearing on the time of death, of great forensic value in determining the opportunity of a person charged with a crime to have committed it. When death has occurred at a time more or less remote from that of the examination of the body, special medical knowledge derived from experience with the changes caused by decomposition, decay and the action of insects, may assist in determining the probable length of the period following death.

Where the death occurred may be self-evident, as well as by what means and at whose hand, the decedent's or another's. The suspending cord about the neck, the illuminating gas tube carefully arranged to remain between the lips following unconsciousness, the blood-stained hand, with near-by knife or razor similarly stained, the bullet wound of the temple by contact shot, or of the mouth, with blood-stained revolver and powder-marked trigger finger in evidence; such, together with other and strongly supportive facts, ordinarily leave no room for doubt in the mind of the medical investigator on either of these points. Far otherwise is the situation in those instances where the body when discovered lies in a position different from that in which it lay at the time of death, as shown by the distribution of post mortem discoloration; or when the immediate surroundings of the body show no evidence of their being the locus of the death; or, again, where the body exhibits disabling and rapidly fatal injuries and yet no implement or weapon for their production is in evidence.

INTERPRETATION OF WOUNDS

Many are the considerations which enter into the interpretation of wounds, notably those caused by small firearms and by cutting implements, and, therefore, into the problems of "reconstruction." In large part these are matters calling for scientific medical knowledge. It may well be a matter of common knowledge that the position of a wound precludes the possibility of its being self-inflicted, for there are parts of the body inaccessible to one's own hand when holding a knife or a revolver. All questions, however, relating to the effects of wounds, their seriousness, the rapidity with which disability, unconsciousness, or death may result therefrom, these and similar questions are such as can be answered only by the medico-legal pathologist.

The scientific study of wounds exhibited by the bodies of persons dead from cutting or stabbing injuries may throw light on the character of the implement used, including its general form and, according to the nature of the wounds, its dimensions. Such study, yielding data as to the depth to which the implement penetrated and the direction which it took, may also throw some light on the direction from which the thrust came and the manner in which it was delivered. In the study of such wounds, collateral study of any articles of overlying clothing may be of great value. The discovery of wounds made by more than one cutting implement or by one such and another implement or weapon of a different sort (bludgeon or firearm) may lead to the inference of more than one assailant.

Similar study of wounds caused by the discharge of firearms, notably revolvers and automatic pistols, yields data of great assistance in "reconstruction" and, therefore, in the differentiation between accident, suicide and homicide as the manner in which the fatal injury was sustained. The part or parts of the body involved, the number of wounds and the effects of each, the proximity of the weapon to the locus of the wound, the course taken by the bullet or the bullets in the body, the differentiation of a wound of entrance from a wound of exit, the direction from which a relatively distant shot came, the kind or kinds of bullets and of powder used, the effects of multiple wounds, and other considerations bearing on the question whether or not either or all of the wounds could have been self-inflicted —these are but some of the matters engaging the attention of the medical examiner whenever he is confronted with the problem of a death from gunshot wound. Careful study of the scene of a shooting, notably when this is indoors, conducted at the outset and again, perhaps, following a further examination of the body and its clothing, and the identification, by autopsy, of the direction and the course into or through the body of the bullet or bullets may enable such "reconstruction" as to show the relative positions of the assailant and the decedent when the weapon was discharged. Investigation of this sort calls for careful objective description of wounds, the recovery from body or clothing of retained bullets, the identification of each bullet with a particular wound, and the determining of the relative importance of each such wound as a factor in the death. In death from multiple bullet wounds (homicidal), technical study of retained bullets may yield facts indicating different weapons as a source. In one such death investigated by the writer, the bullet causing death, differing from three others the effects of which were negligible, likewise retained in the body, was subsequently identified by a firearm expert as having been discharged from a pistol found on the person of a man arrested on suspicion and later convicted of murder.

IDENTIFICATION OF THE BODIES OF THE DEAD

A field of considerable usefulness for medical science as applied to medicolegal inquiry is in connection with the identification of the bodies of persons unknown and grossly mutilated by casualty, partially incinerated by conflagration, altered by decomposition changes incidental to prolonged immersion or otherwise, or found dismembered under circumstances indicative of the intent to conceal death. In some instances the cause of death is self-evident, and the only problem presenting is that of identity, the establishing of which depends on many factors, prominent among which are teeth and evidences of dentistry, when such objects are available for study. In others, the cause of death is likely also to be a subject for inquiry. Familiarity with the various sorts of decomposition changes, ability to distinguish injuries sustained before death in the presence of such changes and to recognize as such, injuries sustained after death are requisites for this work. In one instance, examination by the writer of a body cast up by the sea, showed conditions indicative of previous earth burial, as well as evidence of homicidal injury. Identification of the body, the discovery of a recently filled in and shallow grave near the decedent's seaside home, of a blood-stained axe in near-by bushes, and of blood stains on the walls of his bedroom, together with other facts, led to the arrest of his wife and another and their final conviction of the murder which had been followed by hasty burial of the body, its subsequent exhumation through fear, and attempted sinking in the near-by ocean, unsuccessful from the detaching of a loosely applied weight, the body thereafter drifting ashore.

The identification of the body of a person dismembered post mortem instrumentally and for the purpose of concealing the death by disposal of the body, in the absence of the head may be most difficult. According to the number and the condition of the parts available for examination, and by the use of methods employed in forensic medicine, some attempt may be made to determine sex and to estimate age, stature and weight. Helpful in such instances are cutaneous scars, even though minute, moles or other markings, and the presence of any deformity however slight.

Value of Laboratory Science

Laboratory science is an indispensable adjunct to medico-legal inquiry, alike as an aid in determining the exact nature of certain pathological processes or changes recognized as causing or contributing to death, and as a means of identifying the character of stains of various sorts, which at times is desirable in connection with the investigation of a death. Histological and bacteriological studies in any instance of death from infection are important and form an integral part of the scientific investigation of deaths consequent on the interruption of pregnancy. Here the results of such studies may be of great forensic value.

The examination of stains or other materials for the presence of human blood is now conducted almost wholly by biological methods based on the principles of modern serology. Microscopy yields at most the data differentiating from other stains those made by mammalian blood. For the determination of human blood the biological method, in competent hands, is reliable and productive of authoritative results.

Toxicology, the science of poisons, and pharmacology, the science of drugs, branches of natural science closely allied with medical science, may factor largely in the investigation of death, for without the results yielded by chemical examination made at his direction, the medico-legal pathologist would at times be lacking in the facts needed for well-grounded opinion as to the cause of death. Some poisons leave in their wake but scanty evidence of their action, and in instances where their presence, though suspected, is otherwise incapable of proof, resort must be had to chemistry. Fatal poisoning, under circumstances offering any foundation for the opinion that it might have been due to the act or negligence of another, should lead to thorough and perhaps exhaustive chemical examination of appropriate and significant materials.

The results of medico-legal inquiry thus obtained are always at the service of the police and the prosecuting authorities, in whose hands they may prove reliable aids in their all important duties of conserving public safety.

In the preparation of this article, the writer has been governed perhaps rather more by his instincts than by the suggestions offered by the editor of the Annals. That he has been so governed is due, in part at least, to his abiding faith in the proposition that all genuinely scientific work is fundamentally the search for truth, and his firm belief that in this quest general principles are of greater value than specific directions. In his own work he has found that rigid objectivity in method, a mind free from prejudgment, an ear deaf to theorizing, and the faith that sooner or later truth will crystallize from any mass of facts have served him better than any other and more formal rules of practice.

Psychology in Criminal Investigation

By JOHN A. LARSON, PH.D., M.D.

Henry Phipps Psychiatric Clinic, Johns Hopkins Hospital, Baltimore, Maryland

THE problems of forensic psychiatry which includes all problems involved in the study of abnormal personalities, errors of the witness, judge, jurors or investigating officials made possible by deviations from or variations in the normal components involved in psycho-biological mechanisms cannot be treated here. Rather the following questions are of interest: (1) When a crime has occurred, is the knowledge of psychology of any value to the detective who studies the scene of the crime itself for the purpose of finding some clues to the perpetrator? (2) Can psychology help the detective in capturing or pursuing a suspect? (3) Can psychology help a detective who has captured a suspect to secure from that person a statement of his movements? (4) Can psychology help a detective who has secured such a statement to examine the validity of evidence so secured?

CRIMINAL MODUS OPERANDI

The better trained investigator today makes use of psychology in finding clues at the scene of crime and from the information secured is often enabled to cause the arrest of the criminal. An elaborate system of classification known as the Atcherly *modus operandi* system and modified by Vollmer is based upon the fact that a criminal may be classified and later apprehended by the manner in which he works. In other words—clues to his personality are left at the scene of the crime. Very detailed sheets are filled in by the investigating officer. Thus a burglar may work between seven and nine P.M., attack one-story five-room bungalows, enter through a pantry window, pull down the blinds, turn on all of the lights, wear gloves, and in his search for valuables be very disorderly, throwing the contents of drawers on the floor, take only jewelry, raid the pantry and leave by the front door. The next man may be a porch climber, attack three-story buildings, be a neat worker, operate with the blinds up, and so forth. All of these items are determined by habit and personality differences for no two individuals work in an identical fashion. No one works without leaving so-called clues, and the fact that one man may apparently leave no traces is in itself a description. The reports of the details of the crime are then filed and broadcasted, and the same worker may be located in another state. Often two or more crimes may be committed by the same man, and after going through the records classified by a man in the office special details may be sent out to anticipate the next crime. An illustrative case is that of a group of auto-thieves who terrorized the East Bay region at San Francisco. A group of youths would steal automobiles and commit a hold-up, joy ride (on one occasion they raped a girl), carry away safes and blow them open. An inspector had, long before their final capture, identified the boys by their *modus operandi*. In a short time he showed by maps the identity of the descriptions of the crimes; the suspects would steal Marmon cars from city X, go directly to city Y and there commit a robbery of some kind, drink or joy ride, and abandon the car that night or the next in city Z.

A glove from the girl who had been abducted and raped or a fragment of a safe were found in the stolen car connecting it with the robbery. Checking up on former auto-thieves in the vicinity of Z the inspector found a group of four boys out on parole. The inspector being from city X (the writer worked with him on this case) gave their names to the officials at Z and the boys were brought in, but the girl refused to identify them and they were released. Following their capture she admitted they had threatened to kill her if she told. They were subsequently caught after one of them had shot an officer during a frustrated hold-up. The night of the shooting episode the inspector at X, as soon as he received a complaint that a Marmon had been stolen, notified the officials at Y that there would shortly be a hold-up in that city and he detailed men to block off the highways of X. Because of lack of coöperation at Y the highways were left uncovered and a getaway occurred after the attempted robbery. Upon several occasions the inspector at X placed special details notifying them that a Marmon would be stolen from their beat that evening between seven and nine by four gunmen. This happend each time because of carelessness on the part of some member of the details.

Hans Gross in his volume of Criminal Psychology speaks of nostalgia. There was a series of homes, closely adjacent to each other, which burned on different days. After a careful survey of the first two cases the detectives were informed that the fires were the work of a pyromaniac and that they should be on the watch for a stranger living in the neighborhood or one who had been present at all of the fires. This was relatively easy but required a routine check on everyone present at the fire and his residence.

A stranger, a feeble-minded boy, was found living in one of the homes adjacent to those that had burned. He was away from the place where he had lived all of his life and was very homesick, with no satisfactory method of adjustment.

Not infrequently complaints come in of "boosting" or petty thievery. Attention can usually be turned with success toward the investigation of drug addicts living in the vicinity, especially those addicted to morphine. At times sex maladjustments and antisocial acts may be linked together from a study of the motivation present. Thus a series of inside thefts was being investigated in a girls' boarding house. Suspicion was focused on an adolescent girl who had suddenly commenced to display a splendid wardrobe. She was watched and later caught. Unsuccessful in attracting the boy she wanted, she stole to make herself attractive.

Following unusually vicious assaults or crimes the investigator may with profit canvass the neighborhood for cocaine addicts, epileptics or low grade individuals. Examination of the scene of the crime and determination of the motivation is essential but leads into the field of forensic psychiatry and there is a vast literature in this field. Certain types of crime suggest psychotic conditions. The way in which some thefts are committed may suggest that children are responsible. The manner in which some crimes are committed is suggestive of psychopathic personalities, feeble-mindedness or psychotic factors. The torso of a woman was found in a canyon. The absence of her legs, various mutilations and the manner in which she was killed was suggestive of a sadistic murder. Search was then made for the sadist killer and he was eventually found after having murdered at least twenty-eight women.

Sorority girls in the vicinity of the local campus complained of the theft of underwear from clotheslines and porches. Suspecting the work of a sexual pervert the detectives were requested to question all suspicious characters. A Japanese was located and some two hundred pieces of girls' underwear were found in his room. Again several complaints were received that clothing was being taken from the lines, befouled and abandoned. Inference was made that this was the work of a feeble-minded individual, and a boy out on parole was eventually caught in the act.

A series of anonymous letters were written in which mention of poisoning dogs was made. The contents had persecutory trends. A search was made in the files for known paranoid individuals in the neighborhood, and after a comparison of samples of handwriting the writer was located. A similar study may locate the writer of "poison-pen" letters.

INTERPRETING THE SUSPECT'S STATEMENT

Having found the suspect the task is then that of securing a statement from him. The best time to secure a statement is immediately after apprehension before any attorney or friend has opportunity to coach him. It is then that he is not only willing but at times anxious to confess. He can be requested to give an account of his movements in great detail and then a day or two later repeat his story, when any discrepancy can be noted. All confessions must be carefully checked. No difficulty need be experienced because of alleged "third degree" or rough measures where the police are properly selected and trained and politics excluded.[1]

[1] An excellent description of the psychological nature of confessions, true and false, may be

False confessions often occur in many sensational trials. Thus in connection with the Tesmer murder case, where a gunwoman was supposedly involved and a sex pervert was tried and acquitted, a sexual psychopath in a state hospital confessed that he was guilty. He was brought by the state alienist to the writer and following a deception test he repudiated his confession and proved his innocence. He had confessed falsely hoping to be released from the asylum, tried for the murder and gain some notoriety and attention.

Dying confessions, of course, cannot be relied upon for either accuracy or veracity. It is not infrequent to find a dying confession to be false. Thus in a case known to the writer in Richmond, California, a dying man stated that his brother-in-law was guilty of a murder. This statement was made because of jealousy, was believed to be true by the man himself, but was later found to be erroneous.

Practically, the best results are secured when the suspect is treated with the utmost kindness and interviewed only by the investigating official. Preferably, an interrogator can be trained to assist in the questioning of every suspect. At such times careful notes should be made of all questions, answers, spontaneous actions noted and deception tests employed.

OBJECTIVE EVALUATION OF TESTIMONY

For years psychologists have focused their attention on the problem of se-

found in Hans Gross' *Criminal Psychology*, in Bose's *Juristic Psychology* and in Münsterberg's *On the Witness Stand*. A brief discussion of so-called "third degree" methods, selected from literature and from cases seen in the experience of the writer in contact with different investigating officials, may be found in *Police and Legal Methods of the Determination of the Innocence or Guilt of the Suspect*, Journal of the American Institute for Criminal Law and Criminology, 1925.

curing some objective means of evaluating the testimony of witnesses and of suspects, since such procedures as the oath and the kissing of the Bible are inadequate regardless of the penalties imposed for perjury. The detection of deception, if possible, is one of the most important problems of the criminalist once the suspect is secured.

In India it is alleged that native officials watch the movements of the great toe which varies with deception. The Chinese have long given suspects rice to chew, on the theory that guilty fear would inhibit the salivary flow. The technique of deception tests may be divided into two great groups, association tests and the use of physiological criteria, and these may be listed for convenience as follows, without any chronological significance.

1. Association tests:
   A. Reaction time;
   B. Qualitative response.
2. Hypnosis.
3. Subjective and intuitive methods.
4. Physiological tests:
   A. Sphygmographic and Plethysmographic curves.
   B. Blood pressure:
      1. Quantitative, discontinuous methods;
      2. Continuous, graphic;
      3. Combinations of one and two.
   C. Respiratory changes.
   D. Muscular changes:
      1. Erographic measurements;
      2. Keeler's work;
      3. Work of Luria.
   E. Nerve tonicity—graphic records of knee jerks.
   F. Psychogalvanic reflex.
   G. Moisture changes.
   H. Pupillary changes.
   I. Adrenalin and sugar changes—emotional glycosuria.
   J. Drugs.

For years psychologists have used what is called association tests alone. In undertaking a critical survey of this entire field of the attempts to devise tests for the determination of innocence or guilt of a suspect or a witness, many variables, objections and questions arise, such as whether or not it is possible to eliminate: (1) the fear of the innocent; (2) the anger and the resentment of the innocent; (3) the effect of the experiences of lying, as the lying of a recidivist; (4) the effect of pathological and mental conditions; and (5) the lying of a suspect when something is at stake, as compared with the lying of student subjects in the laboratory;

Again, what should be the legal rôle of a deception test? Should it be used in the police or the district attorney's office, before the judge, in the court room, as evidence *per se* or to furnish leads for further investigation? Should the consent of the suspect be asked? What is the actual rôle or the practical usage of deception tests and how objective can a given test be made, so as to eliminate subjective and intuitive "hunches" and cues on the part of the examiner?

Many questions and criticisms may be raised, but the foregoing have been selected from the comments of thousands, from audiences at legal, police, psychological and psychiatric conventions.

A survey of the literature reveals the fact that the contributions may be divided as follows: (1) class room experiments only; (2) court room demonstrations; (3) experiments in the police laboratory where actual suspects are used and the deception test forms a part of the machinery of criminal investigation.

The workers may be divided into two groups: those who are adequately trained in physiological, psychiatric and in criminal investigation, conducting as well controlled experiments as possible; and the sporadic, sensational seeker who, often untrained, performs isolated and uncontrolled experiments in sensational cases and then generalizes widely in newspapers and magazines. Unfortunately it is the latter type of worker who is known to the public through the medium of the Sunday supplements, the Literary Digest, and other journals.

Although varying degrees of success have been obtained in class room experiments where students, reporters or volunteers are used, it is obvious that the situation is to some extent artificial and that in addition to the effects of lying there are often profound emotional disturbances when the suspect in a criminal investigation lies. In the latter case the uncovering and the proof of deception may result in disgrace, loss of freedom or even of life for the one involved. Therefore, inferences drawn from positive results in the university laboratory where the conditions are at best only artificial cannot be applied to criminal investigation, nor can inferences be made as to the validity of a given method.

ASSOCIATION TESTS

Prior to the War the bulk of the experimentation made was with the so-called association method. Professor Münsterberg, in his book *On the Witness Stand*, describes the technique and the principles involved. He says,

In this way, during the last twenty years, there has developed an exact and subtle study of mental associations, and through such very careful observation of the time differences between associations a deep insight has been won into the whole mental mechanism. The slightest changes of physical connections can be discovered and traced by these slight variations of time. . . .

Marston, a pupil of Münsterberg, and a lawyer, has applied psychological methods to the criminological field. He has written much on the association

method.[2] The literature is tremendous, but the few references given below may suffice for a brief survey of the field.[3]

Crane, Wigmore, Marston and other workers of merit who have used the association word and reaction time method agree in stating that the method as used alone is impractical as far as legal usage is warranted. Wigmore cites the opinion of leading founders of this method and they agree that it is inadequate. However, it may furnish helpful leads if used in conjunction with other methods.

HYPNOSIS

For years hypnosis has been discussed as a possible means of securing confessions, but few attempts have been recorded of its usage in actual cases. Münsterberg discusses the question in his book *On the Witness Stand*. Schilder, of Vienna, an authority in this field, has written on its medico-legal aspects. David Levy of the New York Child Guidance Clinic told the writer of its usage in securing confession from a boy of some sexual episode. Most psychiatrists seem to

[2] *Journal of Experimental Psychology*, Vol. 3, 1920, p. 73.

[3] W. Wundt, *Physiologische Psychologie*. In *Philosophische Studien, I;* J. M. and Bryant S. Catell, *Mental Association Investigated by Experiment*. Mind, Vols. 2 and 14; C. Jung, *Diagnostiche Assoizationsstudien*. In *Beiträge zur experimentellen Psychopathologie*. Ed. 1, 1906; Ed. 11, 1911, Leipzig: Barth; Gertrude Saling, *Assoziation-Massenversuche*, Zeits. f. Psych., Vol. 49; Ferdin and Reinhold, *Beiträge zur Assoziationslehre auf Grund von Massenversuchen*. Zeits. f. Psych., Vol. 54; Grace Kent and A. J. Rosanoff, *A Study of Association in Insanity*, Amer. Jour. of Insanity, Vol. 67, 1910; Crane, *A Study in Association Reaction and Reaction Time, with an Attempted Application of Results in Determining the Presence of Guilty Knowledge;* Wigmore, *Psychology of Testimony*, Ill. Law Rev. 3: 410, 1909; *Principles of Judicial Proof*, p. 571; Wertheimer and Klein, in the *Archiv für Kriminal-Anthropologie*, 1904; R. H. G., in the *Journal of the American Institute for Criminal Law and Criminology* 2: 769, 1911.

agree that since coöperation is so vital, one cannot expect to obtain a confession which will harm the subject or compel the subject to commit an act foreign to his personality. On the other hand, workers agree that while under hypnosis a criminal might be induced to answer questions and give detailed descriptions of his alibi, and he might conceivably incriminate himself or furnish leads for further investigation. Careful experiments, with subsequent checking and investigation, can throw light on this interesting approach. The legality of this or any test procedure in the present status of criminal investigation is not such as to interfere. Although the section, presided over by Captain Duncan Matheson, of the police convention in San Francisco, 1922, went on record as expressing the opinion that deception tests (which were put in the same category as the use of the dictograph) would not be countenanced, there is no objection so long as the suspect consents, knowing the nature of the procedure. The writer has personally tested hundreds of suspects and also used hypnosis therapeutically, consent having been obtained. In three police cases only did the suspects refuse to submit to a deception test, and this was upon advice of their attorneys.

The jurist and the detective with years of experience are not infrequently able to sense that a suspect is guilty and is lying, but are not able to give reasons or objective data whereby other less experienced persons could arrive at the same conclusion. In one suspect it may be a pallor or a form of gesticulation, fainting or the intonation of the voice which gives the lie to the spoken word; while in another it may be the opposite. What seems to be evidences of guilt in one may be due to the fear of the innocent in another. There is no way of measuring, evaluating or of controlling the factors which seem significant to them.

It is incredible to what extent the public and the investigating officials may be influenced by superstition, and the psychologist must be aware of this. In one case, the writer was using a deception test to aid detectives from another city, and one of them, dissatisfied suggested and persuaded the suspects to go to a clairvoyant. Much attention is being given to spectacular solution of cases by alleged mental telepathists. Thus Dr. Langsner, formerly of Vienna, has been very successful in solving sensational and difficult cases by what some have termed mental telepathy or mind reading. The success rather seems to be due to an intuitive faculty based upon much experience in the examination of suspects.

DRUGS

It has long been known that under the influence of narcotics and particularly ether, chloroform, nitrous oxide, and alcohol at a certain stage, inhibition is removed and an individual talks much more freely and may in a braggadocio fashion narrate the details of a crime. It is true that many of the statements may be false or inaccurate, but valuable leads may be secured. Since about 1920, Dr. E. H. House, an obstetrician of Ferris, Texas, has worked on the theory that by the proper administration of scopolamine, following chloroform anaesthesia, a certain stage of narcosis is reached which he terms the "receptive stage" during which one cannot lie, regardless of what may be involved. His experiments and work have received widespread attention, for he has not only worked with reporters and volunteers in demonstrations, but also with suspects held in jail. He has published his theories and results. The writer heard his paper,[4] delivered at the convention of the American Medical Association in San Francisco, 1922, and was present at three of his demonstrations in the penitentiary, as well as later, when he gave a demonstration at the Convention of Identification Experts at Windsor, Canada, in August, 1925. Dr. House has evolved theories of his own to explain the physiological and the psychological mechanisms involved and many persons, including Doctors Kirby and Jelliffe and leading pharmacologists, are said to disagree with his views. In one of the demonstrations a suspect lied about an important detail whenever it was mentioned. Nevertheless, whether an individual can lie or not, he may talk more freely while under the influence of the drugs.

According to editorials, magazine articles and newspaper descriptions, Dr. W. D. Bates, of New York, has made use of the retinoscope in the detection of deception. Apparently the principle involved is that the strain caused by deception causes a transitory myopia (nearsightedness) which is detected by observation of the movements of the shadows during an examination by the use of the retinoscope. Since this movement cannot be prevented by the subject, the method is supposed to be accurate, as it is based upon reflex action which cannot be controlled. It would be very interesting to see controlled experiments whereby deception has been detected in actual cases of criminal investigation.

RESPIRATORY AND BLOOD PRESSURE TESTS

Respiratory and blood pressure changes have afforded another means of study.[5]

Aside from the work of Lombroso with the sphygmograph in the detection of guilt, a distinct advance has been made by the masterly contributions of Benussi.[6]

In describing his method, Burtt writes as follows:[7]

Benussi's subjects were given small cards containing a number of digits, and letters and a picture. They were questioned as to the nature, number and arrangement of the symbols and were asked to describe the picture and to read the symbols in a specified order. In some instances they did this truthfully, but with other cards (marked with a star) they lied upon every point. A number of spectators were present to enhance the subject's emotional state. The breathing was recorded on a kymograph and several breaths immediately preceding and following each reply were measured to compute the I/E.

Benussi found that the average of three to five ratios preceding a false answer was less than the average of three to five ratios following that answer. With truthful replies the reverse was the case—the average I/E before the answer was greater than the average I/E after the answer. The difference between the average ratios before and after a lie varied with the ability of the subject to dissimulate (as judged by the experimenter) and correlated also with the difficulty of lying in specific instances as indicated by the introspection. The results were negative if the audience knew whether the subject was going to lie or not and if the subject was aware of this.

[5] In reference to the use of respiratory changes in emotional studies, the following are of interest: Jung, *Studies in Word Association*, pp. 540; New York: Moffatt, Yard & Co.; Lewis J. Pollack, *Pneumographic Studies of Emotional Reactions in Dementia Praecox*, in The Institute Quart., Vol. 7, no. 3, Sept. 30, 1916; Boris Sidis, *Psycho-Pathological Research in Mental Dissociation*; J. W. Debruyn, *A study of Emotional Expression in Dementia Praecox*, Jour. of Abnormal Psych., Feb.–March, 1909.

[6] *On the Effects of Lying on changes on Respiration.* Archiv. f. die ges. Psych., Vol. 31, 1914.

[7] *Journal of Experimental Psychology*, Vol. 4, Feb. 1921.

[4] *The Medico-Legal and Obstetric Observation of Scopolamine Anaesthesia.*

Benussi found that when the subject tried to voluntarily control the breathing, even following a metronome, the I/E was still diagnostic.

In a review of Benussi's results Whipple wrote:

(a) The human jury, taken on the average, made little better than a "chance shot"—about fifty-five per cent right cases—; (b) the mechanical jury-pneumo-graph—Marey—was practically infallible—nearly one hundred per cent right cases; (c) it also distinguished between good and poor dissimulation; (d) false statements made with full knowledge that the auditors knew their falsity leaves the same record as truthfulness, so that the emotional status of the liar is the essential element in his detection; (e) attempts of the subject to modify breathing do not destroy the significant feature of the respiratory tracing which consists in this that the ratio between length of inspiration and length of expiration is in lying greater after than before the statement, and in truth telling, greater before than after the statement.

In the Journal of Experimental Psychology, Vol. 21, p. 119, Marston wrote:

Benussi's results, indicating as they do great definiteness of lying symptoms, are sufficient to warrant the assumption of the deceptive consciousness as a working hypothesis.

Of the psychologists, Marston and Burtt, who also is a lawyer, have done most in actually attempting to work out a deception test. Whereas several psychologists have written rather positively on the subject and have experimented, no work has been done except artificial experimentation in the laboratory. Lying, by students in the presence of make-believe jurors, is vastly different from and cannot be accurately compared with lying by the criminal about his guilt in order to preserve liberty or life. Marston has

published several papers anent his deception studies in blood-pressure.[8]

On one occasion two attorneys attempted to introduce evidence secured by the blood pressure test to show that their client was innocent. Chief Justice W. L. McCoy of the Supreme Court of the District of Columbia ruled against its usage.

On another occasion Professor New of the University of Maryland is reported to have tested a suspect at the county jail, Paris, Illinois, and has shown that the subject spoke a mixture of truth and falsehood. This inference seems to have been borne out by the officers in charge of the case.

The writer, while a police officer, became interested in Marston's work and obtained considerable success with a modification of his procedure. The following references to various articles prepared by the writer alone or in collaboration with his colleagues describe some of the results obtained:

A Modification of the Marston Deception Test. Journal of the American Institute of Criminal Law and Criminology, Vol. 12, No. 3, 1921; *The Cardio-Pneumo Psychogram and its Use in the Study of Emotions: With Practical Applications.* Journal of Experimental Psychology, Vol. 5, No. 5, Oct., 1922; *Deception Tests and Lie-Detectors*, paper read before the convention of chiefs of police, San Francisco, 1922; *The Berkeley Lie-Detector*, paper read before a section of the American Bar Association, San Francisco, 1922; *Deception Technique*, The Summary, San Francisco, 1922; *The Cardio-Pneumo-Psychogram in Deception.* Journal of Experimental Psychology, Vol. 11, No. 6, Dec., 1923. Reprinted in the Institution Quarterly, Dec., 1923; *Present Police and Legal Methods for the Determination of the*

[8] See *Journal of Experimental Psychology,* Vol. 2, 1917; the *Journal of the American Institute of Criminal Law and Criminology,* Feb. 1921; and *Sex Characteristics of Systolic Blood Pressure Behavior,* in the *Journal of Experimental Psychology* 6: 387–419, 1923.

Innocence or Guilt of the Suspect. Journal of the American Institute of Criminal Law and Criminology, Vol. 16, No. 2, Aug., 1925. In this article the so-termed "third degree" was considered and methods for elimination suggested by the substitution of better personnel, scientific methods of cross-examination, and so forth. The following table cited from this article summarizes some of the results secured by the use of deception technique in police investigation, at the time of the analysis:

TABLE I

Cases All Cleared by Confession or Check, in Berkeley:

Total number of cases cleared	249
Total number of individuals in the above cases	528
Total number who confessed	53
Total number who lied and confessed	129
Total number who lied and were checked	36
Total number of suspects who were cleared	310
Property recovered in cash	$8,000

TABLE II

Distribution of Cases:

Burglary	28
United States Laws, Bootlegging	3
Miscellaneous	11
Sex	36
Larceny	166
Murder	5

TABLE III

Cases Which Because of Lack of Confession or the Disappearance of the Suspects have not been Cleared Up:

Total number of cases not cleared	64
Total number of individuals examined	333

Of these 333, 267 were eliminated by their records.

TABLE IV

Total number of individuals examined	333
Total number of persons tested	861

A Study of Deception in the Penitentiary, by John A. Larson and Herman M. Adler.

Institution Quarterly, June, 1925. A preliminary communication. Further data are being prepared in the form of quantitative tables, and so forth; *The Polygraph in Criminal Investigation.* Paper, illustrated by lantern slides, read before a convention of the International Association for Identification Experts, Windsor, Canada, August, 1925; Tabular summary of some one hundred and twenty juvenile cases. In Annual Report, Institute for Juvenile Research now in press. In addition to testing children when suspected of lying, this technique has been used in probing for complexes in children at the Institute for Juvenile Research and an attempt has been made to devise a questionnaire which would uncover any possible resistances or complexes. Similar work was done by the writer while at Berkeley, complexes being probed by using Kent-Rosanoff association and other words, the Woodworth questionnaire and special questions and the effect upon the polygraphic record noted. Records and data obtained from this type of investigation are now being prepared; *A Classification of Polygraphic Records,* Public Welfare Magazine, Nov., 1926; A complete survey of the literature, observational and legal, and of experimental work on the subject of the *Determination of the Innocence or Guilt of the Suspect and Deception Tests* is now ready for publication by the writer; *Deception and Self-Deception,* by Herman Adler and John A. Larson. Paper read before the American Neurological Association, May 31, 1927, at Atlantic City.

Landis has written about his experiments on deception, but his findings have no value, as the experiments were performed under artificial conditions, with students. Inferences made from these experiments are not applicable to criminal investigation as either confirming or vitiating the results reported by Marston, Larson, and others.

OTHER METHODS

Jung and his co-authors, Darrow, Richter, and others have used the psychogalvanic reflex in psychological investigations. Wechsler has a modified apparatus and is alleged to have used his apparatus in connection with deception, but no controlled experiments in criminal investigation are on record.

C. Darrow, at the Institute for Juvenile Research, with apparatus using the psychogalvanic reflex, blood pressure and respiratory tracings taken simultaneously found that the psychogalvanic reflex was not as accurate and did not show as much in the records where emotions were involved, as did the blood and respiratory tracings.

Keeler has an apparatus of his own and has applied it for years in criminal investigations as well as in class room experiments. He secures continuous blood pressure, respiratory and other curves and has been very successful in his work, performed for the Los Angeles Police Department and in the Psychological Institute at Stanford University. He planned his apparatus while working in Los Angeles before going to Stanford University. Previous to this he had been associated with the writer in the Berkeley experiments.

In discussing his results in a personal communication, Keeler stated that of some eight hundred suspects examined for the Los Angeles and neighboring police departments he did not have a single failure in the interpretations of the records as checked by the facts later discovered. Later he secured records of various psychopathological types in the hospitals about Palo Alto, California, and reported success in differentiating types by the records. At the present time he is working in the same laboratory as Darrow in Chicago and has access to Darrow's apparatus if necessary for the recording of changes in moisture which may be due to emotional or other stimulation. Keeler has been very successful in artificial deception with a card experiment. He shows ten playing cards while records are being secured and by a study of change in the record can tell which card the subject has lied about, after as he has been told to select one and to lie about the selection. He uses this experiment with a questionnaire, designated to test the attitude and the emotions of the inmates of penitentiaries. He has also been interested in studying the effects of deception as recorded by a motor outflow.

Professor McCormick, of the North Carolina Law School, in a special session of a law convention in Chicago, December, 1926, read a paper later published in the North Carolina Law Journal. In this paper he discusses deception tests from a legal viewpoint. He also gives the opinions of many psychologists as to the efficacy of deception tests.

Dr. Alexander R. Luria, assistant professor of psychology at the Second State University of Moscow, has been working for six years with the psychology of deception. He has worked with criminal suspects immediately after their arrest and even before they were questioned by the police. The writer has not had opportunity to familiarize himself with all of his work, but he uses a small simple type of pneumatic indicator, the subject being told to rest his hand upon it and press it when the word is given. He states that the graphic curve produced together with the reaction time shows characteristic reactions following the crucial words. Description of his technique can be secured by writing him.

Many other methods of recording possible physical changes might be devised, such as the measurement of emotional glycosuria and quantitative estimation of the epinephrine output. If it were not possible to differentiate at least to some extent the fear and the anger of the innocent suspect, it would have been impossible to have secured the results reported by the writer and others. The acid test of theories and variables in this case consists in working with the real raw material. The writer has used, in modified continuous tracings of heart beat, variations in blood pressure and respiration, discontinuous estimates of quantitative blood pressure readings and, for a while, reaction time. The success of his interpretation has not depended upon subjective cues received, for often the interpretation and the recommendations for subsequent investigation have been made from records secured by others, and the one who examined the records never saw or heard the suspect or discussed the case with any official. The records are permanent and eliminate subjective factors. So far as the controls are concerned, many are often available in the same investigation. In many cases where the crime was committed by one or more of a group of anywhere from five to one hundred, or even more, suspects in the same house or fraternity, the suspects were all tested under the same conditions and with the same questions, and it was possible to select the record of the guilty and then to check the interpretation by the restoration of the stolen property.

No claims are made by the writer at this stage of the investigation, except that this type of technique is of definite service in criminal investigation. The ultimate accuracy of this or similar technique has not yet been determined. Many psychologists would be satisfied by a series of tests upon one hundred individuals, even with controls and statistical discussion of the results in terms of correlations, but thousands of individuals are necessary, so that the various groupings and reactions of all types, normal and psychopathic, can be ascertained. At the present stage, the technique used has proven its merit as furnishing leads for criminal investigation, but such technique should not now be used in the court room, and a suspect should not at the present time, be convicted or arrested upon the results of deception tests if ever.

SUMMARY

1. Psychological or psychiatric knowledge coupled with a careful investigation at the scene of the crime can aid in the identification and the apprehension of the criminal.

2. Psychology can be of much value in obtaining a confession when the suspect is first apprehended.

3. Deception tests can and have been of immeasurable value in securing objective data of a suspect's guilt or innocence and in eliminating innocent suspects in spite of adverse testimony and even of their own confessions.

INDEX TO SUBJECTS

Académie Internationale de Criminalistique, Lausanne, 204.

Administration, Municipal Police, Bruce Smith, 1–27.

Administration, Police, 96.

Annual Police Report, 96–103; content of, 99–103; reform, 97–8; comparability, 97–8.

Associations, Police; future of, 126–7.

Atcherly Modus Operandi System, 258.

Bertillon System, 205.

Blood analysis, 242–3; methods of, 242–3; blood group, 242–3.

Bureau of Identification, 193.

Bureau of Immigration, see United States Department of Labor.

Bureau of Investigation, see United States Department of Justice.

Criminal Identification, J. Edgar Hoover, 205–13.

Coal and Iron Police, see Private Police of Pennsylvania.

Committee on Uniform Crime Records, 98–9; 123.

Commissioner of Public Safety, Municipal, 5–10.

Control and the Discipline of Police Forces, The, Donald C. Stone, 63–73.

Constable, The, 33; duties and powers of, 33.

Counterfeits, identification of, 246–7; see also Forgeries.

Civil Service Commission, see Municipal Police Administration.

Crime, see under Police, Crime and Politics.

Crime, prevalence and trend of, 76; statistics, 77; rates of, 77–80; trend in Detroit, 80; clearance tables, 81, 82, 95; persons charged with, 86.

Criminal police, Germany, duties and powers of, 225.

Criminal Identification, in England, 221–2; methods of, 221; see also Finger Prints, modus operandi.

Criminal Identification, 237; portrait parlé, 237; footprints, 243; see also Modern Police Technicians.

Criminal Identification, 193–8.

Criminal Identification; history, 205; systems of, 205; international coöperation, 213; handwriting, 211; bullet identification, 210–11; abroad, 211–13.

Criminalistic Institutes of Austria, origin of, 199; in Vienna, 199–201; administration of, 200; curriculum of, 200–1; training for Jurists, 201–3; elementary and specialized, 199–203; where given, 203–4; faculty of, 201.

Criminalistic Institutes and Laboratories, Dr. Seigfried Türkel, 199–204.

Criminal Law, enforcement of, 31–2.

Criminal Modus Operandi, 258–60.

Customs, Bureau of, see United States Treasury Department.

Deception Tests, see Psychology in Criminal Investigation.

Detective, American; methods, 214–5; organization, 216; outwitting professional criminal, 215–16; the court, 217–8; politics, the handicap, 218.

Detective, English; methods, 219–221; specialists, 222; see also Scotland Yard.

Detectives, Private; see Private Police of Pennsylvania.

Detectives, training of, in Belgium, 195–8.

English Police System, The, A. L. Dixon, 177–92.

Federal Police, Albert Langeluttig, 41–54; see Police, Federal.

Fingerprints, 206–13.

Finger Print Identification, England, 221.

Fingerprint Identification, evolution, 206–8; Henry System, in the U. S., 208; abroad, 211–4.

Fingerprint Identification, researches, 240–1; latent fingerprints, 240; foil method, 241; staining fluids, 241; Kögel's method, 241.

Firearms, examination of, 244–5.

Forgeries, 248.

Footprints, 243; Müller's method, 243; Poller's method, 243.

Fraternal Order of Police, 121–5.

Gunpowder, identification of, 245–6.

Handwriting, identification of, 247–8.

Harrison Anti-Narcotic Act, 43.

Holmes Electric Protective Service, 57.

Hypnosis, 262.

Identification, see U. S. Department of Justice; also see Criminal Identification.

Immigration, bureau of, see United States Department of Labor.

Industrial Police, see Private Police of Pennsylvania.

International Association of Chiefs of Police and other American Police Organizations, Lent D. Upson, 121–7.

International Association of Chiefs of Police, history of, 122; purposes of, 122; membership of, 122–3.

International Association for Identification, 124–5.

International Association of Policewomen, 125.

Internationale Kriminal-polizeiliche Kommission, 213.
International Detective Agency, Burns, 57.
International Police Conference, 124.
Investigation of Crime in Germany, division of authority, 223; organization, 224; technical aids, 226–7, 231–4; anthropometry, 227; dactyloscopy, 227–9; new methods, 229; fingerprints, 234–6.
Investigation of death, 250–7.

Journals, Police, 128–34; functions of, 129–33; suggested program for, 133–4.
Journal of the American Institute of Criminal Law and Criminology, The, 128.

Kriminalpolizer, see criminal police.

Laboratories, Austria, 199–204.

Medical examiner, 251–7; see also Medico Legal Inquiry.
Medical Science in the Service of the State, George Burgess Magrath, A.M., M.D., 249–57.
Medical Science, 249–57.
Medico-Legal Inquiry, methods of, 251; in the United States, 251; in Massachusetts, 251; research, 252; outcome of, 253; value of reconstruction, 254–5; interpretation of wounds, 255; identification, 256–7; laboratory science, 257.
Metric photography, 239–40.
Methods of Police Selection, in United States, 147–59; selection standards, 148; origin of, 149; promotion, 149; rating, 149; character investigation, 149; interviews, 149; experience, 149; educational requirements, 149; basis of, 150.
Methods in the Selection of Police in Europe, psychological, 160–5; analysis of qualifications, 160–1; tests, 161–5; list of references, 165.
Modus Operandi Identification, 228.
Modus Operandi System, 210–1.
Modern Police Technicians, 237–8.
Municipal Police, Administration, Bruce Smith, 1–27.
Municipal Police, salaries of, 136–42; clothing allowances, 142; sick leave with pay, 143; vacations, 143; pensions, 144; tenure, 144–6.
Municipal Police Administration, 63–73; by administrative board, 63–4; by commissioner of public safety, 64; by civil service commission, 64–5; patrol supervision, 72–3.
Municipal police control, 4.
Municipal police organization, 3–4.
Municipal Police organization charts, 6–9–13.
Municipal police patrol systems, 25–6.

Narcotic Agents, see United States Treasury Department.

National Conference of Social Work, 121.
National Education Association, 121.
National Safety Council, 101.

Organization charts, municipal police, 6–9–13.
Organizations, Police, state and local, 123–4; unions, rank and file, 125; future of, 126–7.

Philippine Constabulary, 35.
Politics, see under Police, Crime and Politics.
Police Academy of New York City, 170–2.
Police, Annual Report, 96–103.
Police, Crime and Politics, Charles E. Merriam, 115–20; alliance between, 115; industrial relations, 119; future outlook, 120.
Policeman's Hire, The, William C. Beyer, 135–46.
Police Duties, 166.
Police, English, 177–92; historical growth and organization, 177–8; metropolitan police, 178–9; London police, 179; other forces, 179; statistics of, 179–80; salaries of, 180–1; pensions of, 181; central control of, 181–2; police federation, 182–3; selection of, 183–4; type of, 184–6; training of, 186–8; Scotland Yard, 178; promotion of, 191–2.
Police, in Europe, 160–5.
Police, Federal, Albert Langeluttig, 41–54; kinds, 41; salaries, 41–2; suggested reorganization, 52; criticism of, 45; statistics of, 42; opposition to consolidation of, 52.
Police Instructors, abroad, 195–6.
Police Journals, see Journals, Police.
Police Journalism in the United States, Donald Young, 128.
Police Laboratories, abroad, 193–4; in Europe, 193; research of, in Belgium, 194.
Police Laboratory Equipment, 238–9.
Police Matrons, 108.
Police, Private, see Private Police.
Police, Professionalization of, in Europe, 70; in America, 70; need for, 70–2.
Police and Prosecutor, municipal, 15–9.
Police Publications, 127.
Police Research, abroad, 197–8.
Police School of Berkeley, California, 176; organization chart, 175.
Police School of Louisville, Kentucky, 172–6; organization chart, 173.
Police scientifique, 237.
Police, Scottish, 178.
Police, Selection Methods in the United States; see Methods of Police Selection.
Police Statistics, Bennet Mead, 74–95.
Police, State, 136–44.
Police, State, 34–40.
Police Technique, 131.
Police Technique, 237–48; fingerprint researches, 238; examination of stains, 240–1; blood analysis, 242–3; analysis of traces, 243–4; examination of firearms, 244–5; gunpowder,

245–6; counterfeits, 246; questioned documents, 247; other forgeries, 246; hair analysis, 244; dust analysis, 244.
Police Tests, 152–9; in United States, construction of, 152; illustration of, 153–5; trial of, 155–6; probation and promotion, 156–7; character investigation, 157–9.
Police Training School, The, George T. Rogsdale, 170–6.
Police Training, Cornelius F. Cahalane, 166–9.
Police Training, zone system in New York State, 167–8; meeting need for training, 167; training school, 167–9; expense of, 169.
Police Training, municipal, 20–1.
Police, Training of, in Belgium, 193–8.
Police Training in England, 186–91; legal basis of, 186–8; coöperative training, 188–9; Metropolitan Police training school, 189–90; post-probationary, 190–1.
Policewoman, Eleonore L. Hutzel, 104–14; growth of movement, 104–14; duties of, 106–7; protective patrol work, 107–8; organization of work, 108; standards of appointment, 110–1; experience and training, 111–2; salaries of, 112; legal status, 112; position in police department, 112–3; social service relations, 113–4; statistics of, 105–6.
Policewomen, International Association of, 125.
Portrait Parlé, 237.
Postal Inspectors, see United States Post Office Department.
Private Police of Pennsylvania, The, Jeremiah P. Shalloo, 55–62; legal power of, 55; coal and iron police, 55–62; private patrolmen, 56; private detectives, 56–7; railroad police, 57; industrial police, 57–60; legislative reform, 60–2; history of, 58–60; licensing of, 56–62; control of, 56; salaries of, 57–62; detects of, 62.
Private Police, 55–62; in the United States, 55.
Prohibition, bureau of, see United States Treasury Department.
Psychological Methods in the Selection of Policemen in Europe, Morris S. Viteles, Ph.D.,160–5.
Psychology in Criminal Investigation, John A. Larson, P.H., M.D., 258–68; methods of finding suspect, 258–60; interpreting suspect's statement, 260; objective evaluation of testimony, 260–2; deceptive tests, 261; association tests, 262; hypnosis, 262; drugs, 263; respiratory and blood pressure tests, 264–6; statistics, 266; other methods, 266–8.

Questioned documents, 247–8; ink analysis, 247; imitated handwriting, 247–8; Locard's method, 247.

Railroad Police, see Private Police of Pennsylvania.
Recruits, Police, 68–70; selection of, 69; probationary period, 69–70.

Respiratory tests, see Psychology in Criminal Investigation.
Royal Irish Constabulary, 35.
Royal Northwest Mounted, 35.

Salaries, Police, 135–43; rates of, 136, 143.
Science and Criminal Investigation, Harry Söderman, D.Sc., 237–48.
School of Criminology and of Scientific Police of Belgium, Dr. Gustave De Rechter, 193–8; training of, 194; programs and instructors, 195–7.
Scotland Yard, 178.
Secret Service, see United States Treasury Department.
Selection and promotion of Police in United States, 147–59.
Sheriff and the Constable, The, Raymond Moley, 28–33.
Sheriff, The, 28–33; in England, 28; in America, 28; functions of, 29–31; fee system, 29–32; service of writs, 30; enforcement of criminal law, 31–2; legal power, 31–2; restrictions of, 31–2; inadequacy of, 32; establishment of State Police, 32–3.
Sheriff's and Police Officers' Association, 121.
Spoils System in Government, 116.
Stains, examination of, 241.
State Police, The, Major Lynn G. Adams, 34–40.
State Police, 34–40; 135–46; abroad, 35; bibliography of, 40; clothing allowances, 142; functions of, 39–40; in the United States, 35–6; meals and quarters, 142; need for, 34–5; pensions, 144; sick leave with pay, 142–3; salaries of, 38; 136–7; tenure, 144; vacations, 143.
State Police in Pennsylvania, 36–7; training of, 36–7; promotion and discipline of, 37; organization and equipment, 37–8, salaries, 38; pensions, 38–9.
Statistics, Police, Bennet Mead, 74–95; classes and functions of, 74–5; efforts to standardize, 75–6; crime rates and clearances, 77–82; recovery of stolen property, 83–4; personnel and equipment, 84–6; data on crime, 86–9; cost of city police work, 89–91; cost of state police work, 91–4; tables of offences, 94–5; charts, 77–82, 90–5.
Statistics, Police, 100–2.

Technique of the American Detective, Duncan Matheson, 214.
Technique of the Investigation of the English Detective, The, F. J. Crawley, 219–22.
Technique of Criminal Investigator in Germany, The, Dr. Robert Heindl, 223–36.
Technique policière, 237; see also Police Technique.
Tests, Scientific, in selection of Police in the United States; see Police Tests.

Texas Rangers, 35.
Training, Police, see under Police Schools.
Training, Criminalistic, for Jurists, see Criminalistic Institutes of Austria.

United States Civil Service Commission, 147–59.
United States Department of Justice, 41–52; bureau of investigation, 41; organization, 41–2; division of criminal identification, 42.
United States Department of Labor, bureau of immigration, 48; border patrol, 48; organization, 49–50.

United States Post Office Department, Division of inspectors, 50; organization, 50–2.
United States Treasury Department, Secret Service division, 42–3; origin, 42; organization, 42–3; Bureau of prohibition, 43–6; organization, 43; prohibition unit, 45–6; narcotic unit, 45–6; Coast Guard, 46–7; bureau of customs, 47; border patrol, 47–8.

Volstead Act, 43.

Woman's Bureau, The, 109–10.
World Association of Detectives, 122.

INDEX TO NAMES

Adams, Lynn G., 34–40, 62.
Adler, Herman, 266.
Ainsworth, Michael, 247.
Alcock, John H., 76.
Atcherley, Sir L. W., 222.

Bates, W. D., 264.
Barcoski, John, 60.
Bayle, Edmond, 237.
Becker, Howard P., 223.
Benussi, 264, 265.
Beroud, 247.
Bertillon, Alphonse, 193–205, 237–9, 240, 248.
Berwick, 206.
Beyer, William C., 135–46.
Bischoff, M. A., 201.
Branthwaite, J. M., 182.
Burtt, 264 5.

Cahalane, Cornelius F., 63, 166–9.
Campbell, General, 61.
Chavigny, 246.
Cleveland, Pres., 29.
Coke, Lord, 28.
Crane, 262.
Crawley, F. J., 219–22.
Cummings, Homer S., 16.

Darrow, 266–7.
De Rechter, Gustave, 193–8, 237.
Dixon, A. L., 177–92.
Doyle, Sir Arthur Conan, 244
Dumming, Sir Leonard, 188.

Eber, William, 236.
Enright, Richard E., 124.

Faulds, Henry, 207.
Ferrier, 208.
Florence, 243.
Foote, Alfred F., 76.
Fosdick, Raymond, 67.
Freeman, George W., 59.

Goddard, 245.
Galton, Sir Francis, 207, 234, 235, 237.
Gasti, Guestore, 212.
Gilbertson, H. S., 30.
Grammond, De, 238.
Graud, Jacob, 76.
Graville, 245.
Groome, 61.
Gross, Hans, 199, 237, 259, 260.

Hayden, Arthur L., 40.

Heagie, 59.
Healy, Thomas, 76.
Henry, George G., 76.
Henry, Sir Edward, 208, 221, 237.
Heinberger, Josef, 201.
Heindl, Robert, 223–36.
Herschel, Sir William, 206, 234.
Higgins, James, 76.
Hoepler, 199.
Hoover, J. Edgar, 205–13.
House, E. H., 263.
Hulsebosch, Van Ledden, 237.
Hutzel, Eleonore L., 104–14.
Hyde, A. M., 32.

Israel, Harold, 16.

Jelliffe, 264.
Jenkins, L. V., 76.
Jørgensen, 237.
Jung, 266.

Keeler, 267.
King, Clyde L., 59.
Kirby, 264.
Kögel, 241.

Landis, 266.
Langeluttig, Albert, 41–54.
Langsner, 263.
Larson, John A., 258–68.
Lecca-Marzo, 241.
Lee, W. L. Melville, 178.
Lees, Hastings, 188.
Lenz, Adolf, 199.
Levy, David, 262.
Locard, Edmond, 237, 244, 247.
Lombroso, 264.
Lumb, Captain, 61.
Luria, Alexander R., 267.

Magrath, George Burgess, 249–57.
Malpighi, 207.
Marston, 262, 265.
Martin, E. M., 165.
Matheson, Duncan, 214, 218, 263.
Mayo, Katherine, 40.
McBeth, Roderick G., 40.
McCoy, W. L., 265.
McCormick, 267.
McClaughry, R. W., 208.
McDonough, James, 122.
McDowell, Sir John, 35.
McGrath, 188.
Mead, Bennet, 74–95.

Index to Names

Merriam, Charles E., 115–20.
Miehte, 247.
Moley, Raymond, 28.
Moll, A., 165.
Moriarty, Cecil, 185, 188, 189.
Moss, 165, 242.
Moylan, J. F., 178.
Müller, Johan, 243.
Münsterberg, 262.
Musmanno, M. A., 60.

O'Rourke, L. J., 147–59.
Osborn, 247.
Ostrander, J., 165.
Owings, Cloe, 105.

Parke, James H., 208.
Peel, Sir Robert, 166.
Pennypacker, Samuel W., 36.
Piorkowski, C., 165.
Poller, 243.
Purkinje, J. E., 207.
Reiss, R. A., 71, 237.
Richter, 266.
Roscher, 212.
Ragsdale, George T., 170–6.
Rutledge, William P., 76, 105, 112, 114.

Schilder, 262.
Schulte, R. W., 165.
Schneickert, Hans, 165, 237.
Shalloo, Jeremiah P., 55–62.
Smith, Alfred E., 29.
Smith, Bruce, 1–27, 40, 66, 69, 76.
Söderman, Harry, 237–48.

Stevens, 227.
Stockis, 241.
Stone, Donald C., 63–73.
Stryzowsky, 242.
Sylvester, Richard, 122.

Tabor, 208.
Taft, William Howard, 35.
Teichmann, 242.
Telford, F., 165.
Terman, Lewis, 165.
Thompson, Gilbert, 208.
Thurstone, L. L., 165.
Timmerman, L. S., 96–103.
Toerring, Helen C., 135.
Türkel, Siegfried, 199–204, 237.

Uhlenhut, 242.
Upson, Lent D., 121, 127.

Van Winkle, Mina C., 105.
Vincent, 188.
Viteles, Morris S., 160–65.
Vollmer, August, 76–85.
Vucetich, Juan, 207, 234, 237.

Waite, 245.
Warner, Sam B., 75.
Wechsler, 267.
Wentworth, 238.
Wigmore, 262.
Willoughby, W. F., 128.

Young, Donald, 128–34.

POLICE IN AMERICA

An Arno Press/New York Times Collection

The American Institute of Law and Criminology.
Journal of the American Institute of Law and Criminology:
Selected Articles. Chicago, 1910–1929.

The Boston Police Strike: Two Reports. Boston, 1919–1920.

Boston Police Debates: Selected Arguments. Boston,
1863–1869.

Chamber of Commerce of the State of New York.
**Papers and Proceedings of Committee on the Police Problem,
City of New York.** New York, 1905.

Chicago Police Investigations: Three Reports. Illinois,
1898–1912.

Control of the Baltimore Police: Collected Reports.
Baltimore, 1860–1866.

Crime and Law Enforcement in the District of Columbia:
Report and Hearings. Washington, D. C., 1952.

Crime in the District of Columbia: Reports and Hearings.
Washington, D. C., 1935.

Flinn, John J. and John E. Wilkie.
History of the Chicago Police. Chicago, 1887.

Hamilton, Mary E.
The Policewoman. New York, 1924.

Harrison, Leonard Vance.
Police Administration in Boston. Cambridge, Mass., 1934.

International Association of Chiefs of Police.
Police Unions. Washington, D. C., 1944.

The Joint Special Committee.
**Reports of the Special Committee Appointed to Investigate
the Official Conduct of the Members of the Board of Police
Commissioners.** Boston, 1882.

Justice in Jackson, Mississippi: U.S. Civil Rights
Commission Hearings. Washington, D. C., 1965.

McAdoo, William.
Guarding a Great City. New York, 1906.

Mayo, Katherine.
Justice to All. New York, 1917.

Missouri Joint Committee of the General Assembly.
**Report of the Joint Committee of the General Assembly
Appointed to Investigate the Police Department of the
City of St. Louis.** St. Louis, Missouri, 1868.

National Commission on Law Observance and Enforcement.
Report on the Police. Washington, D. C., 1931.

National Prison Association.
**Proceedings of the Annual Congress of the National Prison
Association of the United States:** Selected Articles.
1874–1902.

New York City Common Council.
**Report of the Special Committee of the New York City
Board of Aldermen on the New York City Police Department.**
New York, 1844.

National Police Convention.
Official Proceedings of the National Prison Convention.
St. Louis, 1871.

Pennsylvania Federation of Labor.
The American Cossack. Washington, D. C., 1915.

Police and the Blacks: U.S. Civil Rights Commission
Hearings. 1960–1966.

Police in New York City: An Investigation. New York,
1912–1931.

The President's Commission on Law Enforcement and
Administration of Justice.
Task Force Report: The Police. Washington, D. C., 1967.

Sellin, Thorsten, editor.
The Police and the Crime Problem. Philadelphia, 1929.

Smith, Bruce, editor.
New Goals in Police Management. Philadelphia, 1954.

Sprogle, Howard O.
The Philadelphia Police, Past and Present. Philadelphia,
1887.

U.S. Committee on Education and Labor.
The Chicago Memorial Day Incident: Hearings and Report.
Washington, D. C., 1937.

U.S. Committee on Education and Labor.
**Documents Relating to Intelligence Bureau or Red Squad of
Los Angeles Police Department.** Washington, D. C., 1940.

U.S. Committee on Education and Labor.
Private Police Systems. Washington, D. C., 1939.

Urban Police: Selected Surveys. 1926–1946.

Women's Suffrage and the Police: Three Senate Documents.
Washington, D. C., 1913.

Woods, Arthur.
Crime Prevention. Princeton, New Jersey, 1918.

Woods, Arthur.
Policeman and Public. New Haven, Conn., 1919.

AMERICAN POLICE SUPPLEMENT

International Association of Chiefs of Police.
Proceedings of the Annual Conventions of the International Association of Chiefs of Police. 1893–1930. 5 vols.

New York State Senate.
Report and Proceedings of the Senate Committee Appointed to Investigate the Police Department of the City of New York. (Lexow Committee Report). New York, 1895. 6 vols.

THE POLICE IN GREAT BRITAIN

Committee on Police Conditions of Service.
Report of the Committee on Police Conditions of Service. London, 1949.

Committee on the Police Service.
Minutes of Evidence and Report: England, Wales, Scotland. London, 1919–1920.

Royal Commission on Police Powers and Procedures.
Report of the Royal Commission on Police Powers and Procedure. London, 1929.

Select Committee on Police.
Report of Select Committee on Police with the Minutes of Evidence. London, 1853.

Royal Commission Upon the Duties of the Metropolitan Police.
Minutes of Evidence Taken Before the Royal Commission Upon the Duties of the Metropolitan Police Together With Appendices and Index. London, 1908.

Committee on Police.
Report from the Select Committee on Police of the Metropolis. London, 1828.